The Second Book of Discipline

The Second Book of Discipline

With Introduction and Commentary
by

James Kirk
Lecturer in Scottish History
University of Glasgow

Covenanters

Published by
Covenanters Press

the joint imprint of
Zeticula
57 St Vincent Crescent
Glasgow
G3 8NQ
and
Scottish Christian Press
21 Young Street
Edinburgh
EH2 4HU

http://www.covenanters.co.uk
admin@covenanters.co.uk

Copyright © James Kirk 1980, 2005

The publishers wish to thank both Moira Parker and the Rev Dr Angus Kerr of Newton Mearns Parish Church for their permission to use the Year of the Child 2002 window. Moira Parker can be contacted at Rainbow Glass Artists, 82 Berelands Road, Prestwick, KA9 1ER, Scotland Email: info@rainbowglass.biz; web site:rainbowglass.biz

ISBN 1 905022 19 0 Paperback
ISBN 1 905022 20 4 Hardback

First published in 1980 by The St Andrew Press, Edinburgh
ISBN 0 7152 0439 4

All rights reserved. No part of this publication may be reproduced, stored in a retrieval system, or transmitted in any form or by any means, electronic, mechanical, photocopying, recording or otherwise, without the prior written permission of the publishers.

*For my father and mother
in gratitude*

CONTENTS

Editor's Preface	vii
Abbreviations	ix
INTRODUCTION	1
Antecedents to the second Book of Discipline	3
The first Book of Discipline and its 'rejection'	3
Criticism of the Leith settlement of 1572	23
The search for a 'perfect polity'	35
The drafting of the second Book of Discipline	42
Discussions on jurisdiction and polity	42
Authorship of the book	45
Andrew Melville's contribution	51
The contents and development of the book	57
Church and state	57
'The Office of a Christiane Magistrat in the Kirk'	64
Vocation and ordination	65
The officers of the Kingdom	74
Ministers and bishops	74
The doctor or teacher	84
Elders	88
Deacons	97
Elderships or assemblies	101
The kirk session or presbytery?	102
The provincial synod	114
The general assembly	116
Church patrimony and further reform	122
The book's subscription	124
Implementing the book's proposals	130
The campaign against episcopacy	130
Presbyteries and bishops	133
A reassertion of episcopacy	137

The bishop in presbytery	145
The presbyterian kirk by law established	152
The text and method of editing	154
Illustration	158

THE TEXT AND COMMENTARY — 159

APPENDICES — 245

I Conference on the second Book of Discipline, 1578
II Criticisms of the second Book of Discipline, *c.* 1585
III The election of commissioners to the general assembly

BIBLIOGRAPHY — 291

INDEX — 305

Editor's Preface

The Second Book of Discipline is the first explicit statement of Scottish presbyterianism. Yet it has never been subjected to detailed critical examination. The present work was undertaken in the hope that further study might compensate for this long-standing neglect of one of the primary documents of the Scottish Reformed Church.

My interest in the Second Book of Discipline arose some years ago during research into the presbyterian movement for a Ph.D. thesis in the University of Edinburgh, and I would record my gratitude to Professor Gordon Donaldson and the Rev. Professor A. C. Cheyne, who supervised my work, for stimulating criticism and helpful advice. More recently, I have had opportunity to profit greatly from the assistance and encouragement of the Rev. Professor J. K. Cameron, St Mary's College, St Andrews, and Dr. I. B. Cowan, my colleague in Glasgow, each of whom, with characteristic generosity, has read my typescript and made many helpful comments. I warmly thank them here. I also appreciate the help of Mrs Dorothy Roger and Mrs Kathleen Webster, who are to be congratulated for their unfailing vigilance in typing the manuscript.

November 1978 JAMES KIRK
THE UNIVERSITY
GLASGOW

ABBREVIATIONS

APS	*Acts of the Parliaments of Scotland*
AUL	Aberdeen University Library
BL	British Library
BUK	*The Booke of the Universall Kirk: Acts and Proceedings of the General Assemblies of the Kirk of Scotland*
CR	*Corpus Reformatorum*
CSP Scot.	*Calendar of State Papers relating to Scotland and Mary, Queen of Scots*
CTS	Calvin Translation Society
EUL	Edinburgh University Library
Fasti	*Fasti Ecclesiae Scoticanae*
GCA	Strathclyde Regional Archives incorporating Glasgow City Archives
GUA	Glasgow University Archives
GUL	Glasgow University Library
New Reg. Ho.	New Register House
NLS	National Library of Scotland
OL	*Original Letters relating to the ecclesiastical affairs of Scotland*
Orig. Letters rel. Engl. Ref.	*Original Letters relative to the English Reformation*
PRO	Public Record Office
Peterkin	*The Booke of the Universall Kirk of Scotland*, ed. A. Peterkin. 1 vol. edn. (Edinburgh, 1839)
Reg. Supp.	Vatican Archives, Registra Supplicationum
RMS	*Registrum Magni Sigilli Regum Scotorum: Register of the Great Seal of Scotland*
RPC	*Register of the Privy Council of Scotland*
RSCHS	*Records of the Scottish Church History Society*

INTRODUCTION

ANTECEDENTS TO THE SECOND BOOK OF DISCIPLINE

The first Book of Discipline and its 'rejection'

The essential truth that the late arrival of the Scottish Reformation provided Scots with ample opportunity to absorb the matured ideas of reformers in Europe ought not to obscure the diversity in attitudes among reformers at home. John Knox's belief that 'dyverse men war of dyverse jugementis'[1] is applicable even to the six authors of the first Book of Discipline. Conservative reformers like John Winram and John Douglas in St Andrews, who seem to have arrived finally at protestantism through Erasmian humanism,[2] differed in temperament and outlook from radicals like John Knox and John Willock with their experience of Edwardine protestantism in England and of the Swiss reformers of Geneva and Zürich respectively;[3] Knox also claimed 'great intelligence' with the French church.[4] John Spottiswoode, who knew Archbishop Cranmer during his stay in England and who subsequently accompanied lord James Stewart to France, may have contributed a mediating influence;[5] and John Row, doctor in both laws from Padua, came as an eleventh-hour convert to Calvinism from the papal curia, through contact with Knox and Christopher Goodman.[6]

The formative influences of other reformers were no less varied. Fresh from Geneva, and the 'greyt freynd' of lord James

---

[1] Knox, *Works*, ii, 92.

[2] *Cf.*, J. Durkan and A. Ross, *Early Scottish Libraries* (Glasgow, 1961), 90, 161. The fortunes of Winram, sub-prior of St Andrews and later superintendent of Fife (despite his participation in earlier heresy trials), and lord James Stewart the prior and a leader of the protestant lords of the Congregation, were closely linked. John Douglas had been invited by Archbishop Hamilton in 1547 to become principal of St Mary's college, St Andrews, which acquired a reputation for Erasmian humanism. (Watt, *Fasti*, 382; *cf.*, R. G. Cant, *University of St Andrews* (Edinburgh, 1970), 35.) I am grateful to Professor J. K. Cameron, who has made a special study of St Mary's college for a forthcoming history of the college of which he is a co-author, for allowing me to read his typescript for this period.

[3] Knox, *Works*, i, 231; ii, 16; iii, 33–70, 79, 122; iv, 240; v, 211–16; vi, 16, 123, 133, 562, 613; *Orig. Letters rel. Engl. Ref.*, 314–16, 393–4, 407, 409, 421; Bullinger, *Decades*, v, 544.

[4] Knox, *Works*, ii, 137.

[5] Spottiswoode, *History*, ii, 336.

[6] Row, *History*, 447, 455; *cf.*, Reg. Supp. 2962, fo. 295r.-v.; 2963, fo. 299v.; 2972, fo. 178r.

Stewart, Christopher Goodman played a prominent part in helping to establish a Calvinist discipline in Ayr and in the metropolitan seat of St Andrews.[7] Erskine of Dun and William Christison in Dundee had each been receptive to earlier Lutheran influences,[8] though both were later associated with the second Book of Discipline; and Paul Methven, who had been trained in England by Miles Coverdale, became minister in Dundee and then in Jedburgh until his deposition for adultery in 1562 from his ministry in the Church of Scotland led him to enter the ministry of the Church of England instead.[9] Patrick Cockburn was another Erasmian humanist and teacher of theology at St Leonard's college, St Andrews, who had spent a spell in France in the 1550s, including a stay at Paris and Orléans, before becoming minister at Haddington.[10] John Craig, before joining the reformers, was subjected to a rich assortment of experiences: after graduating from St Andrews he was employed as a pedagogue by lord Dacre in England, then entered the Dominican order, was imprisoned on suspicion of heresy, failed to win a place at Cambridge and so went to France and on to Rome; at Bologna, he taught the Dominican novices, was finally converted by reading Calvin's *Institutes* and was condemned to be burned by the Inquisition, only to escape with some *banditti* in a tumult following the death of Pope Paul IV and so made his way home through Milan, Vienna, Germany and England to become minister of the Canongate near Edinburgh.[11] Plainly, all the ingredients of continental reform – the examples of Germany, Scandinavia, Switzerland, France and England – were known to Scots by 1560.

Outside this main-stream movement for protestant reform lay other potentially disruptive elements. Apart from the continued existence of Catholicism, a factor which no protestant could afford to ignore, there were also individualists like Thomas

---

[7] *CSP Scot.*, ii, no. 316; Knox, *Works*, ii, 87; iv, 66–68; vi, 27, 78, 101; *RStAKS*, i, 4–5, 53, 71, 75, 131, 156, 168, 205, 221.

[8] Melville, *Diary*, 14; *RStAKS*, i, 48–9; T. L. Christensen, 'Scots in Denmark in the sixteenth century', *SHR*, xlix (1970), 138–40.

[9] *CSP Scot.*, i, no. 1163; Knox, *Works*, i, 256, 300, 317; ii, 87, 364–6, 531–2; *BUK*, i, 13, 29, 31–2, 55, 79–81, 125; *Zürich Letters*, i, 131.

[10] *Essays on the Scottish Reformation*, ed. D. McRoberts (Glasgow, 1962), 311, 314, 326; Durkan & Ross, *Early Scottish Libraries*, 83; *CSP Scot.*, i, no. 902; *Fasti*, i, 368.

[11] Spottiswoode, *History*, iii, 92–4.

Methven, prebendary of Kingask and Kinglassie, who rejected papalism and Calvinism alike, boldly affirming that he was 'nether ane Papist nor ane Calvynist, nor of Paul nor of Apollo, bot Jesus Cristis man'. Another nonconformist in 1560 who was 'scornfull aganst the majestie of the Trinitie' claimed to possess the same power as ministers to celebrate communion.[12] The heresy of the 'soul sleepers', which led Calvin to produce his *Psychopannychia*, also reached Scotland, was condemned in the Confession of Faith, and reappeared in 1576 when the general assembly censured as 'erroneous and heretical' a minister's teaching that 'never soule went to heaven before the latter day'.[13] The fear of anabaptism, which haunted all the magisterial reformers and which made Knox compose his treatise on predestination, was never far removed; and by 1561 there was news that a 'playne Anabaptiste' had arrived in Edinburgh from Newcastle with 'fonde and shamfull tawlke'.[14] All this helps to explain the first Book of Discipline's insistence that prospective ministers be thoroughly examined 'in all the chiefe points that now be in controversie betwixt us and the Papists, Anabaptists, Arrians, or other such enemies to the Christian religion'.[15]

Yet the wayward ideas of the sects neither gained strength nor posed a serious menace to the reformed faith in Scotland. Indeed, differences among reformers, to a quite remarkable degree, were subsumed in the Confession of Faith and in the Book of Discipline of 1560 which was submitted to the provisional government 'in unitie of minde'.[16] That agreement in these documents was so readily found is an indication of the skill with which conservative and radical elements were blended in an effort to present a blueprint for the reformed church in both doctrine and organisation. One strand of thought in these composite works owed something to the draft, though abortive, ordinances for the reformation in Cologne prepared by Martin Bucer, assisted in doctrinal matters by Philip Melanchthon, for the archbishop and elector Hermann von Wied in 1543.[17] The work, first translated into English in

---

[12] *RStAKS*, i, 135; 44.   [13] Knox, *Works*, ii, 109; *BUK*, i, 376.
[14] *CSP Scot.*, i, nos. 1023, 1041.
[15] *The First Book of Discipline*, ed. J. K. Cameron (Edinburgh, 1972), 98.
[16] *Ibid.*, 85.
[17] *Canones Concilii Provincialis Coloniensis* (Paris, 1547); *A simple and religious consultation of us Herman by the grace of God Archbishop of Collone and prince Electoure etc.* (London, 1548).

1547, contained articles on doctrine, the church, prayers and fasting, the administration of religion, the sacraments, visitation of the sick, excommunication, the admission of ministers, marriage, burial, holy days, alms, schools and numerous related themes; and in certain aspects it seems to have acted as a model for the authors of the first Book of Discipline.[18]

The similarities between Bucer's proposals for Cologne and the Book of Discipline's plans for Scotland are perhaps most noticeable in the respective sections on marriage, a topic on which Bucer had written at length, but common ground was also found in the appointment from congregations of elders and of deacons, 'provostes of the holy almes' otherwise termed 'the cheife deacons of congregations and wardens of the holie treasure', and in the acceptance of the superintendent's office, though Scottish practice plainly did not follow Bucer's belief that the superintendent should become principal reader of divinity and rector of the divinity school in Bonn; nor were there plans in the Book of Discipline for the introduction of visitors and examiners on the Cologne model; but there was mention in the Cologne scheme of synods and twice yearly convocations of deans and pastors and of the need to carry forward a general reformation of congregations not least through a 'free and christian counsel, universall or national'.[19] At the same time, there was also much in the first Book of Discipline at variance with the mild Cologne reforms, betraying instead more radical influences at work.

For a start, the Book of Discipline's revolutionary proposal to subvert entirely the ancient ecclesiastical structure of benefices and to replace it with another system was quite the reverse of Bucer's plan to retain the system of benefices and patronage as well as the hierarchy of pre-reformation offices in the secular church.[20] For Bucer, it looked almost as if the episcopal order was essential to the church since 'neither it is to be doubted but that bishops were made presidents over all priests', whereas in Scotland

[18] J. K. Cameron, 'The Cologne Reformation and the Church of Scotland', *Journal of Ecclesiastical History*, xxx (January, 1979), 39–64; A. F. Mitchell, *The Scottish Reformation* (London, 1900), 145.

[19] *A simple and religious consultation*, fos. ccxxvi, r.; cxlviii, v., clxxiii, r., clxxvii, r., clxxviii, v.; cclvii, v.ff., cclxxix, r.; cxlviii, v., ccxxi, r.-v.; clxxiv, r., clxxx, v., ccxxvi, r., cclviii, v., cclxxi, r., cclxxiii, r., cclxxiv, r.; ccxxi, v., ccxxii r.-v.; cclxxiv, v., 'The conclution'.

[20] *The First Book of Discipline*, 108ff., 156ff.; *A simple and religious consultation*, fos. cclvii, r., cclxi, v.; ccxxiv, v.; clxxx, v., ccxxiii, v., cclxxv, v., cclxxvii, v., cclxxviii, r.

the superintendent's office, which formed no part of the original drafting of the Book of Discipline, was added only as an afterthought; and the decision 'to make difference betwixt Preachers at this time' was justified, in the Book of Discipline at least, on the purely practical grounds of a shortage of ministers and the consequent need to extend evangelisation throughout the country; hence the acceptance of superintendents as 'most expedient at this time'.[21] Even the adoption of readers was commended on quite different grounds: for Cologne the office was seen to be essential and it was only 'thys scarsnes of ministers of the worde' which meant that 'peculier readers can not be apointed in everie congregation', but in Scotland readers were introduced merely as a temporary measure to serve 'the Churches where no ministers can be had presentlie'.[22] Again, the financial activities of the Cologne deacons were to be confined merely to poor-relief unlike the much wider rôle which the Book of Discipline claimed for the Scottish deacons in collecting and disbursing the whole rents of the church.[23] Excommunication in Cologne, unlike Scotland, need neither incur civil penalties nor even hinder fellowship 'in civile matters' between the faithful and the excommunicated, who might still attend sermons in church.[24] The Book of Discipline also took exception to feast and holy days, and even to the ceremony of ordination, which the Cologne ordinance approved. Nor did the Scots accept Bucer's ideas on the confirmation of children.[25] The more rigorous Scottish attitude detected here is indicative of another strand of thinking which resulted in a rejection of these aspects of Bucer's experiment at Cologne in preference for the adoption of more distinctively Calvinist features. In its advocacy of a system of congregational government based on a consistory with a ministry chosen with congregational consent, with elders elected from the congregation to assist with discipline and deacons to gather the whole revenues

[21] *A simple and religious consultation*, fo. ccxxiv, r.; *The First Book of Discipline*, 49ff., 115. The variant text 'expedient *for* this time' is also noted, *ibid.*, 115. (My italics.)

[22] *A simple and religious consultation*, fo. xv, v.; *The first Book of Discipline*, 105.

[23] *A simple and religious consultation*, fos. cclvii, v.–cclix, v., cclxxxix, r.; *The First Book of Discipline*, 158, 163, 178.

[24] *A simple and religious consultation*, fos. clxxvii, r., ccxxi, v.–ccxxii, v.; *The First Book of Discipline*, 171, 197; Knox, *Works*, vi, 449ff.

[25] *The First Book of Discipline*, 88, 102, 207; *A simple and religious consultation*, fos. ccxliv, r.–ccxlv, r.; ccxxv, v.; clxxi, v.–clxxiv, r.

of the church, the Book of Discipline followed a pattern consistent with Calvin's teaching.[26] Its attitude to excommunication also accorded with Calvin's belief,[27] if not always with Genevan practice, and the exercise for interpreting scripture, which had originated in Zwingli's Zürich and was approved by Bucer, was borrowed from Geneva along with the Book of Common Order, which the Book of Discipline was intended to supplement.[28]

All in all, although the first Book of Discipline – and indeed the second Book of Discipline for that matter – contained much that accorded with Bucer's teaching, including even material borrowed from the *De Regno Christi*,[29] Bucer did not attain in Scotland the influence which he acquired in England, where he was especially consulted on liturgical matters,[30] or which he exercised in Strasbourg, Ulm, Nuremberg, Hesse, Cologne or Bonn;[31] and his impact on the Scottish polity, in particular, was mediated largely through Calvin, who in his exposition of the ministry and in his assertion of an autonomous ecclesiastical jurisdiction was deeply indebted to the Strasbourg reformer.[32] Unlike Luther, Zwingli or Calvin, Bucer left 'no followers who bore his name', and his very ecumenism, which enabled him to transcend differences among the Lutheran, Reformed and Anglican churches and also to display a surprising tolerance of Anabaptism, led him to seek not only protestant unity but even reconciliation between

[26] *The First Book of Discipline*, 168–171; 99, 101; 174ff.; 158, 163, 178; Calvin, *Institutes*, IV, iii, 8; IV, xi, 6; IV, iii, 15; IV, xii, 2; IV, iv, 5.

[27] *The First Book of Discipline*, 167, 171, 197; Calvin, *Institutes*, IV, xi, 3–6; IV, xii, 5; IV, xii, 10.

[28] *The First Book of Discipline*, 187–191 and notes; G. D. Henderson, *The Burning Bush* (Edinburgh, 1957), 44, 46; *A simple and religious consultation*, fo. cclxxiv, 1.; Knox, *Works*, iv, 178; vi, 287ff., 294.

[29] *The First Book of Discipline*, 129, 133, 164ff.; see also below, X. 9.

[30] C. Hopf, *Martin Bucer and the English Reformation* (Oxford, 1946); G. J. Cuming, *A History of Anglican Liturgy* (London, 1969); T. M. Fallow, *The Order of Baptism . . . illustrated from the Use of Salisbury, the Religious Consultation of Herman* (London, 1838); *Common Places of Martin Bucer*, ed. D. F. Wright (Appleford, 1972), 24–28.

[31] J. Courvoisier, *La Notion d'Église chez Bucer* (Paris, 1933), 135ff., and *passim*; H. Eells, *Martin Bucer* (New Haven, 1931), *passim*; M. U. Chrisman, *Strasbourg and the Reform* (New Haven, 1967), 201ff.; F. Lau and E. Bizer, *A History of the Reformation in Germany to 1555* (London, 1969), 95–6, 114–122, 164–5, 178ff., 187ff.

[32] H. Strohl, 'La théorie et la pratique des quatres ministères à Strasbourg avant l'arrivée de Calvin', *Bull. de la Soc. de l'Hist. du Protest. franç.*, lxxxiv. (Paris, 1935), 123–140; and 'Bucer et Calvin', *ibid.*, lxxxvii. (Paris, 1938), 354–360; W. Pauck, 'Calvin and Butzer', *Journal of Religion*, ix (1929), 237–256.

protestant and Catholic.³³ Yet, by the 1560s opponents of the Reformation in Scotland were agreed that the leading ministerial reformers had become 'Calvinians';³⁴ and the earlier phase of rapprochement which permitted humanists to conform to the Reformation without too sharp an awareness of the contrast with reformist Catholicism had finally disappeared.

The radicalism of the reformers in effecting a reformation in defiance of the crown and in their rejection of the existing ecclesiastical system – despite Archbishop Hamilton's plea to Knox that the ancient structure, 'the work of many ages',³⁵ should not be hastily overturned – held out little immediate prospect that the reformers would conform, as some contemporaries in England suggested they might, to the examples of either Scandinavia or England. By all accounts, the reformers were less than enthusiastic about the possibility of imitating the example of Denmark; and the ministers were found 'so severe in that that theie professe, and so lothe to remytte any thyng of that that theie have receaved' that little hope was seen 'how uniformity might be had in religion' between the English and Scottish churches. The explanation offered by the same English observer why the Scots wished to have their first draft of the Book of Discipline approved by Calvin, Viret and Beza in Geneva and by Martyr and Bullinger in Zürich, but not by any English divine, was simply that 'I see not their opinion to England to be such that they will "stonde to their judgement herein", yet they will not refuse to commune with any "lerned in our nacion".'³⁶

In the regulation of its ministry, the Scottish church found no place either for the provost or for the ministerial deacon of the Danish system. Not did Scottish reformers assert, as did the English, that 'from the Apostles' time there hath been these three orders of ministers in Christ's Church: Bishops, Priests, and Deacons'. Departing from the examples of Denmark and England, the Scots maintained the scriptural validity of a ministry including elected elders and deacons, the latter as financial officers, an order which, it was claimed, God had 'now restoired unto us agane

---

³³ W. P. Stephens, *The Holy Spirit in the Theology of Martin Bucer* (Cambridge, 1970), vii; *Common Places of Martin Bucer*, 17–52.

³⁴ Leslie, *Historie*, ii, 447, 449, 464; Winzet, *Certane tractatis for reformatioun of doctryne and maneris in Scotland* (Edinburgh, 1835), 37, 55, 56, 58, 69, 74, 79, 87; *Catholic Tractates of the Sixteenth Century* (Edinburgh, 1901), ed. T. G. Law, 17, 25, 27, 34–6, 41, 44–6, 51, 55–9, 68, 78, 80, 83–6, 89–91, 98, 101, 103, 109, 114.

³⁵ Spottiswoode, *History*, i, 372.   ³⁶ *CSP Scot.*, i, nos. 506, 525, 891.

efter that the publict face of the Kirk hes bene deformed by the tyrany of that Romane Antichrist'.[37] The Scottish superintendent, unlike his counterpart in some Lutheran countries, remained purely an ecclesiastical officer and never became a royal official or instrument for royal control of the church. Nor did ecclesiastical discipline in Scotland become a function merely of the magistracy, and those continental precedents, both Lutheran and Reformed, where it did so become were clearly set aside in favour of what came to be the essentially Calvinist dichotomy of minister and magistrate, following the examples set by Oecolampadius and Bucer.

If there was much on which the first Book of Discipline was categorical, there were also matters on which it was indeterminate. There was certainly ample discussion of the ministry of the Word and sacraments, of schools and universities, of elders and deacons of the exercise of ecclesiastical discipline and the care of the poor, of the temporary need for readers and exhorters to serve until sufficient fully qualified ministers were to be had, of superintendents, to whose streamlined provinces 'ten or twelve' were to be selected 'to plant and erect Kirkes, to set, order and appoint Ministers';[38] and consideration was also given to the delicate problem of the church's proper patrimony as well as to a review of such matters as interpreting scripture, marriage, burial and the repair of churches. At the same time, little thought was evidently given to the wider structure which a national church should assume. Although it distinguished the local congregation as the 'inferiour Church' from the 'counsell or greater church' in language which suggests a concept fatal to any belief in the right of individual congregations to function independently of any higher ecclesiastical authority, the Book of Discipline still remained vague on any organisation beyond the kirk session and superintendent's court, to which specific mention was made. The only indication of an awareness of higher courts occurs in five incidental references to 'the whole Church or the most part thereof', to the 'consent of the whole Kirk', the 'consent of the whole counsell of the Kirk', to 'the great councell of the Kirk' and, most significantly, to the 'Assemblie of the Universale Kirk gathered within the

---

[37] E. H. Dunkley, *The Reformation in Denmark* (London, 1948), 54, 85, 89; *The Two Liturgies . . . of Edward VI*, ed. J. Ketley (Cambridge, 1844), 16; Knox, *Works*, ii, 153.

[38] *The First Book of Discipline*, 115.

Realme',[39] by which is to be understood the general assembly which came into being as the Book of Discipline underwent revision during 1560 and whose antecedents may be sought in the convention of ministers, nobles and burgesses which met for ecclesiastical purposes in July 1560.[40] A foreshadowing of the later provincial synod, which was certainly recognised by 1562 if not earlier, may be detected in the superintendent's subjection to the 'censure and correction of ministers and Elders, not of his chiefe towne onely, but also of the whole Province over the which he is appointed overseer' and possibly in the requirement that an elder and deacon from each church in the province should submit a report of their minister's diligence each year 'unto the ministers of the Superintendents kirk'.[41]

A second area where ambiguity, or at least a certain lack of clarity, may be discerned was the Book of Discipline's attitude towards the reformed church's relationship with the government where the kind of establishment which the reformers sought is implied rather than stated. Even so, the Book of Discipline, it is sometimes necessary to recall, was a report commissioned by the provisional government which the protestant lords of the Congregation had called into being. Its plans were therefore based on the assumption that the new church would operate in partnership with the new state, and not as hitherto when it functioned 'under the cross' in times of adversity. Already the 'reformation parliament' had prepared the way when it tackled the religious question, not only by prohibiting the celebration of mass and abolishing papal jurisdiction but also by approving a reformed Confession of Faith, though it settled neither polity nor endowment; hence the commissioning of an expanded Book of Discipline which offered a solution to both of these problems.[42] The prospect, then, to which the Book of Discipline addressed itself was one of full establishment and state recognition for the reformed church and of the implementation of its proposals.

The magistracy, in the form of the 'great council of the realm', was therefore assigned a rôle in the distribution of ministers and was even expected to compel those with the necessary qualifica-

[39] *Ibid.*, 99, 103, 120, 127, 164, 200.
[40] Knox, *Works*, ii, 84-87; Calderwood, *History*, ii, 11; Spottiswoode, *History*, i, 325.
[41] *The First Book of Discipline*, 127, 177.
[42] *APS*, ii, 526-535; Knox, *Works*, ii, 128.

tions to undertake a ministry 'where your wisdoms and the Church shal think expedient', but this extension of the ministry, it was made clear, was to take place 'with the consent of the Church'. Although the Book of Discipline recommended the appropriate salaries for superintendents, it was nonetheless conceded that these stipends might be adjusted 'at the discretion of the Prince and councell of the Realme'. Again, initial nomination of superintendents, was attributed to the 'great council of the realm', or to those to whom it might give commission, but this was regarded only as a temporary arrangement in recognition that 'in this present necessity the nomination, examination and admission of the Superintendent cannot be so straight as we require and as afterwards it must be'; and so the Book of Discipline had recommended that, with the establishment of the office after three years, any right of nomination by the privy council should be withheld and transferred instead to the church and town council of the locality.[43]

The unstable situation with which the reformers were confronted may account in part for assigning to the great council some duties which were of a purely transitory character and which were clearly designed to lapse once the future was more assured. In any event, the assistance of the civil power in reforming the church was never allowed to obscure the separate identities of civil and ecclesiastical councils. The existence of two co-ordinate but distinctive jurisdictions is postulated not least in the Book of Discipline's division of offences into those which 'ought to be taken away by the civill sword' and those which 'openly appertaine to the kirk of God to punish' through the imposition of ecclesiastical discipline including excommunication.[44] It was plainly envisaged that the 'council of the church' would function independently of the 'prince and council of the realm'. In emphasizing the magistrate's responsibilities to the church, the Book of Discipline displays no trace of subservience; nor is there even a serious hint that supreme authority over the reformed church should be vested in the great council. Indeed, the general assembly, which came into being between July and December 1560, was already a reality before Scots had opportunity to reflect on the repercussions following the death of Francis II of France on 5 December 1560 and the probable return of Mary as

[43] *The First Book of Discipline*, 104–5, 109–110, 123, 125–6.
[44] *Ibid.*, 166–7.

a sovereign hostile to the Reformation. The 'Assemblie of the Universall Kirk gathered within the Realme', to which in an *additio* the Book of Discipline referred, was clearly distinguished in the minds of contemporaries both from the great council of the realm and from any other organ of civil government, with which it ought not to be confused. It was recognised as an essentially ecclesiastical gathering of ministers, nobles and burgesses. It was not the magistracy in council, parliament or convention; it was not even just the magistracy in the church; it was manifestly an assembly representing the whole church; and if its composition mirrored the three estates, this is surely because the assembly was the Christian community, or rather its representatives from the dominant interests in society, planning for the church's future in a capacity quite independent of existing political institutions, and accordingly represented the 'church' as distinct from the recognised organs of the 'state'. It was, in short, the new church assuming a central directive rôle in partnership with the new state.

Thirdly, in its revolutionary financial proposals, the Book of Discipline was less than explicit on the means of achieving its quite forthright objective of dismantling the whole structure of benefices and of reallocating ecclesiastical finances, uplifted by the deacons, for the support of the ministry, schools and poor. Such a programme could not be attempted, far less realised, without the goodwill (which, in the event, was not forthcoming) of those whose claims the Book of Discipline so studiously disregarded, for the rights of patrons and beneficed men alike were not acknowledged. Nor was recognition given to the interests of the crown, nobility and lairds whose outstanding success in secularising church property was matched only by their wholehearted reluctance to relinquish those possessions which, by one means or another, they had acquired. In its claim for the church to inherit the major portion of this patrimony, the Book of Discipline proposed to separate the spirituality, consisting chiefly of teinds, from the temporality, or lands and their rents, by dissolving the benefices, and the only concession to circumstances was the conspicuous silence on the fate of the monastic temporalities which alone were not assigned for ecclesiastical purposes.[45]

[45] *Ibid.*, 156–164. Winram, who helped to devise the Book of Discipline, was prior of Portmoak and sub-prior of St Andrews, and lord James Stewart was commendator of the priories of St Andrews and Pittenweem.

The decision in favour of dissolving the benefices, rather than utilising them, is perhaps all the more surprising in view of the five bishops who conformed to the Reformation, three of them agreeing to undertake service as 'overseers' in the reformed church. That almost half the episcopate should conform to the Reformation by August 1560 – for Brechin was still technically unprovided and the archbishop of Glasgow had removed himself to France[46] – could hardly have been wholly discouraging to more conservative reformers who might have wished to follow the English example by making protestant appointments to the sees. Yet this pattern was not repeated in Scotland where the provisional government made no attempt on behalf of the crown to nominate a protestant successor to any bishopric deemed vacant or to question the tenure of those bishops who were merely bishops elect, postulates or administrators of their sees, far less to seek to compel the more intransigent bishops, kinsmen of the greatest families in the land, either to conform or to demit; and the report in August 1560 that Willock had become 'bishop' in Glasgow is a misreading, or loose reading, of the situation by the chamberlain to the Catholic archbishop of Glasgow.[47]

The intention to dissolve the benefices was consistent with the Book of Discipline's rejection of any identification between the reformed church and the ecclesiastical structure of the old church which still remained in being. Even the names to denote office in the reformed church were chosen for their freedom from association with the old order, similarly 'kirk' and 'congregation' were used in preference to 'parish', and consistently the Book of Discipline made no attempt even to advance a case for protestant successors to the bishoprics; instead superintendents, with rationalised provinces not coterminous with the antiquated diocesan boundaries, were charged to perform the work of true pastors and overseers of the flock.[48] Finance, or rather the lack of it, appears to have been a major obstacle preventing the appointment of the full complement of superintendents on the pattern envisaged in the Book of Discipline, for only five were so appointed, with stipends allotted from the fruits of benefices by the crown collectory,[49] from the spring of 1561 onwards; so that supervision of ministers and congregations within the reformed church came to be entrusted to five superintendents in areas which

[46] Watt, *Fasti*, 41, 150.
[47] Keith, *History*, iii, 10.
[48] *The First Book of Discipline*, 115ff.
[49] *Thirds of Benefices*, 54, 95, 128.

coincided only approximately with the sees of the more unyielding bishops, to the three conforming bishops who undertook service in the reformed church and who subsequently acquired from the general assembly commissions for visitation, and, thirdly, to ministers commissioned by the assembly to undertake visitations for a term. Here, as elsewhere, the Book of Discipline's proposals were only imperfectly realised.

Although its recommendations were accepted not only by the general assembly, which, as best as it could, attempted to give effect to its ideas, and by a convention of nobility and barons which met in January 1561, but also, with qualifications, by an act of privy council, the first Book of Discipline still failed to achieve the parliamentary approval which its authors, and others, had anticipated.[50] This was essentially because its claims to the extensive patrimony of the pre-reformation church proved anathema to the vested interests of the crown and nobility who for long had exploited ecclesiastical resources to the full and who had no intention of allowing this profitable source of income to diminish. Even the act of privy council approving the Book of Discipline felt constrained to add the provision that, on condition that they undertook to support ministers from their revenues, existing benefice holders should remain in possession of their benefices for life.[51] This measure effectively postponed, and ultimately frustrated, any attempt to subvert the structure of benefices, for a generation or more would be required before all the benefices became vacant through the deaths of existing incumbents. An added complication was the return from France in August 1561 of Mary, who showed no immediate predisposition to lend her support to the reformed church or to accord it state recognition. Maitland of Lethington plainly foresaw the difficulties, believing that 'our exactenes and singularitie in religion wyll never concurre with her judgemente; I thynke that she wyll hardely be broughte under the rule of our discipline, of the which we cane remytte nothynge to anye estate or persone'.[52] Without firm support from Mary's government, the revolutionary financial programme outlined in the Book of Discipline, intent as it was on separating teinds from other ecclesiastical revenues, had no possibility of success; and the

[50] Row, *History*, 16; Knox, *Works*, ii, 129–30, 181, 257–8, 297; *CSP Scot.*, i, nos. 958–9, 1056; *Diurnal*, 63.
[51] Knox, *Works*, ii, 257–8.   [52] *CSP Scot.*, i, no. 964.

government showed no signs of conceding the claims advanced. Another solution to the urgent financial problems of the reformed church, on principles at variance with those of the Book of Discipline, had therefore to be sought, and for success any solution had clearly to be acceptable to the crown and nobility as well as to satisfy the needs of the reformed church.

One temporary expedient reached in February 1561/2 was the 'assumption of the thirds of benefices', whereby a third of the revenues of all benefices was assigned to the support of the crown and reformed ministry, with existing benefice holders retaining two-thirds of their revenues. The origins of this measure can be traced to the privy council's efforts to reach agreement on how the revenues of benefices might be best apportioned to meet the requirements not only of existing benefice holders but also of the crown and reformed church with the summoning in December 1561 of a convention of the whole ecclesiastical estate of beneficed men to determine the appropriate concessions. Pressure for some financial solution had been steadily mounting from the protestant barons who threatened to prevent beneficed men from gathering their rents unless provision for the ministry was forthcoming. The threat was no idle boast, for during an earlier phase many lords 'held into thair awin handis the fructis that the Bischoppis and otheris of that sect had befoir abused; and so some parte was bestowed upoun the Ministeris. But then the Bischoppis began to grypp agane to that which most injustlie thei called thair awin; for the Erle of Arrane was discharged of Sanctandrois and Dunfermeling, whairwith befoir, be verteu of a factorie, he had intromitted: and so war many otheris'. Benefice holders, for their part, were anxious to find a solution which would leave them in secure possession of at least a portion of their revenues. 'The bishops sought to be restored', it was said, and so had offered a 'large contribution to be put in possession' of their revenues, agreeing to 'departe yearlye from vij partes of their lyvinges, wherof iiij shalbe imployede to the mayntaynance of preachers, fyndinge of schollers, and supporting of the poore, and the other iij to the increace of the Crowne, or more yf neade be (for those are the wordes!)'. At the same time, the privy council had ordered the superintendents, ministers, elders and deacons of the reformed church to submit a full list of ministers with an account of the finances necessary for sustaining them; and by February 1561/2, the privy council found that the needs of the crown and ministry amounted to as much as a third of all ecclesiastical revenues. Such a compromise was of course contrary to the ideals of the Book of Discipline which sought to streamline the chaotic state of ecclesiastical finances through a dissolution of the whole antiquated system of benefices, and John Knox showed no hesitation in condemning this device as not only unfair but ungodly.[53]

Mere criticism, however, did not prevent operation of the scheme which went some way towards reducing acute financial hardship among ministers. Even so, such an arrangement was inadequate and merely temporary. Yet, it did offer the possibility that, in the years ahead under a thoroughly protestant regime, ministers would be permitted to succeed to benefices as they fell vacant and that instead of subverting the benefice structure, the reformed ministry would gain access to it and so utilise it in the interests of the kirk. A realistic appraisal of the situation might therefore suggest that the needs of the reformed church would be better served by abandoning the financial theorizing of the first Book of Discipline in favour of reallocating the benefices of the old church for use by the new. There was already talk of revising the contents of the Book of Discipline in 1563,[54] so that its judgment on this matter, as on others, could scarcely be regarded as final. The general assembly, moreover, had come to recognise by 1565 the advantages which would accrue by incorporating the existing benefice system within the structure of the reformed church. The attainment of such an aim was facilitated first by an act of privy council in October 1566, which proposed that ministers should succeed to the lesser benefices worth less than three hundred merks a year as they became vacant, and, then, following the deposition of Mary and the accession of James VI, by an act of parliament in December 1567 which gave full effect to these proposals.[55]

Securing possession of the benefices, thereby arresting the trend toward secularisation, had been pursued as the only readily available answer to financing the work of the reformed church, but the assembly noticeably still declined to recognise as a permanent solution the inheritance of the old ecclesiastical structure and continued to assert a claim to the teinds as the proper patri-

---

[53] Knox, *Works*, ii, 298–310; *CSP Scot.*, i, no. 1056; *RPC*, i, 192–4, 196–7, 199–200, 202–3, 204–6; Keith, *History*, iii, 360–368.
[54] *BUK*, i, 41.   [55] *Ibid.*, 59, 62, 70; *RPC*, i, 487–8; *APS*, iii, 23.

mony of the kirk. Indeed, as events were to show, the ideals of the Book of Discipline, though temporarily set aside, were by no means abandoned. So far, the reformed church had had to co-exist and function as best it could with a sovereign who remained less than sympathetic to its requirements and who chose to conciliate the ministers in 1566 only for the political advantages which might ensue. The revolution of 1567, however, completely transformed the political situation and increased the general assembly's expectation that the reformed church would be finally accorded full support from the state which had been hitherto denied. Not content merely to acquiesce in the expediency of the thirds or in succeeding to the lesser benefices, the assembly in July 1567 resumed its campaign that 'ane perfyte ordour may be tane and establischit toward the full distribution of the patrimonie of the kirk according to Gods word', and reiterated the Book of Discipline's earlier claim that the kirk be put 'in full libertie of the patrimonie of the kirk according to the booke of God and the ordour and practise of the primitive kirk'.[56]

The ultimate objective of reforming ecclesiastical finances on a basis at variance with the existing benefice system was evidently still to the fore, and the assembly continued to press for a dissolution of the prelacies. Although the Regent Moray in 1569 was 'most willing that the kirk sould have been put in full possessioun of the proper patrimonie', a serious obstacle still existed in parliament's refusal to dissolve the greater benefices as the assembly required.[57] The problem, therefore, remained unresolved, for the provision of ministers to bishoprics had never formed any part of the assembly's programme. The reformed church had played no part in the crown's provision of Alexander Campbell, a minor, to the bishopric of Brechin in 1566, and the general assembly in 1569 had criticised John Carswell, superintendent of Argyll, 'for accepting the Bishoprik of the Isles not making the Assemblie forseene'.[58] Similarly, the crown's nomination, after Beaton's forfeiture, of a protestant candidate to the archbishopric of Glasgow according to a formula devised in January 1570/1[59] formed no part of the assembly's strategy in either polity or endowment, and indeed was flatly in contradiction to its plans for dismembering the prelacies and disentangling the revenues of the appropriated churches. Throughout, the

[56] BUK, i, 107–8.
[57] Ibid., 151; cf., 59–60.
[58] Watt, Fasti, 41, 206; BUK, i, 144.
[59] RSS, vi, no. 1107.

assembly's policy towards the fate of the bishoprics was consistent and unambiguous, and the crown's decision to make a fresh appointment to Glasgow in 1571 is to be regarded essentially as an exercise in magnate politics and not as part of a grand design to complete the process of identifying the reformed church with the ancient structure.

The nominee, John Porterfield, minister at Kilmaronock in the Lennox, enjoyed the support of the earl of Glencairn, who in 1568 had commended Porterfield to the assembly as a minister then 'banischt from Dumbartan', where the castle was held by the Hamilton supporters of the queen's party, and Glencairn himself had besieged the castle in 1569 on behalf of the king's party. By July 1569, the Regent Moray informed the assembly that Porterfield had been recommended 'be diverse great men' for presentation by the crown to the vicarage of Ardrossan, to which he had been presented as early as April 1568, and to the vicarage of Stevenston, to which he received a presentation in June 1569, despite the assembly's protest.[60] Both churches had been annexed to Kilwinning abbey whose control passed to Glencairn's son, Alexander Cunningham, in July 1571, with the death and forfeiture of Gavin Hamilton. Another son, James Cunningham, who served from 1571 as Scottish envoy to the English court for both Lennox and Mar, already had a claim, never wholly secured, to the commendatorship of Lesmahagow priory in 1557 and ended up as pensioner of Kelso abbey, which controlled Lesmahagow, only to discover in January 1570/1 that the Hamiltons had appropriated his pension from the fruits and rents of Lesmahagow.[61] But with the costly set-back suffered by the Hamilton supporters of the Marian cause after the triumph of the king's men, Glencairn and his family were poised to further their own cause in the west, and apart from the family's acquisition of monastic property, the nomination of the earl's own 'servitor' to succeed the forfeited Beaton,

---

[60] *Fasti*, iii, 5, 340, 350; *BUK*, i, 132, 153–4; *CSP Scot.*, ii, no. 1125; *RSS*, vi, nos. 256, 661, 2409. (A kinsman, Mr John Porterfield of that Ilk, with John Cunningham of Drumquhassill had an interst in the revenues of the provostry of Dumbarton, held by Cuthbert Cunningham. SRO, Register of Acts and Decreets, vol. 45, fo. 316v.)

[61] I. B. Cowan, *The Parishes of Medieval Scotland* (Edinburgh, 1967), 8, 187; I. B. Cowan and and D. E. Easson, *Medieval Religious Houses Scotland* (London, 1976), 68–9; *CSP Scot.*, iii, nos. 608, 695, 713, 764, 782, 820–21, 848–49 *et passim*; cf., Thirds of Benefices, 259n.2.

who was Mary's emissary in France, could hardly have been other than attractive to Glencairn, who had earlier shown an interest in the temporalities of the archbishopric,[62] and probably also to the Lennox Stewarts whose chief, as Regent, had sanctioned the appointment. Nor was there anything exceptional in the bid by a prominent layman for control of a bishopric, effected usually through the device of accompanying the bishop's nomination with the reservation of pensions from the see, as much earlier and some subsequent history all too clearly reveals.

No word of Porterfield's candidature for the archbishopric is to be found in the acts of the assembly, but a hint of the episode is probably suggested in the proceedings of March 1570/1 when Glencairn's son, 'Captain James Cunninghame, servitour to my Lord Regents Grace presented a letter to the brethren' of the assembly with a request that the next assembly be held in Glasgow to assist discussions on 'the estate and affairs of the Church; as also the Kings Majesty, and common wealth of this countrey'. This led the assembly to reply by requesting *inter alia* that 'his Grace and Counsell grant and consent that no disposition of any benefice or presentation be made of any person without the admission and collation of the Kirk', which would indicate an awareness that some such move was afoot.[63] Certainly, a response from the church to the government's action in making appointments to bishoprics could scarcely be further postponed when the crown in August 1571 provided the aged John Douglas, principal of St Mary's college and not a minister, to the archbishopric of St Andrews, vacant since the execution of John Hamilton for treason in April 1571.[64] In a sweeping attack on the abuses which he detected within the kirk, John Knox prepared the way in August 1571 by urging the assembly never to 'suffer unworthie men to be thrust in into the ministrie of the Kirk under quhat pretence that ever it be' but to 'resist that tyrranie as ye wald avoyd hells fyre' and so 'gainstand the mercilesse devorers of the patrimonie of the Kirk'.[65] For its part, the assembly decided to appoint a commission to meet the Regent at Stirling, and on 8 September in an effort to avert criticism of the failure to take account of ecclesiastical opinion the Regent Mar's newly formed government appointed its own commission, composed of substantially the same personnel as the assembly's, to examine the

[62] *BUK*, i, 132.   [63] *Ibid.*, 185, 188.
[64] Watt, *Fasti*, 299.   [65] *BUK*, i, 199.

fitness of the two archbishops 'be ressoun thay ar to have the charge and oversicht of the inferiour ministeris'.[66]

The decision, anticipated here, that the kirk should inherit the bishoprics and that the crown's nominees after due examination should undertake active service was logical enough but nonetheless startlingly novel, and it had yet to be debated by the assembly which was still committed to dissolving the bishoprics. At the same time, the government's action in granting James Paton the bishopric of Dunkeld by simple gift on the same day that it announced its commission to examine the fitness of the two archbishops seemed to betray its declared intention of promoting suitably qualified candidates. Paton, at least, had served as a minister, unlike some other appointees, but he was thought to have owed his appointment to the influence of the earl of Argyll with whom he was suspected of having entered into a simoniacal agreement.[67]

Both the archbishops appeared in parliament in September 1571, despite the superintendent of Fife's warning to Douglas that he should not attend, on pain of excommunication, until he be 'admitted by the kirk'. Once more, the barons and gentry defended the ministers' cause by condemning the tyranny whereby 'the kirk sall be compelled to admitt dumbe dogges to the office, dignitie and rents appointed for sustentatioun of preaching pastors and for other godlie uses', and in their address to the Regent and council they proceeded to censure the practice whereby 'erles and lords become bishops and abbots, gentlemen, courteours' babes, and persons unable to guide themselves, are promoted by you to suche benefices as require learned preachers. When such enormiteis are fostered, we say, what a face of a kirk sall we looke for ere it be long within this realme?' The impasse was accentuated when the collectors of the thirds of benefices, who were accountable to the assembly, refused to allow Douglas of St Andrews to gather certain rents from the archbishopric on the grounds that he lacked the 'consent, assent or admission' of the church; and the situation was saved only by the intervention of Erskine of Dun, the superintendent of Angus, who offered the Regent Mar a firm but acceptable compromise in November 1571.[68]

[66] *Ibid.*, 200; *RSS*, vi, nos. 2810-11.

[67] *RSS*, vi, no. 2812; *BUK*, i, 270, 300, 314; Keith, *Bishops*, 97.

[68] *APS*, iii, 70; Bannatyne, *Memoriales*, 183, 197; Calderwood, *History*, iii, 138, 144-46, 156-62.

After attacking 'that great misorder used in Stirling at the last parliament, in creating bishops, placing them, and giving them vote in parliament as bishops, in despite of the kirk, and high contempt of God', Erskine argued reasonably that all benefices, greater and lesser, possessing teinds had spiritual offices attached, and that it therefore lay within the power of the church alone to examine and admit all candidates presented to benefices. Any hint that the church sought possession of the greater benefices from 'avarice and ambition' was effectively dispelled by recalling that it had always been the church's policy to dissolve the prelacies and to separate the appropriated churches. 'But if this cannot be granted', he continued, 'I meane the dismembring (as they call it) of great benefices, I trust, in respect of this confused troublous time, the kirk will consent (the benefices joyned therunto being givin after the order before spokin, that the priviledge and libertie of the kirk be not hurt) to assigne suche profites as may be spaired above the reasounable sustentatioun of the authoritie and commoun effaires for the present, whill further order may be tane in these maters'. In less conciliatory tone, Erskine defended the continued existence of superintendents, 'notwithstanding anie others that intruse themselves, or are placed by suche as have no power in suche offices', for unless 'that misordered creation of bishops be not reformed, the kirk will first compleane unto God, and also unto all their brethrein, members of the kirk within this realme, and to all reformed kirks within Europe'.[69]

Anxious to reach agreement, the Regent Mar, in reply, recognised the need for 'reforming of things disordered in all sorts, als farre as may be, reteaning the priviledge of the king, crown, and patronage', and attributed the whole misunderstanding to the belief that 'the policie of the Kirk of Scotland is not perfyte'. He therefore asked whether a conference of commissioners from the crown and kirk could be arranged to meet at Leith in order to resolve outstanding problems. The confrontation between church and state was thus averted with the summoning of the Convention of Leith in January 1571/2, which reached agreement on the procedures to be followed for appointments to the greater benefices; but in achieving this compromise, it also set aside many of the assumptions of the first Book of Discipline, and led Knox to protest that the 'kirke of Scotland suld not be subject to that ordore which then was used, consiidering the

[69] Calderwood, *History*, iii, 156-62.

lordis of Scotland had subscryvit, and also confirmed in parliament the ordore alreadie and long agoe appointed, in the buike of discipline'.[70]

Criticism of the Leith settlement of 1572

After more than sixty delegates – superintendents, ministers, barons, and commissioners of provinces, towns and kirks – convened at Leith in January 1571/2 to give their deliberations the force of a general assembly, eight superintendents and ministers were selected, or any four of them, to negotiate with eight commissioners, or any four of them, appointed by the Regent and privy council, and they were then to report their conclusions to the next general assembly for approval. In the 'quiet conference' which ensued, agreement was reached on the structure which the church's endowment should assume. Access to the lesser benefices had been established by 1567, and this principle was extended in 1572 by assigning the church an active rôle in appointments to the greater benefices which, far from being dissolved, were to remain unaltered. The ancient diocesan structure was thus to be incorporated within the reformed church. Candidates of at least thirty years of age, nominated by the crown within a year and a day of the vacancy occurring, were to be provided to the bishoprics after due examination and election by a chapter of ministers. The newly created bishops were to exercise no greater jurisdiction than the superintendents 'quhill the same be agreit upoun' and were to be subject to 'the Kirk and Generall Assembly' in spiritual matters as they were to the king in temporal matters.[71]

Arrangements were also made for settling procedures governing the monastic property. No further appointments were to be made until the teinds were distinguished from the lands and their rents so that adequate stipends might be allotted, with the advice of the bishop or superintendent, to the ministers of the appropriated churches. The title and rest of the revenues were to be assigned to suitably qualified candidates who, after examination by the bishop or superintendent, would represent the ecclesiastical

[70] *Ibid.*, 163–5, 168–9, 207; Bannatyne, *Memoriales*, 256–7, The Book of Discipline had been approved not by parliament, as Knox is reported to have remarked, but by the convention of nobles and barons which met in January 1561. See above, 15.

[71] *BUK*, i, 203–9; *CSP Scot.*, iv, no. 149.

estate in parliament, or even act as senators, thereby replenishing the ecclesiastical element, in the college of justice, or be employed in other aspects of royal service. On the extinction of surviving monastic chapters, ministers from the annexed churches were to form new chapters to assist the commendator in administering the revenues.[72]

As with the monastic property, the spirituality pertaining to deaneries and provostries of collegiate churches was to be distinguished from the temporality to provide suitable stipends for ministers, and the prebends of these foundations were explicitly reserved for the support of students at university. Nor were the needs of the poor overlooked, for it was recommended that all persons promoted to ecclesiastical livings should be liable to a levy of a tenth of their income derived from teinds for the support of the poor.[73]

The rights of patronage to benefices appropriated to prelacies were also secured. Access to these benefices having the cure of souls was to be confined to ministers found to be fit by the superintendent or bishop and of at least twenty-three years of age who were required to take up residence, and pluralism was expressly forbidden. Vicarages with an annual value of £40 or less were to be conferred on readers, who were now to be permitted to conduct baptisms and marriages; and surplus funds from wealthier benefices might be properly reallocated by the ordinary to augment inadequate stipends elsewhere.[74]

Such a comprehensive settlement, which skilfully sought to accommodate the interests of the crown and needs of the kirk, was not without its advantages, though it had its defects too, and above all it had still to be subjected to the assembly's scrutiny. Knox's undisguised hostility towards the settlement, his warning that the church should never be subjected to that order, and his declared preference for adhering to the earlier proposals of the Book of Discipline, which he had helped to devise in 1560, already suggested that the agreement might be received with less than wholehearted approval. This was confirmed when the Perth assembly of August 1572 expressed serious misgivings about many aspects of the new constitution. By then, even the original commissioners from the church who negotiated the terms had second thoughts on sanctioning the proposals without emendation Indeed, when all but one of these negotiators were appointed, with

[72] *BUK*, i, 210.   [73] *Ibid.*, 213–16.   [74] *Ibid.*, 211–13.

six others, to an assembly committee to examine the Leith agreement, to assess the attitudes of assembly members who were invited to submit criticisms, and to advise on those articles of the settlement which should be 'retained or altered', they took the unprecedented step of issuing a formal 'protestation' which attacked many of the assumptions accepted at Leith. The protestation, which may be stated at length, ran as follows:[75]

'For sameikle as in the Assemblie of the Kirk haldin in Leith in January last, ther was certaine Commissioners appointed to travell with the Nobilitie and their Commissioners to reason and conclude upon diverse articles then thoght good to be conferritt upon: According to the quhilk commission they have proceidit to divers dyatts and conventions, and finallie concludit for that tyme upon the saids heids and articles, as the same produceit in this Assembly proportis. In the quhilks beand considderit and red are found certaine names, sick as Archbishop, Deane, Archdeane, Chancellour, Chapter, quhilks names were found slanderous and offensive to the ears of many of the brethren, appeirand to sound to papistrie: Therfor the haill Assemblie in ane voyce, asweill they that were in Commission at Leith as uthers, solemlie protests, that they intend not be useing sick names to ratifie, consent and aggrie to any kynd of Papistrie or superstition, and wishes rather the saids names to be changeit into uthers that are not slanderous or offensive. And in lyke manner protests, that the saids heids and articles aggreit upon be only receivit as ane interim, untill farder and more perfyte ordour be obtainit at the hands of the Kings Majesties Regent and Nobilitie; for the quhilk they will prease as occasion sall serve: Unto the quhilk protestation the haill Assemblie presently conveened in ane voyce adheres.'

The assembly's decision to accept the Leith settlement only on a temporary basis 'as ane interim untill farder and more perfyte ordour be obtainit' quickly dispelled any impression that the settlement was expected to have permanence. The dissatisfaction expressed was evidently strong, and the ideals of the Book of Discipline, to which Knox now appealed, were not to be readily disregarded. The reaction of the assembly, at this point, proved to be crucial, for this was the first real test of ecclesiastical opinion. After all, the sixty or so members of the Convention of Leith,

[75] *Ibid.*, 244–47.

other than the eight commissioned to negotiate, had not been consulted on the terms agreed, and the next assembly at St Andrews in March 1571/2 had merely selected a committee to meet, significantly enough, in John Knox's house (presumably in St Andrews where Knox was then resident) to consider how far the settlement was 'agreeable to Gods word and to the utility of the Kirk'.[76] By August 1572, there had been ample time for reflection, and even Erskine of Dun, who had been the driving force in favour of a settlement, evidently withheld express approval; not only did he help to produce the 'protestation', he also acted as moderator of the same assembly which declined to accept the Leith agreement as a lasting settlement.[77] All in all, the church's matured judgment was both cautious and qualified in its attitude towards the 'concordat of Leith', and a reflection of the ambivalence with which it was received was the failure to accord the agreement the parliamentary approval which its creators had anticipated. English diplomatic reports immediately after the Leith agreement had indicated that the Regent was fully prepared 'to have it enacted by Parliament as a law', and it was thus believed that there would 'not be great let to have it allowed by parliament'.[78] That it was not presented to the three estates is clearly an indication of the subsequent lack of unanimity on the subject, and a measure of the church's misgivings towards certain aspects of the settlement. Such a conclusion was voiced in the privy council, some time later, when it was acknowledged in 1576 that the Leith settlement was merely a 'prevat constitutioun as is the said pretendit ordinance maid at Leyth, quhilk is nayther constitute be the Estaittis as a law, nor yit is it ressavit be the ministerie universalie, bot oppugnit and callit in doubt be thame selffis in divers the maist substanciall pointis of the same'.[79]

The critical reception accorded to the Leith arrangements was no doubt a setback for those who sought to identify the old ecclesiastical structure with the new, but it certainly did not prevent the scheme from operating, for the assembly at least had consented to adhere to it until a more agreeable alternative could be devised. In these new circumstances, Knox allowed his earlier hostility somewhat to abate, and showed himself ready to acquiesce in the assembly's interpretation of the agreement merely as a temporary measure, provided the plan operated to the church's

[76] *Ibid.*, 238.   [77] *Ibid.*, 243–5.
[78] *CSP Scot.*, iv, no. 149; *cf.*, *ibid.*, no. 519.   [79] *RPC*, ii, 565.

benefit; hence his concern for the elimination of abuses and for ensuring that only qualified candidates be presented to the greater benefices;[80] but such a realistic appraisal of the situation did not require Knox to abandon his hopes for the ultimate supersession of 'that ordore' – the Leith episcopacy – by another more carefully attuned to the reformation principles of 1560.

It is by no means difficult to understand the reservations expressed and, in particular, the assembly's reluctance to accord the settlement any permanence. For a start, the scheme devised was manifestly at odds with the church's declared aim, reaffirmed as recently as 1571,[81] of securing the abolition of bishoprics and abbacies, and there was little indication that such an objective had been abandoned. Concern was also expressed at the intention of incorporating within the church such 'slanderous and offensive' pre-reformation titles as archbishop, dean, archdeacon and chapter. The assembly's reservation that by using such obnoxious titles ministers were not intending to sanction 'any kynd of Papistrie or superstition' is itself indicative of a more general apprehension that the adoption of alterations in titles might presage further, more drastic, changes to come.[82] Bishops, after all, though subject to the assembly, were only to have no greater powers than superintendents until further agreement was reached. Again, if the contention held good that archbishoprics and bishoprics had ecclesiastical offices attached to the livings and that the holders ought to possess a function in the kirk, it was just as plausible to argue, and hard not to concede, that archdeacons and the successors of other pre-reformation dignities should also be permitted to exercise their traditional ecclesiastical offices. There was to say the least a confusion or illogicality in thought in a compromise which accepted the bishop's rôle in ecclesiastical administration while denying the same to the holders of other benefices which had denoted office in the pre-reformation church. The general assembly, as best it could, sought to distinguish the legal styles signifying possession of benefices from the ecclesiastical titles denoting office and the exercise of a spiritual ministry in the kirk, as it had largely succeeded in doing since the incorporation of the lesser benefices from 1566, and in an effort to clarify matters had recommended that 'archbishop' should be replaced by 'bishop', which of course did have scriptural

[80] *BUK*, i, 247–9.
[81] Calderwood, *History*, iii, 159.   [82] *BUK*, i, 246.

warranty, 'in these things concerning the function of the Kirk'; but, then, this of course was one of the reasons why the first Book of Discipline had avoided any identity between the two structures in the first place, and had approved the dismantling of the pre-reformation system of benefices. Other modifications, sanctioned by the assembly, included the substitution of 'bishop's assembly' for 'chapter', of 'moderator' for 'dean'; alternatives were to be found for 'archdeacon' and 'chancellor', which were 'so offensive to the ears of a great number of the Kirk'; 'abbot' and 'prior' were also to be changed to 'other names more agreeable to Gods word and the policies of the best reformed Kirks'; and further thought was to be given to the functions of these offices.[83]

The conservatism of the styles devised by the lawyers and borrowed from pre-reformation practice was also apparent in the formulae and rites for 'consecration' and for the imposition of hands, which the reformers had repudiated in 1560 in the belief that it was 'neither the clipping of their crownes, the greasing of their fingers, nor the blowing of the dumb dogges called the Bishops, neither the laying on of their hands that maketh Ministers of Christ Jesus'.[84] Indeed, so much of the earlier terminology was now to be reused that it was evidently thought advisable by those who drafted the Leith articles to refer, lest unnecessary confusion should arise, to the 'election of the trew bishop' and to the 'trew reformit Kirk'; yet while there was much talk of 'reverend fathers in God', of ordinaries and of metropolitan and cathedral kirks,[85] little concern was shown for effective pastoral oversight, now all the more urgent with the adoption of the obsolete diocesan framework with its irrational boundaries and irregularities instead of the streamlined provinces for superintendents proposed by the Book of Discipline. Nor were suspicions by members of the assembly who found aspects of the settlement 'appeirand to sound to papistrie' altogether groundless, for even the seal of the protestant archbishop of Glasgow depicted a mitred figure in episcopal vestments, presumably St Kentigern, enthroned and flanked by several crosses with crozier before him

[83] *Ibid.*

[84] *RSS*, vi, nos. 1473, 1474, 1672; vii, nos. 101, 186, 1254, 1646; Calderwood, *History*, iii, 207; Bannatyne, *Memoriales*, 224; *The First Book of Discipline*, 102, 207.

[85] *BUK*, i, 219, 221, 226–7.

all of which could be readily mistaken for the 'papistrie' which the assembly so professedly abhorred.[86]

Another departure from the principles of 1560 was the exclusion of the Christian community from any direct voice in episcopal appointments, for the method now approved was essentially restrictive, consisting as it did in nomination by the crown and election (or rejection) by a chapter of ministers, a procedure which departed from the Book of Discipline's belief that, with the establishment of the office, superintendents should be nominated by at least the kirk session and town council of the chief town in the province and then be elected with 'publick consent' by the votes of ministers and congregations.[87] Nor was consent by the people intended to be a mere formality, as Alexander Gordon, bishop of Galloway, discovered when he tried to bribe the electors in an unsuccessful bid to become superintendent of Galloway in 1563; and even though he claimed nomination by the privy council, the general assembly judged this to be insufficient, refusing to 'acknowledge him for a superintendent lawfullie called for the present', and had inquired whether the churches of Galloway 'craved anie superintendent or not, and whom they sought', all of which effectively demonstrates that a claim to nomination by the civil power was insufficient to guarantee provision as a superintendent.[88] Similarly, although the privy council's advice was sometimes sought by the assembly in the various abortive negotiations to appoint additional superintendents, nomination effectively lay not with the privy council but with the assembly, which drew up leets of candidates.[89]

The contrast between the reformers' ideals and the prevailing procedure for electing bishops after 1572 is all too apparent, and what is equally evident is that the machinery for nominating bishops by the crown did not always work in the best interests of the church. Too often appointments of the unreformed variety continued to be made, and none of the ablest ministers became bishops. The Earl of Morton seemed particularly intent on securing dynastic or unreformed appointments. Two fellow Douglases were advanced to the sees of St Andrews and Moray;

[86] GUA, Blackhouse MS. 422; cf., J. H. Stevenson and M. Wood, *Scottish Heraldic Seals* (Glasgow, 1940), i, 114–5.
[87] BUK, i, 217–19; *The First Book of Discipline*, 125–6.
[88] Knox, *Works*, ii, 374–5; BUK, i, 15.   [89] BUK, i, 27, 28, 30, 32, 54.

the earl of Montrose's kinsman, though not even a minister, was provided to Dunblane; Argyll was influential in the appointment to Dunkeld; and in Glasgow, where Porterfield failed to secure his earlier appointment, James Boyd, the nephew of lord Boyd, an ally of Glencairn, was 'inducit be his Cheiff to tak the bishoprie, the gift wharof the said Lord Boid, being a grait counsellour to the Regent, haid purchassit for his commoditie'. All this certainly lends substance to the protest voiced by Patrick Adamson, then 'a zealus preatchour against Bischopes', who in 1572 had distinguished three sorts of bishop: the papal prelate or 'my lord bishop', the 'tulchan bishop' who was 'my lord's bishop', and 'the Lord's bishop' whom he identified with 'the trew Minister of the Gospell'.[90]

The failure of chapters effectively to resist improper or even scandalous nominations by the crown could scarcely be concealed, though efforts were sometimes made to oppose unsatisfactory nominees. Great difficulty was experienced in securing the chapter's agreement to Douglas's re-election to St Andrews, for it was said that 'many of the godlie ministeris were against it', one member of the chapter made a formal protest, and Knox showed his disapproval by refusing to take part in the inauguration, but Douglas, 'ane agit learnad man', nonetheless secured his appointment.[91] As further sees were filled, the assembly expressed particular concern in 1574 over the chapter's rôle in the election to Moray of George Douglas, the earl of Angus's illegitimate son and an adventurer from pre-reformation times, long known as postulate of Arbroath, who had great difficulty in satisfying an assembly committee of his formal qualifications; and the assembly also intervened in the appointment of Andrew Graham to Dunblane and of Alexander Hepburn to Ross.[92] In an effort to prevent further abuse in March 1574/5, the assembly prohibited all chapters from proceeding to episcopal elections until the nominees had first satisfied the assembly of their fitness in 'doctrine life and conversation'; and in St Andrews the archbishopric was left vacant on Douglas' death in 1574 'because the [electoral] College will not agree to choose a man of the Regent's nomina-

[90] Keith, *Bishops*, 39–40, 97, 151, 181, 261; Melville, *Diary*, 31–32, 47; Calderwood, *History*, iii, 206; Hume, *History of the Houses of Douglas and Angus*, 320–1.
[91] Bannatyne, *Memoriales*, 223, 256–7; Calderwood, *History*, 206–7; *CSP Scot.*, iv, no. 149.
[92] *BUK*, i, 288, 300–2, 303–4, 308, 315, 317, 320–21, 323, 325–6.

tion'.[93] Amidst the disquiet surrounding episcopal appointments, an Edinburgh minister and member of the Convention of Leith, put before the assembly in 1575 the not inappropriate question 'whither if the Bischops, as they are now in the Kirk of Scotland, hes thair function of the word of God or not, or if the Chapiter appointit for creating of them aucht to be tollerated in this reformed Kirk'.[94] Yet, it was not merely the method by which bishops were appointed or even the fitness of the candidates which caused criticism. Bishops, on their own admission, proved unable to administer their dioceses to the standards set by the assembly, and chapters, whose consent was required in dispositions of episcopal property, proved as ineffective in preventing dilapidation of the bishoprics as in preventing inappropriate nominees.

Since the superintendents, even with the benefits of their streamlined provinces, had found their office arduous and unrewarding, repeatedly asking the assembly to relieve them from office,[95] it was not surprising that the new bishops experienced even greater problems in supervising their antiquated sees which sometimes possessed detached parishes as enclaves in other dioceses. In particular, the disproportionately large sees of St Andrews and Glasgow were hardly conducive to efficient pastoral oversight. The respectable though aged Douglas of St Andrews, who still retained his university offices, soon realised 'because the bounds are great and he not able to doe his office in his own person' that 'some of the Godliest and best learned' would require to be appointed, as he informed the assembly, to assist 'in taking order how the whole Diocie may be served'. It was obvious that the services of the existing superintendents and commissioners could not be summarily dispensed with; and though the Regent Morton might ignore their complaints and claim that with the election of bishops their office was no longer necessary, the assembly saw matters differently and continued them in office alongside the bishops.[96]

Although the assembly proceeded to criticise Douglas for visiting 'by others and not be himself', the elderly archbishop was by no means unique, for younger and more energetic men found

[93] *Ibid.*, 326–7; *CSP Scot.*, v, no. 187.
[94] *BUK*, i, 340; Spottiswoode, *History*, ii, 200.
[95] *BUK*, i, 39, 77, 120, 242, 296–7, 302–3; Bannatyne, *Memoriales*, 227.
[96] *BUK*, i, 242, 243–4, 286, 296–7, 302–3, 318, 338; Spottiswoode, *History*, ii, 195–6.

their duties no less severe. The archbishop of Glasgow admitted in 1575 that the 'bounds belonging to his jurisdiction was so large and wide that one person was not able to visite and oversee them', and so the assembly appointed two commissioners to assist him.[97] Other bishops with smaller dioceses were also criticised. In 1573, Paton of Dunkeld was accused in the assembly that 'he had received the name of a Bishop, but they had not heard that he had used the office of a Bishop within his bounds', and a minister was subsequently appointed to visit the diocese at the bishop's expense.[98] The young bishop of Brechin had to be instructed to accompany Erskine of Dun, the superintendent of Angus, at visitations 'that he may see the order and proceeding used by the Superintendent in his office'; and in Moray an additional commissioner was appointed 'to support the visitation of Murrey, and consider the Bishop's diligence with the complaints of the Ministers of the countrie against him, during his residence there'.[99] As bishop of Dunblane, Andrew Graham seems to have played little part in diocesan administration, and later confessed that 'he never gaif ony collatioun to beneficis to na persone sen his admissioun to the foirsaid bishoprie as the foirsaid brethrein in Dumblane present knew, and being demandit thairof affermit the same'.[100] By the early 1570s, then, commissioners and the three surviving superintendents had still to operate in virtually every diocese, despite the appointment of protestant bishops to eleven of the thirteen sees; and in a practical reappraisal of this complicated, inconsistent and even chaotic system of oversight, the assembly finally resolved in 1576 that:[101]

> 'the great and intollerable burden lying to the charge of Bishops, Superintendents and Commissioners, is, and hath been, the very cause that the whole Kirk within thir bounds could not be duely overseen, consequently good discipline unexercised within the same for lack of visitation'.

It was therefore decided to scrap the dioceses as units for visitation and to introduce visitors (ministers commissioned by the assembly for a term) to undertake supervision of smaller, more manageable districts.[102] The prospect, in short, was a return to something like

[97] BUK, i, 270, 286–7, 317–18.   [98] Ibid., 270, 337.
[99] Ibid., 318, 337.
[100] SRO, CH2/722/1. Stirling Presbytery Records, 25 December 1582.
[101] BUK, i, 353.   [102] Ibid., 353–9.

the system of ecclesiastical administration which operated with effect in the 1560s.

The financial loopholes associated with the Leith settlement, which permitted the alienation for secular purposes of revenues from the bishoprics and abbacies, gave grounds for further concern. The main opportunity afforded by the agreement had been the prospect that the church would inherit a greater portion of what it claimed was its proper patrimony. That this had been a sufficient inducement to secure co-operation, on at least a temporary basis, was suggested by David Ferguson's sermon preached before the Convention of Leith in which he had renewed the church's claim for a restoration of its full patrimony.[103] In practice, however, through pressure or persuasion bishops were prevailed upon by their kinsmen to feu lands or set in tack teinds or grant and confirm pensions in money or kind from episcopal property.

There were already precedents, for in the assembly of March 1569/70 Adam Bothwell of Orkney had been accused of simony and he admitted to setting in tack the fruits of his bishopric,[104] though such a confession did not deter him from feuing lands belonging to his see or from granting pensions on a substantial scale from the abbey of Holyrood,[105] by an arrangement of 1568 in which he exchanged the temporalities of the bishopric for the commendatorship of the abbey,[106] and he was ready to consent to the charters of others who wished to indulge in similar activities.[107] Another conspicuous dilapidator was Paton of Dunkeld, who had been accused in the assembly of August 1574 of making a simoniacal pact with Argyll. His reply was that he had refused the earl's overtures, but he did admit to yielding certain pensions from the bishopric, which he had since revoked, and to dilapidating his benefice by setting a nineteen years' tack of teind victual to Argyll; and as part of his defence pled that he had been forced to make the agreement on account of 'his house being beseiged, and his son taken away'. His activities are known to have included the feuing of episcopal lands to other parties besides Argyll, and although he ingeniously suggested

---

[103] Ferguson, *Tracts*, 57–80.   [104] *BUK*, i, 162–3, 166–7.
[105] *RSS*, vii, no. 988; vi, nos. 1302, 1317; vii, 1495, 1776, 2196.
[106] G. Donaldson, 'Bishop Adam Bothwell and the Reformation in Orkney', *RSCHS*, xiii, 85–100, at 100; *RSS*, vi, no. 506.
[107] *Ibid.*, vii, nos. 1711, 2206, 2130, 2558, 2559.

that an act of assembly against dilapidation applied only to ministers and not to bishops, the assembly dismissed his excuses and first suspended, then finally deprived, him from office in 1576, a decision with which the Regent could find no fault.[108]

As bishop of Brechin, the young Alexander Campbell was liberal in bestowing feu charters including one to his chief, the earl of Argyll;[109] and Robert Stewart, as bishop of Caithness and commendator of St Andrews priory (after Moray's death), was lavish in his grants,[110] whereas James Boyd, as archbishop of Glasgow, at least made some attempt to keep grants of feus and pensions within his family,[111] though the Regent Morton was clearly not to be outdone.[112] After his accession to St Andrews, Patrick Adamson, who had been minister of the Regent's household, was no exception in feuing episcopal lands, and he proved to be positively generous in assigning pensions, particularly to retainers and servitors of the Regent Morton.[113] From the evidence of the privy seal and great seal, Andrew Graham of Dunblane appears to have been almost respectable, but a glimpse into his financial transactions from another source casts a very different light on Graham's career. In the parliament of July 1578, the kindly tenants of Dunblane complained that Andrew Graham, 'provost of the bishopric', had set the temporalities of the see in feu to his kinsman, the earl of Montrose, whereby a thousand 'commonis and pure people wilbe put to uter heirschip and extreme beggartie . . . quhen as sa grite rowmes quhairupoun sa mony ar sustenit salbe reducit in the handis of ane particular man'.[114]

In the light of these developments, it is not surprising to find that contemporary opinion condemned a settlement which permitted the nobility to acquire:[115]

---

[108] *BUK*, i, 300, 314–15, 331–2, 340–1, 350–2; *RMS*, iv, nos. 2236–2244, 2318, 2397, 2504, 2631, 2719, 2871, 2989; *RSS*, vii, nos. 426, 2367.

[109] *RMS*, iv, nos. 1745, 1764, 2228, 2443, 2833.

[110] *RSS*, vii, nos. 987, 2696; vi, nos. 1144, 1285, 1564, 1721, 2059, 2438; vii, 812, 1198, 1234–5, 1358, 1675–6, 1735, 1894A, 1901, 1983, 2319, 2696.

[111] *RMS*, iv, nos. 2382, 2407, 2881, 2937; SRO, CH4/1/2, Register of Presentations to Benefices, fos. 83v.–84r.

[112] *RMS*, iv, nos. 2727, 2764. For further grants, see *ibid.*, nos. 2199, 2416, 2938, 3012; *RSS*, vii, nos. 180, 1413, 2075, 2126.

[113] *RMS*, iv, nos. 2703–2706, 2725, 2831, 3030; *RSS*, vii, nos. 1137, 1139; 827, 864, 868, 941, 1614, 1726, 1746, 2015, 2182, 2226, 2493, 2497; 824, 862–864, 866, 867, 869, 902, 916.

[114] *APS*, iii, 111–12; *cf.*, 165–6.   [115] Pitscottie, *Historie*, ii, 283.

'sic proffeit be thir counterfet bischopis that thay obtenit fewis, takis and teindis as thay pleisit. And thir bischopis war namit throche the cuntrie the lordis counterfett bischopis and nocht men of the kirk of god nor guid religion.'

The Leith agreement had been tested and its defects revealed. The evils of tulchanism – the milking of the bishoprics – were doubtless modest by pre-reformation standards, but their existence in a church which professed to be reformed could be scarcely condoned. Other ministers, it is true, were also guilty of dilapidating their benefices on a smaller scale, but the very wealth of the bishoprics and abbacies made the resulting abuses all the more glaring and intolerable. Moreover, the transference of episcopal functions from bishops to visitors in 1576 made the retention of the revenues of the sees nominally in the possession of individual bishops all the less defensible, and it was harder to justify the continued existence of bishoprics as ecclesiastical entities. The earlier ideal of the reformers for the elimination of the bishoprics had not been abandoned, and it threatened to eclipse the Leith episcopacy.

The search for a 'perfect polity'

Behind the financial arrangements of 1572 there had indeed emerged a formal episcopate professedly based on imitation of Anglican procedure, on following as far as possible, so it was said, 'the order of the kirke of England'; and critics were no doubt justified in seeing the concordat as part of the government's policy of 'conformity with England', of approximating the structure of the Scottish church to that of England.[116] Yet the adoption of the ancient financial structure by itself did not affect the machinery of government, other than the substitution of bishops for superintendents, since the ecclesiastical courts remained unchanged by the Leith settlement: general assemblies, to which the bishops were subject, synods and kirk sessions continued as before, and even the machinery of the superintendent's court was not allowed to lapse.[117] The similarities with English practice, in any event, were purely superficial, for church government, as distinct from the financial framework, came no closer to that of England; and any equation of the Scottish superintendent (or

---

[116] *CSP Scot.*, iv, no. 149; Melville, *Diary*, 45.
[117] *RStAKS*, i, 367, 377, 381, 387, 421–2.

bishop), minister and reader with the English bishop, priest and deacon can be made only with reservation, since the Anglican church also possessed readers,[118] and the Scottish church still had exhorters in addition to readers, two temporary offices until sufficient ministers were had, as well as the distinctive offices of elders and deacons as an integral part of its constitution.

If the Regent Mar had detected in 1571 that 'the default of the whole standeth in this that the policie of the Kirk of Scotland is not perfyte' and had sought agreement for 'reducing of thingis disorderit to a perfite rule and uniformitie', the assembly declined to acknowledge any improvement after the arrangements of 1572 and preferred the prospect of their supersession by a 'farder and more perfyte ordour'.[119] But, in any case, continuing debate on the implications of the Leith settlement inevitably raised other related issues directly affecting the church's government and jurisdiction. There were questions of accountability, of the relationship of the new bishops to the existing superintendents, none of whom curiously then became bishop, of diocesan administration, of oversight and visitation, of ecclesiastical representation in parliament, privy council and college of justice; and in the aftermath of the civil war the whole question of the church's relationship to the state and the issue of royal supremacy required fresh examination.

The Convention of Leith itself had sought to remove any ambiguities which might arise between the bishops and superintendents by requiring the former to 'exerce na further jurisdictioun in spirituall functioun nor the superintendentis hes and presently exerces, quhill the same be agreit upoun'. In theory, therefore, the bishops like the superintendents were subject to the censures of the ministers and elders of each province, as the first Book of Discipline had recommended; in practice, they were certainly subordinate to the assembly, for it was agreed at Leith that 'all Archebischoppes and Bischoppis be subject to the Kirk and Generall Assembly thairof *in spiritualibus*, as thay ar to the King *in temporalibus*'; and it was possibly a certain apprehension lest bishops acquired greater powers which led the assembly in March 1573/4 to reassert that the bishops' jurisdiction should 'not exceid the jurisdictioun of Superintendents, quhilk heirtofoir

---

[118] Strype, *Annals*, I, i, 515–16; ii, 496.
[119] Calderwood, *History*, iii, 164; Bannatyne, *Memoriales*, 205–6; *RPC*, ii, 90; *BUK*, i, 246.

they have had and presentlie hes; and that they salbe subject to the discipline of the Generall Assemblie as members therof, as the Superintendents hes bein heirtofor in all sorts'.[120]

Difficulties in ecclesiastical administration were resolved, first, with the assembly's decision to retain commissioners and superintendents as overseers and as assistants to the bishops, then, with the introduction in 1576 of visitors or commissioners for smaller areas to replace the outdated diocesan machinery inherited at Leith. Even so, bishops still possessed powers not enjoyed by other overseers since they were entitled to sit in parliament as successors to the pre-reformation episcopate, and they were eligible for election to the privy council, all of which confounded the separate jurisdictions of church and state which the earlier reformers had sought to distinguish. Both Henry Balnaves and John Knox had emphasized how it was no part of a bishop's, or minister's, office to meddle with secular affairs; the first Book of Discipline had declared ministers ineligible for membership of the privy council; and the general assembly from 1564 had proceeded against the conforming bishops of Orkney and Galloway for accepting appointment on the privy council and court of session.[121] Although the assembly was prepared in 1572 to make an exception in the case of one minister whom the Regent had requested to serve also as a senator of the college of justice, the experiment was not repeated, nor, as the assembly explained, was it to be interpreted as a 'preparative to other ministers to procure sick promotioun'; and the assembly, in 1573, proceeded to the more general affirmation that:[122]

> 'It is neither aggrieable to the word of God nor to the practise of the primitive Kirk that the speciall administratioun of the Word and Sacraments, and the ministration of the Criminall and Civill Justice be so confoundit that ane person may occupie both the cures.'

In the 1560s, even under the 'godly' regime of James VI, the general assembly had repeatedly urged that 'the jurisdictioun of the Kirk may be separat frome all that is civile';[123] the appeal to the laity in such a claim plainly lay not in any incipient clericalism

---

[120] *BUK*, i, 209, 294; *The First Book of Discipline*, 127.
[121] Knox, *Works*, iii, 26, 532; v, 519; *The First Book of Discipline*, 178; *BUK*, i, 52-3, 112, 114, 131, 150, 162, 166, 261, 273-77.
[122] *BUK*, i, 206, 264, 267.   [123] *RPC*, ii, 7; *BUK*, i, 140, 146.

but in a freedom from clericalism through the elimination of clerical administrators and bureaucrats from secular politics; and consistently the reformers had expressed no wish for ecclesiastical representation either in the 'reformation parliament' of 1560 or in subsequent parliaments during the 1560s. John Knox had already declared his opposition by 1559 to episcopal representation in the English parliament;[124] and his advice did not go unheeded north of the border where no claim was made for the presence in parliament of superintendents or commissioners from the general assembly. Instead, the church had found an alternative means of formulating its programme, independently of the machinery of the state, in the general assembly where representatives of the Christian community, though subject to the guidance of the ministry as the official interpreters of scripture and as the 'mouth of the kirk',[125] determined policies for the church in the expectation that a truly 'godly' magistracy would promote and reinforce the resolutions of the church.

The spiritual estate in parliament, even after the accession of James VI, was thus confined to the surviving and conforming bishops of 1560, over whom the assembly could exercise little direct control, and the abbatial representatives in the form of the lay commendators, who were even less accountable to the assembly; but, by confirming these arrangements for ecclesiastical representation, the Leith settlement offered a practical solution attractive to conservative and orderly minds, particularly in the aftermath of a civil war and with the statutory imposition in 1573 of a religious test for all benefice holders.[126] The division in ecclesiastical opinion which subsequently emerged on this issue, therefore, may be best explained in terms of those who adhered to the reformation principles of 1560 and who denied the need for representation, and of those who were disposed to yield to tradition and to expediency by deferring to the requirements of a 'godly' government. Even so, the assembly's concern in 1574 lest bishops assumed further powers than superintendents was far from unwarranted, since Morton's government plainly hoped that in future ecclesiastical matters would be resolved not by the assembly, whose legality it questioned, but by the king and bishops in parliament.

As part of his policy of post-war reconstruction and of con-

[124] Knox, *Works*, v, 519.
[125] *BUK*, i, 84.
[126] *APS*, iii, 72; *BUK*, i, 212.

formity with England, Morton sought to restrain the assembly's freedom and even to supress it. He revived the earlier arguments of Mary and Maitland of Lethington that the assembly constituted an illegal convocation of the lieges without licence from the crown; and his dislike of assemblies was said to be such that he 'wald haiff haid the name thairof changit that he might abolishe the previlage and force thairof'.[127] At every opportunity, he was ready to subordinate the assembly to the machinery of the state; he refused to attend assemblies and declined to send representatives, preferring that commissioners from the church should discuss matters with the privy council, and in 1574 he appointed, in effect, an ecclesiastical committee of the privy council to which the assembly was required to remit certain matters for final judgement.[128] In keeping with his attempts to reduce the assembly's status, Morton decided, in 1573, to inspect the acts of assembly to see 'how many of them be perpetuall, and how many temporall', and the outcome of his investigations became apparent three years later, when the privy council dismissed an act of assembly as 'bot prevat, na publicatioun being maid thairof, nor yit authorizit be Parliament as it aught to be befoir it tak effect; and thairfoir is null'.[129]

If the government expressed doubts about the assembly's continued existence, as a gathering of nobles, laity and ministers, and hinted that it had outlived its usefulness under the rule of a 'godly' prince, prevailing opinion evidently thought otherwise and justified the assembly as 'decidedly necessary, to wit, that the nobles, advancing the faith with all zeal and effort, may be present in assemblies as assisters and helpers to the ministers and bear witness to others with regard to their own life, the morals of the people and so on'.[130] Moreover, in March 1573/4, the assembly itself had already advanced an emphatic claim to existence by divine right on the grounds that:[131]

'For preservatioun of the holie Ministrie and Kirk in puritie, the Lord hes appointit Assemblies and Conventiouns, not only of the persons of the Ministrie, but also of the haill members of the Kirk professing Chryst: The quhilk Kirk of God hes con-

[127] Calderwood, *History*, iii, 306; Melville, *Diary*, 61.
[128] *BUK*, i, 365, 392–4; Melville, *Diary*, 59; *RPC*, ii, 346–9, 434–5.
[129] *BUK*, i, 262, 381; *RPC*, ii, 560.
[130] *SHS Miscellany*, viii, 105.   [131] *BUK*, i, 292.

tinuallie usit, and uses the same Assemblies, sanctified be the word of God, and authorized be the presence of Jesus Chryst.'

All in all, even despite fluctuations in attendance, the assembly showed little sign of withering away, as some would have wished.

The continued existence of the general assembly certainly remained an obstacle to direct control of the church by the crown in parliament; and the disinclination to accept magisterial supremacy in ecclesiastical matters – already implicit first, in the claim for separation of civil and ecclesiastical government, secondly, in the political theories which reformers espoused to justify the revolution of 1567 and to limit the terms of the prince's rule in civil government, and, thirdly, in their belief that even princes were subject to ecclesiastical discipline[132] – was made indubitably explicit at a conference called by the Regent Morton in March 1573/4 to debate the proposition 'whether the supreame magistrate should not be head of the church as well as of the common-wealthe', at which the ministers present refused to concede the case and the meeting broke up when Morton found 'no appearance of obtaining that point'.[133] In another somewhat picturesque account of the episode, the Regent insisted that 'the king and his counsall sould be suppreme heid of the kirk under God', and the ministers in turn asserted that they were 'supreame heid of the kirk and that nane sould have jurrisdictioun ovir thame bot thair sellffis and generall counsall under God'.[134]

Clearly, the rule of a 'godly' prince had brought no nearer any recognition of the king's supremacy over the church, but instead had led to a narrowing of ecclesiastical supremacy to the ministry and to the general assembly. Besides, it is all too apparent that the oath devised in the Leith articles of 1572, which had recognised the king as 'supreme Governour of this realme, as well in things temperall as in the conservatioun and purgatioun of religioun', deliberately departed from the English oath, on which it was otherwise modelled, acknowledging the prince as 'supreme governor of this realm ... as well in all spiritual and ecclesiastical things or causes as temporal', in order to avoid offending ministers' susceptibilities and in recognition of their reluctance to accept the unequivocal and uncompromising terms of the English oath; hence the thoughtful substitution for this English phraseology of

[132] See below, 59ff.
[133] Hume of Godscroft, *History of the House of Douglas*, 334; *cf.*, BUK, i, 295–6.
[134] Pitscottie, *Historie*, ii, 313–4.

the language of the Scots Confession of Faith.[135] The rejection of papal headship in 1560 had not required any recognition of royal supremacy; nor was it forthcoming, as such, either in 1567 or 1572, as reformers gradually discovered, first under Mary and then during the minority of James VI, that royal control could be just as harmful as papal headship to the church's wellbeing, a conviction expressed by Erskine of Dun in 1571 when he observed that 'of old the Papists called the truthe heresie; and some now call the truthe treasoun'.[136]

The course which Morton had charted was patently modelled on developments in England where the Tudor monarchs in their exercise of kingship had ended convocation's historic rôle as an independent ecclesiastical legislature;[137] but the application of such policies to Scotland did little to settle the basic issue of the church's relationship to the state under the rule of a 'godly' prince, and rather initiated a period of controversy within the church. The accuracy of the description by one critic of Morton's 'purpose to restrean the fridome of application in preatching, and authoritie of the Generall Assemblies, and bring in a conformitie with Eingland in governing of the Kirk be Bischopes and injunctiones'[138] is wholly supported by English diplomatic reports in 1575 to the effect that:[139]

'the misliking between the Regent and the ministers is on this ground. The Regent would "induce" into the Church of Scotland the liberty used by the magistrates and bishops of the Church of England, which they like not of, and so it stands between them as yet undecided. In the meanwhile the Church fast holds her own....'

Morton's policy of conformity with England had plainly run into difficulties, and in recognising defeat the Regent sent word to the assembly in 1576:[140]

'to require of them whether they would stand to the policy agreed unto at Leith; and if not, to desire them to settle upon

---

[135] *BUK*, i, 220; *Statutes of the Realm*, IV, i, 350–55; Knox, *Works*, ii, 118.

[136] Calderwood, *History*, iii, 160.

[137] E. T. Davies, *Episcopacy and the Royal Supremacy in the Church of England in the XVIth Century* (Oxford, 1950), 68–9.

[138] Melville, *Diary*, 45.

[139] *CSP Scot.*, v, no. 187.   [140] Spottiswoode, *History*, ii, 202.

some form of government at which they would abide. The Assembly taking the advantage of this proposition answered, that they were to think of that business, and should with all diligence set down a constant form of church-policy, and present the same to be allowed by the council.'

Here were the firm beginnings of the first drafting of the second Book of Discipline.

THE DRAFTING OF THE SECOND BOOK OF DISCIPLINE

Discussions on jurisdiction and polity

The claims which the reformed church consistently pursued for the exercise of an independent ecclesiastical jurisdiction, even when established under the rule of a 'godly' magistracy, fully accorded with the beliefs expressed by Oecolampadius, Bucer and Calvin, though obviously not with English practice where the *potestas jurisdictionis* including the *ius liturgicum* which the church possessed was understood to be derivative from and dependant upon the authority of the crown; and Archbishop Cranmer, who had recognised the possible use even of civil excommunication, underlined the erastian nature of the English compromise when he acknowledged that 'all Christian princes have committed unto them immediately of God the whole cure of all their subjects, as well concerning the ministration of God's word for the cure of souls, as concerning the ministration of things political and civil governance. In both these ministrations they must have sundry ministers under them, to supply that which is appointed to their several offices'.[141]

In Scotland, where the church courts had come into being without authority from the crown, there already existed a tradition of ecclesiastical independence which the church was unwilling to forego even after the accession of a 'godly' prince. Earlier discussions on the extent of ecclesiastical jurisdiction had

---

[141] *BUK*, i, 140; 146; Calderwood, *History*, iii, 158-9; A. Demura, 'Church Discipline according to Johannes Oecolampadius' (Princeton Th.D. thesis, 1964); Courvoisier, *La Notion d'Église chez Bucer*, 65, 125; Calvin, *Institutes*, IV, xi, 1, 3, 5; IV, xii, 4; Davies, *Episcopacy and the Royal Supremacy*, 7, 61; Cranmer, *Works*, ii, 116; *cf.*, Whitgift, *Works*, ii, 246: iii, 176; Hooker, *Laws of Ecclesiastical Polity*, VII, xv, 3.

been recognised in parliament's approval in 1567 of the church's jurisdiction in preaching of the Word, administration of the sacraments, and correction of manners. A commission was also established by parliament 'to considder quhat uther speciall points or clausis sould appertene to the jurisdictioun, privilege, and authoritie of the said Kirk'; and the general assembly not only appointed its own committee to investigate the matter with a deputation chosen by parliament or by the Regent but proceeded, in March and again in July 1569, to assert a claim 'that the jurisdictioune of the Kirk may be separate fra that quhilk is civille'. Little progress was evidently made in discussions with the government, and in March 1570/1 the assembly presented to the Regent a fresh list of articles on the church's jurisdiction seeking recognition of the church's judgment on doctrine, admission to ecclesiastical office and to benefices, church discipline including excommunication, matters relating to the ministry, benefices and church revenues, 'and because the conjunctioun of marriages pertaines to the ministrie, the causes of adherents and divorcements aught also to pertaine to them, as naturallie annexit therto'. John Knox, in his last letter to the assembly in August 1572 in which he expressed such solicitude for the church's welfare, also desired that the question of the church's jurisdiction which had been so long postponed might be finally resolved without further delay.[142]

An agreement acceptable to the church and government alike was not readily achieved, though the Leith settlement, which was primarily an agreement on endowment, did not deflect the assembly's determination to secure the government's approval on the extent of the church's jurisdiction, which in so wide an area as that affecting faith and morals was bound to rival as well as limit the competence of the secular courts and the administration of the magistrate's authority. Further discussions during 1573 and 1574 convinced Morton of the necessity 'for setling of the Policie of the trew Reformit Kirk' and led, in March 1574/5, to the preparation of draft articles on polity as well as jurisdiction, which the assembly presented to the government. At exactly the same time, a convention of estates nominated sixteen officials headed by lord chancellor Glamis, and including three superintendents, two bishops, two ministers and the principal of

[142] *APS*, iii, 24-5; *BUK*, i, 29, 50, 113, 140, 146, 185-7, 249; *RPC*, ii, 7; Calderwood, *History*, ii, 426; Spottiswoode, *History*, ii, 93.

King's college, Aberdeen, to convene and so 'put in forme the ecclesiasticall policie and ordour of the governing of the kirk'. It was evidently as a member of this commission set up by the estates to examine the church's polity that lord Glamis took the step of writing to Theodore Beza in Geneva for guidance and advice on framing a workable and durable constitution for the church.[143]

As Morton himself had made clear in January 1573/4, the need to achieve a 'gude ordour and provisioun of the Policie of the Kirk in thingis ambiguouss and irresolute' arose not from extraneous circumstances or from the advocacy of novel ideas, but from the initial failure in 1560 to reach full agreement and to the continuation thereafter of 'na setlit Policie, partlie throw want of the allowance of the auctoritie at the first Reformatioun, and partlie because the benefices of cure wer of lang tyme sufferit to be possest be personis repugnant to the said [reformed] religioun'.[144] The same explanation was offered by lord Glamis in his letter to Beza, written probably in the spring of 1576, in which Glamis related how:[145]

'the form of government which for some time was practised by our ancestors was overthrown some years ago along with the popish superstition and in its place it has not hitherto been possible to substitute a convenient and fitting form of church government, particularly because our sovereigns either were hostile to the true faith or, after they had begun to accept the chief points of Christian doctrine, were yet hindered by internal strife from being able to pay attention to the matter as they wished. Now, however, we are free from all those earlier hindrances; we have secured peace and enjoy the rule of a king whose outstanding ability and upbringing in the true faith promise us as much as could be looked for from anyone of his age; and we are striving to establish some ecclesiastical constitution'.

The advice which Glamis sought was, first, whether bishops were any longer required 'since the power of all ministers in the church of Christ seems to be equal and identical', and the only case advanced for their retention was 'the unruliness of the people'

[143] *BUK*, i, 280. 293, 295, 325–6; *Wodrow Society Miscellany*, i, 289–90; *APS*, iii, 89; *SHS Miscellany*, viii, 95–113.
[144] *Wodrow Society Miscellany*, i, 289–90.   [145] *SHS Miscellany*, viii, 100.

and the tradition which assigned to bishops a seat in parliament as 'one of the three orders and estates of the realm'; secondly, whether the general assembly as presently constituted had become unnecessary under a 'godly' prince or whether it ought to remain as a safeguard lest 'a prince not attached to the faith should ascend the throne in the future'; thirdly, the authority for summoning assemblies and the matters on which assemblies might properly legislate; fourthly, which offences should incur excommunication and whether Catholics should be so punished or merely by a lighter penalty; and finally whether the wealth of the prelacies, excluding teinds, might be assigned to the prince's service. Beza's reply was unequivocal in its denunciation of 'the bishop ordained by man', and of episcopal attendance at parliament which he considered 'a manifest abuse, contrary to the Word', and so advised that 'this device of man' should cease with the deaths of existing incumbents. The 'censures of the church and the authority of the magistrate' were seen as sufficient restraints on unruly behaviour, and churches might be visited 'without any great cost and bishoplike pride' by delegates from 'elderships' chosen with the king's authority. Excommunication should be pronounced only on obdurate and unrepentant offenders. To allot the goods of the church for secular use was sacrilege, but excess revenues, once the ministry, poor, schools, universities and hospitals were fully provided, might be 'bestowed for the service of the kingdom when the public necessity thereof doth require it'.[146]

Whether Glamis found the advice from Geneva wholly acceptable is open to question, but the timely appearance of the reply, with a discussion of its contents, did 'mikle guid'[147] as the general assembly set about the task of producing an independent report of its own on the church's constitution, which emerged as the 'Headis and Conclusionis of the Policie of the Kirk', otherwise known as the second Book of Discipline.

Authorship of the Book

The all but universal belief which insists in attributing the second Book of Discipline to one individual by assigning its authorship to Andrew Melville is simply not supported by the facts of history, and its abandonment is long overdue. The Book was not even the product of six individuals, as was the first Book of

[146] Ibid., 100–113.   [147] Melville, Diary, 55.

Discipline (though two of the surviving authors of that book certainly participated in it), for it emerges that over thirty ministers, under the assembly's general guidance, were active in formulating and revising the contents of the work.

A start was made in April 1576 when the assembly charged a number of commissioners from Aberdeen, Angus and the Mearns, Fife, the Lothians and the west of Scotland with the task of 'making an overture of the policie and jurisdiction of the Kirk, and uttering the plain and simple meaning of the Assemblie therein'. Glasgow, Edinburgh, St Andrews, Montrose and, presumably, Aberdeen were to serve as centres for the respective regional committees; a 'generall meiting and conventioun' of delegates from the regional committees was to be held at Stirling 'to communicat and cognosce upon thair haill travells and labours taken heirin and to conferre universallie heirupon together'; and their report was to be submitted to the next assembly or, if parliament should be called before then, to a specially convened assembly to be intimated by the ministers of Edinburgh.[148]

Even the most cursory examination of the membership of these committees readily discloses that of the twenty-two participants all but three (Archbishop Boyd, James Lawson and Andrew Melville) belonged to the earlier generation of reformers who had accepted the reformation principles of 1560. They were sober, level-headed representatives of the reformation church, men of no known doctrinaire bias, who from the early 1560s had played a prominent part in assemblies. The Aberdeen committee was formed by John Craig, then minister at Aberdeen, Alexander Arbuthnot, principal of King's college, and earlier licensed to minister and teach by the assembly in 1560, and by George Hay, who had studied with his brother, Andrew, in Paris before 1560 and served as minister first at Eddleston and then at Rathven, and as commissioner of Aberdeen and of Caithness. Five veterans of 1560 sat on the committee for Angus and the Mearns: Erskine of Dun, the superintendent, William Christison, minister at Dundee, John Row, minister at Perth, William Rhind, minister at Kinnoull, and John Duncanson, minister at Stirling. The Fife committee consisted of John Winram, the superintendent, and the 'principall masters' of St Andrews university, by which is understood Robert Hamilton, principal of St Mary's college and minister at St Andrews, John Rutherford, principal of St Salvator's,

[148] *BUK*, i, 362.

and James Wilkie of St Leonard's, who had all attended the assembly from the 1560s. The Lothians were represented by Robert Pont, who had been present in the earliest assemblies as an elder from St Andrews before he became successively minister at Dunblane, Dunkeld, commissioner for Moray and provost of Trinity college in Edinburgh, James Lawson, sub-principal of King's college from 1569 and successor to John Knox as minister at Edinburgh in 1572, David Lindsay, minister of South Leith, and two Edinburgh advocates, Clement Little and Alexander Syme, who were also procurators for the kirk. In the west, Archbishop Boyd, chancellor of Glasgow university and a 'lover of lerning and lernd men',[149] Andrew Melville, the college principal, Andrew Hay, George's brother, university rector and minister at Renfrew, David Cunningham, then dean of the faculty of arts and minister at Cadder, and James Greig, minister at Colmonell, were all appointed to the Glasgow committee.

Most of the committee members had taken part in earlier discussions on ecclesiastical jurisdiction or polity, and they included all but one of the original negotiators for the church of the Leith agreement, as well as a majority of those who issued the subsequent protest against aspects of the settlement in 1572.[150] Other members had been involved in the examination of bishops whose qualifications the assembly had questioned, or had taken part in the debate on episcopacy in 1575,[151] and it is apparent that besides the two professional lawyers there were present men like Row, Arbuthnot, Boyd and Melville who had studied civil or canon law.[152] In geographical terms, representation was far from inequitable: six members came from north of the Tay, six from the area between Perth and Stirling, five from the Lothians and five from the west.

By October 1576, the committees 'to consult upon the matter of the Policie of the Kirk' had presented 'their judgment contained formalie in writt to this Assemblie'. A new committee of eleven (composed of lord Glamis, the laird of Lundie, Andrew and George Hay, Melville, Lawson, Durie, Pont, Row, Wilkie

---

[149] Melville, *Diary*, 47.

[150] *BUK*, i, 50, 113, 185, 204–5, 208, 238, 244, 293, 295, 325–6.

[151] *Ibid.*, 288, 301, 303, 308, 314–15, 317, 320–1, 337, 340, 361.

[152] Row, *History*, 447; Spottiswoode, *History*, ii, 319; Wodrow, *Collections*, i, 206, 208, 210; Melville, *Diary*, 39–40; J. Durkan and J. Kirk, *The University of Glasgow, 1451–1577* (Glasgow, 1977), 267–8, 272.

and Clement Little) was formed to review the draft articles and to advise the assembly on the material presented. At the same point, the Regent Morton presented the assembly with forty-two questions on the church's constitution, partly in an effort to gauge the assembly's reaction and to test its weaknesses; this underlined the scope of subjects under examination, and answers to many of the questions raised were certainly forthcoming in the final version of the second Book of Discipline in 1578.[153]

Morton's enquiries related directly to the issues under discussion: to imparity among ministers, the election of elders and deacons for life, the exercise of excommunication, the problem of oversight and the diocesan structure, the competence of church courts, the convening and composition of general assemblies, the confounding of the ecclesiastical and secular jurisdictions, ecclesiastical representation in parliament and privy council, the church's patrimony, benefices and the collection and distribution of revenues, and even, in effect, the work of the commissary courts. The assembly selected seventeen members (substantially those involved in earlier discussions) to answer the Regent's questions and to further 'the matter of the Policie'. The 'heids of the Policie', which this committee considered, were evidently nearing completion, for the work was presented to the next assembly in April 1577, which proceeded to approve the contents except for 'thrie heids' on the diaconate, patronage and divorce which were 'callit in doubt be certaine' members, and so were referred for further disputation, but 'as to the rest, nothing was thoght to the contrair, nor opponit'.[154]

The procedure which the assembly adopted to ensure that the draft Book of Discipline was fully understood and thoroughly debated was for every section, each prepared by a separate individual, to be read aloud before the whole assembly and be approved or remitted at the assembly's discretion. In the surviving register of the assembly, compiled from various sources, brief mention is made of the sections written or revised by Row, Lawson, Erskine, Andrew Hay, David Ferguson, Pont, Lindsay and Craig. Melville's name is curiously absent from this list, but is included in Calderwood's account where the variant reading that 'nothing was alledged against the heeds committed to Mr Andrew Melville, Mr Robert Pont, Mr David Lindsey' replaces the sentence 'the pairts committit to Mr Andro Hay, Robert

[153] *BUK*, i, 365, 368–72. [154] *Ibid.*, 373–4, 389.

Pont, David Lindesay: nothing alledgit in the contrair'. Since Andrew Hay's contribution, by all accounts, had been already considered by the assembly and 'nothing was opponit against the same, except the article anent the Suspension of Ministers, referrit to farther reasoning', it is plain that Calderwood's text which includes Melville is to be preferred.[155] It is still not possible, however, to identify authorship of the separate sections or chapters, since the draft headings do not correspond with the final version, which *inter alia* contains no section on divorce nor any extended treatment on patronage, two topics earlier included.

On the generous assumption that no further chapters were added, that only the section on divorce was deleted, and that the assembly examined the chapters of the Book consecutively from start to finish, it is possible tentatively to suggest that John Row, whose section was discussed first, may have been responsible for the introductory material distinguishing the ecclesiastical and secular jurisdictions, and that James Lawson's contribution, examined next, may have been the second chapter on the administration of ecclesiastical polity. The topic assigned to Erskine of Dun, possibly on the admission of office-bearers, was 'thocht be him obscure and mystick', so further consultation was needed 'that he may be resolvit of the meaning therof'. Andrew Hay's section evidently concerned the ministry, since his 'article anent the Suspension of Ministers' was remitted for discussion, and may be therefore equated with the fourth chapter. Then came David Ferguson's section, possibly on elders or elderships, whose eighteenth article was referred, indicating that his was one of the more lengthy chapters. Further sections were assigned to Melville, Pont and Lindsay, possibly on doctors, elders and the magistracy respectively, and finally 'the heids committed' to Craig, possibly on the diaconate and patrimony, were thought worthy of either contraction or 'farther reasoning'; this, at least, is consistent with what is known to have been the continued failure to reach full agreement on the chapter on the diaconate. All this, of course, is purely speculative, for the select committee (of Lawson, Melville, Craig and George Hay) which the assembly immediately established to ensure that the Book's contents were well 'digestit and disposit in good and convenient ordour' might have readily rearranged the order in which the various chapters should finally appear; and there was also the concluding section

[155] *Ibid.*, 384; Peterkin, 163; Calderwood, *History*, iii, 381.

on the reformation of abuses which must have been added without delay.[156]

Since 'the matter of the Policie of the Kirk collectit be the brethren is not yet in sick perfyt forme as is requisite', the assembly before closing chose Pont and Lawson to inspect the articles once more and remove any weaknesses or inconsistencies in the text, by 'avoyding of superfluitie and obscuritie, the substantialls beand keipit'. A further watchdog committee (of Erskine, Arbuthnot, Melville, Craig, Andrew and George Hay, Row, Lindsay and Duncanson) was charged to supervise the work entrusted to Pont and Lawson. Care was taken to ensure free access to the committee for any with points to raise or criticisms to make; and the commissioners of provinces were instructed to inform the barons that the 'warke is in hand' and to request 'thair presence and concurrence therto'.[157]

The next assembly, in October 1577, devoted further attention to the Book of Discipline which the committee of the last assembly had presented for critical examination. Despite pressing invitations, the Regent Morton declined to attend the assembly, though on learning how 'the Kirk is labourand in the Policie', he encouraged the assembly to 'gang fordwart earnestlie and put the same to end'. Accordingly, in the thirteenth session, 'the heids of the Policie and Jurisdictioun of the Kirk beand haillilie red in the audience of the haill Assemblie', it was decided to present the Regent with a copy of the Book of Discipline, 'saifand the head, de Diaconatu, quhilk is ordained to be givin in with a note that the same is aggreeit be the most part of the Assemblie, without prejudice of farther reasoning'. Typical of the meticulous attention to detail and of the painstaking care with which the Book was drafted was the assembly's commission to Lawson, Pont and Lindsay, with the clerk to the assembly, to 'sett in good ordour' the copy to be presented to the Regent, and to ensure that it corresponded in every detail 'to the originall'. Not content with this, the assembly also required the copy to be checked and inspected by Duncanson, Ferguson, Brand and James Carmichael, and by Erskine of Dun if present, and 'beand found be them according to the originall', the work was finally to be handed to the Regent by Lawson, Pont and Lindsay. Anticipating the discussions with the government which would follow, the assembly before dissolving decided to nominate

[156] *BUK*, i, 384–5, 389.   [157] *Ibid.*, 391.

Patrick Adamson, Erskine, Craig, Row, Arbuthnot, Melville, Lawson, Pont, Lindsay, Duncanson and Andrew and George Hay to be ready to convene when instructed to do so by the Regent.[158] After all the intensive committee work which preceded it, the second Book of Discipline had at last arrived. The 'work of establisching a perfyte ordour and policie in the Kirk' had finally emerged for appraisal by a wider public.

Andrew Melville's Contribution

That the authorship of the second Book of Discipline should be ascribed either solely or even principally to Andrew Melville is plainly not supported by the evidence available, and even his admiring nephew and diarist assigns no greater rôle to Melville than to other participants in composing the work. Indeed, the very considerable participation of the first generation of reformers in a document which has gained the reputation, not undeservedly so, of being a substantially presbyterian work suggests that the principles on which the Book was founded were by no means incompatible with reformation thought, with which they have been sometimes contrasted, and can be said to represent rather the logical extension of earlier ideals. Certainly, the only prominent reformer of 1560 still active in the church whose name is not associated with the second Book of Discipline was Spottiswoode, the superintendent and father of the archbishop. And the unanimity of opinion in the assembly in approving the Book of Discipline as early as 1577 (apart from the chapter on the diaconate reserved for further study) is explained more satisfactorily not by postulating that Melville converted to his novels views the men of 1560 but by recognising that in their estimation of priorities no fundamental divergence in the consensus of viewpoints existed among ministers.

From a survey of the evidence, it is demonstrable that the theory of the two kingdoms, the rejection of royal supremacy over the church, the insistence on the general assembly's continued existence irrespective of the sovereign's religion, the disinclination to adopt the model of the English church, even the acceptance of parity among ministers, implicit at national level in the institution of the moderator's office and explicit in Adamson's identification of the parish minister alone as the truly 'godly' bishop, were all principles which had been affirmed by leaders of the Knoxian

[158] *Ibid.*, 393–5, 397–8.

church and therefore cannot be said to have been introduced by either Andrew Melville or the second Book of Discipline.[159] Too much credit is sometimes given to Melville for supposedly introducing those ideas when in reality it was in the church of his predecessors that they first found expression. His influence, which was by no means negligible, lay rather in his ability to apply those earlier tenets of reformed thought at a time when the crown was actively engaged in a concerted effort to recover that control and initiative in ecclesiastical matters which it had lost at the Reformation.

Returning home in the summer of 1574, after a decade's study in France and Switzerland, Melville attended the assembly in August 1574, which confirmed his appointment as principal at Glasgow university. His arrival coincided with the continued search for a settled ecclesiastical constitution, and to attribute renewed debate solely to Melville's intervention, as Archbishop Spottiswoode was later to do, is to misrepresent the problem.[160] Even though he was well placed to offer stimulating advice, through his continental experience both of France and of Beza's Geneva, the evidence scarcely suggests that he arrived with a blueprint for remodelling the church's polity. At least, if he had a plan of action in mind, he did not immediately disclose it. When appointed in the assembly of March 1574/5 to two committees for examining the aptitude of the bishop of Moray and the bishop elect of Dunblane, Melville seems to have expressed no disapproval of the episcopal office, or even to have voiced an objection when 'it was remembred be some of the brethren' at the bishop of Moray's examination 'that the question is yet undecided if he be Bishop lawfully chosen or not'.[161] As a member of the committee, Melville was concerned not with ending all episcopal appointments but with recommending how the examination and election of candidates could be made more effective. The meaningful sobriquet of 'episcoporum exactor',[162] which Melville was to earn, still lay with the future.

Melville's attitude to episcopacy was based at least as much on observation and experience of Scottish practice – practice which already had led to a denunciation of 'thir counterfett bischopis' – as on any doctrinaire argument inherited from Geneva, but his

[159] See above, 45ff.
[160] Melville, *Diary*, 47–8; *BUK*, i, 310; Spottiswoode, *History*, ii, 200.
[161] *BUK*, i, 315, 317, 320–21, 325.   [162] Melville, *Diary*, 52.

introduction to the episcopate through the bishops of Moray and Dunblane, two quite improper promotions criticised by the assembly since neither had been a minister, was singularly unfortunate though possibly revealing. It was, however, precisely because of prevailing dissatisfaction over episcopal appointments and the method of capitular election that John Durie, a minister in Edinburgh, questioned in 1575 both the rôle of chapters and the office of the newly appointed bishops, and found support in the assembly from 'uther brether of his mynd'. Durie's critical appraisal of the rôle of bishops 'as they are now in the Kirk of Scotland' was said by Archbishop Spottiswoode (whose testimony is unsupported) to have been seconded by Andrew Melville, who appeared not to have had prior notice of the motion but who nonetheless drew the assembly's attention to the views of Calvin and Beza on ecclesiastical polity. After commending Durie's zeal, and with his knowledge of biblical philology, Melville showed how the New Testament bishop was 'not to be taken in the sense that the common sort did conceive, there being no superiority allowed by Christ amongst ministers', and ended by affirming (as Beza had earlier warned Knox) that the church could not remain in purity unless the corruptions which had crept into the estate of bishops were completely removed.[163]

Melville's speech, which was 'applauded by many', was clearly given a sympathetic reception in the assembly. This strongly suggests that many shared the criticisms of both Durie and Melville, and certainly seems to dispel any notion that there existed any consensus of opinion for an exclusively episcopal system. The Leith episcopacy, after all, only dated from 1572. Indeed, to Spottiswood's evident dismay, not only did the assembly, after discussion, fully approve Melville's standpoint but even the bishops present in the assembly voiced no opposition to the proceedings. It remains something of a curiosity that Spottiswoode's account of Melville's discourse lacks documentary support from strictly contemporary sources, for neither the acts of assembly nor James Melville, who was always ready to demonstrate his uncle's opposition to episcopacy, mentions the purported speech in support of Durie's criticisms. Yet evidence of Melville's attendance, if not of his speech, at the assembly is afforded by his appointment to a committee, composed also of Craig, Lawson, Row, Lindsay and George Hay, to debate Durie's proposition whether bishops,

[163] *BUK*, i, 331, 340; Spottiswoode, *History*, ii, 200; Knox, *Works*, vi, 614.

as they existed in Scotland, had scriptural validity and whether the chapter could be tolerated in a reformed church. Though considering it 'not expedient presentlie to ansuer directlie to the first questioun', Melville and the other members of the panel readily reached agreement, and by implication answered the question indirectly, for the name of bishop, they agreed, was common to all ministers of the Word and sacraments, and while this was their 'cheife functioun of the Word of God', some still might be chosen with 'power to oversie and visite sick reasonable bounds, besydes his awin flocke, as the Generall Kirk sall appoint'.[164]

The implication of their report was plainly that those chosen as overseers should retain a congregational charge and that authority for their commission of oversight should be vested in the general assembly, which would also designate the bounds of their visitation. Such a recommendation implied a return to something like the system operating in the late 1560s when visitation was very largely entrusted to commissioners appointed by the assembly. Certainly, if the bishop or overseer was to retain a congregational charge, he could not be expected to perform his office of visitation on a permanent basis, and the committee's recommendation that the assembly should assign to the overseer 'reasonable bounds' for visitation suggested a departure from the old diocesan structure inherited at Leith.

The next assembly in April 1576 'resolutelie approvit' the report on bishops and gave effect to its proposals by redefining the office and duties of 'visitors' or 'commissioners of provinces', and by emphasizing how the 'power stands not in the Visiter, but in the Kirk'. Many, though not all, of the bishops, who had raised no objections to Durie's criticisms or to the report on episcopacy, were willing to accept a congregational ministry and so were selected with other ministers to supervise for a term much smaller districts achieved by dividing the country into more than twenty new administrative units designed to replace the unwieldy boundaries of the thirteen traditional dioceses which the reformed church had only begun fully to utilise in the four years after the Leith settlement.[165] The intention in 1576 was to return more closely to the principles of oversight which operated in the 1560s.

[164] Spottiswoode, *History*, ii, 200–1; *BUK*, i, 340, 342–3.
[165] *BUK*, i, 349, 352–61.

Of Melville's 'exceeding grait peans' in regularly 'keiping Assemblies and dyettes of conference, reasoning and advysing with brethring anent that wark', there is sufficient testimony. Nor is his aversion to 'pseudo-episcopacy' in dispute. Yet in the Glasgow regional committee, where his influence might be expected to prevail, it was neither the archbishop nor Melville who chaired the meeting, but David Cunningham, in whose house the committee met, who 'moderat the reasoning, gatherit upe the conclusiones, and put all in wrait and ordour to be reported to the Assemblie'. His main contribution, however, was probably his advocacy of the eldership or presbytery, though his nephew's boast that ministers were merely 'informed mair throwlie be Mr Andro of the unlawfulnes of Bischopes and the right maner of governing of the Kirk be Presbyteries' rather suggests that even here his ideas were already shared by others; and Andrew Hay is named as one 'wha lyked never those bischopries and wha specialie was the ernest suttar for Mr Andro Melvill'.[166]

The arguments advanced by Melville and his colleagues, and so familiar to readers of Calvin's *Institutes*, seem to have been that the New Testament bishop was not a great diocesan prelate who sat in parliament and council, the 'lord-like bishop' for whom Knox had shown such distaste, but rather an overseer and shepherd of the flock. In the primitive and apostolic church, the bishop had become president for order's sake in an assembly of presbyters; but just as bishops had brought forth archbishops, patriarchs and the papacy so now false bishops would introduce fresh abuses, already demonstrable in the evils of tulchanism and in the widespread contempt for the new 'counterfett bischopis'; hence the renewal of the earlier assertion, first by the assembly in 1565 and then by Patrick Adamson in 1572, that the true bishop was the pastor of the flock, the minister of the congregation.[167]

Reformed thought in Scotland had always recognised that there could be no higher ministry than the ministry of the Word and sacraments; and rejecting as they did any belief in episcopal ordination, reformers found no reason either to insist that ministers should be admitted by bishops or to accept an order of

[166] Melville, *Diary*, 48, 52, 56.
[167] Spottiswoode, *History*, ii, 200; Calvin, *Institutes*, IV, iv, 2–4; IV, vi, 1; Knox, *Works*, vi, 434, 559; *CSP Scot.*, iv, no. 452; Pitscottie, *Historie*, ii, 283; Calderwood, *History*, iii, 206.

bishops distinct from that of ministers.[168] There was no trace of any belief that bishops possessed a plenitude of sacramental power which other ministers did not share. All ministers were held to have equal power to preach the Word and administer the sacraments. In jurisdiction, it was recognised that superintendents and other ministers commissioned by the church should exercise such additional duties as visiting congregations, examining and admitting ministers, inspecting schools and universities, preaching where no ministers existed, summoning synods and helping to select commissioners to the assembly, but lordship was emphatically condemned. Superintendents were counselled to 'usurpe not dominioun nor tyranicall impyre over thy brethrein'; they were subject to the general assembly, and to correction by their fellow ministers, and by the elders of their province; they were often accompanied at visitations by assessors and were required to seek the advice of the ministers of the province, and they gave judgment usually with advice of the synod or of the principal kirk session of their province.[169] The whole emphasis was on conciliar government, on collective decisions by kirk session, superintendent's court, synod and general assembly, with the operation of an appellate jurisdiction from the lower to the higher courts. Hence Melville's determination to ensure that power continued to lie with assemblies of the church, which Morton threatened to subvert, and not with a new order of bishops whose powers were only limited until further agreement was found.[170] The concern expressed was doubtless justified, for one bishop from 1576 declined to acknowledge his subordination to the general assembly;[171] and as early as March 1572/3, possibly in a reaction to the Convention of Leith, the synod of Lothian had criticised the undemocratic manner in which decisions had been sometimes taken without full consultation and so proposed that the exercise become an administrative unit for determining opinion between synods and assemblies in order that 'weighty matters of the Kirk be not concluded be a few, as often times they are without knowledge or consent of the brethren'.[172] The pros-

[168] *The First Book of Discipline*, 102, 207; Knox, *Works*, ii, 144.

[169] Knox, *Works*, ii, 150; *BUK*, i, 25, 43, 75, 123, 161, 193, 237, 241, 284; *The First Book of Discipline*, 127; *RStAKS*, i, 145, 151, 183–4, 189, 221, 229, 233, 257; Knox, *Works*, vi, 450; *CSP Scot.*, i, no. 1136.

[170] See above, 23, 36–7.

[171] *BUK*, i, 367, 377, 385–6. [172] *Ibid.*, 265.

pect of 'governing of the Kirk be Bischopes and injunctiones'[173] was not to be readily realised.

THE CONTENTS AND DEVELOPMENT OF THE BOOK

The thirteen chapters which form the second Book of Discipline present a particularly orderly exposition of the church and its ministry. Definition of the church and of the difference between ecclesiastical and secular government is succeeded by discussion of the call and admission to the ministry, of pastors, doctors and elders, of elderships or assemblies, deacons and the distribution of church goods, the Christian magistrate, and finally the reformation of abuses and the benefits which thereby would ensue.

Church and State

The concise definitions of the church, first, as a fellowship of professing Christians in whose ranks, side by side with the godly, exist an unknown number of 'hypocrittis professing alwayis outwartlie ane trew religioun', and, secondly, in more exclusive terms as the godly and elect alone, are respective descriptions of the visible and invisible church,[174] though the third expression of the church in terms of the ministers was less characteristic of protestant confessions, for Catholics, like Quintin Kennedy readily accepted that 'sumtyme the Kirk is tane mair specialie for the cheif pastores of the universale Congregatioun',[175] but it was consistent with the Calvinist emphasis on the church as an institution, with its ministry and ecclesiastical organisation.[176] Without an ecclesiastical polity, the first Book of Discipline had declared 'there is no face of a visible kirk'; and Erskine of Dun spoke indiscriminately of 'thair mother the holie kirk' and of 'thair mother the holie ministerie', insisting that 'quhat is menit be our mother is befoir declarit, to wit the ministere of the holy mystereis quhilk God hes placed amangis us'.[177]

Arising from the church's definition lay the problem of its authority and jurisdiction on which the Book was quite forthright. It recognised that the spiritual jurisdiction and government,

[173] Melville, *Diary*, 45. [174] See text below, I. 1–2, and notes 2–3.
[175] *Wodrow Society Miscellany*, i, 117–18.
[176] *Cf.*, Calvin, *Institutes*, IV, viii, 9. See text below, I. 3, n. 4.
[177] *The First Book of Discipline*, 180; *Spalding Club Miscellany*, iv, 95.

granted to the church by God through Christ the Mediator, should be exercised not by the membership at large but by those members appointed by the Word to specialised functions within the congregation of the faithful. Such a restriction recalls the first Book of Discipline's claim that ministers were 'promoted to the regiment of the Kirk', and accorded with the teaching of Calvin and Bullinger.[178] Distinction was drawn between *potestas ordinis*, exercised individually, in preaching the Word and dispensing the sacraments, and *potestas jurisdictionis*, exercised corporately, or 'conjunctlie be mutuall consent of thame that bear the office and charge', an implicit acknowledgment of the necessity of church courts or elderships for the exercise of ecclesiastical discipline. As Calvin had shown, this power of discipline in the primitive church 'did not belong to an individual who could exercise it as he pleased, but belonged to the consistory of elders, which was in the Church what a council is in a city'.[179]

No less significant was the affirmation that all power ecclesiastical is derived 'immediatelie frome God, and the Mediatour Chryst Jesus', without any earthly intermediary. The church was not deemed to have received its jurisdiction from God intermediately through the prince, as was claimed in England where the Henrician act for the restraint of appeals had declared that all jurisdictions, spiritual and temporal, were derived from the crown, and the acts of supremacy underlined this approach. Instead, the Book postulated the existence of two parallel, divinely ordained jurisdictions, separate and distinct, yet co-ordinate. The phraseology of the 'two kingdoms' was not employed to describe the relationship, but the implication was there, for if Christ were 'the onlie spirituall king and governour of his kirk' – a proposition which could not be denied – then it followed that the church was his kingdom ruled 'throw his Spirite and word, be the ministrie of mene'. Any notion of intermediate, earthly headship of the church, either papal or princely, was positively denounced as 'ane title falslie usurpit be antichrist', which 'aucht not to be attributtit to angell or to mane of quhat estait soevir he be, saiffing to Chryst, the heid and onlie monarche in this kirk'. Accordingly, while kings might be called lords of their subjects 'quhom thay governe civilie', in the spiritual government of the church Christ alone is lord and master, and those who bear

---

[178] *The First Book of Discipline*, 100.
[179] See text below, I. 5–7, and notes 6–9; Calvin, *Institutes*, IV, xi, 6.

office must not usurp dominion or be called lords for they are 'onlie ministeris, disciplis and servandis'.[180]

Such an authoritative statement on the church and its ministry, though fatal to any belief in a 'godly' prince ruling church and state alike, was quite compatible with earlier Scottish attitudes. As early as May 1559, reformers had reminded Mary of Guise, as queen regent, that God had committed to her charge the government of 'ane kingdom temporall' to be ruled within the limits of the Word, and solemnly warned her to:[181]

> 'tak heid that ye pas nocht the limittis and boundis of your awin office, nother entyr be impir in Christis kingdome usurpeand forther powr unto you nor he hes gewin, ffor thocht all kingdomes bayth temporall and spirituall pertenis to God, yit hes God distributit the ministerie diverslye, that is the temporall kingdomes in the government of mortell men, and makis thame princes of the erthe, for the mentenance of commoun welthis and civill polaceis. Bot the government of the spirituall and hevinlie kingdome, the kirk of God we mein, he hes onlie committit to his sone Christ, ffor he is the heid thairoff, all uther ar her memberis under him'.

Clear distinction was drawn between the state governed by the prince and the church ruled by Christ the Mediator who, the reformers insisted, is and can be the church's only head. Within 'Christis kingdome', the queen regent was but:[182]

> 'ane servand and na quein, havand na preheminence nor authoritie above the kyrk, or onye power in that kingdome, to oppin your voce to command onye uther thing nor Christ hes techeit, ffor that kingdome as sayis Sanct James hes bot ane law gevar. Be war thairfor that ye tak na authoritie upone you

---

[180] See text below, I. 10, 12, 13 and notes 12, 14–16 (where the views of continental reformers are also considered); *Statutes of the Realm*, IV, i, 350–55. In Geneva, Jean-Raymond Merlin preached in 1564 against the 'tyranny' in the claims to earthly headship of the church advanced by the papacy and by Henry VIII in England; and in 1571 the French national synod also censured the opinions of those who 'maintained the supremacy of the magistrate as head of the church' and who sought to eliminate ecclesiastical discipline by confounding it with the jurisdiction of the civil magistrate (E. Choisy, *L'état chrétien calviniste à Genève au temps de Théodore de Bèze* (Geneva, 1902), 20–24; R. M. Kingdon, *Geneva and the Consolidation of the French Protestant Movement, 1564–1572* (Geneva, 1967), 21, 98, 104; Quick, *Synodicon*, i, 92).

[181] *Spalding Club Miscellany*, iv, 89.
[182] *Ibid.*

abwe the kirk of Christ, for than seik ye to be equall with him quha can hef na merrowis'.

Emphasis, too, was placed on the fall from grace of those overmighty princes in antiquity who sought to rule the church and on the disaster which would befall any prince foolish enough to meddle in Christ's kingdom:[183]

'Be thir exempillis we wald your grace suld keip you within the boundis of your awin vocatioun, exerceand iustlie the authoritie temporall gevin to your maiestie, and suffer Christ trewlie be his word to reuill his awin kingdome.'

The significance of the reformers' claim lies also in what it refrained from stating. If they had wished to do so, the reformers could well have invalidated the queen regent's interference in ecclesiastical matters on the grounds that only a 'godly' or protestant prince could govern the church and claim supremacy, but it is an interesting indication of their train of thought that no such assertion was made; instead they implied that the administration of the church on earth was vested through the ministry of the Word in the preaching of men 'send of God and ordinarilie callit to Christis ministerrye'.[184] An even earlier protestant claim to similar effect had been made by Henry Balnaves in 1548 when he distinguished the prince's 'jurisdiction of people in the civil ordinance', which included the suppression of superstition and establishing true religion, from 'all power ecclesiastical', which properly resided 'in the office of the administration of the Word of God'.[185] Much later, even under a 'godly' prince, the same distinction was observed by Erskine of Dun who sought to repel secular interference by affirming that:[186]

'there is a spirituall jurisdictioun and power which God hath given unto his kirk, and to these who beare office therein; and there is a temporall power givin of God to kings and civill magistrats. Both the powers are of God, and most agreing to the fortifeing one of another, if they be right used'.

The tradition of ecclesiastical independence established at the Reformation persisted under a 'godly' prince and led in March 1573/4, at a date antecedent to Melville's return, to an explicit

---

[183] *Ibid.*
[184] *Ibid.*, 90.
[185] Knox, *Works*, iii, 526–29.
[186] Calderwood, *History*, iii, 158.

refusal by ministers to concede any claim to royal supremacy advanced by the government. Such a forthright denial rather suggests that the exception which the assembly had taken in 1568 to the title in a book which named James VI 'supreame head of the primitive kirk' related not so much to the unusual wording – for reformers, after all, had sought to restore in Scotland the 'grave and godlie face of the primitive Churche' – but to the issue of royal supremacy itself.[187] In any event, the disinclination to accept royal supremacy was already implicit in earlier attitudes which reformers had exhibited in their political thought, in their wish to establish a separate ecclesiastical jurisdiction distinct from the civil, and in their insistence that king and people alike were subject to ecclesiastical discipline administered by ministers and elders.

The political theories espoused by reformers on winning the revolution of 1567 which had led them to prescribe to the king the terms of his rule, whether they were modelled on the contractual ideas revived by Buchanan or on the biblical precedents advanced by the assembly, quite forcefully emphasized the constitutional limitations on royal power and suggested a belief that sovereignty was delegated to the prince by God through the people, to whom the prince remained responsible.[188] If the prince's rule in civil government was conceived to be curtailed by human and divine law alike, it is not surprising that an equally critical view was taken to claims of royal supremacy over the church. Similarly, the exercise of an independent ecclesiastical jurisdiction, where elders on kirk sessions as 'ecclesiastical magistrates' assumed an 'authoritie to judge in the kirk of God' and to supervise 'the manners and conversation of all men within their charge',[189] denied to the civil magistrate control of ecclesiastical affairs, just as the continued existence of the general assembly proved difficult for the crown to establish its claims in

---

[187] See above, 40; *BUK*, i, 125–6. (No copy of Bassandyne's work is known to exist, but the book in question possibly may be identified with *Here begynneth a boke called the faull of the Romyshe church*, c. 1540–1550 (*STC*, nos. 21304–21307), to which Bassandyne, as printer, may have added a dedicatory preface to James VI); Knox, *Works*, i, 303, 306; ii, 264; *BUK*, i, 94, 107, 267, 311; ii, 419; *RStAKS*, i, 311.

[188] *De Jure Regni*, LXXIV; cf. LII; *BUK*, i, 108–9; *RPC*, i, 536; *APS*, iii, 39, cf., 23–4.

[189] A. Maxwell, *The History of Old Dundee* (Edinburgh, 1884), 72; *The First Book of Discipline*, 174–6.

the church. Again, long before the Heidelberg debate took place between George Withers and Thomas Erastus in 1568 on whether 'to a minister with his eldership power is given by the law of God to excommunicate whomsoever, yea even kings and princes themselves', reformed opinion in Scotland had decided that 'to discipline must all the estates within this Realm be subject, as well the Rulers, as they that are ruled'.[190] In 1561, Knox had repeated his conviction that princes as well as people were subject 'unto God, and unto his trubled Churche'; and the same belief was strikingly illustrated in the assembly's repeated insistence in 1562 and in 1571 that the civil magistrate, being subject to the rule of Christ, could not be exempt from excommunication.[191] Reformed opinion in Scotland gave the prince no immunity from church discipline and accordingly denied his supremacy.

The theory of the church and its relationship to the civil power formulated in the second Book of Discipline was certainly consistent with earlier thought and practice. The church was seen to be ruled by Christ the Mediator through the preaching of his Word by a ministry lawfully called and approved both by God and the congregation. The ministers, through their vocation, were the appointed ambassadors and messengers, the instruments of Christ's rule, the expounders and official interpreters of the Word. This high doctrine of the ministry had been earlier expounded by both Calvin and Knox; and in the first Book of Discipline the ministers had been commended as the 'servants and Embassadors of the Lord Jesus', for 'whosoever rejecteth and despiseth their ministerie and exhortation, rejecteth and despiseth Christ Jesus'. Erskine of Dun ascribed to the ministry no less exalted a position when he complained that 'a proud confessione to be of the kirk in contemptioun, or comparing with thame quhilk beiris spirituall cuir and office thairin, is maist damnabill, and cumis of ane hie presumptione, and schawis disobedience and rebellioun to God and his ordinance'.[192]

In accord with an earlier pronouncement by Knox, the second Book of Discipline recognised the church, and more particularly the ministry, to possess the power of the keys, 'quhilk our Maister

---

[190] *Cf.*, Hooker, *Laws of Ecclesiastical Polity*, Preface, ii, 9; *The First Book of Discipline*, 173.

[191] Knox, *Works*, ii, 283; *cf.*, v, 516–20; *BUK*, i, 16, 195.

[192] Calvin, *Institutes*, IV, iii, 1–2; IV, vi, 10; Knox, *Works*, v, 486; *The First Book of Discipline*, 102; *Spalding Club Miscellany*, iv, 93–98.

gaif to his apostles and thair trew successouris', to preach the gospel, dispense the sacraments and to bind and loose, while to the temporal arm pertained the power of the sword whereby the evildoer might be forcibly restrained and coerced.[193] There was still much, however, which required elucidation; but it was a logical application of reformation principles to require that the exercise of office in both jurisdictions should not be united in the same person. Calvin, in particular, had shown how 'if in this matter we seek the authority of Christ, there can be no doubt that he intended to debar the ministers of his word from civil domination and worldly power', since 'he intimates not only that the office of pastor is distinct from the office of prince, but that the things differ so widely that they cannot be united in the same individual'. Such an ideal had been given prominence by Scottish reformers in the 1560s, and had been widely observed until the Leith settlement led bishops to exercise a temporal as well as spiritual jurisdiction which many found objectionable.[194]

At the same time, the second Book of Discipline made no attempt to provide the ministry with any immunity from the normal processes of law, either civil or ecclesiastical; and the general assembly already had recognised in 1570 that a minister, if guilty of a secular offence, was liable to punishment by the temporal authorities. Accordingly, ministers were held to be accountable to the magistrate in civil affairs just as the magistrate was responsible to the church in ecclesiastical matters. Yet ambiguity remained in determining precisely which matters were strictly civil and which were properly ecclesiastical, and as late as 1596 ministers were still aware of the need for the assembly to define 'the limits of the two jurisdictiouns, civill and spirituall'. The conflicting claims which could arise had been well illustrated in October 1573 when the privy council challenged the church's decision to depose a schoolmaster by claiming that the action was merely 'civill and prophane' and that the 'Bischope and Minister ar na judgeis competent thairto; and na law yit establischit or approvit that gevis thame sic power'; and it discharged the church from proceeding to excommunicate the offender lest such a sentence be 'extendit to all uther maner of actionis of quhatsumevir qualitie thay wer; and be that way the ministeris of the Kirk suld mak

[193] Knox, *Works*, i, 333; see text below, I. 16, and n. 19; X. 8 and n. 166.
[194] Calvin, *Institutes*, IV, xi, 8; see text below, I. 15 and n. 18, and Introduction, 37–8.

thame selffis judgeis in all caussis, outher be direct or indirect meanes, quhilk wer ane grit absurditie'.[195]

It could not be reasonably expected that the second Book of Discipline should offer firm guidance on the niceties of civil and ecclesiastical law. It was devised essentially as a digest of the principles on which the church should operate. The offices of minister and magistrate, though distinct, were complementary, each assisting and fortifying the authority of the other. Accordingly, although they were forbidden from usurping each other's function, the magistrate was still to ensure that ministers fulfilled their duties according to the Word, and the minister's responsibility was to 'teach' the magistrate how to exercise his office as God's Word required. Here, perhaps, were the makings of a theocracy; but, then, this ought also to be read along with Knox's reported sermon in 1561, when he as minister of the Word had expounded 'the duty of all kind of magistrates in a good reformed commonwealth'.[196]

'The Office of a Christiane Magistrat in the Kirk'

The belief that the second Book of Discipline excluded the magistrate from authority in the church is quite without foundation, for although full discussion of the magistrate's office was relegated to a later chapter, it was indubitably acknowledged, in language which recalls the words of the Scots Confession of Faith, that Christian princes and magistrates had chief responsibility as nourishing fathers, to advance Christ's kingdom by upholding and defending the church against all enemies, by ensuring that ecclesiastical discipline was supplemented by appropriate civil punishment, by protecting the integrity of the church's patrimony and even by legislating for the church's welfare, though an earlier restriction forbade the magistrate from prescribing any rule in either doctrine or discipline. Though much of the phraseology was commonplace, the exposition contained similarities with Beza's Confession of Faith, where the Christian magistrate, as a principal member of the church, was held even to exercise a ministry in the church by maintaining and protecting it; and there was much which was directly borrowed from Bucer's *De Regno Christi*.

[195] See text below, I. 14, 23 and n. 17; *BUK*, i, 179; Calderwood, *History*, v, 492; *RPC*, ii, 288–9.

[196] See text below, I. 17, 21–22, and notes 20, 23–25; Keith, *History*, ii, 87–88.

The prince, it was observed, had a right to intervene by his own authority to reform a church corrupted; but it was carefully pointed out that when 'sum godlie kingis in Judea' had taken this step, they had done so only 'be direction of Prophets', and when godly emperors and kings had reformed the church in times past, this they had done only 'in the lycht of the New Testament'. In a church reformed and possessing a lawfully constituted ministry, princes and magistrates must proceed more warily and be willing to hear God's will revealed through his messengers and ambassadors, the ministers of the Word, and so 'reverence the majestie of the sone of God speaking be thame'. All this was literally borrowed from Martin Bucer. Yet here, and not for the last time, was the recurrent theme of the ministers as the official interpreters of scripture; and it is indeed important 'to note the tendency which so early entered into the Reformed practice of practically abandoning the original emphasis on the priesthood of believers in the matter of exposition of scripture and insisting upon educated ministers alone undertaking this work'. All might be priests and read the Bible, but not all were prophets or expounders of the Word.[197]

The treatment accorded to the Christian magistrate's office evidently found widespread acceptance, for the verdict of the king's conference called to discuss the book's contents was that 'the whole chapter is thought good';[198] and there appears not even to be slender foundations for any belief that the second Book of Discipline significantly altered the church's political doctrines. What the work did provide was a succinct summary of earlier strands of thought.

Vocation and Ordination

In defining procedures for admitting candidates to ecclesiastical office, the third chapter of the book strongly emphasized the concept of vocation or divine calling, an idea deeply rooted in renaissance and reformation thought and not confined to a calling to the ministry. Each individual as a member of society had a variety of functions to perform to which he had been called by God and through which he could serve both his creator and his community. Henry Balnaves, in 1548, had accordingly

---

[197] See text below, X. 1-9, and notes 157-167; G. D. Henderson, *The Burning Bush* (Edinburgh, 1957), 45.

[198] Calderwood, *History*, iii, 439; Spottiswoode, *History*, ii, 247.

divided 'the estate of man' into the 'four offices, dignities or special vocations' of prince, minister, parent or householder, and servant or subject.[199] It was, however, with the particular calling to ecclesiastical office, through which candidates were 'rasit up be God' to a public function in the church, that the second Book of Discipline was primarily concerned.

This calling, upon which the validity of the ministry rested and without which none might enter ecclesiastical office, might be extraordinary, as the prophets and apostles had witnessed when they experienced a call immediately from God, but in a reformed and established church a second form of call, besides the internal call of God, consisted in the 'lauchfull approbation and outward jugement of men'. The first Book of Discipline had indicated earlier how 'Ordinarie Vocation consisteth in Election, Examination and Admission', and the second Book of Discipline similarly defined 'ordinarie and outward calling' as election and admission after due examination 'be the jugement of the eldarschip and consent of the congregatioun', to be followed by ordination or the solemn setting apart of the candidate to his office in the church, 'the separatioun and sanctifeing of the persone appointit of God and his kirk'.[200] By 'eldership' is understood the assembly of ministers, doctors and elders from several contiguous congregations; and by 1582 the general assembly had assigned the examination of candidates to 'particular presbyteries'. The proposed procedure somewhat resembled the practice of the French reformed church, whose national synod had required that 'no minister for the present shall be chosen by one only minister or by his consistory, but by two or three ministers and their consistories, or by the provincial synod, or by the colloquy, which in those places (where they be already established) shall be, if possible, called together for this purpose'.[201]

In their condemnation of a candidate's intrusion without the congregation's express consent, the first and second Books of Discipline were in full agreement, though a difference in emphasis emerged on the question of 'ordination', for whereas the second Book defined the 'ceremonyis' to be observed at ordination as 'fasting and eirnest prayer, and impositioun of handis of the

---

[199] Knox, *Works*, iii, 522-42.

[200] See text below, III. 1-12, and notes 42-54; *The First Book of Discipline*, 96.

[201] See text below, VII. 22 and note 117; *BUK*, ii, 570; Quick, *Synodicon*, i, 3; Aymon, *Tous les synodes*, i, 2.

elderschippe', the first Book had deliberately avoided the term 'ordination', and thereby any sacramental concept, speaking only of 'admitting' a candidate to a particular charge, and had rejected any ceremony other than the consent of the people and 'declaration of the chiefe minister'. The doctrine of the ministry and its validity rested not upon any theory of personal succession or the transmission of orders, episcopal or otherwise, but on 'the Spirit of God inwardly first moving the hearts to seek Christs glorie, and the profite of his Kirk, and thereafter the nomination of the people, the examination of the learned, and publick admission' which alone made 'men lawfull ministers of the Word and Sacraments'.[202]

The initial rejection, in 1560, of the imposition of hands, later to be reversed, is perfectly intelligible and seems to have been borrowed from Genevan practice where the ceremony was omitted from the definitive text of the 'Ordonnances' of 1541 and from the 'Forme of Prayers', used by Knox and the English exiles, on account of the current superstition surrounding the rite. Though he did not deem it essential, the rite for Calvin was nonetheless to be preferred where superstition was avoided, since it possessed apostolic sanction; and he justified its use on the grounds that:

> 'though there is no fixed precept concerning the laying on of hands, yet as we see that it was uniformly observed by the apostles, this careful observance ought to be regarded by us in the light of a precept. And it is certainly useful, that by such a symbol the dignity of the ministry should be commended to the people, and he who is ordained, reminded that he is no longer his own, but is bound in service to God and the Church. Besides, it will not prove an empty sign, if it be restored to its genuine origin. For if the Spirit of God has not instituted any thing in the Church in vain, this ceremony of his appointment we shall feel not to be useless, provided it be not superstitiously abused'.

The French reformed church in 1559 also had given qualified approval to the ceremony, 'yet without superstition, or opinion of necessity'; and in Scotland where a more critical attitude was adopted, the imposition of hands soon found acceptance once

[202] See text below, III. 2, 5, 12 and notes 43, 46, 54; *The First Book of Discipline*, 96-107; 102, 207; *cf.*, Knox, *Works*, iii, 460-1; vi, 497-8.

the phase of superstition associated with the rite had passed away.[203]

The reintroduction of the ceremony, however, is not attributable merely to the second Book of Discipline, for in this, as in much else, that document mirrored attitudes already present in reformed thought. The general assembly, after all, had expressed no disapproval of the rite as sanctioned in the second Helvetic Confession which it proceeded to endorse in 1566; and the suggestion that the assembly either read the confession imperfectly or shrank from criticising another church's order is at odds with the assembly's own belief that it had 'considered each chapter by itself and left nothing unexplored, and diligently examined everything respecting God, the sacred laws and rites of the church', and also with the assembly's criticism of that portion of the confession which approved the observance of festivals, to which the Scots took exception. Nor is there ambiguity in Erskine of Dun's advice in 1571 that admissions should proceed 'be impositione of handis be the pastouris, with admonitionis, fasting, and prayers passing befoir'. Again, as a result of the Leith settlement in 1572, the newly elected bishops were to receive the imposition of hands at their consecration; later mention was made in 1577 of the 'ordinars and inaugurers' of Adamson as archbishop, and if there were ordainers it is clear that there had also emerged an acceptance of the idea of ordination.[204]

That there was diversity of practice in the admission of ministers is suggested by the assembly's efforts to secure a uniform procedure. In 1570, the assembly had felt it necessary even to enact that all inaugurations should be conducted in public; and in October 1581, the synod of Lothian petitioned that 'ane universall ordour be tane and made be the Generall Assemblie for examinatione, tryall, admissioun and ordinatioun of Ministers'. Although an assembly committee, which included Andrew Melville, was formed to discuss the matter, nothing is known of its recommendations, though the succeeding assembly regulated the age of entry to the ministry; and by April 1589 the synod had

[203] 'Ordonnances Ecclésiastiques', 1541, *CR*, XXXVIII, i, *Calvini Opera*, X, i, 18; Knox, *Works*, iv, 174–6; Calvin, *Institutes*, IV, iii, 16; Quick, *Synodicon*, i, 3; Aymon, *Tous les Synodes*, i, 2.

[204] Cochrane, *Reformed Confessions*, 224–301; D. Shaw, 'The Inauguration of Ministers in Scotland, 1560–1620', *RSCHS*, xvi. (1966), 44–6; *Zürich Letters*, ii, 363–4; *Spalding Club Miscellany*, iv, 100; Calderwood, *History*, iii, 207; *BUK*, i, 386.

formulated its own rules for entry: a candidate had normally to be aged twenty-five, he must have participated for a year in the exercise and have attended the kirk session of the principal town of the presbytery 'to the end that he may grow in the gift of government alsweill as in doctrein', and at his admission a representative from every presbytery in the province was to be present to examine the candidate's qualifications, and after offering prayers 'handis salbe laid on' the person appointed, provided he had the approval of his flock.[205]

It is also evident that ordination by the imposition of hands, as directed in the second Book of Discipline, soon became an accepted practice. At the admission of George Byres to Barro in June 1589, Haddington presbytery first appointed a minister to 'mak the prayer and gif hime ordinatioun', but then cancelled its instruction and asked the minister instead to search 'out of the book of God and custom of the primityve kirk quhat haiv bene the rycht forme of ordinatioun of ministeris and ryttis usit thairin, and to report the samin the nixt day that thay micht proced thairin in sic forme as mycht be warrandit be Godis word and may be usit in all tymes cuming'. All that is known of the form of Byres' admission is that he received 'ordination according to the buik concerning admitting of ministeris', which may or may not refer to the second Book of Discipline; but, at least, use of the term 'ordination' by then had become common.[206]

Dalkeith presbytery conscientiously sought to adhere to the synod's ordinance of April 1589, and in Peebles presbytery at the admission of Robert Livingston in 1597 'for the mair verificatioun Adam Hepburne, Mr David Neirne withe the rest of the brethreine laid handis upoun him and admittit him to the ministrie at Skirling'.[207] There is no record, however, that entrants to the ministry in Stirling presbytery received the imposition of hands, until the admission of Henry Forrester to Larbert in July 1597 when the presbytery appointed four ministers 'to plaice him pastor at the said kirk be impositione of handis according to the

---

[205] *BUK*, i, 176; ii, 535–7, 559; iii, 924–5; *Synod of Lothian*, 8–9.
[206] SRO, CH2/185/1. Haddington Presbytery Records, fos. 27v., 47v. 4 June 1589, 8 Oct. [1589].
[207] SRO, CH2/424/1. Dalkeith Presbytery Records. [11] March 1590/1, 15 April, 21 April, 12 Aug. 1591, 20 April, 4 May, 11 May, 24 Aug. 1592; *cf.*, *Synod of Lothian*, 26–7; SRO, CH2/295/1. Peebles Presbytery Records, fo. 9v. 1 April 1597, *cf.*, fo. 18v. 31 Aug. 1597.

ordur'.²⁰⁸ This complied with the assembly's enactment of May 1597 that ordination ceremonies should include the imposition of hands.²⁰⁹ Thereafter, the ceremony became customary in that presbytery, but in Fife, where the imposition of hands gained acceptance more slowly, representatives from presbyteries were chosen merely to 'inaugurat and authorise' ministers 'according to the form subscryvit in the buik of Discipline'.²¹⁰ In the west, however, the synod in Glasgow resolved in 1587 that none should serve in the ministry without the 'imposition of the hands of the presbyterie, conform to the canon of the Apostle'; accordingly Patrick Sharp, the university principal and minister of Govan, was selected by Glasgow presbytery in November 1589 to admit Andrew Boyd to Eaglesham 'be impositione of handis according to Godis word', and in Glasgow 'admissioun be impositioun of handis according to the canon of the apostel' was regularly observed.²¹¹

If the practice to ordain candidates entering the ministry accorded with the principles of the second Book of Discipline, it was not unknown for ministers already serving to be ordained on translation from one parish to another. Andrew Law received the imposition of hands at his induction to Neilston, though it was not his first charge; John Davidson, a seasoned minister, received 'ordination' at his admission to Prestonpans in 1595; and Walter Hay, who had been deposed from the ministry at Bothans, was 'ordanit' at his readmission to the ministry in 1589.²¹² At the same time, Edinburgh presbytery condemned William Watson's admission to the ministry of Edinburgh in 1585 as highly irregular:

---

²⁰⁸ SRO, CH2/722/2. Stirling Presbytery Records, 20 July 1597; CH2/722/3. 8 Feb., 14 Feb. 1598/9; 25 July, 1 Aug. 1599; 27 April, 25 May, 13 July, 20 July 1603.

²⁰⁹ *BUK*, iii, 925.

²¹⁰ St Andrews Presbytery Records, 11 March 1590/1; 1 April 1591; 14 Oct. 1596. (On 13 September 1604, the presbytery deputed two ministers to 'give Mr John Carmichaell ordinatioun to the ministerie of Kilconquhar the nixt Saboth according to the act of the synode'.)

²¹¹ Porteous MS., 4 April 1587. SRO, CH2/722/2. Stirling Presbytery Records, 4 July 1592 (containing an extract from Glasgow Presbytery Records dated 18 November 1589, no longer extant); GCA, Glasgow Presbytery Records, entry preceding that of 14 May 1595; 17 June, 15 July, 29 July 1595; 10 July 1599; 30 April 1600.

²¹² GCA, Glasgow Presbytery Records, 15 July 1595; SRO, CH2/185/1. Haddington Presbytery Records, 29 Oct., 19 Nov., 24 Dec., 31 Dec. 1595; 7 Jan. 1595/6; (Hay) 29 Oct. 1589.

'be ressoun Patrik callit bishop of St Androis was moderatour and thairfore it was concludit that the said Mr William suld acknowledg the sam, quhilk the said Mr William did in presence of the brether, and efter long ressoning had of his doctrin and diligent inquisitione of his lyf ffinding him now lauchfullie to be callit and admittit to the functioun of the ministrie to the said toun ffand no uther thing nather in his calling, lyf, conversatioun and doctrin nor said is that unqualefeit or ony way makis him unable to continew in the office of the ministry at the said kirk of Edinburgh'.

Yet there was noticeably no attempt at Watson's formal readmission in 1589 to include the imposition of hands.[213] Again, if exception was taken to inaugurations presided over by Adamson, as archbishop, a more favourable view was taken by Dalkeith presbytery of John Bonar who in 1592 'producit his testimoniell concerning his lyfe and doctrine direct fra the faythfull brether of the ministerie in Ingland'. When John Gibson, who had served in the ministry of the church of England, sought to become minister at Athelstaneford in 1601, Haddington presbytery was uncertain whether he should be 'admittit as ane new intrant in the ministrie or as ane that had alreddy usit the office of the ministerie', but any doubts were soon resolved when Gibson 'producit ane letter of his admissione to the ministerie in England be the Bischop of Canterberrie', with which the presbytery declared itself satisfied and 'thinkis it provin thairbe that he was ane actuall minister'.[214]

With the division of Edinburgh into several parishes in 1598, the unfortunate Watson who had been twice admitted, first by the archbishop and then by the presbytery, was required to undergo readmission yet again, as were his colleagues. Not only so, but on the king's personal intervention Robert Bruce, one of the ministers who lacked the imposition of hands, was required to receive the ceremony before he could be readmitted as minister. Although his colleagues had agreed to 'take impositioun of handis als weill as he', Bruce refused to accept the ceremony other than as a confirmation of his ministry. To do otherwise, and to accept it as ordination, would seem to call in question his

---

[213] SRO, CH2/121/1. Edinburgh Presbytery Records, 27 Oct. 1589.

[214] SRO, CH2/424/1. Dalkeith Presbytery Records, 17 Aug. 1592; CH2/185/2. Haddington Presbytery Records, 29 April 1601.

earlier ministry. When the king therefore pressed Bruce 'to take a new ordination', Edinburgh presbytery was ready to acknowledge that Bruce 'was and is yit a lauchfull pastor of the kirk of Edinburgh having ane lauchfull calling of the generall assemblie thairto and as to this impositioun of handis, the use is not as a ceremonie of ordinatioun to the ministrie, bot as a ceremonie of ordinatioun to his particular flock'.[215]

Yet, even before this episode, it is evident that ordination by the laying on of hands was widely observed, and there can be little doubt that the second Book of Discipline, which presbyteries had subscribed by the early 1590s, was largely influential. There was, however, still no notion that the ceremony itself conferred authority or bestowed on the recipient any special grace; nor does there seem to have been any awareness of what Samuel Rutherford, in the seventeenth century, called the 'succession of pastors to pastors, and elders by elders'. In reply to the king's enquiry in 1597 whether a minister was a 'lawfull Pastor who wants *impositionem manuum*', the synod of Fife had declared that 'impositioun, or laying on of hands, is not essentiall and necessar, but ceremoniall and indifferent, in admission of a pastor'; and Patrick Galloway's judgment, as minister at Perth, was that 'the ceremonie is indifferent, if the apostolick duteis of ordinatioun be weill observed and followed'. In the seventeenth century, too, George Gillespie, enlisting the support of Calvin, interpreted the imposition of hands not as an act but as a sign of ordination, which 'is left free' and by no means essential. Although Martin Bucer, like Calvin, had approved 'l'imposition des mains sur ceux qui sont eleus et deputez au sainct ministere', the complete omission by Bucer of any mention of the gifts of the Holy Spirit imparted in ordination has suggested the belief that Bucer possessed 'a doctrinal conception of ordination different from that of the Anglican Ordinal'.[216]

Certainly, in Scotland what spiritual grace a candidate possessed was thought to be observable before his admission in his performance on the exercise and not to be the product of any ordination ceremony. The imposition of hands was not held to

[215] Calderwood, *History*, v, 711ff.; SRO, CH2/121/2. Edinburgh Presbytery Records, 2 May, 16 May 1598.

[216] Rutherford, *The Due Right of Presbyteries* (1644), 187; *cf.*, *BUK*, ii, 431; *BUK*, iii, 905; Calderwood, *History*, v, 586, 597; Gillespie, *An Assertion of the Government of the Church of Scotland* (1641), 103; Bucer, *Opera Latina*, xv: *De Regno Christi*, ii, 69; C. Hopf, *Martin Bucer and the English Reformation*, 91.

convey the gifts of the Holy Spirit but acted only as a recognition and seal of the spiritual gifts already present. Accordingly, Glasgow presbytery, in 1597, had inquired whether William Livingston, as a prospective minister at the exercise, 'perceavit him self inwardlie callit to the ministerie or not, quhilk Mr Williame answerit that he was inwardlie movit and callit to the said ministerie'; and in Paisley, Walter Whiteford was licensed in 1604 to preach publicly in the church where he sought admission 'to the exerceising that gift quhilk God hes gevin him to the calling of the ministrie'. Again, George Sloan was recommended by Edinburgh to Glasgow presbytery as 'ane profitabill instrument in the Lordis vyneyard quhair it sall pleis God to call him bot especialie within the presbiterie of Glasgw within the quhilk boundis the Lord is apperandlie to drawe him'; and Glasgow presbytery itself had deposed a minister in 1597 for 'inhabilitie in his persone of spirituall graces'.[217] No less significant was Alexander Borthwick's declaration to Edinburgh presbytery in 1592 that he had deserted his ministry:[218]

> be ressoun he fand in his conscience that nather had he ane inward calling nor yit giftis able to discharg sick ane hie calling and in respect he fand him self greifit that without licence of the kirk had left the said office for the quhilk he submittit him self to the judgment of the presbyterie that gif efter tryell of his giftis thai thocht his travellis mycht yit do gude in the kirk he wald glaidly offer thame, gif utherwayes his giftis efter tryell wer fand unmeitt that thai wald author-ize him with thair testimonial of his honest mening and gude willinnes'.

Clearly, as the second Book of Discipline had illustrated, what remained paramount was not the imposition of hands but the idea of vocation and the two aspects of the call to the ministry. Even so, there can be little doubt that ordination with the laying on of hands had become an accepted practice within the church of Scotland before the end of the sixteenth century.

[217] GCA, Glasgow Presbytery Records, 4 July 1597; CH2/294/1. Paisley Presbytery Records, 10 May 1604; Glasgow Presbytery Records, 8 April 1600; 4 July 1597.

[218] SRO, CH2/121/1. Edinburgh Presbytery Records, 31 Oct. 1592. For discussion of the ordination of elders and deacons, see below, 91ff., 99–100.

The Officers of the Kingdom

The substance of the church's polity over which the officebearers presided was summarily described as consisting in doctrine, discipline and distribution, which had been earlier recognised in the first Book of Discipline, and from this division there arose a threefold permanent order of ministers, bishops or preachers, elders or governors, and deacons or distributors, each of whom was seen to exercise a ministry within the church. Yet out of this threefold order, there emerged the four offices of minister, doctor, elder and deacon, since both pastors and doctors were understood to exercise ministries of the Word in expounding doctrine and explaining scripture. This particular exposition of the ministry was derived directly from Calvin, though it also accorded with Bucer's teaching in Strasbourg, from which Calvin had elaborated his fourfold ministry, and with the ecclesiology of Heinrich Bullinger.[219] Only those offices recognised to have scriptural warrant were to be adopted, and all others introduced merely by human device were rejected as unscriptural.

1. *Ministers and Bishops*

In its interpretation of the functions of pastor, bishop, minister and presbyter, the second Book of Discipline acknowledged the highest ministry to be that of the Word and sacraments (for doctors were declared ineligible to dispense the sacraments), and in its identification of *episcopi* and *presbyteri*, the book was merely reiterating a rediscovery of the Reformation which Calvin had carefully expressed when he wrote that 'in giving the name of bishops, presbyters and pastors indiscriminately to those who govern churches, I have done it on the authority of Scripture, which uses the words as synonyms. To all who discharge the ministry of the word, it gives the name of bishop'. Elsewhere, Calvin had expressly stated that only the offices of pastor, doctor, elder and deacon possessed divine warrant; and he recognised the custom which had allowed a bishop to become 'president in an assembly' to be purely a 'human arrangement'.[220]

The widespread acknowledgment at the Reformation that diocesan episcopacy was simply a human arrangement for

---

[219] See text below, II. 2-3, 10 and notes 29-31, 38-39.

[220] Calvin, *Institutes*, IV, iii, 8; IV, iv, 2; *Comm. Tim.*, 75; *Comm. Philipp.*, 23-4; *Comm. Catholic Epistles*, 145, 293-4; *Comm. Acts*, xx, 28; *CR*, XXXVIII, i, *Calvini Opera*, X, i, 15-17; *Institutes*, IV, iii, 4-5.

regulating church order meant that it was only a matter of expediency or convenience, and not of necessity, whether a church should have bishops and be episcopally governed. Far from there being any compulsion to adopt an episcopal system, the latitude was such that Matthew Parker of Canterbury was content that 'the standing or falling' of episcopacy in England should be left to Elizabeth and Burghley.[221] The opposite of a 'false' bishop was certainly a 'true' bishop, but the true bishop evidently did not have to be a diocesan bishop, a pastor of pastors and bishop of many flocks yet with no particular flock of his own. Episcopacy, then, by all accounts was not understood to be essential to the church or ministry. On what were the essential requirements, reformers were wholly explicit. Provision for the cure of souls and further evangelisation through the ministry of the Word and sacraments, for discipline through the oversight of elders, for instruction by teachers and for the care of the poor by deacons was regarded by reformers at home and elsewhere to reside in permanent and specialised ministries sanctioned by divine or dominical command.[222]

In a considered exposition of the ministry, as late as December 1571, written a month after his earlier letter to the Regent Mar, Erskine of Dun found scriptural validity for the work of pastors and teachers yet conspicuously refrained from commending the need for diocesan episcopacy on divine grounds or otherwise and instead identified the duties of bishop and minister by citing St Paul's injunction which 'requeris a bischop, or ministere, to keip hospitalitie'; but this, of course, was purely in line with the assembly's pronouncement in 1565 that 'every true preacher of Jesus Christ is a Christian bishop'. Similarly, in a sermon preached before the opening of the Convention of Leith, David Ferguson expounded how the Lord 'hes ordanit Ministeris, Pastouris and Teicheris quha aucht be the ordinance of Christ him self to have thair rewaird for thair labour', and he had indicated how 'cair-

[221] *Luther's Works*, vol. 29, 16–17; Calvin, *Institutes*, IV, iv, 2; Bullinger, *Decades*, 112; Parker, *Correspondence*, 454; N. Sykes, *Old Priest and New Presbyter* (Cambridge, 1957), 1–29.

[222] *CR*, XXXVIII, i, *Calvini Opera*, X, i, 15–17; Calvin, *Institutes*, IV, iii, 1–5, 8–9; IV, iv, 1; Bullinger, *Decades*, v, 108–9; Knox, *Works*, ii, 151–4; iv, 174–7; vi, 300, 315, 433, 441. (In 1568, Knox claimed that 'our Kirk is no new found Kirk... but that it is a part of that holy Kirk universall, which is grounded upon the doctrine of the Prophetes and Apostlis; having the same antiquitie that the Kirk of the Apostles hes as concerning doctrine, prayers, administratioun of sacramentis, and all other thinges requisite to a particulare Kirk'. *Works*, vi, 492.)

fullie the Primitive and first Kirk under the Gospell provydit for thair Ministeris and pure'. Much earlier, Ferguson had spoken in 1563 of the 'poore preachers of the Gospel, or Bishopes call them as ye list', and had illustrated how, through archbishops and patriarchs, there had ensued the primacy of the papacy, 'the Beastes sait', and with it the papal claim to be 'universal Bishop or head of the Church'.[223]

To distinguish the true bishop from the false bishop required, as Alexander Seton had observed in the 1530s, a recognition that 'it behoved a Bischope to be a preachear or ellis he was but a dume dogg and fed not the flocke but fed his awin bellye'; and the belief that 'the principall office of a Bischop is to preach the true Evangell' was shared by Henry Balnaves a decade later when he defined 'the office of a Bishop or Minister of the Worde of God' as preaching 'the pure and syncere worde to the flocke committed to thy charge', comforting the weak and infirm and ministering the sacraments according to the Word. John Knox was no less emphatic that the 'great dominions and charge (impossible by one man to be discharged)', which pertained to 'prowde prelates' were 'no parte of Christ's ministerie' for the 'office of preaching' existed to 'fede the soules of the hungrie shepe'; and his pointed contrast in 1568 between the protestant 'lord-like Bishop' and the 'painfull Preacher of his blessed Evangell' suggests a belief that even a reformed bishop was not always a true bishop.[224] George Buchanan similarly had remarked in 1579 that 'whilst a bishop is said to have only one church, others are commended to his care and all are plundered', and the inference that such a defective episcopacy might be best reformed by assigning to the bishop only the cure of his own church could scarcely have startled contemporary opinion. Indeed, Adam Bothwell, the conforming bishop of Orkney, whose mixed career had led to his suspension in 1567, could even have profited from similar advice when he informed the assembly in March 1569/70 that 'he only keeped his own parish kirke, where he received the sacraments'.[225]

Such a critical attitude towards diocesan episcopacy is wholly

[223] *Spalding Club Miscellany*, iv, 92–101, at 96; Knox, *Works*, vi, 434; Ferguson, *Tracts*, 70; 13.
[224] Knox, *Works*, i, 46; iii, 531–4, *cf.*, 538–9; v, 518–9; vi, 559; *cf.*, Calderwood, *History*, iii, 207.
[225] Buchanan, *De Jure Regni*, XXXI; *BUK*, i, 168.

comparable in the writings of Tyndale and Hooper in England; Cranmer himself had recognised that bishops and priests were 'both one office in the beginning of Christ's religion', and had justified degrees within the ministry only by an appeal to custom and tradition, not to divine prescription. John Jewel, in 1559, sought to impress the Zürich divines by insisting that 'we require our bishops to be pastors, labourers and watchmen', while Thomas Sampson told Peter Martyr that he was prepared to undertake the office of preacher wherever Elizabeth might choose but yet declined to 'take upon myself the government of the church, until, after having made an entire reformation in all ecclesiastical functions, she will concede to the clergy the right of ordering all things according to the word of God, both as regards doctrine and discipline, and the property of the church'.[226] Plainly, a preaching ministry was seen to be essential to the church in a way in which diocesan episcopacy was not, and some like Knox and Buchanan in Scotland, and Sampson in England evidently considered the latter office to need further reform.

A search for the approval of diocesan episcopacy (or for its outright condemnation) in the writings of Scottish reformers has proved unrewarding, and is somewhat inapposite since a formal episcopacy, it is sometimes necessary to recall, formed no part of the Scottish church's polity of the 1560s. The Scottish solution to the problem of supervision had been ingenious, for it neither adopted bishops on the English model, whose further reformation some still craved, nor rejected without trial the merits of individual oversight. The decision 'to make difference betwixt Preachers at this time'[227] on the purely practical grounds of a scarcity of ministers and the need to extend evangelisation throughout the country had led reformers to entrust supervision to superintendents and to ministers commissioned by the assembly (in which latter category were placed the three conforming bishops who had undertaken service in the reformed church); and such a convenient compromise might have persisted had the experiment not been eclipsed by the Leith settlement and by the introduction of bishops *per se* to whose ranks none of the superintendents or commissioners was then promoted.

[226] Tyndale, *Doctrinal Treatises*, 229-30; Hooper, *Early Writings*, 19, *cf.*, 480; Cranmer, *Works*, ii, 117; *cf.*, à Lasco, *Opera*, ii, 117; *Zürich Letters*, i, 51; 1-2, *cf.*, 63.
[227] *The First Book of Discipline*, 115.

The oft-quoted remark at Winram's election as superintendent of Fife in April 1561 that 'of Crist Jesus and of his apostolis we have command and exempill to appoynt men to sic chergis' receives no support from the Book of Discipline or from the Form and Order of the Election of Superintendents and its uniqueness needs admitting; but it is, in any event, too slender a foundation upon which to advance a claim for the *ius divinum* of episcopacy, for what the remark was surely intended to convey was the necessity of evangelisation through an energetic preaching and itinerant ministry for which Winram had special responsibility as 'cheef minister';[228] and what the remark did not anticipate was the supersession of superintendents by bishops in 1572.

The highly critical attitude which the assembly itself displayed towards the conforming bishops whose title it declined to acknowledge in any sense other than as a title in law is apparent, first, in its insistence that they were only charged with a preaching ministry to which the assembly had added a commission of oversight for specified territories; then, in its grudging reference in 1562 to 'them that are callit bischops' and in 1563 to 'Alexander Gordon stiled Bishop of Galloway'; thirdly, in its criticism of the bishop of Orkney in 1570 for styling himself with 'Roman titles as Reverend Father in God which pertaineth to no Ministers of Christ Jesus, nor is given them in Scriptures', to which the bishop consented that he had 'never delighted in such a stile nor desired any such arrogant title' since he was but 'a worm of the earth not worthy any reverence', and yet again in the assembly's censure of Carswell, superintendent of Argyll, for accepting from Mary a gift of the bishopric of the Isles in 1567 without 'making the Assemblie forseen'.[229] All in all, the reformed church of the 1560s had displayed little enthusiasm for bishops in the commonly accepted sense of that term.

Only in November 1571, when the government attempted to appoint bishops without consulting the church did Erskine of Dun seek to repel the entry of the new bishops by arguing that the admission of candidates to ecclesiastical office belonged to bishops or superintendents 'by the Scriptures of God', and 'as to the questioun if it be expedient a superintendent to be where a qualified bishop is, I understand a bishop and superintendent to be but one office; and where the one is the other is'; yet the existing superintendents ought still to oppose bishops intruded on

---

[228] *RStAKS*, i, 74–5.   [229] *BUK*, i, 27, 31, 162, 166; 144.

the church who were not true pastors.[230] It is not easy to reconcile Erskine's assertions in November 1571 with either his subsequent exposition of the ministry in December 1571 or with his later contribution to the second Book of Discipline; but it is quite evident that the emergence of a formal episcopacy was immediately followed first by a criticism of bishops – it certainly would have been odd had criticism preceded the existence of the office – and then in 1578 to the first emphatic defence of episcopacy on purely scriptural grounds by the archbishop of Glasgow who maintained 'the name, office and modest reverence borne to a Bischop to be lawful and allowable be the Scriptures of God; and beand electit be the Kirk and King to be Bischop of Glasgow, I esteime my calling and office lawful', and so was content to be examined 'be the Canon left be the Apostle to Timothie, I epistle and 3 cap., seing that place was appointit to me at my receipt, to understand therfra the dueties of a Bischop'.[231]

The extent to which individual oversight can be equated with episcopacy is a matter which requires careful consideration, for if the superintendent's office can be identified with a reduced form of episcopacy then so must the commissioner or visitor be seen as a bishop of sorts, so that the debatable area between episcopacy and presbyterianism is considerably narrowed when it is recalled that the commissioner was by no means incompatible with a presbyterian structure, and the second Book of Discipline itself had acknowledged that 'everie assemblie hes power to send furth frome thair awine nomber ane or ma visitouris to sie how all thingis be reulit in the boundis of thair jurisdictioun'.[232] Throughout, the church's concern had been with perfecting a delicately balanced structure of conciliar government, which permitted individual initiative yet guarded against lordship in the ministry; a concern which required a superintendent at his election to acknowledge both his need for 'correctioun and admonitioun',

[230] Calderwood, *History*, iii, 156–162, at 160. If Erskine of Dun identified the superintendent with the bishop, Spottiswoode in 1574 equated the superintendent with the visitor or commissioner. (*BUK*, i, 296–7.) In a work published in 1580, the Scottish Jesuit, John Hay, enquired 'sen that the name Superintendent is drevin from ane Latine wourd, and the name Bischop from ane Greek wourd, quhow is it that ye admit the ane and refuses the wther?' (*Catholic Tractates*, 62.)

[231] *BUK* ii, 423; David Lindsay's approval in 1573 of 'the book devised in Leith wherein the order of the election of bishops, with many other good articles, is contained' noticeably refrained from adducing scriptural warrant for diocesan episcopacy. (*CSP Scot.*, iv, no. 519.)

[232] See text below, VII. 7, and n. 103.

and his subjection to 'the hailsume disciplin of the Kirk', since 'the vocatioun of God to bear charge within his Kirk makethe not men tyrantes, nor lordis, but appoynteth thame Servandis, Watchemen and Pastoris of the Flock', an attitude which led to the assembly's insistence in 1576 that the power of visitation belonged to the church and not to individuals; hence the second Book of Discipline's belief that 'pastouris, in safar as thay ar pastouris, hes not the office of visitatioun of ma kirkis joinit to the pastureschip without it be gevin thame'.[233]

Such an ecclesiology drew much of its inspiration from Calvin whose primary concern had been to prevent dominion and superiority, lest one minister should usurp lordship over his brethren, since scripture had provided that 'no one should dream of primacy or dominion in regard to the government of the church'. The practice of 'applying the name of *bishop* exclusively to the person whom the presbyters in each church appointed over their company', Calvin taught, originated purely 'in a human custom and rests on no Scripture authority', and he was no less explicit in his belief that 'from the corrupted signification of the word this evil has resulted that, as if all the presbyters were not colleagues, called to the same office, one of them under the pretext of a new appellation, usurped dominion over the others'. All this would go far to explain the second Book of Discipline's concern that 'in the corruptioun of the kirk this name as utheris hes bene abusid and yit is lyk to be', until its meaning be properly restored, 'for it is not the name of superioritie and lordship, bot of office and watching'. It therefore behoved 'trew bischopis' not to 'usurp lordship ovir thair brethrene and ovir the inheritance of Chryst as thais men do'.[234]

Whatever his advice to Poland on the matter of episcopacy, it is significant that Calvin found no place for bishops in Geneva or France, the two churches with which he had been most closely concerned; and Hooker may not have greatly erred in his belief that Calvin was 'an enemy unto regiment by bishops'. Certainly, Calvin's emphasis (all too clearly mirrored in the second Book of Discipline) on the eldership, on how discipline was 'not to be administered at the will of an individual but by a lawful consistory' which was 'ordained by the Spirit of Christ', together

---

[233] Knox, *Works*, ii, 147; *BUK*, i, 357; see text below, XI. 13, and n. 186.

[234] Calvin, *Institutes*, IV, iv, 4; IV, iv, 2; *Comm. Philipp.*, 23–4; see text below, XI. 10–12, and notes 182–5.

with his stress on 'governing and maintaining the church by ministers', amongst whom there could be no monarchy, strongly suggests that only the most reduced form of individual oversight could be accommodated within such a structure.[235]

Reinforcing Calvin's misgivings on the corrupt use of the word bishop, Theodore Beza, as his successor, left no room for ambiguity as to his views on diocesan episcopacy: he warned the Scots in 1572 and again in 1576 that 'bishops ordained by man and brought into the church by little and little so as to establish government by a few' would degenerate into a new popedom, and had therefore urged 'chasing away this device of man' since the issue had been resolved by Christ who had allowed no superiority among his own disciples.[236] In place of bishops, the Geneva of Calvin and Beza had found a more acceptable alternative in the appointment for order's sake of a moderator; and, indeed, Calvin's description of the early bishop – whose duties as 'president in an assembly' of presbyters had been 'to bring matters before them, collect their opinions, take precedence of others in consulting, advising, exhorting, guide the whole procedure by his authority, and execute what is decreed by common consent' – bears a decided similarity to the rôle of moderator as exemplified not only in Geneva but in the national synod and general assembly of the reformed churches of France and Scotland. In Scotland, in particular, the appointment of a moderator, elected by the whole assembly, had been justified in 1563 'for avoyding confusion in reasoning, but that everie brother sould speake in his awin rowme', and it represented a practice which many would find hard to reconcile with episcopal government.[237] Acceptance of individual oversight at regional level apparently did not preclude the rejection of imparity at national level. It was not for nothing, therefore, that the second Book of Discipline had commended moderators of assemblies 'chosine be commoun consent of the haill brethrene convenit quha sould propone materis, gather the voitis and caus guid ordour be kepit in the assembleis'.[238]

All in all, it is hardly surprising that in Scotland the belief came

[235] *CR*, XLIII, *Calvini Opera*, XV, no. 2057; Hooker, *Laws of Ecclesiastical Polity*, VII, vi, 9; Calvin, *Institutes*, IV, xi, 5–6; IV, iii, 2; IV, vi, 10.

[236] Knox, *Works*, vi, 613–14; *SHS Miscellany*, viii, 102–4.

[237] Calvin, *Institutes*, IV, iv, 2; Quick, *Synodicon*, i, 2; Aymon, *Tous les Synodes*, i, 1; *BUK*, i, 38, 52.

[238] See text below, VII. 5 and n. 101.

to prevail that unity in doctrine and discipline might best be safeguarded by assemblies presided over, for order's sake, by a moderator among colleagues, and not by a distinct office of bishop as such;[239] and this attitude was strengthened with the second Book of Discipline's attempt to found the ministry directly on Christ's institution where no place properly might be found for an office which professedly was merely of human appointment. The existence of any permanent or exclusive system of *pastores pastorum* could not be conceded, since superiority and lordship were seen to form no part of the ministry, and diocesan episcopacy must therefore be reformed by restoring it to what was conceived to be its original purity. The truly godly bishop, as Adamson had earlier remarked, was none other than the pastor of the congregation, and a corporate or collegiate episcopacy must therefore take the place of the recently introduced diocesan episcopacy, which the authors of the book, following Calvin, regarded as a corrupted form of episcopacy.[240]

Throughout, importance was attached to functions rather than titles, and the power of oversight and visitation of more churches than one was adjudged to be no intrinsic part of a pastor's, or bishop's, office, since it properly resided not in an individual but in the church. Authority to appoint commissioners or visitors, empowered by the corporate body, to undertake supervisory duties appropriately lay with the elderships or assemblies; but, then, all this was no more than an acceptance of the assembly's conclusions in 1576; and the theory behind these developments remained the same as that which had led to the assembly's appointment of commissioners and visitors from the early 1560s. The call for parity among ministers, so conspicuous in the writings of English presbyterians, was less noticeable in Scotland where the existence of any imparity during the 1560s was less apparent, and the assembly's approval of the identity in function of minister and bishop in 1565 and again in 1576 was such that the authors of the second Book of Discipline saw little reason to argue a case for 'equalitie of power' among ministers. After all, at no time since the Reformation had the government of the church been committed solely to superintendents or bishops, and it is too readily forgotten that even after the Leith settlement

---

[239] Knox, *Works*, ii, 296; *BUK*, i, 292.

[240] See text below II. 7, and n. 35; XI. 10–12, and notes 182–185; see also above, 55, 75–6.

commissioners continued their work in a majority of dioceses.[241]

On the ordinary duties of minister, there was little which required explanation in the second Book of Discipline, though objection was taken to ministers who deserted their vocation, a matter which had caused the assembly some concern, and care was taken to ensure that ministers did not proceed unadvisedly in such matters as excommunication, absolution and the 'solemnising' of marriage contracts without 'lauchfull proceding be the elderschip', in recognition of the earlier distinction between *potestas ordinis* and *potestas jurisdictionis*. But in all this, little novelty can be detected.[242]

By implication, the expediency of the temporary offices of exhorter and reader, which had been introduced until fully qualified ministers were available in sufficient strength, was no longer conceded. Exhorters had been permitted to preach and even to baptise and conduct marriage services, but not to administer the sacrament of communion. Initially, readers were confined merely to reading the common prayers and possibly a scriptural text. The Concordat of Leith, however, permitted readers, if found qualified, to minister the sacrament of baptism and to officiate at marriages, two duties which the assembly hitherto had denied them; but by 1576 the assembly again required that 'no Reider within this realme minister the holie scaraments of the Lord except sick as hes the words of exhortatioun in their mouths'. The synod of Lothian informed the assembly in 1579 that 'the haill brether hes inhibite all Readers from ministring the sacraments and solemnization of marriage, permitting nothing unto them but proclamatioun of the bands and simple reiding of the text', and asked for a uniform order to be established by act of assembly. Such a measure was forthcoming in 1580 when the assembly concluded that the reader's office was 'no ordinar office within the Kirk of God' and after considering 'whether in respect of thair necessitie and circumstance of tyme they sould be sufferit to continue', resolved that readers after examination should either become ministers or be deposed from all office; and in 1581 the assembly prohibited the admission of further readers. Similarly, when a commissioner admitted an

[241] See text below VII. 7-8, and notes 103-104; XI. 12-16, and notes 184-189; see also above, 32.

[242] See text below II. 6, and n. 34; IV. 4-5, and notes 63-64; IV. 11-12, and notes 71-72; see also above, 58ff., 66ff.

exhorter to Eddleston, the assembly in 1580 declined to recognise such an office to be within 'the Kirk of God'. Although some depositions occurred as presbyteries and commissioners took account of readers' abilities, the office was still not abolished in practice, and indeed new readers were even recruited.[243]

2. *The Doctor or Teacher*

A minor innovation in the second Book of Discipline was the renewed emphasis on the doctor's office, 'ane of the twa ordinar and perpetuall functionis that travell in the word'. In effect, the doctor or teacher (also termed 'prophet', 'bishop', 'elder' and 'catechiser') was the theology professor, and if the minister were the 'messinger and herauld betwene God and the people', the doctor had the scarcely less important task of interpreting scripture: 'to oppine up the mynd of the Spirit of God within the Scripturis simplie without sic applicationis as the minister usis'.[244] For Melville, as doctor and theology professor first at Glasgow and then at St Andrews, the true meaning of scripture was discovered not by studying the traditional fourfold sense of the text nor merely by inspiration but by applying the tools of philology to biblical exegesis. The sacred texts had to be studied in their original tongues, and by so doing scripture became 'perfect, clear in itself, its own interpreter, the supreme judge of all controversies; it is of divine authority, comprehended in the canonical and divinely inspired books of the Old and New Testaments, written down in Hebrew and Greek letters, editions of which alone are authentic, from which to resort to Latin or vernacular editions in controversies is practically foolish and impious'.[245]

Unlike the minister who might also serve as schoolteacher, the doctor unless orderly called could not act as minister or dispense the sacraments, and it was apparently not until the Westminster

---

[243] *The First Book of Discipline*, 105–6, 111–12, 130, 163; *BUK*, i, 63, 82, 124, 211, 276, 372; ii, 438–9, 455–7, 464, 479, 513; iii, 927; *RStAKS*, i, 177–8; ii, 529, 594, 600–1; *Synod of Lothian*, 7, 60, 101, 103, 120, 127, 152, 166, 200; L. MacBean, *Records of the Burgh of Kirkcaldy*, 120–1; SRO, CH4/424/1. Dalkeith Presbytery Records, fos. 15r., 17r., 26r., 31v., 32v., 97v.–98v., 99v., 100v., 103r., 105r., 108v., 111r.; SRO, CH2/121/2. Edinburgh Presbytery Records, 18 Jan., 15 Feb., 8 March, 22 March 1596/7; 21 June, 19 July, 6 Sept. 1597; SRO, CH2/550/1. Glasgow Kirk Session Records, fo. 88r. (7 March 1587/8).

[244] See text below, IV. 13, and n. 73; V. 1–2, and notes 74–75.

[245] Melville, *Scholastica diatriba de rebus divinis* (Edinburgh, 1599), *aphorismi de rebus divinis*, III.

Assembly of 1644 that Scottish presbyterians formally conceded the doctor's right to administer the sacraments. In 1580, and again in 1582, the assembly had permitted a minister to set aside his own duties for a spell to enable him to undertake the office of doctor; but ever since John Douglas had retained the provostry of St Mary's college on his promotion to the archbishopric of St Andrews, there had been criticism of the concurrent exercise of both offices by the same person. This was exemplified in the assembly's insistence in 1576 that Robert Hamilton, minister at St Andrews and the new provost of St Mary's, should demit one or other office.[246]

In personnel, there was much interaction between the two offices; there were both ministers who became doctors and there were those who in effect were doctors and who became ministers. James Lawson, John Davidson, James Melville, Robert Rollock, George Robertson, Peter Blackburn, Theodore Hay and Oliver Colt are all well-known men who held university appointments before they undertook a parish ministry; and there were others like Robert Wilkie who were ministers before they became university teachers.[247] At the same time, the principal at Glasgow university was required to preach each Sunday in the kirk of Govan in accord with the charter of *nova erectio* of 1577 by which the crown had annexed the benefice of Govan to the college for its support. Melville, as principal, must therefore have preached regularly at Govan, a practice which the second Book of Discipline did not envisage, but whether he also served as minister at Govan and administered the sacraments is less than clear, though later principals were explicitly designated to have been ministers of Govan, and one is even known to have celebrated communion there.[248] A somewhat similar situation occurred in St Andrews where the principal of St Leonard's college was also appointed minister for St Leonard's parish. In Edinburgh, Rollock as college principal also preached on Sundays in the 'new kirk'

---

[246] See text below, V. 6, and n. 82; R. W. Henderson, *The Teaching office in the Reformed Tradition* (Philadelphia, 1962), 202; *BUK*, ii, 469, 597; i, 241–2; ii, 375.

[247] *Fasti*, i, 28, 37, 51, 54, 131, 170; iii, 162; v, 212, 231; vi, 36.

[248] Durkan and Kirk, *The University of Glasgow* (Glasgow, 1977), 286–7, 349, 442; GCA, Glasgow Presbytery Records, fos. 51v., 148v.; *Select Biographies*, i, 134. The difficulties surrounding such a practice were revealed at a presbyterial visitation of Govan in 1596 when the complaint was voiced that 'thair is na residence of a minister at the kirk of Govan quhilk [wes] havelie lamentit be the elderis of the kirk of Govane'. (GCA, Glasgow Presbytery Records, 1 June 1596.)

before his appointment as parish minister there in 1596. Similarly Alexander Arbuthnot was concurrently principal of King's college, Aberdeen and minister at St Machar's, as in turn was David Rait; and in 1602 it was even envisaged that the 'maisteris of the college' would assist John Chalmer, the sub-principal, in 'teaching' or preaching on Sunday afternoon in the kirk of Old Aberdeen. With the foundation of Marischal college in 1593, Robert Howie, as first principal, continued to act as a city minister, while in Fraserburgh Charles Ferme was appointed to serve both as minister of the town and as principal of the ill-fated college there.[249]

The integration of the doctoral office into the church's constitution was accomplished without difficulty or dislocation. As an elder, the doctor had the task of assisting in the government of the church. It was therefore expected that he would take his place on the courts of the church.[250] From 1561 university teachers had found a place as elders on St Andrews kirk session – indeed their names took precedence over the names of other elders – and it is known that in Glasgow the regents of the university from 1583 sat as members of the general session.[251] With the creation of presbyteries in 1581, it was reported in April 1582 that St Andrews presbytery consisted of pastors and teachers, but 'not of these that hes not the cure of teaching'. In practice, regents and masters of theology and philosophy, together with the master of the grammar school, gained seats on the presbytery along with the ministers.[252] Only in 1587 did the church decide to exclude philosophy regents from attending presbytery meetings, and it was not until the king's injunctions against the attendance of doctors in 1597, in an effort to diminish Melville's influence, that

---

[249] St Andrews Presbytery Records, 14 Oct. 1591; *Fasti*, v, 243; SRO, CH2/121/1. Edinburgh Presbytery Records, 5 Sept. 1587; *Fasti*, i, 37; New Reg. Ho. OPR. 168A/12. Aberdeen Old Parochial Register, 31 Oct. 1580 (where Arbuthnot 'inaugurated' the elders and deacons after their election to the kirk session); SRO, CH2/1/1. Aberdeen Presbytery Records, 7 Aug. 1601; 2 July 1602; *Fasti*, vi, 13, 18, 22; G. D. Henderson, *The Founding of Marischal College, Aberdeen*, 63; *Fasti*, vi, 220-1.

[250] See text below, V. 5, and n. 81; VI. 2, and n. 85; VII. 1, 23, 27.

[251] *RStAKS*, i, 2, 4, 5, 323, 342, 350, 368, 382, 399, 412, 419, 427, 431, 442, 453 and *passsim*; SRO, CH2/550/1. Glasgow Kirk Session Records, fos. 2r., 20v., 52r., 80r., 100r., 119r., 137v., 158v., 181r. (Smeaton, Sharp, Lawrie, Patrick Melville). See also SRO, CH2/1/1. Aberdeen Presbytery Records, 2 July 1602, where John Chalmer, the sub-principal, is on record as an elder on the kirk session of Old Aberdeen.

[252] *BUK*, ii, 549; St Andrews Presbytery Records, fo. 1r.-v.

doctors or divinity lecturers were prevented from giving their presence at presbytery meetings,[253] though Melville and his colleagues continued to frequent the exercise.[254] Regents from Glasgow university, as was to be expected, also attended the presbytery, and the same may have happened in Edinburgh, for in 1597 the presbytery decided that 'in tyme cuming na persone sall remaine in the presbyterie bot actuall ministeris and sick as hes gevin up their names to be upon the exerces'.[255] Since 'under the name and office of ane doctour we comprehend also the ordour of scoles in collegis and universiteis', it was logical enough that schoolmasters as well as ministers, university teachers and elders should take their place in presbyteries.[256] At regional level, too, the synod of Fife regarded doctors as eligible to attend meetings of the synod, for not only is Andrew Melville's presence recorded on various occasions, but his nephew James is known to have been appointed moderator of the synod when still a theology master; and, in 1597, the church under cross-examination from the king, reaffirmed its belief that doctors had an inherent right to sit and vote in synods.[257]

Since the election of a majority of the commissioners to the assembly was conducted by presbyteries or synods, it is not surprising that doctors with ministers and lairds were chosen to attend the assembly. Although evidence for the election of commissioners from St Andrews presbytery is somewhat scant, Andrew Melville seems to have been present at most assemblies, and certainly Melville, John Johnston and Patrick Melville from the university are on record among the commissioners from St Andrews presbytery in 1593. Similarly, John Robertson from St Mary's college had been chosen commissioner in 1590;

[253] St Andrews Presbytery Records, 23 April 1590 (containing an extract of an act of general assembly dated 23 June 1587, and an extract of an act of the synod of Fife dated 8 April 1590, neither of which is extant), 15 July 1597; SRO, CH2/121/2. Edinburgh Presbytery Records, 8 Feb. 1596/7; Calderwood, *History*, v, 651; *Evidence*, iii, 197.

[254] St Andrews Presbytery Records, 4 Aug., 8 Sept. 1597; 19 Jan. [1597/8]; 9 Nov., 16 Dec. 1598; 30 June 1599; 21 Feb., 14 Aug., 21 Aug. 1600; 1 July 1602, and *passim*.

[255] GCA, Glasgow Presbytery Records, e.g. 8 April, 15 July, 18 Aug. 1595; SRO, CH2/121/2. Edinburgh Presbytery Records, 8 Feb. 1596/7.

[256] See text below, V. 4, and n. 78; IX. 9, and n. 153; e.g. St Andrews Presbytery Records, fo. 11.(Monipenny); SRO, CH2/722/1. Stirling Presbytery Records, 31 Oct. 1581 (Yule); GCA, Glasgow Presbytery Records, fo. 148v.

[257] Melville, *Diary*, 245, 359, 395; Calderwood, *History*, iv, 494–5; v, 436, 590.

Melville, as rector, and Homer Blair from St Salvator's college were elected in 1594; and in 1596 Melville was once more appointed; while in Glasgow, Patrick Sharp, the university principal, also found himself deputed by the presbytery on several occasions as commissioner to the assembly.[258]

Familiar as he must have been with the doctoral office both in Geneva and in France, Melville was no doubt instrumental in reviving its Scottish counterpart, but responsibility for incorporation of the office in the second Book of Discipline need not be attributed to one individual for university representation at the committee stages of the book's composition was undoubtedly strong. There was certainly a renewed stress upon the doctor's office immediately after Melville's arrival which found expression in the assembly's appeal, in August 1574, that 'doctours may be placit in Universities, and stipends grantit unto them; querby not only they quho are presentlie placit may have occasion to be diligent in thair cure, but also uther learned men may have occasion to seik places in Colledges within this realme'. Yet such a claim also contained a recognition that doctors already existed; and long ago John Knox and his colleagues in the Genevan 'Forme of Prayers', subsequently incorporated in the Scottish Book of Common Order, had explicitly recognised the scriptural validity of the doctor's office 'where tyme and place dothe permit'.[259]

3. *Elders*

Although ministers and doctors were each regarded, in some sense, as 'elders', the pastorate was nonetheless distinguished from the doctorate, and both were differentiated from the eldership, since 'in this our divisioun we call thais eldaris quhome the apostles callis presidentis or governouris'.[260] There therefore existed, as Calvin had illustrated, a functional difference between ruling and preaching presbyters, though such a distinction plainly did not preclude the recognition in 1592 that a minister was also 'ane elder', or even prevent the election of both ministers and doctors to sit as elders on Glasgow general session.[261] As an

[258] St Andrews Presbytery Records, 31 July 1590; 19 April 1593; 2 May 1594; 11 March 1595/6; GCA, Glasgow Presbytery Records, 5 March 1594; 17 Feb. 1595/6, 11 March 1600. See below, Appendix III, 276–9, cf., 289.

[259] *BUK*, i, 305; Knox, *Works*, iv, 177; vi, 293–4.

[260] See text below, VI. 1–3, and notes 84–6.

[261] Calvin, *Institutes*, IV, xi, 1; St Andrews Presbytery Records, 22 Feb. 1591/2; SRO, CH2/550/1. Glasgow Kirk Session Records, fos. 2r., 20v., 52r., 80r., 100r.

ordinary and perpetual office 'alwayis necessar in the kirk of God', elders once called and elected from the congregation were obliged not to leave their office, but such a restriction did not eliminate the possibility of re-election to specific commitments, annual or otherwise, and the second Book of Discipline itself recognised the need for special provision to be made that 'ane part of thame may releif ane uther for ane resonable space, as was amang the Levittis undir the law in serving of the temple'.[262]

Discussion of the elder's office led one contemporary to remark that:[263]

'We reade of theyr institution, good lives and office but no thing of theyr chang nor yet of theyr continuance ather in that office. It appeareth to me by the historie of the primityve kyrk that they wer men of grater bearing besyds the gyft of regiment then they ar now; some of them did teache and out of that numer teachers wes chosen and they continueth and had some payment for theyr service as it may appeare by the wydows wherof Paule doeth writ to Timothie, and I see not why the gyft of God and lawfull calling of the kirk sould not urge mens conscience to continue in theyr office, nor yit do I see any good cause wherefore the kyrk shoulde discharge him whom they have once called so long as the gyft endured or some othir impediment come not....'

At the same time, it was recognised that the election of elders for life did not 'so stretly bynd mens conscience to continue' without some 'releef and demission' of their duties for a spell, so that:[264]

'otheris that hath the same or greater gyftis be called for theyr releaf for a certayne tyme nor but the former when neid required shall assiste and serve for the confort of the kyrk. This ordour wes kept amang the prestis and Levites who still remayneth prestis and Levits and yet serveth but theyr tyme about. This ordour is kept amangis the preacheris whare many are in our kyrk one of them doeth releaf the rest for a tyme thogh theyr dismission be shortter then the other. This ordour

---

119r., 137r., 158v., 181r. For Scottish usage of 'presbyter', see J. Kirk, 'The Development of the Melvillian Movement in late sixteenth-century Scotland' (Edinburgh Ph.D. thesis, 1972), i, 344–6.

[262] See text below, VI. 6–7, and notes 89–90.
[263] NLS, Adv. MS. 29.2.8, fo. 122r.   [264] *Ibid.*

being kept nether shal the brethren be byrdyn[eth] uncheritably nor gyftis givin unto them remayne idle nor the fyrst calling and gyft be absolutly discharged'.

The example in the Old Testament to which allusion is made appears to be the priestly rota system described in *I Chronicles* 24: 1–19, the operation of which is illustrated in the case of Zechariah in *Luke* 1:23.

The proposal to appoint elders for life differed only in detail, and not in principle, from the earlier practice of election for a specific term, usually for a year. The belief, shared by the first Book of Discipline, that elders were called by God to a special vocation and office in the church made it difficult to deny that the call which an elder experienced was likely to be enduring rather than transistory, and certainly not one which abruptly ended each year. In any event, the first Book of Discipline had accepted that an elder might be 'reteaned in office moe years then one'. The case for annual election had been twofold; it interfered less with an elder's occupation and his ability to earn a livelihood, and it lessened the prospect that some might 'presume upon the liberty of the kirk'. The practice had been borrowed from the order observed in the 'privy kirk' of Edinburgh during the 1550s where elders and deacons had been elected to office which 'thay patiently susteaned a yeir and mair: and then, becaus they could not (without neglecting of thair awen private houses) langer wait upoun the publict charge, they desyred that they micht be releaved, and that uthers micht be burdeined in thair roume: quhilk was thocht a petitioun ressonabill of the haill Kirk'. The concession that elders and deacons might be released from their duties for a spell was wholly consistent with the second Book of Discipline's recognition that among elders 'ane part of thame may releif ane uther for ane resonable space'.[265]

Any initial fear of dominion by a few must soon have faded, with the establishment of a full system of church courts and with the exercise of fraternal correction and mutual censuring, for substantially the same people were returned to office each year and formal election served rather to confirm them in office. In St Andrews kirk session alone, some elders and deacons first elected in 1559 were still serving in the 1580s, and when the register closes in 1600 there was one survivor from 1559 who had

---

[265] *The First Book of Discipline*, 175, 179; Knox, *Works*, ii, 151–4.

been an elder for some forty years.[266] Nor did Andrew Melville express criticism at his own annual election as an elder on St Andrews session where he was repeatedly elected to office each year between 1591 and 1596.[267] In Anstruther, the procedure adopted in 1592 was for the elders to convene and enter into 'tryell and censuring of everie one in particular concerning ther dewetie in ther office publicklie and privatlie, and ther eftir sic as wes fund meit wes continued and exhorted to a greatter diligence in tym coming and utheris wer named' to fill any vacancies which arose; while in Burntisland elections were seemingly held only every other year.[268]

Here again, the modifications suggested in the second Book of Discipline were less drastic than have been sometimes allowed; and when the king asked the assembly in 1597 whether elders should be elected for life, the reply was that elders were already elected for life, unless otherwise deprived, and it was only because no financial assistance was forthcoming that elders could ill afford to neglect their occupations every year while attending to their ecclesiastical duties; hence the practice that from 'a number lawfully elected successivelie, some releeve other, yitt all abide kirk officers'. The suggestion was that elders ought to have been reimbursed, for their loss of earnings, from the proper patrimony of the church, but the lack of adequate finance prevented any allocation of funds for elders or deacons, and the decision to favour annual elections in 1560 was taken in the knowledge that a 'publick stipend' for elders and deacons would not be necessary 'because their travell continues but for a yeare, and also because that they are not so occupied with the affaires of the kirk but that reasonably they may attend upon their domesticall businesse'.[269]

It is possible, of course, to mistake the elder's office for an order in the ministry. Elders were to be elected for life; they were to receive ordination; and their office was 'ane functioun spirituall, as is the ministrie'.[270] Yet this alone is too slender a foundation for

---

[266] E.g., Thomas Balfour, George Black, Martin Geddie, John Motto, Thomas Walwod; William Cook; *RStAKS, passim.*

[267] *RStAKS*, ii, 694, 751, 760, 788, 802, 816.

[268] New Reg. Ho. OPR. 403/1. Anstruther Wester Old Parochial Records, 19 Aug. 1592; SRO, CH2/523/1. Burntisland Kirk Session Records, 7 Nov. 1602, 3 April 1608, 17 Feb. 1611, 28 July [1611], 9 Nov. 1617; 14 Nov. 1619, 4 Nov. 1621, 21 Dec. 1623.

[269] Calderwood, *History*, v, 588; Melville, *Diary*, 394; *The First Book of Discipline*, 179. [270] See text below, VI. 5–6, and notes 88–89.

contrasting the elders of the second Book of Discipline with those of the first, especially when it is recalled that from 1560 onwards elders frequently served for many years, were acknowledged to possess a vocation, of which ordination came to signify merely a recognition, and they were understood to exercise a ministry in serving the community. The prayer at the election of elders in Edinburgh from the 1550s specifically mentioned how God 'hes alwayis usit the ministry of men, alswell in preiching of thy word, and administratioun of thy sacraments, as in gyding of thy flock, and provyding for the puir within the same'; in St Andrews the elders and deacons were comprehended under 'the ministerie in ther sessione'; and not only had Knox and his friends grouped the elders 'with the rest of the ministers' in their Genevan 'Forme of Prayers', but the English exiles in Frankfort had also spoken of the elders' 'ministry or office', which was to end on 1 March each year, in their second New Discipline of 1557. Again, the English in Frankfort proposed ordaining their annually elected elders with the imposition of hands, a ceremony which à Lasco also practised in his strangers' church in London, but all this was no more than an outward sign of an elder's vocation, a recognition of the spiritual grace which he already possessed.[271]

If the elder of the second Book of Discipline conceivably could be mistaken for an order in the ministry, if an elder, as is sometimes argued, now ceased to be a layman as generally understood, then it was neither his election for life nor even his ordination which made him a 'minister', but only that divine calling which was of course common to the elders defined in both Books of Discipline. Although the ordination of elders in Scotland remained an exception rather than a rule, it is apparent that the elders of Burntisland in 1608 and again in 1611, though still elected for a term, were required to 'receave ordination to their callings and work according to the forme in all poyntis'; and the elders so elected, whose number included several skippers, a wright, a cooper and a maltman, must have been popularly regarded as lay persons.[272] They did not form what in any sense could be regarded as a professional, full-time ministry. Even in

[271] Knox, *Works*, ii, 153; *RStAKS*, i, 196–7, 264, 266 and *passim*; Knox, *Works*, iv, 176; *A Brief Discourse of the Troubles at Frankfort*, 186; à Lasco, *Opera*, ii, 75; *Orig. Letters rel. Engl. Ref.*, ii, 571.

[272] SRO, CH2/523/1. Burntisland Kirk Session Records, fos. 32r., 47r. 10 April 1608, 11 Feb., 24 Feb. 1611.

presbyteries, where elders were elected for life,²⁷³ it would have been scarcely possible for contemporaries to regard Adam Erskine, the lay commendator of Cambuskenneth, or the lairds of Garden and Blairlogie, who were among the elders on Stirling presbytery, or the laird of Cockpen on Dalkeith presbytery – men whom contemporaries called 'gentlemen elders' – as anything other than 'laymen' who happened to be office-bearers in the church.²⁷⁴ Neither in theory nor in practice is there sufficient evidence to confirm the view that the elder of the second Book of Discipline received indelible character, a belief which the reformers had plainly denounced and discarded.²⁷⁵ Patrick Adamson in his commentary on the second Book of Discipline in 1583 understood the proposed elders to be 'laick men'; and Andrew Melville distinguished pastors and doctors, who in effect formed a professional ministry, from elders or 'governors, to which office gentlemen and other qualified persons that are not ministers may be called'.²⁷⁶

If it is possible to mistake the elder's office for an order in the ministry, it is no less a mistake to regard it as clerical. The office was recognised to be both spiritual and ecclesiastical, but it was not understood to be clerical. Apart from reference to the use of the term 'clergy' in the ancient canon, the word was conspicuous by its absence, since the Scottish reformed tradition was disinclined to accept any rigid distinction between clergy and laity. James Melville, as a presbyterian, once censured Archbishop Adamson in 1586 for his acceptance of that 'distinction betwixt the Priests and the people: the one sorte being tearmed the Cleargie and the other the laitie' and affirmed his own belief that 'that distinctioun of yours betwixt the clergie and laicks ... smelles of the antichrist, who esteems themselves to be the holie inheritance of the Lord allanerlie, and the people to be, in respect of them, profane and unholie'; but in all this James Melville was at one with Calvin who had illustrated the fallacy in ministers appropriating

---

²⁷³ SRO, CH2/722/1. Stirling Presbytery Records, 8 Aug., 22 Aug., 10 Oct. 1581.

²⁷⁴ *Ibid.*, 8 Aug. 1581; SRO, CH2/424/1. Dalkeith Presbytery Records, fo. 71r., 27 June 1583; NLS, Adv. MS., 6.1.13, fo. 40r.

²⁷⁵ *Cf.*, Knox, *Works*, iv, 127: 'for now, we haif na Leviticall Preistheid' (1556); J. L. Ainslie, *Doctrines of Ministerial Order*, 192. When ministers and elders were deposed, they were deprived from all office and function in the kirk and not merely from the administration of their office.

²⁷⁶ Calderwood, *History*, iv, 51, 54; 290.

to themselves the name of clergy when 'the whole church is by Peter denominated *clerus*, that is, the inheritance of the Lord'.[277]

The progression towards a belief that an elder should be appointed for life, though subject to re-election to a specific charge, was scarcely innovatory, and it is not surprising that 'the perpetuitie of the persons of the Elders' was readily accepted by the assembly in 1578, and by a 'Conference had be the Commissioners appointit be the Kings Majestie and Counsell', whose report was submitted to the assembly by June 1578.[278] The judgment of one contemporary, possibly lord Menmuir, on the election of elders for life, though favourable, was somewhat severe:[279]

> 'quhen he makis the office of ane elder perpetuall, I think it should be so, and yit it is playne contrarie the ordor that hes bene observit quhair eldaris hes bene yeirlie electit through the haill realm.'

Yet lord Menmuir, elsewhere, had plainly taken a less critical view of elders elected for life. In 1597 he declared: 'I have borne the office of ane elder dyvers yeiris in the principall kirk of this realme quhilk makis the office to continew with me for my lyftyme.'[280] Menmuir may have been pleading a special cause, for he was resolutely opposing the claim of Robert Wallace, minister of St Andrews, to special privilege as an 'elder', which Menmuir contended ought not to prejudice his own position as an elder;[281] but, at the same time, his words reveal a deeper truth. Here was an implicit acceptance of the theory of the eldership propounded in the second Book of Discipline, and a realisation that an elder's vocation ought to be enduring.

Not only did the underlying concept of the elder's office remain substantially the same in both Books of Discipline, but later elders were endowed with essentially the same powers as those assigned to their predecessors. It is true, of course, that the king's inquiry, drafted by lord Menmuir, in 1597 on whether kirk sessions might judge a minister's doctrine led the ministers – taking as their text *I Corinthians* 14: 32, 'the spirit of the propheits is subject to the propheits' – to insist that pastors and doctors alone, as expounders of scripture, were judges of doctrine.[282]

[277] *Ibid.*, 517; Calvin, *Institutes*, IV, iv, 9. [278] *BUK*, ii, 415.
[279] NLS, Adv. MS. 29.2.8, fo. 128v. [280] *Ibid.*, fo. 83v.
[281] *Ibid.*, fos. 55–111. [282] Calderwood, *History*, v, 588, 597, 601.

Yet it is easy to read too much into this statement without considering other evidence. In 1597, the church was decidedly on the defensive, after the Edinburgh riot in December 1596, and its primary objective was to repel any attempts at royal interference in doctrinal matters. The summoning before the privy council in 1596 of David Black, minister in St Andrews, for purported treasonable speeches uttered in pulpit, had been regarded by ministers as a 'preparative quhairby the haill auctoritie of Chrystis kingdome mycht be overthrawin be subjecting to the judgment of the Civill Magistrat the censuring of the preiching of the word and saitting of injunctionis thair upone and upone the haill discipline of the kirk'.[283]

In more normal times, however, in a more relaxed and less inflammatory atmosphere, it is evident from visitations that elders were expected to judge and to give an account of their minister's doctrine. In December 1591, Robert Rollock as visitor had 'demandit of the eldaris of Dalkeith anent the doctrine and lyfe of thair minister', and in reply the elders reported that Archibald Simson, their minister, had 'taught the undoutit truthe of God sensiblie till all', that 'he growis in doctrine and edifying' and that they found 'in him a gud example of lyfe and conversatioun'.[284] Similarly at a presbyterial visitation of the kirk of Haddington in 1589, after being solemnly 'chargeit to declair the trewth as thay wald answer to God in the day of jugment', the gentlemen and elders announced that they could find no fault with their minister, nor any insufficiency in his doctrine 'but that he behavit him self in all thingis as becomes the Minister of Goddis Word in doctrene and example of lyfe', though the parishioners did suggest that their minister's doctrine, though sound, was nonetheless 'ovirleirnit above the commoune pepillis capacities', and they recommended that it was time for the minister, with the advice of the kirk session, to change the scriptural text for his sermons. The minister, James Carmichael, was therefore 'ordanit to change and tak upone the Lordis day befoir none with the advyse of his sessioun sum of the Evangelistis or of the Epistillis and efternone the Catechisme and on Thuirsday to begine the Genesis and red every ordinar day ane haill chapter to the end quhairof he may gather the haill in sum heidis with

[283] SRO, CH2/722/3. Stirling Presbytery Records, 24 Nov. 1596; Calderwood, *History*, v, 460.
[284] SRO, CH2/424/1. Dalkeith Presbytery Records, 16 Dec. 1591.

nottis, applicationis and exhortationis as the text sall offer swa familiar plane as may be'.²⁸⁵

Not only were the minister's imperfections revealed by elders and parishioners, but those of his wife, family and servants came under the closest scrutiny; and it was not unknown for the moderator of the presbytery to admonish a minister 'maist gravelie' to reform his wife and family. At Aberlady, the 'gentlemen' of the parish adjudged their minister's doctrine to be 'cauld and not edificative'; at Gullane, the laird of Saltcoats with other parishioners found their minister 'sumtymis lycht in language'; and at Tranent the parishioners felt the minister's doctrine 'edificative' but wished it were 'mair pithie'.²⁸⁶ At a presbyterial visitation of Nigg in Kincardineshire, the minister 'being removit and censurit, receavit a guid testimonial of his eldaris and remanent of the paroche and thairfor commendit and allowit'; but at Skene the minister was accused that 'he delyveris nocht the doctrine of salvatioun to the edificatioun of that flok as thair neid requirit'.²⁸⁷ In addition to visitations, St Andrews presbytery, like its counterpart in Stirling, required commissioners, usually elders, from the churches of the presbytery to present themselves before the presbytery to 'testifie of the doctrein, lyfe and disciplin exercisit be thair minister and to complain upon thaim gif ony occasioun thei hed'.²⁸⁸

Under the presbyterian system, elders were plainly expected to examine and judge their minister's life and doctrine in precisely the same manner as that outlined in the first Book of Discipline; and just as no minister under the earlier system could be deposed except with the consent of the superintendent, synod or general assembly, so also had consent to be sought from the presbytery, synod or assembly²⁸⁹ under the presbyterian system before a minister could be removed from his charge. The element of congregational initiative was certainly present, as presbyterial

---

²⁸⁵ SRO, CH2/185/1. Haddington Presbytery Records, fo. 34r.-v., 2 July 1589.

²⁸⁶ *Ibid.*, 35r., 36v., 38v.

²⁸⁷ SRO, CH2/1/1. Aberdeen Presbytery Records, 10 July 1601; 3 Aug. 1599; *cf.*, 11 July, 18 July 1600.

²⁸⁸ St Andrews Presbytery Records, 27 Aug., 3 Sept., 17 Sept. 1590; 15 Sept., 23 Sept., 30 Sept., 14 Oct. 1591; SRO, CH2/722/1. Stirling Presbytery Records, 12 Aug., 26 Aug. 1589; CH2/722/2. 22 Sept. 1590.

²⁸⁹ *Cf.*, SRO, CH2/722/1. Stirling Presbytery Records, 1 July 1589 containing an extract of an act of the general assembly, no longer extant in the records of assembly, dated 6th session, 21 June 1589.

visitations so readily indicate, and it was not only the elders but the parishioners, too, whose judgments were sought on their pastor's doctrine and diligence. Much depended on whether a church had a receptive or rebellious congregation, on whether it possessed a determined or docile kirk session, and on whether its minister was domineering or easy-going; but there can be little doubt that it was possible for elders to gain the upper hand, particularly where a minister was inexperienced or ineffective. At St Ninians near Stirling, the gentlemen elders had 'insistit in urgein' their new minister, Henry Livingston, to baptise an illegitimate child of Murray of Touchadam without obtaining the father's repentance, which involved the humiliating experience of standing bareheaded in sackcloth at the pillar of repentance on successive Sundays. 'Allaigein it hes bein the commone practeis usit in thair assembleis befoir his cuming to thame and that thai knew na act of the kirk made in the contrar', the elders had warned their new minister that 'he did thame wrang gif he refusit the samin, thruch the quhilk he was constranit ather to bapteis the said bairn, or than to suffir seditione to arys betuix him and thame, and sua the haill disceplein of thair kirk to gang lows'.[290] Not all ministers might aspire to becoming popes in their own parishes, and a survey of the evidence lends little support to the contention that the powers of elders in 1560 were withheld from those operating under a presbyterian system.

4. *Deacons*

If ministers, doctors and elders were all, in a sense, elders and entitled as such to sit and vote on the eldership, they might also be regarded, through their service and ministry, as 'deacons'. Recognising the philological problems present in interpreting the office and functions of the 'deacon', a term which, it was conceded, could be taken to include 'all thame that beir office in the ministrie and spirituall functioun in the kirk', the authors of the second Book of Discipline, like their predecessors in the first Book, proceeded to define the deacon proper as a financial officer whose duties consisted in collecting the church's revenues and in distributing alms among the poor and needy.[291] Such an exposition coincided with the teaching of Calvin and Beza, and the Scots noticeably showed no inclination to adopt the interpretation offered in Walter Travers' *Disciplinae ecclesiasticae* . . .

[290] *Ibid.*, 16 April 1588. [291] See text below, VIII. 1–2, and notes 138–9.

explicatio which distinguished two ministries of bishop and deacon from which were extrapolated two functions within each ministry: under bishop were included the functions of pastor and teacher, and under deacon were comprehended the functions of elder and distributor or deacon proper.[292]

In practice, the deacon's financial duties never became so comprehensive as those envisaged in either the first or second Book of Discipline, and the office was largely confined to the collection and distribution of alms. Yet, while this remains true, it is significant that as early as April 1561 the deacons of St Andrews were directed 'to resave and intromit wyth the frutis' of certain prebends and to distribute them 'at the discrecion and sycht of the holl ministerie', to whom the accounts were to be rendered.[293]

Although the first Book of Discipline had conceded that deacons 'may also assist in judgement with the Ministers and Elders', a practice which Beza approved in his letter of 1576, the second Book of Discipline, on a strict definition of function, denied to the deacons any place on 'presbytereis or elderschippis', since the office was purely a financial and not a disciplinary one.[294] Although the deacons were assigned no rôle on the new district presbytery, they continued to sit on the kirk session as they had done in the past, but even here practice was far from uniform. In St Andrews kirk session, disciplinary cases from 1559 were initially heard by the minister and elders and only subsequently were deacons admitted; in Perth judgment in disciplinary cases continued to be reserved to 'the assembly of the minister and eldaris'; in Elgin matters were referred to 'the assemblie of the eldaris'; and in Old Aberdeen the decision was taken somewhat later, in 1601, that 'nane haiff vote in the sessioun bot onlie the Ministerie of the Kirk and eldaris'.[295] The practice which permitted deacons, and elders, to serve at the communion tables

---

[292] Calvin, *Institutes*, IV, iii, 8–9; *Comm. Acts*, cap. vi, 3; Beza, *La Confession de foi du chrétien*, V, xxx; S. J. Knox, *Walter Travers, Paragon of Elizabethan Puritanism* (London, 1962), 32–7.

[293] *RStAKS*, i, 76–7, 138–9.

[294] *The First Book of Discipline*, 178–9; *SHS Miscellany*, viii, 106; see text below, VIII. 7, and notes 143–4.

[295] *RStAKS*, i, 1–202 (ministers and elders); 203, 213, 220, 261, 264 and *passim* (and deacons); SRO, CH2/521/1. Perth Kirk Session Records, 6 Sept. 1577; 29 June, 8 Dec. 1578; 12 Jan. 1578/9; SRO, CH2/141/1. Elgin Kirk Session Records, fo. 1r. 8 Jan. 1584/5 and *passim*; SRO, CH2/1/1. Aberdeen Presbytery Records, 7 Aug. 1601.

continued to be observed, but it received no support from either Book of Discipline.

The restrictions on the deacon's rôle in church government was an issue which had wider ramifications than the Scottish polity. Although Beza had commended to lord Glamis in 1576, the presence in synods of 'an elder or a deacon' from every church in the province, he had nonetheless supported the French church's decision at the synod of La Rochelle in 1571, where he presided as moderator, to limit the essential composition of consistories to ministers and elders, and to permit the presence of deacons only if 'the consistory do judge it fitting', in opposition to Morély and Peter Ramus who favoured the deacon's inclusion and the adoption of a more democratic polity. At the following synod of Nîmes in 1572 it was also resolved that:

'the Ministers of God's Word, together with the Eldership, do constitute the Churches consistory, in which the Ministers ought to preside; and Deacons may and should be present in the Consistory, that so by their Advice the Church may be served, as hitherto in these difficult times we have happily employed them in the Government of the Churches, and called them forth into the Eldership. And for time to come all Deacons thus chosen or continued, shall joyntly together with the Pastors and Elders have the Rule and Conduct of the Churches'.

Beza, moreover, accused Ramus of stirring up 'a very serious discussion concerning the whole government of the church' when the latter had argued that it 'ought to be more democratic, not aristocratic, leaving to the council of elders only the proposal of legislation; wherefore, the synod at Nîmes, in which I participated, upon by advice condemned that view, which is most absurd and pernicious'.[296]

In Burntisland, at the beginning of the seventeenth century, the deacons, like the elders, received 'ordination to thair callingis', as the second Book of Discipline had recommended, though as early as 1571 Erskine of Dun had pointed the way when he observed that 'the deacouns, which were chosin in Jerusalem by the whole congregatioun, were receaved and admitted by the

[296] Quick, *Synodicon*, i, 96, 106; F. P. Graves, *Peter Ramus and the Educational Reformation of the Sixteenth Century* (New York, 1912), 200–201.

Apostles, and that by laying on of their hands, as Sanct Luke writteth in the sixt chapter of the Acts of the Apostles'.[297] Care was also taken in the second Book of Discipline to ensure that deacons, though elected for life, were subject to the same restrictions which governed the activities of their predecessors; hence the requirement that 'becaus this vocatioun appeirs to mony to be dangerous let them be oblisit (as thay war of auld) to ane yeirlie compt to the pasturis and elderschip'. The safeguards proposed in the second Book of Discipline, in some respects, surpassed those of the first Book of Discipline, since it was now envisaged that 'gif the kirk and prince think expedient lat cautioneris be obleist for thair fidelitie that the kirk rents onnawyse be delapidat'.[298]

In kirk sessions it was common practice for auditors to be appointed to scrutinise accounts rendered by deacons. Besides this, in Edinburgh general session one elder, in particular, was appointed treasurer; in Perth one of the deacons was appointed 'distributer to the ordinar pure'; and in some rural areas, such as Fossoway, the familiar pre-reformation term 'kirkmaster', in effect churchwarden, was used to denote those who were elected with the elders for a term to carry out the deacons' duties.[299] Sessions normally took the additional precaution of giving custody of the poor's box to a particular individual, perhaps a reader or elder, while entrusting the key or keys to different elders, but even this device was not infallible, and in one case it was not the deacons but the minister himself, the decrepit Alexander Livingston of Kilsyth, who confessed to Glasgow presbytery that he had appropriated 'the penalties of offenderis', and in Ayr any fear of corruption in the popular imagination found embellishment in the accusations of one woman who, in 1606, was 'convict of grit blasphemie in saying that no bodie had the rycht of the pure folkis silver bot the devill and the proveist'.[300]

[297] SRO, CH2/523/1. Burntisland Kirk Session Records, fos. 32r., 47r. 10 April 1608, 24 Feb. 1611; Calderwood, *History*, iii, 157.

[298] See text below, XII. 19, and n. 228.

[299] SRO, CH2/450/1. Edinburgh General Session Records (Robert Gourlay), entry preceding that of 1 July 1574; 16 May 1574; 3 March 1574/5; CH2/521/3. Perth Kirk Session Records, 7 Oct. 1594; 12 Oct. 1601; 11 Oct. 1602; New Reg. Ho. OPR. 461/1. Fossoway Old Parochial Records, 1 Jan. 1609 (where the names of 15 elders, six kirkmasters and the beadle are recorded); see also SRO, PS1/50, Register of the Privy Seal, fo. 122r. (where mention is made on 22 April 1584 of the elders and kirkmasters of Baldernock).

[300] SRO, CH2/1026/1. Stirling Kirk Session Records, 7 Dec. 1598; CH2/450/1.

Eldershipps or assemblies

The second Book of Discipline's treatment of elderships or assemblies preceded its exposition on the diaconate which was linked instead to discussion of the church's patrimony. This was logical enough since deacons were purely financial officers possessing no competence in disciplinary matters which properly resided within the jurisdiction of ministers, doctors, and elders. Of the four office-bearers postulated, only three were thus entitled to sit on the courts of the church: 'eldarschippis or assembleis ar constitute commounlie of pasturis, doctouris and sic as commounlie we call eldaris that laubour not in the word and doctrene'. This definition somewhat resembled the practice already adopted by the French church at its synods of La Rochelle and Nîmes in 1571 and 1572, but unlike the French church which came to possess four separate ecclesiastical courts, the second Book of Discipline clearly distinguished only three courts within a nation: first, the local eldership composed either of one congregation or of several contiguous congregations; secondly, the provincial synod; and thirdly, the national or general assembly.[301] Despite the rise of national churches and the apparent fragmentation of the universal church as a visible institution, the Scots had not lost sight of the catholic church; they remained conscious of their bond with the 'best reformed churches' overseas; and in the second Book of Discipline, they upheld the vision of an ecumenical general council 'representing the universall kirk of Chryst', composed of 'all and divers nationis professing ane Jesus Chryst'.[302] The legacy of the conciliarist tradition was evidently still strong.

The sovereignty of the church courts, so defined, their power to exercise ecclesiastical discipline independently of any civil jurisdiction and their right to convene without tarrying for the magistrate's permission were all affirmed in the book, but this amounted to no more than a confirmation of earlier practice, and it was only with the 'Black Acts' of 1584 that the prince's licence was first required for convening kirk sessions, synods and

---

Edinburgh General Session Records, 6 [Feb.] 1574; CH2/523/1. Burntisland Kirk Session Records, fo. 50r., 4 Aug. [1611]; GCA, Glasgow Presbytery Records, fo. 70v., 10 Aug. 1591; CH2/751/1. Ayr Kirk Session Records, 19 May 1606.

[301] See text below, VII. 1-2, and n. 99; Quick, *Synodicon*, i, 96, 112-13.

[302] See text below, VII. 40-41, and notes 135-137; *BUK*, i, 246; SRO, CH2/121/1. Edinburgh Presbytery Records, 26 Sept. 1587.

assemblies.[303] All along, the kirk consistently had declined to follow the 'erastian' example which denied the need for an independent ecclesiastical authority for discipline where the magistrate was 'godly', and instead had adhered to the Calvinist insistence on the necessity of church discipline, including excommunication, regardless of the magistrate's persuasion in religion.[304]

1. *The Kirk Session or Presbytery?*

No aspect of the second Book of Discipline's programme has caused greater confusion, and perhaps needlessly so, than the issue of whether the presbytery can be said to receive support from that document. Opinions have varied from the authoritative statement that 'the institution of the Presbytery was the main achievement of the *Second Book of Discipline*' to the no less assertive remark that 'there was no word of the presbytery in the book'.[305] Neither view seems consistent with the evidence presented in the second Book of Discipline itself. For a start, the word 'presbytery', if not the institution, is mentioned twice, though without distinction from the 'eldership'.[306] Knowledge that the second Book of Discipline underwent some kind of revision at a date after its completion in 1578[307] might even suggest a possibility that the presbytery, if not present in the original drafting, emerged only in subsequent versions, but such speculation is to no avail, for no significant variant readings are to be found in surviving texts.

Equipped with the retrospective knowledge that Scottish presbyterianism was a system of church government by kirk session, presbytery, synod and general assembly, historians usually have looked in vain in the second Book of Discipline for a definition of all four courts, have found only three described (eldership, synod and general assembly), and by identifying the eldership with the kirk session, which already existed, have too readily concluded that the district presbytery was not to be found. The mistake, however, is to assume the complete identity of

[303] *APS*, iii, 293; SRO CH2/550/1. Glasgow Kirk Session Records, fo. 19r., 22 April 1585; CH2/521/1. Perth Kirk Session Records, 10 Aug. 1584; *RStAKS*, ii, 529.

[304] See above, 40, 59ff.

[305] J. G. MacGregor, *The Scottish Presbyterian Polity* (Edinburgh, 1926), 118; G. Donaldson, *The Scottish Reformation* (Cambridge, 1960), 203.

[306] See text below, VIII. 7, and XI. 15.   [307] See below, 129.

eldership and kirk session. Congregational elderships, after all, were defined as assemblies of pastors, doctors and elders either of one church or of several contiguous churches, since not 'every particular paroche kirk cane or may have thair awin particular eldarschip, especiall to landwart, bot we think thrie or four, ma or fewar, particular kirkis may have ane commoun eldarschip to thame all to judge thair ecclesiasticall causes'.[308]

Something akin to the common elderships advocated here already operated in the general sessions of the larger burghs where the ministers, elders and deacons from each district met together in a joint assembly for discipline.[309] Yet here the common elderships were especially commended for rural districts where the problems of ecclesiastical administration were particularly severe. In many country areas, there was still a marked shortage of ministers; it was customary for three or four churches, each possessing readers, to be grouped together under one minister, as the registers of ministers' stipends so clearly testify; in some districts, too, kirk sessions failed to operate and discipline consequently remained lax. As late as 1575, the assembly had recommended the appointment of elders and deacons 'in every principall congregation quher ther is none', and the implication seems to have been that smaller congregations should not possess a kirk session of their own.[310]

Practical considerations, such as these, may have suggested the suitability of introducing common elderships of 'thrie of four, ma or fewar, particular kirkis' in areas where the shortage of ministers was acute and where no sessions had been established. Not only so, the decision to unite three or four churches into a common eldership also coincided with the practical problem of 'the platt of the four churches' served by one minister, and it had a relevance, too, for the phasing out of readers, as the assembly was later to recommend. At the same time, the envisaged elimination of bishops as overseers placed a further emphasis on the need to develop closer links among churches to permit conference and discussion among neighbouring ministers. The creation of common elderships fulfilled this additional requirement though the second Book of Discipline still seemed to concede that

[308] See text below, VII. 14, and n. 111.
[309] See SRO, CH2/450/1. Edinburgh General Session Records, 3 May 1574; CH2/550/1. Glasgow Kirk Session Records, fo. 2r.
[310] *BUK*, i, 343.

some churches might retain their own 'particular eldership', presumably in areas where flourishing kirk sessions were already established. Yet even here the idea may have been to link weaker neighbouring churches to one with a stronger tradition of congregational government. Certainly, the projected existence of 'particular elderships' for individual churches was soon qualified, if not contradicted, by the additional statement to the effect that only in 'townis and famous places' were 'eldaris of particular kirkis' to convene in their common elderships.[311] The incorporation of this further restriction on both the existence of single elderships in towns and on common elderships of 'thrie or four, ma or fewer, particular kirkis' in the countryside suggests a distinct development in the notion of a district eldership or presbytery centred on the main burgh of the area and composed of ministers, doctors and elders from the constituent churches, perhaps a dozen or more, which would no longer possess their own kirk sessions.

The communal eldership or presbytery, in short, was designed to replace individual kirk sessions and was based not on doctrinaire abstractions but on the need to solve practical problems. The second Book of Discipline's concern was that 'in every paroche of resonable congregationis there wald be placit ane or ma pasturis to feid the flok and na pasture or minister aucht to be burdenit with the particular charge of ma flokis or kirks thene ane allanerlie'. At the same time, an awareness that 'it wilbe thocht hard to find out pasturis or ministeris to all the paroche kirkis of the realme, alsweill in landwart as in borrows townis' led to the recommendation that a commission should be set up with the king's authority to advise on how parochial reorganisation should proceed so that 'parochis in landwart or small villagis may be joinit twa or thrie or ma in sum places togidder and the principall and maist commodious kirkis to stand and to be repairit'. The commission significantly was also to 'nominat and designe places quhair the assembles of particular elderschippis sould convene'.[312] The creation of elderships or presbyteries was thus to coincide with the reorganisation of parishes. Here, too, was the germ of the scheme in April 1581 which proposed reducing around a thousand parish churches to a mere six hundred churches, divided into elderships or presbyteries, each served by a resident

---

[311] See text below, XII. 6–7, and notes 207–8.
[312] See text below, XII. 3–4, 8, and notes 204–5, 209–10.

minister.[313] The equation of eldership and presbytery received further confirmation in 1586 when the assembly defined the presbytery in language borrowed from the second Book of Discipline's description of the eldership, and this was again repeated in the 'Golden Act' of 1592.[314]

As early as October 1578, the assembly had required bishops to 'impyre not above the particular Elderschips, but be subject to the same' and 'that they usurp not the power of the presbytries'. Although variant manuscript readings of the text sometimes replace 'presbytries' with 'pastors', 'presbytries' does seem to be preferred as the authentic version;[315] and an explanation of the use of 'presbytries' at a point before the appearance of presbyteries as a distinctive court intermediate between kirk session and synod is to be sought in the use of 'presbytery' as a synonym for 'eldership', in the second Book of Discipline's sense of an eldership of one congregation or several. Only in July 1579 did the assembly finally decide that 'the exercise may be judgit a presbyterie'.[316]

As a meeting of ministers with some elders for interpreting scripture in the main town of the district, the exercise had already assumed administrative duties by the early 1570s; it acted as a convenient meeting point for conference and deliberation; and it offered a ready-made solution to the problem of substituting a common eldership for individual kirk sessions thereby forging closer links between neighbouring churches in each district. In March 1572/3, the synod of Lothian had sought approval that 'sick matters as falls out betwixt the Synodall Conventiouns and Generall Assemblies salbe headed and notit at every Exercise'; again, in 1576, the assembly agreed that in

---

[313] *BUK*, ii, 480–7; *cf.*, Bancroft, *A Survay of the Pretended Holy Discipline* (1593), 99.

[314] See text below, VII. 17–21; *BUK*, ii, 665; *APS*, iii, 541.

[315] *BUK*, ii, 425; NLS, Adv. MS. 17.1.8, fo. 108 (*cf.*, Peterkin, 184); GUL, MS. General 1122, fo. 89v.; MS. General 1132, fo. 130. It should be noted that Adv. MS. 17.1.8 is a transcript of the acts of assembly made after 1616 and which later came into Wodrow's possession. The two copies in GUL are seventeenth-century transcripts. An earlier copy compiled by James Carmichael in the 1590s corresponds with the text in *BUK*, ii, 425 (AUL, MS. 227, fo. 79). A seventeenth-century transcript belonging to the earl of Cromarty also reads 'presbyteries' (SRO, CH1/1/2, fo. 107), as does a copy made by James Melville (EUL, MS. La. III. 335). The not dissimilar contractions for 'pastors' and 'presbyteries' may have contributed to a misinterpretation of the text. A further variation occurs in Spottiswoode's *History*, where bishops were stated neither to 'empire over presbyteries', nor to 'usurp the power of presbyteries'. (Spottiswoode, *History*, ii, 258.)

[316] *BUK*, ii, 439.

urgent cases a visitor 'may conveen them that are upon the exercise in that Province' to suspend a minister, and it also recognised that ministers might be admitted to benefices by the visitor 'with the advice of the Ministers of the Exercise within that Province'. Similarly, in 1578, the 'Brethren of the Exercyiss of Edinburgh beand convenit with the Commissionar of Lowthiane' undertook certain administrative duties, and in 1579 the assembly instructed a commissioner 'with the assistance of the brethren of his Exercise' to execute the assembly's injunctions in a case of non-residence.[317] Such was the transition from exercise to presbytery, which really entailed a change of name rather than a change in function, that the 'brethren of Dunblane', on being asked to attend Stirling presbytery, protested in September 1581 that 'we haif a presbyterii of our awin erectit of a lang tyme past in Dunblane be the ordur approvit be the generall kirk affoir our visitor standand undischargit, our assembleis and conventionis mentenid, our exerceis haldin and keipit and the matteris of our kirk intreattid'.[318] This, of course, was an allusion not to the presbytery, as such, but to the administrative and disciplinary functions conducted at the exercise as a result of the visitor's articles of 1576.

The expedient of identifying the presbytery with the exercise led the assembly in October 1580 to devise a formal scheme for 'establischnig and constituteing of Presbyteries', and the king reported to the next assembly in April 1581 that the privy council and ministers had reached agreement on 'how Elderships may be constitute of a certaine number of parochines lyand togither; small parochines to be united and the great to be divydit, for the better sustentatioun of the Ministrie and the more commodious resort of the commoun peiple to thair kirks'. The assembly understood that the total number of parish churches was to be reduced to six hundred; these churches were to be divided into groups of twelve or so to form elderships or presbyteries to be established in the main towns; and three presbyteries 'or moe or fewer as the countrey lyis' were to form a diocese.[319]

Throughout, the crown had played a prominent part in issuing instructions for revising diocesan and parochial boundaries 'that

---

[317] *Ibid.*, i, 265, 357; ii, 430; *Wodrow Society Miscellany*, i, 407-8; see also *BUK*, ii, 465, 466-7, 468; *RStAKS*, i, 464.

[318] SRO, CH2/722/1. Stirling Presbytery Records, 12 Sept. 1581.

[319] *BUK*, ii, 469-70, 477, 480-7.

thairefter presbitereis or elderschippis may be constitute'. On the king's directions, a group of nobles, lairds and ministers was to meet in each locality to elect from its ranks some who would 'considder and try the ancient and present estaites of all particular kirkis and parochinnis in thair boundis' in order that presbytries might be established.[320] This course of action gave effect to the proposals of the second Book of Discipline, and it is true to say that the development of the eldership or presbytery is directly attributable to the recommendations advanced in the twelfth chapter of the Book of Discipline.

The creation in 1581 of only thirteen model presbyteries mainly in towns in the lowlands, which were 'to be exemplars to the rest'[321] meant that kirk sessions could not be permitted to lapse, and their continued existence went uncontested. The only surviving presbytery records for 1581, those of Stirling, indicate that the presbytery consisted of ministers from neighbouring churches with 'twa or thre elderis' from each particular session who were elected elders of the presbytery for life. The presbytery or 'elderschip of Striviling', formally erected on 8 August 1581, initially contained the ministers of Stirling, St Ninians, Falkirk, Dunblane, Logie, Alva, Fossoway and Muckhart, to which others were added, first four, and then six, elders from Stirling, three from St Ninians, two from Logie, and one elder each from the kirks of Alva, Fossoway and Glendevon, who 'promesit faythfullie to exerceis thair officis thairin unto the end of thair lyvis as God sall minister to them the giftis of his spirit'.[322] All this gave effect to the claims of the second Book of Discipline for establishing 'common elderships' in towns where the 'eldaris of particular kirkis about may convene togidder', but it was less easy to concede that kirk sessions should cease to function as they had done in the past. The assembly itself in 1581 had proposed that Stirling presbytery should contain as many as twenty-four churches.[323] Many of these, such as Kippen, Tullibody, Glendevon and Muckhart, only possessed a resident reader, and only occasionally were visited and served by a minister 'according to the platt of the four kirks', while other churches in the area like the Port

---

[320] *RPC*, iii, 383; *BUK*, ii, 519–21.

[321] Calderwood, *History*, iii, 523; *BUK*, ii, 482.

[322] SRO, CH2/722/1. Stirling Presbytery Records, 8 Aug., 15 Aug., 22 Aug., 12 Sept., 10 Oct. 1581; 16 Jan. 1581/2.

[323] *BUK*, ii, 484.

of Menteith had no ministers, 'na eldaris, deacones nor forme off disciplein ... quhairthrow sin and vyce gretlie abundis amangis thame'.[324]

The creation of a 'common eldership' centred on Stirling certainly offered a practical solution to the problem of supervising so many churches lacking ministers, though attempts to reduce the number of parish churches in the area inevitably met with local resistance. The small congregation of Bothkennar protested at plans for union with either Airth or Falkirk, and promised instead to repair their church, provide a stipend of a hundred marks and even make a horse available for the minister if the presbytery would only find them a resident minister.[325]

The failure to reduce the number of parishes on the scale proposed and the relatively slow process of establishing common elderships throughout the country were all conducive to the continued existence of kirk sessions as 'particular elderships'. The result was that a two-tier system of kirk session and presbytery, both confusingly called elderships, came into being, though such a development had not been fully foreseen in the second Book of Discipline, and Scottish presbyterianism ended up with four courts instead of the three proposed by the second Book of Discipline.

The relationship of the kirk session to the eldership or presbytery during this formative phase in 1581 is not readily determined, for no records for this initial period survive to illustrate the operation of both courts for the same district. The records of the 'particular elderschip of the kirk of Striviling', or kirk session, begin only in 1597; St Andrews kirk session records which are extant show no dislocation,[326] though the presbytery records commence only in 1586, and St Andrews presbytery in 1582 was said to consist only of 'Pastours and Teachers, bot not of these that hes not the cure of teaching'.[327] Again, although Glasgow presbytery records start in 1592, the session records begin rather earlier in 1583, a mere two years after the creation of presbyteries, and the vestiges of some kind of transitional arrangement in the direction of a common eldership of several congrega-

---

[324] EUL, MS. La.II.14, Visitation of the Diocese of Dunblane, visitations of Kippen (18 Aug. 1586), Port of Menteith (19 Aug. 1586), Glendevon and Muckhart (15 Sept. 1586), Tullibody (16 Sept. 1586).
[325] *Ibid.*, visitation of Bothkennar (12 Aug. 1586).
[326] *RStAKS*, i, 464; ii, 494.   [327] *BUK*, ii, 549.

tions, as proposed in the second Book of Discipline, may possibly be detected in the continued presence as elders on Glasgow general session of the ministers from neighbouring parishes. This arrangement is unique, and it may reflect earlier changes effected between 1578 and 1581 designed to replace sessions with a common eldership based on the chief burgh of the district. This, at least, is one explanation why Andrew Hay, minister of Renfrew, Andrew Polwarth and John Bell, successively ministers at Cadder, Robert Darroch, minister at Kilmaronock, and Thomas Jack, minister at Eastwood, should all be elected elders of the general session, though many of them also had close connections with the university.[328] It is certainly true that the assembly in 1581 had projected that Glasgow presbytery should be assigned twenty-four churches, but such a scheme was evidently harder to achieve, for as late as 1596 Glasgow presbytery complained that it possessed only six churches whereas neighbouring presbyteries could claim fifteen.[329]

The initial plan to replace separate elderships with combined or common elderships must soon have been abandoned as presbyteries began to function only in certain burghs from 1581; but reluctance to concede the principle is evident in the persistence of the term 'eldership' to denote either court. Although Knox had earlier equated the eldership with elders of the kirk session, the terms 'session', 'assemblie' and 'consistorie' were common descriptions for the congregational court.[330] By the 1580s, however, with the operation of both presbyteries and sessions, Elgin kirk session saw itself as 'the assemblie of the elderschip of Elgin'. Stirling kirk session described itself as 'the eldarship of the kirk', and Stirling presbytery, which also assumed the title of 'elderschip of Striviling', distinguished its own meetings from those of the 'particular elderschip' of what was, in effect, the session, but it continued to speak of the 'elderships' of Tullibody and St Ninians, and rather quaintly of the elders and deacons of the 'eldership' of Logie.[331] Haddington presbytery also equated

---

[328] SRO, CH2/550/1. Glasgow Kirk Session Records, fos. 2r., 20v., 52r., 80r., 100r., 119r., 137v., 158v., 181r.; Durkan and Kirk, *The University of Glasgow*, 409, 415, 418.

[329] *BUK*, ii, 484–5; GCA, Glasgow Presbytery Records, 16 March 1595/6.

[330] Knox, *Works*, ii, 152 (eldership); 364, 519; *RStAKS*, i, 82, 196, 205, 338 (session); 266; *Buik of the Kirk of the Canagait*, 6, 9 (assembly); *BUK*, i, 29; *RStAKS*, i, 38 (consistory).

[331] SRO CH2/145/1. Elgin Kirk Session Records, fos., 1r., 2v., 3r., 3v., 4r.–v.,

eldership with both presbytery and session, referring to the 'presbyterie of Edinburgh and elderschip of the same' and to the 'particular sessioun of the elderschip' or 'sessioun and elderschip'; and in Dalkeith, the presbytery made no effort to differentiate the presbyteries or 'elderships' of Edinburgh and Haddington from the session or 'elderschip of Cranstoun'.[332]

Yet behind this apparent inconsistency lay a deeper truth. To an age accustomed, if not addicted, to writing in Latin, 'presbytery' was simply the Latin equivalent of the vernacular 'eldership', denoting a consistory or assembly of presbyters or elders. Archibald Simson, minister of Dalkeith, in his manuscript Latin history of the church translated the title of the seventh chapter of the second Book of Discipline, 'of eldarschipis and assembleis and of discipline' as 'presbyteriis, synodis et disciplina'; and the passage where 'eldarschippis and assembleis ar constitute commonlie of pasturis, doctouris and sic as commounlie we call eldaris that labour not in the word and doctrine' is rendered 'presbyteria constant ministris, doctoribus, senioribus qui non laborant in verbo'.[333] The eldership or presbytery was seen to represent the scriptural 'presbuterion' or 'presbyterium', which, it has been observed, was translated in the Genevan bible as 'eldership' and in the Authorised version of 1611 as 'presbytery'.[334] Its existence was therefore justified on the model and 'practise of the primitive kirk quhairas eldaris or colleges of seniouris wer constitute in citeis and famous places'; and by assigning to elderships the power of excommunication, which pertained not to an individual to pronounce unadvisedly, and also the examination, admission and ordination of ministers,[335] the second Book of Discipline can only be properly understood to refer to common elderships or presbyteries erected in the burghs and market towns where people from the rural hinterland were accustomed to congregate.

Although elders on kirk sessions continued to be elected for a

---

7v., 11v.; CH2/1026/1. Stirling Kirk Session Records, 24 Nov. 1597; CH2/722/1. Stirling Presbytery Records, 8 Aug. 1581; 6 March 1581/2; 21 Sept. 1591; 13 June 1599; 17 April 1594.

[332] SRO CH2/185/1. Haddington Presbytery Records, fos. 17v., 19v.; CH2/424/1. Dalkeith Presbytery Records, fo. 87v.

[333] NLS, Wodrow MSS., Quarto vol. xiii, no. 1, fo. 16r.-v.

[334] A. F. Mitchell, *The Scottish Reformation* (London, 1900), 231-2; G. D. Henderson, *Presbyterianism* (Aberdeen, 1954), 94.

[335] See text below, VII. 21; III. 7, 9, 12.

term thereby permitting some to be released for a spell from their duties, it is nonetheless significant that presbytery elders, in accord with the second Book of Discipline, were elected for life, though recruitment of presbytery elders in some areas possibly proved difficult. By 1582, a presbytery of ministers had been established in the Merse 'but not as yet of any Gentlemen or Elders', and in St Andrews the presbytery consisted of 'Pastouris and Teachers, bot not of these that hes not the cure of teaching'.[336] The reluctance of elders to serve all but continuously on presbyteries certainly explains the assembly's concession to elders in April 1582 that:[337]

> 'thair resort to the Presbyterie salbe no farther straitit but as the weghtines and occasioun upon intimatioun and advertisement made be the Pastours and Doctours sall requyre; at quhilk tyme they sall give thair godlie concurrence; exhorting them alwayse that may commodiouslie resort to be present at all tymes'.

In Stirling presbytery, however, where elders from the local churches were appointed to the presbytery for life, the sederunts indicate the regularity with which some life-elders attended meetings of presbytery from 1581 until the onset of the 'Black Acts' of 1584 which proscribed presbyteries from meeting.[338] A similar picture emerges in Dalkeith where elders attended the presbytery in the years immediately after its foundation, though it was sometimes necessary for the elders to be reminded of their duty to attend.

In May 1582, the presbytery warned the 'haill elderis with the ministeris quha absentes thame selfis from the elderschip to be present this day aucht [days] becaus of sam wechtie effaris'; at a presbytery meeting in October 'the brether ministers and eldaris wer convenit in thair sessioun hous' to select a moderator; by November 'a gret nomber of eldaris quha had giffin thair aythis in thair admissione to thair office' were reported to be absent from presbytery meetings, and one elder understood his attendance to be necessary only 'anis or twys in the yeir', though 'being now informit of the trewth of thingis, he suld at all tymes concur with his presence ... quhen health of body and uther

[336] *BUK*, ii, 549.　　　[337] *Ibid.*, 567.
[338] SRO, CH2/722/1. Stirling Presbytery Records, 28 Nov., 5 Dec., 19 Dec., 26 Dec. 1581; 16 Jan., 13 Feb. 1581/2; 27 March, 8 May 1582 and *passim*.

urgent bissines' permitted; in May 1583 the presbytery was addressed as 'the ministeris and eldaris of the presbiterie of Dalkeyth'; in June the 'gentilmen and elderis of the presbiterie of Dalkeyth' convened with the ministers; and in July 'sindrie gentilmen present eldaris of the presbyterie' were again on record, but in August:[339]

> 'the moderatour proponit to the brethren the continuall absence of the eldaris quha not withstanding thair ayth and promiss maid for assisting thame, the ministeris, wes continewallie absent quhairthrow they wantit assistance and in respect willit the brether to interpone thair jugementis quhat they thocht best. Efter reasoning haid thairupone they concludit the mater suld be minuted and giffin in at the sinodall assemble as ane generall questione'.

The eclipse of elders from regular attendance at presbyteries might readily have occurred by default rather than by design had Archbishop Adamson not attacked in 1583 the 'great confusion' and 'continuall seditioun' arising from the presence of 'gentlemen, lords of the ground and others' with ministers on presbyteries, and had the Arran regime not taken the deliberate step in 1584 of undoing the work of the two previous administrations by prohibiting presbyteries from meeting.[340]

If the effect of the Arran regime discouraged the subsequent resumption of elders on presbyteries, Edinburgh presbytery continued to show an awareness of 'the greit necessitie that thair is of the baronis and gentilmen quha wer anes nominat and chosin eldaris to concure with the brethren of the ministrie', and it decided in 1587 that 'the baronis and gentilmen quha wer chosin to be eldaris at the first erecting of the presbyterie salbe desyrit be the brethren of the ministrie to be present the last of this instant to the effect foirsaid'.[341] The church evidently viewed with concern the absence of elders from presbyteries, and even after the king finally barred elders from presbyteries in 1597,[342] the issue came to the fore again in 1601 when Edinburgh presby-

---

[339] SRO, CH2/424/1. Dalkeith Presbytery Records, fos. 17v., 28r., 29v., 30v., 42r., 66r., 71r.-v., 76r., 78r.

[340] Calderwood, *History*, iv, 54; 258–61, 265–6; *APS*, iii, 293; *RStAKS*, ii, 529.

[341] SRO, CH2/121/1. Edinburgh Presbytery Records, 17 Oct., 1587.

[342] St Andrews Presbytery Records, 15 July 1597; SRO, CH2/121/2, Edinburgh Presbytery Records, 8 Feb. 1596/7.

tery raised the matter in the synod of Lothian 'that thair advyse may be had concerning the reparing of the unpreiching eldaris to the presbytereis according to the first institutioun'.[343] Indeed, having rid St Andrews presbytery of Andrew Melville's influence, the king himself in 1602 saw the advantages to be gained in making presbyteries more amenable to royal influence through his own nomination of some 'godlie and unsuspect elderis' to sit on St Andrews presbytery, a move which the presbytery countered by permitting only their presence 'without voting or melling with ony mater of doctrine or discipline'.[344]

All this effectively dispels any notion that elderships or presbyteries were designed initially to be purely clerical or ministerial; and any parallel between the Scottish kirk session and presbytery, on the one hand, and the Genevan consistory and venerable company of pastors, on the other, is at best only accidental, since the second Book of Discipline recognised one local or district court, not two, and it permitted the inclusion of elders on presbyteries, whereas the venerable company, as a meeting of pastors, was primarily concerned with matters of doctrine and less with disciplining delinquents which was the basic function of the consistory.[345] The second Book of Discipline neither slavishly imitated the Genevan example here nor directly copied French practice where four courts had come into being. Nor did it altogether accord with the theorizing of English presbyterians for whom the 'presbytery' denoted the congregational consistory. Walter Travers understood that 'the Consistory or Councell off the churche is the company and assemblye off the Elders off the churche'; the 'Second Admonition to the Parliament' in 1572 believed that a 'consistorie' should 'be had in every congregation' and it distinguished three further courts, the conference or classis, the provincial synod and national synod, within a kingdom.[346] By contrast, the second Book of Discipline declined to acknowledge that every church should have its own consistory; by defining only three courts, it adopted a programme consistent with Beza's advice to lord Glamis; and in its advocacy of an

[343] SRO, CH2/121/2. Edinburgh Presbytery Records, 4 March, 1601.
[344] St Andrews Presbytery Records, 15 July 1602.
[345] *Registres de la Compagnie des Pasteurs de Genève*, ed. J.-F. Bergier, *et al.*, 5 vols. (Geneva, 1962–1976), *passim*. The Venerable Company nonetheless undertook at regular times in the year the examination and disciplining of ministers.
[346] Travers, *A full and plaine declaration*, 159; *Puritan Manifestoes*, 97, 118–9.

eldership (neither restricted to one congregation nor yet sufficiently enlarged to form the classis or presbytery, as it developed) the Book of Discipline exhibited an indebtedness to Oecolampadius Bucer and to Calvin, and not least to Beza's *Annotations* on the New Testament, first published in 1557, and widely acclaimed, where the eldership or presbytery, as the company of elders or presbyters, was seen to be an essential element in church government.[347]

2. *The Provincial Synod*

The synod, defined as a lawful convention of the pastors, doctors and elders of a province, was recognised as the 'conference of kirkis and brethrene'. Here, in a phrase, was perhaps a hint of the corresponding movement which was developing in England, where the term 'conference' was applied to the classis. The 'Second Admonition' in 1572 had defined the conference, interposed between the consistory and provincial synod, as a 'meeting of some certaine ministers and other brethren, as it might be the ministers of London, at some certaine place as it was at Corinth, or of some certaine deanrie or deanries in the countrie, as it might be at Ware, to conferre and exercise them selves in prophesying or in interpreting the scriptures'. The disproportionate size of the English and Scottish provincial synods goes some way towards explaining why the second Book of Discipline chose to style the synod as the conference. The 'Second Admonition' had recognised that an English synod might even be as large as 'Canterburies province' or more modestly might consist of 'one or moe dioceses';[348] but even so, the English dioceses were enormous by Scottish standards, and the Scottish synod was frequently much smaller than a Scottish diocese: the synod of Glasgow and the west in 1594 consisted only of five presbyteries (Lanark, Hamilton, Glasgow, Paisley and Dumbarton) and the synod of Lothian and Tweeddale, which included territory from the archdioceses of St Andrews and Glasgow contained six presbyteries (Linlithgow, Edinburgh, Dalkeith, Haddington, Dunbar and Peebles) with perhaps around eighty churches.[349]

[347] Beza, *Annotationes maiores in Novum Dn. Nostri Iesu Christi Testamentum* (1594), 456 (*I Tim.* 4: 14).

[348] See text below, VII. 27; *Puritan Manifestoes*, 107–110.

[349] GCA, Glasgow Presbytery Records, 30 July 1594; *Synod of Lothian*, x and *passim.*

No indication of the frequency with which synods should meet is forthcoming in the Book of Discipline, but in practice synods continued to convene twice yearly, as in the past, which made them singularly unsuitable instruments for conference and regular prophesying. Consequently, interpreting scripture became a function of the presbytery with the assembly's decision in 1579 that the exercise should be judged a presbytery.[350] This development, however, occurred only after the composition of the second Book of Discipline, which had not foreseen the creation of an expanded eldership comprehending some twenty churches; and only at this stage, by 1581, did the scale of the Scottish presbytery come to approximate the English classis with perhaps between ten and twenty churches.

Any modifications to the synod's composition which the second Book of Discipline proposed could be readily accommodated within the existing structure without significant dislocation. An elected moderator, as observed in the general assembly since 1563, superseded the rôle of superintendent or commissioner as permanent moderator of synods. From 1562, 'the minister with ane elder or deacon' from each church was expected to attend synods, though lay attendance may have been sometimes lax, and little difficulty could have been experienced in restricting access of deacons.

In a letter to Erskine of Dun written possibly in 1579, John Hepburn, minister of Brechin, indicated how 'we have ordenit our commissionaris and hes authorised them with our commissione and instructions' to a synod of Angus held at Montrose. Later, in 1586, Archbishop Adamson, who objected to gentlemen having the right to vote in synods, was said to have been 'dashit in conscience and terrified with the number of gentilmen conveined' in the synod of Fife; and James Melville enumerated how in that synod there were present 'twenty-eight elders, labouring in the Word and doctrine, by the gentlemen, elders of the congregatiouns and commissioners of touns'. By 1597, a fuller definition of the synod's composition was forthcoming in the statement that 'Pastors, Doctors and sic as hes commissioun from particular Sessionnes of Congregationnes hes vott, except in maters of doctrin, wherin onlie they that labors in the Word may vott and judge'. Yet, even here, practice throughout the country

---

[350] *BUK*, ii, 439; see also NLS, Adv. MS., 6.1.13. fo. 39r.

was probably not uniform, and no elders are recorded as present in the synod of Lothian for this period.[351]

The apparent omission of elders in the synod of Lothian stands in marked contrast to their inclusion in Fife, where St Andrews presbytery in March 1594 instructed ministers to 'nominat commissionaris in thair awin sessionnes for the nixt synodall'; in September, it asked ministers 'to adverteis the gentill men within the perische to be present on Twysday nixtocum at the provinciall assemble'; and in 1600 when the barons chose a commissioner to the general assembly of their own accord, the presbytery required 'this to be remembred that the baronis be adverteist in all tymis heirefter to be present at synodall assembleis to the intent the ancient forme of electioun of commissioneris may be kepit'. It is also known that in St Andrews itself, the kirk session elected commissioners to the synod, and those so appointed were all current elders of the session.[352] All in all, the second Book of Discipline's proposals for the synod could be readily achieved without drastic revision.

3. *The General Assembly*

Since the assembly itself already had advanced a claim in March 1573/4 for its continued existence by an appeal to divine right,[353] it was not surprising that the need for the assembly, even under a 'godly' prince, should receive support from the second Book of Discipline, which defined the assembly as 'ane lauchfull conventioun of the kirkis of the haill realme or nation quhair it is usit and gadderit for the commoun effairis of the kirk and may be callit the generall elderschip of the haill kirkis within the realme'.[354] From the outset, the general assembly had been recognised as an ecclesiastical gathering. It was, as Knox described the meeting of 1561, 'the Generall Assemblie of the Churche'. This being so, the primary element in its composition was the ministers and commissioned members. Although the original records of the assembly are no longer extant, it is evident both from strictly contemporary sources and from transcripts of the acts of assembly made later in the sixteenth century, that an

---

[351] *Spalding Club Miscellany*, iv, 63–4; Melville, *Diary*, 247; Calderwood, *History*, iv, 496, 498, 520; Melville, *Diary*, 395; *Synod of Lothian*, xi.

[352] St Andrews Presbytery Records, 21 March 1593/4; 19 Sept. 1594; 6 March 1600; *RStAKS*, ii, 590, 817, 856.

[353] *BUK*, i, 292; see also above, 39–40.   [354] See text below, VII. 32.

essential element in assemblies from 1561 was 'the principall Commissionaris of the Churches, the Superintendents and some Ministeris' (1561), the 'superintendentis and ministeris of the Evangell of Jesus Christ within this realme together with the commissionaris of the hoill churches' (1562), 'the Mynisteris and Commissionaris of Kirkis' (1563). In 1564, the assembly is reported even to have claimed that the judgments of 'thair superintendantis and cheif ministeris' were 'so necessarie that without thame the rest sould sit as it wer idill'; in 1565, it was said that there 'convened in Edinburgh the Commissioners of the churches within this Realme for the Generall Assemblie', and in 1566, 'the Generall Assembly of the Ministers and Commissioners of the Churches Reformed within this Realm' is once more recorded to have met.[355]

Such descriptions wholly accord with the assembly's own estimation of its essential composition; from 1562 its letters were executed in name of 'the superintendentes, ministers and commissioners of kirkes reformed within the realme of Scotland', or sometimes merely 'the superintendents of kirks and ministers of the reformed kirk within Scotland'.[356] In 1562, certain business was 'concludit be the haill ministers assemblit'; later, in 1571, a petition to the assembly was addressed to the 'Superintendentis, Ministeris and Kirk of God presently assembled within this burcht for reformatioune'; and, again in 1571, Knox spoke plainly of 'the Assemblie of Christian ministers'.[357] It was not for nothing that ministers in the assembly were described as the 'mouth of the kirk', and all but invariably moderators were recruited from the ministry itself.[358] No dubiety, therefore, need exist about the central position occupied by the ministry in early assemblies. Equally, in the sederunts of these assemblies, reconstructed from later transcripts, the presence of commissioners of provinces or shires, and of kirks and burghs, and sometimes of universities is entirely consistent with contemporary evidence. The nobles and barons who frequented assemblies seem to have attended as individuals and not as commissioners, and by July 1567, with the revolution against Mary, nobles were individually invited to attend

[355] Knox, *Works*, ii, 295, 337, 363, 412, 421, 423, 515–18.
[356] Knox, *Works*, vi, 423, 431, 437, 438; *BUK*, i, 20, 84–5, 190.
[357] *BUK*, i, 15; Bannatyne, *Memoriales*, 92, 94; Knox, *Works*, vi, 586ff.; Calderwood, *History*, iii, 50.
[358] *BUK*, i, 84; Calderwood, *History*, viii, 306–11.

by letters missive.³⁵⁹ Not only so, but the nobles who did attend were repeatedly said to be present only for the 'assistance of the mynisteris'. Later, lord Glamis also acknowledged the nobles' presence in assemblies as 'assistants and helpers to the ministers', which hardly suggests that their influence was allowed to predominate, though their presence continued to be sought; and even the privy council, which had sometimes participated in assemblies, was likewise requested in 1564 merely 'to assist the Assemblie with their presence and counsell', but it was not understood to form an integral or regular part of assemblies.³⁶⁰ In any event, such language hardly argues in favour of effective secular or state control of the church, and in practice the initiative was seen to lie with the ministry.

If the assembly thus came to be recognised as 'the Church National', as Knox described it in 1565, or as the 'nationall assemblie (quhilk is generall to us)' as the second Book of Discipline defined it in 1578, there was plainly a parallel between the assembly and national synods in other protestant countries, not least in France where ministers and elders, assisted by nobles and sometimes by judges and magistrates from the town council attended national synods.³⁶¹ Nor need there by any doubt that in Scotland, too, elders attended assemblies in the 1560s. Lord Glamis in his letter to Beza remarked on how it became an 'accepted custom' after the Reformation for elders to be selected to attend the assembly, and he asked Beza whether under a 'godly' prince ministers alone should attend the assembly or whether it was still possible for 'the elders who are chosen among us yearly from the people and also from the nobility, to come to such assemblies without the king's command'. Contemporaries were well aware that protestant nobles like lord Ruthven in Perth and lairds in parishes up and down the country were elders on their local kirk sessions.³⁶² All this goes far to explain the presence of the 'Ministrie and uthers, Elders of the Kirk' at the Convention of Leith in

---

[359] *BUK*, i, 3, 13, 20, 25, 31, 38, 46, 52, 57, 65, 77, 82, 84–5, 93, 96, 100, 112, 123, 132, 134, 141, 157, 175, 184, 198, 203; *CSP Scot.*, ii, no. 44; iii, no. 251; *BUK*, i, 93–96, 100–102.

[360] Knox, *Works*, ii, 421, 484, 515, 516–7, 531; vi, 444; *SHS Miscellany*, viii, 105; *BUK*, i, 46, 77, 93, 181–2; ii, 404.

[361] Knox, *Works*, ii, 484; see text below, VII. 32; J. Kirk, 'The Influence of Calvinism on the Scottish Reformation', *RSCHS*, xviii (1974), 157–179, at 170.

[362] *SHS Miscellany*, viii, 105; J. Kirk, 'The Development of the Melvillian Movement', i, 310–16.

1572, to which Archbishop Boyd referred in 1576. Indeed, it is tempting to identify the elders who attended these assemblies with commissioners of kirks, of whom so much is heard but so little is known; and it was logical enough that elders who helped govern their local churches should be selected as representatives to the general assembly.

In an effort to redefine its composition, the assembly in 1568 had restricted its voting membership to superintendents, commissioners for visiting churches, and ministers 'brocht with them', along with commissioners from burghs, shires and universities. Ministers and commissioners from the shires were to be chosen at synods, and burgh commissioners were to be appointed jointly by the town council and 'kirk of their awin townes'; only those with a written commission were to be admitted.[363] The participation of the kirk session in the election of burgh commissioners and of the synod in the choice of shire commissioners from 1568 is likely to have strengthened the tendency to elect elders, and in his unpublished history, Archibald Simson, who began his ministry at Dalkeith as assistant to his father in 1586 and who had access to the original acts of assembly, recorded the right of elders to attend the assembly as a result of the act in 1568.[364]

Elders in some capacity or another were certainly present in early assemblies. In accordance with the act of 1568, Edinburgh town council, in July 1580 (perhaps following the precedent of February 1570/1) chose burgh commissioners with the 'avyse of the minister, eldares and deikynes of the kirk of this burgh', and the record of St Andrews kirk session shows that from at least as early as 1572, and regularly thereafter, it was the kirk session, and not the town council, which elected commissioners to the assembly; indeed, in every instance (save one isolated occasion when the session chose the provost, who was not an elder, along with two elders, or any one of them as representatives) the candidates commissioned by the session were always current

[363] *BUK*, i, 124.
[364] NLS, Wodrow MSS, Quarto vol. xiii, no. 1, fo. 8r.-v. '1568: Anno sexagesimo octavo sacra synodus Edinburgi habita in quam tot omnium ordinum confluxerunt ut pro numero (quibus debeantur suffragia) expectante synodo molestias darent: consilio habito synodus concludit episcopis, superintendentibus, ministris, barronibus et presbyteris missis, burgorum delegatis, et a senatu ecclesiastico oppidorum suffragia deberi proviso tamen ne terriarium numerum excedant'.

elders on the session.³⁶⁵ A further restriction on the assembly's membership is also apparent in the assembly's decision in 1575 to decline admission to an advocate, as procurator for a bishop, 'nor nane uthers quho are not of the functioun of the Kirk'. Such a development went even further than the second Book of Discipline's proposal to restrict voting membership of the assembly to 'ecclesiasticall personis' (to ministers, doctors and elders, that is, who had a function or office in the kirk), and only to admit 'uther personis that will repair to the said assemblie to propone, heir and resone'.³⁶⁶

The second Book of Discipline did not intend to transform, or even severely to limit, the assembly's traditional membership, and a firm precedent for its proposals to restrict those eligible to vote is clearly to be found in the act of 1568. Nor did the book attempt to deprive the assembly of its characteristic composition as a meeting of representatives from the Christian community, but sought rather to combine the traditional representation with the added requirement that voting members should consist of ministers, doctors and elders. All in all, at a time when most protestant lairds and gentlemen were elders and were appointed commissioners first at synods and then at presbyteries, where elders were also expected to be present, and when burgh representatives were chosen by, or with the advice of, the kirk session, such a restriction offered little difficulty and could be accomplished without any perceptible dislocation. Nor was university representation eclipsed, for university teachers were now understood to sit as doctors in the assembly, and St Andrews presbytery claimed within its number most of the teaching staff in the university, where six masters from St Leonard's, including the master of the grammar school, and four masters each from St Mary's and St Salvator's colleges were entered members of the presbytery.³⁶⁷

The restrictions on voting members seem to have commanded substantial support. They were largely conceded by the convention called by the king to discuss the book's proposals in 1578 which recommended that other members 'sall not have libertie to vote

---

³⁶⁵ *Edinburgh Burgh Records*, iv, 167; *RStAKS*, i, 367–8, 406 (*cf.*, 459–60), 478–9; ii, 526, 748–9, 798, 921; see Appendix III below, 281–9.

³⁶⁶ *BUK*, i, 333; see text below, VII. 33.

³⁶⁷ St Andrews Presbytery Records, fo. 1r. For earlier elections of commissioners from St Andrews University, see Appendix III below, 289–90.

above the number of fifteen', and in the aftermath of the 'antipresbyterian dictatorship' of the Arran regime, the assembly in May 1586, in presence of the king:

> 'found that all such as the Scripture appointeth Governours of the Kirk of God as, namelie, Pastours, Doctours, and Elders may conveine to Generall Assemblies and vote in ecclesiasticall matters; and all uthers that hes any sute or uther things to propone to the Assemblie, may be ther present and give in thair sutes, and propone things profitable to the Kirk, and heir reasoning, but sall not vote'.[368]

All this was a resounding endorsement of the recommendations of the second Book of Discipline; and here was one way of avoiding, or at least of lessening, the charge repeatedly made in the past that the church by convening its assemblies was guilty of convoking the king's lieges. Not only so, there is evidence that the Book of Discipline's proposals operated in practice. A contemporary account indicated how 'ministers and gentlemen elders' were present in the assembly as commissioners from presbyteries, and the king himself addressed a speech in the assembly of 1590 to 'my good people, ministers, doctors, elders, nobles, gentlemen and barons'.[369] It is also plain that the limitations on voting rights, which the presbyterians supported, were far less innovatory than the plans proposed by their episcopal opponents, who, had they succeeded, would have altered the whole character of the assembly's composition, reducing and transforming it into an exclusive 'conventioun generall of clergie', properly termed, since it would have been merely an 'assemblie of bishops or clerks', severely subordinated to the crown in parliament.[370] Here, in this latter case, were all the makings of a clerical oligarchy, with which the second Book of Discipline's proposals can be fairly contrasted; but as was so often the case, Archbishop Adamson, and not Andrew Melville, proved the real innovator.

---

[368] See Appendix I below, 249; *BUK*, ii, 650.

[369] NLS, Adv. MS. 6.1.13, fo. 40r.; Calderwood, *History*, v, 106.

[370] Calderwood, *History*, iv, 145–6; Melville, *Diary*, 196. For a later instance see Spottiswoode, *History*, iii, 211. At congregational level, episcopalian proposals became no less restrictive: on 22 October 1609, the archbishop informed Glasgow Kirk Session that his diocesan synod had decided that elders and deacons in all sessions were to be chosen in future by the ministers themselves. (GUL, Wodrow MS. Biographies, Life of David Wemyss, fo. 29.)

Church Patrimony and Further Reform

The claim for a full restoration of the church's patrimony lay at the centre of the Book of Discipline's reforming programme. The resumption of ecclesiastical property to its legitimate uses, from which it had been diverted and 'devoirit be idle belleis' in the past, was to provide the necessary finances to make the scheme effective. Ecclesiastical revenues, collected and distributed by the deacons, were allocated to the support of the ministry, the schools and poor. In this way, parish churches, reorganised to suit the needs of the population, were to be staffed with fully qualified, resident ministers, appointed with the congregation's consent and not by a system of patronage, and provided with adequate stipends. The schools and universities were also to receive sufficient aid to recruit more teachers to instruct the youth, for whom bursaries might be found, and to train aspiring ministers, who would fill parishes hitherto served by readers. Additional funds were to be bestowed on the poor and the hospitals that their welfare might receive greater attention than in the past; and excess revenues, once churches had been repaired, were to be assigned to the support of king and commonwealth.[371]

In an inventory on the abuses and defects requiring further reform, prominence was given to the continued appointment by the crown of titular abbots, commendators, priors and prioresses, and of similar cathedral dignitaries, who neither served nor had office in the reformed church, a practice condemned as a plain abuse. It was also found to be repugnant that so many 'abuseris of the patrimony of the kirk of Chryst' should represent the spiritual estate in parliament and council. The continued operation of cathedral and monastic chapters was seen to serve no useful purpose, and only permitted the further secularisation of ecclesiastical property instead of conserving it. Churches appropriated to prelacies ought to be separated and their benefices assigned to qualified ministers.[372] Benefices were defined as 'nothing els bot the stipend of the minister that is lauchfullie callit and electit'.[373] Yet, there were signs of inconsistency. Some passages of the book favour dissolving the prelacies and subverting the system of benefices by redistributing the goods of the church, at the hands of the deacons, according to the famous

---

[371] See text below, IX. 1–9; X. 7; XII. 1–5, 8, 12–22.
[372] *Ibid.*, XI. 1–8.   [373] *Ibid.*, III. 10.

fourfold division in the ancient canons; but another section of the book seems prepared to accept the structure of benefices and to argue only that benefices should be assigned to 'sic as ar qualifeit to teache Goddis word havand thair laufull admissioun of the Kirk' and not to those 'quha ar not myndit to serve in the kirk, bot leid and leve ane idle lyf as the utheris did quha bruikit thame in tyme of blindnes'. A qualified approval was even given to the Leith agreement, if correctly interpreted and operated in the church's interest.[374] All along, the authors were no doubt well aware of the difference between what they hoped to attain and what they knew they could attain.

At the same time, diocesan episcopacy was to be reformed, and true bishops were to undertake a congregational ministry; visitation was to become a function of the corporate body or eldership; a pastor's assumption of any criminal jurisdiction was censured as a 'corruptioun'; and the consistorial jurisdiction exercised by the secularised commissary courts whose competence extended to certain ecclesiastical matters including matrimonial suits and litigation concerning benefices was seen to need curtailment.[375]

The benefits of the projected reforms offered no tangible inducements to secure the co-operation of the nobility who were threatened with a loss of their rights to ecclesiastical property and to ecclesiastical patronage, but they did contain an appeal to the middling interests in society – to many burgesses, smaller lairds and tenant farmers – who might be expected to approve the prospect of an end to patronage and its replacement with greater safeguards against the intrusion of unwanted or unworthy candidates. The burden on congregations of what was, in effect, voluntary support for the poor, the hospitals and the repair of churches was to be eased by direct contributions from ecclesiastical resources. Again, the return to the ideal that every man should have his own teinds, by reforming the practice of setting teinds in tack, and by distinguishing the spirituality from the temporality of appropriated churches, had an obvious benefit to farmers and labourers of the ground who had been 'hitherto rigorouslie handlit be thame that war falslie callit kirkmen, thair takkismen, factouris and extortioneris'; and, more generally, it was envisaged that the king and country would be well served by devoting

[374] Ibid., VIII, 2; IX, 2, 5–9; XII, 16–17 (subversion); XI. 8–9 (retention).
[375] Ibid., XI. 10–20, 26.

surplus ecclesiastical revenues for public works.³⁷⁶

Yet, for success, the programme required the unequivocal support of both crown and nobility, who had acquired so much of the church's wealth and who consequently had withheld support from the similar proposals advanced in the first Book of Discipline. As Melville informed Beza in 1578, and again in 1579, 'those who have grown rich by sacrilege and loaded themselves with the spoils of Christ deny that ecclesiastical discipline is to be derived from the word of God'; and the nobles are said to have defended their interests by maintaining that 'if the ecclesiastical goods are restored to their legitimate use, the royal treasury will be exhausted'.³⁷⁷ Ecclesiastical patrimony was clearly the central issue which remained the 'chief impediment' to the second Book of Discipline's ratification by parliament.³⁷⁸

The Book's Subscription

In October 1577, the assembly had presented a copy of the second Book of Discipline to the Regent Morton; this was evidently little more than a final draft version, for there was still continuing discussion on the diaconate, and in July 1578 the assembly even made further emendations to the text.³⁷⁹ This was apparently the product of negotiations with the privy council which on 2 June had made arrangements for a convention to meet at Stirling on 10 June to consider what parliament ought to discuss when it assembled at Stirling in July. The convention, which preceded parliament, is known to have nominated a committee (of nine lords, two bishops and five ministers) which was to convene at Edinburgh on 23 June to examine the copy of the Book of Discipline presented to the king; and the members were said to have reached agreement 'in all things except in foure heeds whiche were explained' to the assembly when it reconvened in July.³⁸⁰ The minutes of the two assemblies which met during June and July and again on October 1578 are not fully extant, apparently due to the 'wilful destruction' of certain

---

³⁷⁶ *Ibid.*, XIII. 3–5.

³⁷⁷ NLS, Wodrow MSS, folio vol. xlii, fo. 11v.; 111r.; T. McCrie, *Life of Andrew Melville* (Edinburgh, 1899), 71–72.

³⁷⁸ Calderwood, *History*, viii, 34.

³⁷⁹ *BUK*, i, 393–5, 397–8; ii, 406–7, 414–15; Calderwood, *History*, iii, 410ff.

³⁸⁰ Calderwood, *History*, iii, 415; *BUK*, ii, 415; Melville, *Diary*, 63; *RPC*, ii, 763.

enactments when the pro-episcopal party gained possession of the registers in 1584, but it is known that in July 1578 'when the booke of policie was discussed and examined' some ministers favoured individual subscriptions to the Book of Discipline; Archbishop Adamson himself was induced to assent to the document; and the assembly 'all in a voice hes concludit the haill articles and propositiounes of the Buik of the Polecie of the Kirk to be conform to the Word of God, and meit for the Esteat of the Kirk in this land'.[381] The decision by the assembly, and possibly also by the convention, to submit the work to parliament must soon have followed.

When parliament met in July, 'ane buik of the policie of the kirk being presentit be the ministeris', the lords of the articles found many of the chapters of such 'great wecht and consequence' that no immediate resolution could be made. The twelve commissioners from the kirk who had presented the Book of Discipline 'tooke this answere for a shift or rather a refusall, becaus the booke was allowed before by these who conveened in Edinburgh except in foure heeds, which craved not muche disputation'; and when Morton suggested that selected extracts from the Book of Discipline might be 'established by law', the ministers declined their consent, since 'their commisision would not suffer them so to doe' and argued instead that:

> 'it became the Assemblie to collect out of the booke of God a forme of discipline and policie ecclesiasticall, to propone it to the prince, and to crave it to be confirmed as a law proceeding from God, and that it became not the prince to prescrive a policie to the kirk, and if they would appoint anie, they would not consent to it'.

Disregarding the protest, the lords maintained that the king might choose whom he wished and with their advice make a law; and accordingly parliament proceeded to appoint a committee of several earls and lords from the privy council with the two archbishops and one bishop, three lay commendators, three barons and three commissioners from the burghs, two advocates, the king's tutors, the principal of King's college, Aberdeen and six ministers, or any eighteen of their number, to convene at

---

[381] Melville, *Diary*, 62–3; Calderwood, *History*, iv, 55–60.

Stirling in August there to compare the Book of Discipline with the Leith agreement and to report their conclusions.[382]

At the same time, the continuing political instability throughout 1578 had provided an unfavourable climate for an early acceptance of the Book of Discipline. The dislocation caused by the 'alteration of the Authoritie'[383] had become marked in March when Morton's opponents had engineered an end to the regency, but in April Morton had regained custody of the king, and after a struggle which threatened to erupt into open hostilities in the summer, Morton's ascendancy was once more achieved by the autumn; and when talks on the Book of Discipline were resumed, they took place at a conference which the king had arranged to meet at Stirling in December 1578. Of the original committee members, chosen by parliament in July, who were due to meet in August, only eleven (with two new members) convened at Stirling in December; and while they had many detailed comments to make, they noticeably refrained from approving the Book of Discipline without emendation.[384]

Much of the section distinguishing the ecclesiastical and secular jurisdictions was accepted without serious alteration, and so too was the substance of the chapters on vocation and ordination, and the subsequent treatment of the minister's office, though the word 'bishop' was referred for further discussion in relation to the proposals for visitation. The fifth chapter on doctors, however, was wholly reserved for more detailed examination, but the claim was later admitted that doctors should attend synods, and be appointed in universities, colleges and schools to 'oppen up the meaning of the Scripturis and to have the charge of scoles and teache the rudiments of religioun'. On the elder's office, there was little to which outright exception was taken, apart from referring 'the perpetuitie of elders to further deliberatioun'. It was recognised that elders and doctors should sit in synods, and that the visitor of each province with a minister, two elders and a commissioner from each burgh chosen by the synod should attend the assembly, to which access by nobles and others might be permitted, though no more than fifteen might have liberty to vote. Some

---

[382] *APS*, iii, 105–6; Calderwood, *History*, iii, 414–17. Calderwood's account of the committee's composition varies slightly from the parliamentary record.

[383] *BUK*, ii, 404–5.

[384] See Appendix I below, 245ff.; Calderwood, *History*, iii, 433–442; Spottiswoode, *History*, ii, 232–253.

of the powers attributed to church courts, such as the appointment of visitors, were again referred, and care was taken not to prejudice the outcome of discussion on the rôle of the bishop or visitor.

The chapters on the diaconate and patrimony, significantly, were set aside while the remainder of the book was examined. No criticism was offered on the chapter concerning the Christian magistrate's office in the church, as 'the whole chapter is thought good'. It was agreed, too, that continuing abuses ought to be ended, that the church's patrimony should be protected from further secularisation, and that a petition for dissolving the prelacies, and assigning the separated churches to qualified ministers, 'at least after deceasse of the present possessors', should be submitted to the king and three estates, but the question of diocesan episcopacy was once more reserved for further consultation. It was conceded, however, in accord with the assembly's scheme for visitors in 1576, that bishops should undertake a congregational ministry and that parliament might consider dividing the dioceses into smaller units for oversight. The need for parochial reorganisation was likewise recognised, but not the abolition of patronage, which instead was referred; and the final chapter on the benefits to be gained by the proposed reforms seems to have passed without comment.[385]

The area of apparent disagreement between government and assembly looked rather as if it had been substantially narrowed to the issues of patrimony and episcopacy. Andrew Melville in a letter to John Row referred to the 'archiepiscopal skirmishing', which he heard had taken place at the king's conference in Stirling; to Arbuthnot, he expressed his dismay at how 'little success' had been achieved first by being 'called sometimes to Stirling and sometimes to Edinburgh, now by letters from the king and then by letters from the council, at one time by an order from the estates, and at another by appointment of the assemblies of the church'; and to Beza, he explained in 1579:[386]

'We have presented to his Majesty and three estates of the kingdom at different times, and recently to the parliament which is now sitting, a form of discipline to be enacted and confirmed by public authority. The king is favourably inclined

---

[385] See Appendix I below, 245-53.
[386] NLS, Wodrow MSS, folio vol. xlii, fos. 11-12; McCrie, *Andrew Melville*, 71-72.

to us; almost all the nobility are averse. They complain that, if pseudo-episcopacy be abolished, the state of the kingdom will be overturned; if presbyteries be established, the royal authority will be diminished; if the ecclesiastical goods are restored to their legitimate use, the royal treasury will be exhausted. They plead that bishops, with abbots and priors, form the third estate in parliament; that all jurisdiction, ecclesiastical as well as civil, pertains solely to the king and his council, and that the whole of the ecclesiastical property should go into the exchequer.'

By 1579, the government showed no signs of recognising the assembly's claims for the book's approval, and in July the king advised the assembly to proceed no further until the matter was determined by parliament, which, when it met in October, was persuaded only to recognise the church's jurisdiction in the ministry of the Word and sacraments, and in discipline, until a further commission reported its deliberations. On failing to secure the government's support, the assembly in April 1581 formally registered the Book of Discipline among the acts of assembly, and required copies to be distributed to presbyteries. Besides this, the changing political situation was illustrated first in the sudden overthrow of the Lennox regime by the strongly protestant Ruthven raiders in August 1582, followed ten months later by the anti-presbyterian Arran government which remained in power until the formation of a coalition ministry by 1586 finally led Maitland of Thirlestane to recognise the growth of a presbyterian system in the country by the 'Golden Act' of 1592.[387]

On the eve of this measure, the assembly itself had pressed forward in August 1590, and again in July 1591, with plans for the formal subscription of the second Book of Discipline by presbyteries. In September 1590, Dalkeith presbytery asked the clerk of assembly for an extract of the Book of Discipline so that it might be subscribed in accordance with the act of assembly. Although copies of the book were available, the extractor required twenty shillings before he would deliver a copy, and the presbytery agreed 'to provyd the silver... to ressaif the book, pay for it and subscryve the sam'. A year later, a copy had evidently been acquired, for in November 1591 the presbytery decided that the book should 'be red and eftir conference to be

[387] *BUK*, ii, 428; *APS*, iii, 137–8; *BUK*, ii, 487–8; *APS*, iii, 541–2.

subscryvit'. Yet something occurred to prevent subscription, and in June 1592 the presbytery appointed a minister to speak to James Ritchie, clerk of assembly, 'willing him to recognos and correct of new agane our copy be collationing it with the last editioun of the buik of discipline'.[388] Since no copy is known to have been printed before 1621,[389] the presbytery must have received a manuscript copy in some way defective, which required collation with the authentic text in the acts of assembly; and if any revision took place after 1578 it must have occurred before 1581, when the assembly engrossed the book in its register. At any rate, there is no significant variation in the surviving text of the Book of Discipline which Haddington presbytery subscribed in September 1591 from the copy known as 'Maister James Carmichel's Book', which it may be presumed, Carmichael, as minister of Haddington, took to England during his exile in 1584.[390]

In 'executione of the act of the generall assemblie made anent subscryving the buik of Polecie', Stirling presbytery also decided in November 1590 'to send to the clark of the generall assemblie for ane of the saidis buikis subscryvit be him that may be auttentik to the end the samin may be subscryvit according to the act'. Yet, in Andrew Melville's own presbytery of St Andrews, difficulties soon emerged regarding subscription. Even though 'the moderator of the presbitrie, as of befoir, hes this day proponit and desyrit the Buik of Polecie to be subscryvit be the brethering, according to the act of the generall assemblie', the members of the presbytery who 'tuik avys xx dayis quhilk now ar expyrit' had nonetheless reported that they 'as yitt findis thame selfis not resolvit in all poyntis'.[391]

In October 1590, the synod of Lothian asked moderators of presbyteries to acquire 'just and autentik' copies of the book, and to present them 'to their presbitereis to be subscryvit'. By April 1591, the majority of presbyteries in the province had evidently obtained copies, and Linlithgow was the only presbytery censured for failing to possess a copy. In August, Edinburgh presbytery

---

[388] *BUK*, ii, 773, 780; SRO, CH2/424/1. Dalkeith Presbytery Records, 24 Sept. 1590; 11 Nov. 1591; 15 June, 3 Aug. 1592.

[389] *STC*, no. 22015.

[390] See below, 154; PRO, SP.52/29. (State Papers, Scotland, Elizabeth.)

[391] SRO, CH2/722/2. Stirling Presbytery Records, 3 Nov. 1590; St Andrews Presbytery Records, 25 Aug. 1591.

announced its decision to subscribe the Book of Discipline, though by October it still had to fulfil its intentions. Haddington presbytery, on the other hand, had made its subscription in September; and by October, Dunbar, Haddington, Linlithgow and Dalkeith had all reported to the synod their formal ratification of the book. Only Peebles presbytery, along with Edinburgh, had still to sign the document.[392]

The Book of Discipline's subscription by individual members of presbyteries followed by parliament's authorisation of a presbyterian polity (but not the Book of Discipline) in 1592 each went far towards confirming 'the work of establisching a perfyte ordour and policie in the Kirk'.[393]

IMPLEMENTING THE BOOK'S PROPOSALS

The Campaign against Episcopacy

The implementation of the provisions laid down in the second Book of Discipline and not least the organisation of presbyteries and the consequent eclipse of episcopal jurisdiction were all cardinal aspects of the assembly's campaign for the supersession of the Leith settlement by an undisguisedly presbyterian constitution for the church. This programme had been approved and ratified by successive assemblies, and initially there was little indication of the conflict which emerged between church and state. The government had not intervened in the assembly's decision in 1576 that bishops should accept a congregational ministry, and many bishops like Dunblane, Ross, Moray and even Glasgow agreed to do so, though some like Adamson of St Andrews proved less compliant. After his provision to the archbishopric by 1576, Adamson firmly declined to submit to the assembly's jurisdiction and refused to accept a parochial ministry despite the assembly's injunctions, and it was only in 1580 that he finally was compelled to adhere to the will of the assembly.[394]

Similar proceedings were instituted against John Campbell, bishop of the Isles, Alexander Campbell, bishop of Brechin, Neil Campbell, whom the crown had provided to Argyll in

[392] *Synod of Lothian*, 21, 25, 30–2, 34; SRO, CH2/121/2, Edinburgh Presbytery Records, 10 Aug. 1591; *Wodrow Society Miscellany*, i, 403.
[393] *BUK*, i, 390.
[394] See above, 54; *BUK*, i, 367, 376–7, 385–6; ii, 422–3, 432–4, 453, 464, 467–8.

1580, and against Adam Bothwell of Orkney and Robert Stewart of Caithness, two of the conforming bishops at the Reformation who had long abandoned their active ministry in the reformed church; and while it is clear that most of these bishops finally submitted, the precise terms on which they did are largely obscured by the destruction of the documentary evidence for the bishops' submissions of 1580, along with other acts of assembly injurious to the episcopal cause, by the episcopal party in 1584.[395] After censuring the use of the title 'bishop' and insisting that bishops 'be callit be thair awin names, or Brethren in tyme comeing', the assembly in April 1578 had prohibited chapters from electing further bishops before the next assembly; it, in turn, forbade episcopal elections 'for all tymes to come, ay and quhill the corruptioun of the Estate of Bischops be alluterlie tane away'; and the assembly in July 1580 condemned diocesan episcopacy outright as having no authority in scripture, being merely a device 'brocht in by the folie and corruptions of mens invention to the great overthrow of the Kirk of God'.[396]

The assembly's decisions, first, that bishops should accept a congregational ministry and, then, that diocesan episcopacy should be abolished were doctrinal or theological judgments within the church's competence, in which the government might expect to have little say, but the claim for the complete extinction of the episcopate threatened to overthrow the whole machinery which the government operated, and no government could afford to view with equanimity the surrender of the last vestiges of influence in a system of church government which proclaimed a sovereignty and autonomy not of the king's making. Unlike the old superintendent, the new bishop exercised a temporal as well as a spiritual jurisdiction: not only might he serve on the privy council, he was also expected to take his seat in parliament, where the presence of bishops (or of other commissioners from the church) seemed almost indispensable were parliament to continue to be what the king claimed in 1605 was 'the representative bodie of the state'.

In any event, it was obvious that the fate of episcopacy could not be decided by the assembly unilaterally without approval from the government. The assembly might remove bishops from ecclesiastical administration, but as legal entities the bishoprics

[395] *BUK*, ii, 434, 453-5, 467-8, 589-90.
[396] See above, 30; *BUK*, ii, 404, 408-9, 413, 453.

continued in being; and although the church possessed the right of admitting qualified candidates, it was only a right of admission to spiritual office. Where the church declined or neglected to admit a candidate, the government might still have recourse to its legal right of presenting a candidate to the benefice, and even though he might be devoid of ecclesiastical office, the person provided *iure devoluto* could nonetheless possess the title and revenues of the see and sit as a member of the spiritual estate in parliament.

Even so, at least as late as April 1581, the privy council had agreed that:[397]

> 'all benefices of cure presentlie vacand and that heirefter sal happin to vaik and be at his Hienes presentatioun afoir the first day of November nixtocum sall remane vacand and undisponit quhill the samin day that in the meyntyme it may be considerit and aggreit upoun the forme of dispositioun of the saidis benefices and the estate and qualiteis of the personis to quhom the samin benefices and all uther that sal happin to vaik thairefter salbe disponit'.

Not only so, the government also accepted the necessity for a dissolution of 'the ancient boundis of the diocyes'.[398] Yet, by the summer of 1581, an abrupt change in the government's attitude occurred; and at a time when the assembly was preoccupied with abolishing episcopacy and pressing ahead with plans for the erection of presbyteries, the government took up the assembly's challenge and proceeded to make an appointment to the vacant archbishopric of Glasgow by issuing a licence to elect a successor to Boyd as archbishop on 1 August 1581.[399] The crown's nominee was Robert Montgomery, minister of Stirling and a man of somewhat unorthodox views; but Montgomery's bargain with the duke of Lennox, whereby the duke gained access to the temporalities of the see, did little to commend him to the church; and the refusal by all thirty members of the chapter to elect the crown's nominee left the government with little option, short of acknowledging defeat, than to declare that the right of disponing the bishopric had devolved into the king's hands. The church replied by instituting proceedings against Montgomery; and rioting students from the university prevented

[397] *RPC*, iii, 377; *BUK*, ii, 519.
[398] *RPC*, iii, 383-4; *BUK*, ii, 519-21.   [399] Watt, *Fasti*, 151.

Montgomery from entering the cathedral whose pulpit they reserved for Thomas Smeaton, their principal, who chose as his text 'He that enters not by the door but by the window is a thief and a robber', and so preached against Montgomery's 'simoniacal entry and the levity he had showed in all his proceedings'.[400] Yet in the same month in which the assembly ordered 'that no Acts be past in parliament repugnant to the true Word of God, and namelie concerning bischops with sharp admonitiouns therin to be pennit' by Andrew Melville and Thomas Smeaton, the privy council, in October 1581, positively approved the Leith arrangements of 1572 for electing bishops and appointing candidates to benefices. Meanwhile in the assembly, Andrew Melville opened the case for the prosecution against Montgomery; and though forbidden by the crown to proceed against him, the assembly in April 1582 finally declared Montgomery deposed and excommunicated 'to the effect that his proud flesh being cast into the hands of Satan he may be win againe if it be possible to God'. But apparently undaunted by the severity of the assembly's sentence, Montgomery obtained from the privy council in July 1582 a decree confirming him in his emoluments from the archbishopric.[401]

Presbyteries and bishops

Along with the church's resolve to eliminate the episcopal office came the assembly's plans for the development of presbyteries; and the government's initial concurrence in setting up presbyteries in the period immediately preceding the Montgomery case may be best explained as political concessions from an administration somewhat unsure of the policy which it ought to pursue, as ultra-protestant feeling became prominent with the ascendancy of Esmé Stewart and the ensuing popish scare which had led in January 1580/1 to the signing of the Negative Confession, a document scarcely excelled in its violent denunciation of all things popish.[402]

In accord with the government's intention of revising the old diocesan and parochial boundaries to make way for the creation

---

[400] Melville, *Diary*, 75; Spottiswoode, *History*, ii, 320; *RPC*, iii, 474–6; Durkan and Kirk, *University of Glasgow*, 335–7.

[401] *BUK*, ii, 524–5, 528, 533–4, 538, 541–7, 557–62; *RPC*, iii, 476–7, 496–7, 770.

[402] Calderwood, *History*, iii, 501–5.

of a streamlined system of presbyteries 'constituted for a dossone parochins or therabout', the privy council reported in May 1581 that a group of lairds and ministers in the Haddington area (a district designated by the assembly for the erection of one of the thirteen model presbyteries) had been appointed to discuss the reorganisation of eighteen parishes in the area. Nor was it accidental that these churches formed part of the assembly's scheme drafted in the previous month for establishing a presbytery at Haddington out of some twenty churches in the district. Although the exact date at which Haddington presbytery came into being is uncertain, two other model presbyteries were erected at Edinburgh and Stirling on 31 May and 8 August 1581. As early as April, the assembly had announced that already 'certan Presbyteries ar be them erected', and the assembly in October 1581 reaffirmed its opposition to episcopacy and reviewed its plans for the expansion of presbyterial organisation. That a number of presbyteries were already established in the Lothians may be inferred from the synod's recommendation in October 1581 that schoolmasters should have a place on presbyteries, that a uniform procedure should be adopted for summoning parties to compear before presbyteries, and that the designation of manses and glebes should fall within the jurisdiction of presbyteries.[403]

By April 1582, further presbyteries were operating in Ayr, Irvine, Linlithgow, Dunfermline, St Andrews, Perth, Dunkeld, Dundee, Brechin, Montrose and also in Tweeddale and in Strathearn. As a competitor for the jurisdiction which bishops had partly exercised, the presbytery provided a particularly useful instrument in the assembly's campaign against diocesan episcopacy. In October 1582, a group of presbyteries was empowered by the assembly to proceed against the bishops of Moray, Aberdeen, Brechin, Dunkeld, St Andrews, Dunblane and the Isles.[404] Stirling presbytery, in particular, to whom the bishops of Dunblane and the Isles were assigned for examination, had also taken action against Montgomery on his provision to Glasgow, and it was somewhat ironical that the presbytery, itself established by Montgomery and Andrew Graham, bishop of Dunblane, should institute proceedings against its founder members.

[403] *Ibid.*, viii, 34–6; *BUK*, ii, 485, 514, 523–4, 530–3, 535; SRO CH2/722/1. Stirling Presbytery Records, 8 Aug. 1581.

[404] *BUK*, ii, 549–50, 593.

Montgomery's principal offence in the eyes of the presbytery had lain in his attempt to 'aspyr to the bishoprie of Glasgw' but a variety of other accusations were also levelled against him. Fellow members of his presbytery complained that 'he was bruittit with intemperance of his mouthe sa that sumtymis eftir meikill drink his sensis wald feall him', that 'his doctrein is not formall nor sensablle to the commone pepill, and that his jestur in pulpet is nocht decent at sum tymis'. Though he strenuously denied that he was ever 'swa ovircumit with drink that his sences faillit him', Montgomery did confess 'that sumtymis thruch laik of memorie and negligence in his studie . . . he keipit not sic furmalitie and sensebilnes in doctrein'; he agreed that 'he hes bein sumtymis langer deteinit in cumpany than become him'; and he 'did not proceislie deny' lending money at a high rate of interest. The presbytery seemed determined to discredit Montgomery whom it accused of stirring up 'ane lamentablle schisme and trublle in the kirk' and whose 'insatiablle greid and stinking pryd' it so roundly censured; and its actions in many ways anticipated the proceedings of the Glasgow assembly of 1638.[405]

If the verdict in the Montgomery case was something of a triumph for the presbytery, the activities of the bishops of Dunblane and the Isles, which it proceeded to investigate, proved to be less reprehensible. Although nothing could be found 'in his lyf bot godliness and honestie', Graham's reputation as a dilapidator was certainly confirmed after the presbytery examined his rental book;[406] but no less significant was the verdict in the case of the bishop of the Isles. A report from Glasgow presbytery revealed 'no thing at all in lyf and conversatioun of the bischop of the Ylis in this our countrie bot honestie', and Stirling presbytery absolved the bishop from all accusations lodged against him in the general assembly:[407]

'excep the disjunctioun and separatioun of the abbacie of Ycolumkill fra the bischoprik of the Yllis laitlie procurit be

[405] SRO, CH2/722/1. Stirling Presbytery Records, 8 Aug., 5 Sept., 12 Sept., 19 Sept., 10 Oct., 21 Nov., 28 Nov., 5 Dec., 19 Dec., 26 Dec. 1581 ; 2 Jan., 6 Feb., 13 Feb., 27 Feb., 13 March, 20 March 1581/2; 17 April, 3 July, 17 July, 31 July, 7 Aug., 25 Dec. 1582; 16 July, 23 July, 20 Aug. 1583.
[406] *Ibid.*, 11 Dec., 18 Dec., 25 Dec. 1582; 1 Jan., 8 Jan., 15 Jan., 22 Jan., 29 Jan., 1 Feb., 19 Feb., 26 Feb., 5 March 1582/3; 26 March, 16 April, 23 July, 20 Aug., 3 Sept., 24 Sept., 8 Oct., 3 Dec. 1583; 14 Jan. 1583/4.
[407] *Ibid.*, 11 Dec. 1582; 15 Jan., 22 Jan. 1582/3; 26 March, 16 April, 16 July, 23 July, 13 Aug., 20 Aug. 1583.

the said Mr Johnne as also ane confirmatioun gevin be him to the erll of Argyll of the landis of Skirkennyth quhilkis befoir was sett in few be Mr Johnne Carswall his predicessur as he allegis and continewis the decisioun of the samin to the nixt generall assemblie of the kirk'.

Unlike some of his colleagues, John Campbell, as bishop of the Isles, seems to have measured up to the reformed ideal of a pastor and overseer of the flock.

Where presbyterial organisation was established, the assumption of the jurisdiction which the assembly hitherto had assigned to visitors or commissioners went ahead uninterrupted. As early as April 1582, Stirling presbytery chose its own commissioners to the general assembly; in March 1582/3, the presbytery suspended a reader and proceeded in July to depose another outright; and by 1583 Stirling, Edinburgh and Dalkeith presbyteries were all conducting visitations.[408] An unforeseen stimulus to the presbyterian campaign came as a consequence of political developments, for in August 1582 the Lennox regime was overthrown by the Ruthven raid; and while personal and political factors contributed to forming the alliance of the Ruthven lords, many of the key figures in the new government, like Gowrie, Glencairn and lord Lindsay, were staunchly protestant, and the affiliations of many who supported the Ruthven raid reveal strong undercurrents of religious radicalism.

The complexion of the new administration, which received a wide measure of popular support, was undisguisedly sympathetic to the presbyterian movement. This was illustrated by the triumphal return to Edinburgh in September, with the government's full approval, of its minister, John Durie, who had been banished from the capital by the previous regime. Once in power, what the new government did was not so much to give legal countenance to the continued development of presbyteries but rather to issue a proclamation which was generally favourable to the presbyterian campaign. In it, the government guaranteed the church's right to hold 'generall, synodall and particular assembleis at all times convenient', and declared that it was never the crown's intention 'to resist or putt stay or injunctioun to the free preaching of God's Word in reproving of sinne and iniquitie'. All this

---

[408] *Ibid.*, 10 April 1582; 19 March 1582/3; 9 April, 2 July 1583; *Wodrow Society Miscellany*, i, 459; SRO, CH2/424/1. Dalkeith Presbytery Records, fo. 71r.-v.

went far towards recognising the church's claims to exercise an independent jurisdiction; and just as the Ruthven lords readily condemned the attempts of the previous regime to silence the preaching of leading presbyterian ministers, so too did the assembly justify the Ruthven raid as the 'late actione of the Reformatione'.[409]

The palace revolution which had thus gained the church's approval 'brought a grait relieve to the Kirk, and the honest breithring of Glasgw and Edinbrucht that war soar troublit' by Lennox's government, but in terms of statute law, the establishment of a presbyterian system still gained no further recognition, if only because no parliament met during the Ruthven lords' ten months in power; and when reaction came it took the form of the 'anti-presbyterian dictatorship' of the Arran regime. If it did little else, Arran's government, by proscribing presbyteries and establishing episcopacy brought into sharp focus two conflicting and seemingly irreconcilable systems of church government.[410]

A Reassertion of Episcopacy

Even before his assumption of power in July 1583, Arran already had gained the reputation of being 'a scorner of religion, presumptuous, ambitious, covetous, careless of the commonwealth, a despiser of the nobility, and of all honest men' and in April 1583 a petition to the assembly had condemned the misdeeds of 'that ungodlie man'.[411] But, encouraged by the conservative reaction which set in under Arran's rule, Archbishop Adamson passed from defence to attack and, after a scathing assault on presbyterian theory, proceeded to give a terse and lucid exposition of his own ideas on church government, which opposed all that the second Book of Discipline approved. In a series of articles penned for the benefit of the churches of Geneva and Zürich, and of the French church in London, Adamson expounded an ecclesiology which was deferential to monarchy, erastian in outlook, episcopal in form, and essentially 'Anglican' in spirit. He began by asserting that it lay within the prince's power to appoint a form of polity for the church, since the prince, under Christ, was chief head of the church as well as of the state, and his judgment was sovereign in both. Such a theory contrasted sharply

[409] *CSP Scot.*, vi, nos. 62, 112, 113, 120, 142, 160; Calderwood, *History*, iii, 646–7, 650–1, 655–6; *BUK*, ii, 594.
[410] Melville, *Diary*, 134.   [411] Melville of Halhill, *Memoirs*, 242; *BUK*, ii, 619.

with the views of both Knox and Melville who claimed that it pertained not to kings to appoint their own rules for the church since the laws of God, and not of man, were alone applicable. What Adamson was advocating, in effect, was the notion of the 'one kingdom' theory where sovereignty was understood to be committed indivisibly to the crown. Under the king, church government ought to be entrusted to diocesan bishops who alone would be empowered to conduct ordinations.[412]

Adamson's rigid notions were quite out of keeping with the reformers' flexible ideas, and downright contrary to some of their proposals. The exclusive right to ordain or inaugurate ministers which he attributed wholly to bishops had never been characteristic of the activities of superintendents and commissioners, and Knox himself had publicly inaugurated James Lawson, as his successor, to the ministry in Edinburgh in 1572.[413] By reasserting the traditional right of the pre-reformation bishops to a seat in parliament, Adamson was reverting to a practice which could only lead to a confounding of the two jurisdictions which the first reformers had sought to keep separate and distinct. At the same time, Adamson's claim that bishops were of apostolic origin was not easy to reconcile with his belief that bishops were delegates of the crown. By appealing to the practice of the early church, Adamson appeared to be departing from the theory of the royal supremacy, which he was in the process of advancing, for if bishops were understood to derive their authority directly from the apostles, then they could scarcely be said to have received their authority intermediately as officers of the crown.

Bishops, the archbishop asserted, possessed an exclusive power of oversight and visitation, though he did allow that they might delegate their authority to others. Here again, however, Adamson's inflexible and dogmatic approach was quite contrary to the whole character of the Scottish polity where the church or more usually the general assembly (and not an individual superintendent) commissioned ministers to undertake supervisory functions. Visitation was regarded as a function delegated by the general

---

[412] Calderwood, *History*, iv, 50–55, 165; Knox, *Works*, iii, 41; iv, 232; v, 37, 515–16, 519–20. The letters which the presbyterian leaders wrote to Geneva and Zürich to counter Adamson's account of events are still extant in Bibliothèque Publique et Universitaire Genève, MS. Fr. 410, fo. 26r.-v., and in Staatsarchiv des Kantons Zürich, MS. E.II.382, fos. 1057r-1059v. One version is given in Calderwood, *History*, iv, 158–67.

[413] Bannatyne, *Memoriales*, 280–1.

assembly and other courts; but Adamson himself had declined to acknowledge the assembly's authority, and the formulation of his attitude to the assembly was predictably stimulating, for, in effect, his proposals left no room for a regularly constituted assembly, such as had met in the past, which he was intent on subverting. The independence and representative nature of the general assembly, presided over by an elected moderator, where decisions were reached by a plurality of votes, had always obstructed unimpeded episcopal rule. Adamson, therefore, proposed to abolish the rôle of an elective moderator, and wished to end the assembly's autonomy and to reduce its status by having it meet only 'upon a great and weightie occasioun', under strict licence from the prince, and by prohibiting it from formulating any enactments of its own save those which had the prince's approval.

What Adamson seemed intent on doing, as was made explicit in 1584, was to transform the assembly into an exclusive 'conventioun generall of clergie', an 'assemblie of bishops or clerks', subservient to the king in parliament.[414] After October 1583, no assembly, significantly, met for the duration of the Arran regime. All this was at variance with the assembly's traditional rôle, but if parallels are to be sought in England, it is plain that Adamson's proposals were consistent with the Henrician 'submission of the clergy' which eclipsed convocation's historic rôle as an independent ecclesiastical legislature.

The participation of barons and lairds on presbyteries was also condemned by Adamson as introducing 'a great confusion in the kirk, and an occasioun of continuall seditioun'; and it looked rather as if his whole train of thought was towards the exclusion of the Christian community (other than the ministry) from a place on church courts, for what he was advocating can only be described as a clerical oligarchy. Even more startling were his views on the eldership which Knox and the first reformers had justified as an order which 'O Lord, thou of thy mercie hes now restoired unto us agane efter that the publict face of the Kirk hes bene deformed by the tyrany of that Roman Antichrist'. Provocative from the start, Adamson insisted that 'seniors, or elders of the laick sort, are not agreeable with the Scriptures, nor ancient puritie of the primitive kirk'. This went even further than the views of Whitgift or Bancroft in England who had recognised

[414] Calderwood, *History*, iv, 145-6; Melville, *Diary*, 196.

the expediency of elders and of presbyteries in apostolic times when the church was persecuted and 'under the cross', and in Scotland Adamson's novel views on the eldership could scarcely be taken seriously. Even the reputedly godless Arran was not prepared to give effect to Adamson's extreme notion of abolishing elders, and instead issued a proclamation allowing kirk sessions to continue functioning.[415]

Though condemning elders, Adamson was nonetheless prepared to sanction the office of doctor, but according to his own definition doctors would have no say in governing the church and have 'no power to preache, but by the appointment of bishops'. Here was the archbishop's reply to Andrew Melville and the second Book of Discipline. No less intriguing were Adamson's views on ecclesiastical patrimony. With a reverence for statute law and constitutional practice, he believed that it was no business for a reformed church to claim for her own the whole patrimony of the Roman church, as indeed the second Book of Discipline had done. Instead, he argued that the church should be content to accept what the laws of the land allowed; and, as was to be expected, he strongly supported patronage and the system of benefices in its entirety.[416] The appeal of his proposals, it is evident, was aimed particularly at the crown, the aristocracy and the landed interest, who could scarcely fail to be attracted by such a defence of lay patronage and of the secularisation which had taken place of church patrimony, which went far to consolidate the social and political status of the nobles in their own territories.

In so far as his proposals were founded upon a recognition of the royal supremacy and upon an exclusive and uncompromising form of episcopacy, and in so far as they rested upon a repudiation of the eldership, a rejection of the independence of the two jurisdictions, and upon a denial of the assembly's traditional rôle, it is evident that Adamson's novel theories were quite contrary to the main stream of Scottish reformed thought. The whole drift of his argument took no account of Scottish reformation principles, and in many ways were the obverse of the ideals for which the first reformers stood. The tone and emphasis of his

---

[415] Knox, *Works*, ii, 153; Calderwood, *History*, iv, 54, 72-3; Whitgift, *Works*, i, 472; iii, 180; *Tracts ascribed to Richard Bancroft*, 111; *RStAKS*, ii, 529-30; SRO, CH2/521/1. Perth Kirk Session Records, 10 Aug. 1584; CH2/550/1. Glasgow Kirk Session Records, 22 April 1585.

[416] Calderwood, *History*, iv, 54-55.

proposals were undisguisedly and unapologetically 'Anglican' in outlook. Nor is this surprising, for his articles were initially formulated for consumption outside Scotland, and Whitgift, the new primate of England, was among the recipients.[417] Adamson's embassy to England in 1583 was understood by James Melville to have had as its purpose 'the alteration of the haill esteat and discipline of the Kirk', and once there he 'practised with the Bischopes for Conformitie, and gaiff tham *dextra societatis*'. Nor does this account materially differ from that by another contemporary who, displaying no apparent presbyterian bias, remarked that:[418]

> 'the King directit Patrick Archebishop of Sanctandrois to Ingland, to tak sure cognitioun of the ecclesiasticall policie of that cuntrie, and to report the same to his Majestie at his returne, that he mycht frayme the kirk of Scotland conforme; bot this tuik na gude succes, for albeit this Bishop was a man of rare learnyng, and of excellent doctrine in the kirk, yit his actions and proceidings in lyff and conversatioun war nawayis correspondent; and the baneist Ministers of Scotland had certefeit sum of the counsall and prelatis of Ingland heirof, sa that the man was the les regairdit in his negociatioun'.

Although he succeeded in meeting the bishop of London, the archbishop of York, and Whitgift himself with whom he continued to correspond, Adamson's diplomatic mission proved something of a failure, and on finding Whitgift aloof and Walsingsham unsympathetic, he returned home empty-handed.[419]

Even so, Adamson's articles and his trip to the south are symbolic of his policy to approximate the church of Scotland to that of its southern neighbour. His ideal seems to have been a uniformity in both government and worship; and picking up

[417] G. Donaldson, 'The Attitude of Whitgift and Bancroft to the Scottish Church', *Transactions of the Royal Historical Society*, 4th ser., xxiv (1942), 95–115, at 98–99.

[418] Melville, *Diary*, 141; Melville of Halhill, *Memoirs*, 274–5; *The Historie and Life of King James the Sext*, 205.

[419] BL, Add. MSS, 32092, fos. 75v., 76v., 80r; Harl. MSS, 7004, fo. 3r.-v. (where Adamson, in a letter from St Andrews dated 16th June 1584, kept Whitgift informed of how king and parliament 'hathe restored *in integrum* the estate of Bishops and hathe contramandet the seignoreis, presbitereis, not onele be good reasoun of scripture and antiquite, bot likwayis in respect his hienes had livelie experience that they were gret instrumentis of unquietnes and rebellioun be there populare disordour'.)

the threads of Morton's discredited policy of conformity with England, Adamson presented in a new guise an alternative, if controversial, solution to church polity. Whether his ideas commanded any widespread support from the ministry may be doubted and, apart from Montgomery who shared some of his views, no one of outstanding merit came forward to join the archbishop in his wholesale assault on the presbyterian discipline. Where his views did find substantial support was with the government which again resolved to secure that initiative which it had lost at the Reformation and to reassert its traditional authority in both church and state, which could be traced back at least as far as the Indult which Pope Innocent VIII had granted to James III in 1487. One solution, therefore, was to create an episcopate dependent upon, and directly responsible to, the crown alone; and, with some justice, Adamson could illustrate how 'the order and state of the kirk, as within thir few yeares, has beene frome superintendents to bishops, from bishops to visitors, from visitors to commissioners, and frome commissioners to presbytereis and moderators'.[420]

Yet although Adamson's views were founded on an uncompromising and doctrinaire form of episcopacy, the flexible attitude of his opponents to the rôle of visitor, as defined by the assembly in 1576 and subsequently by the second Book of Discipline, was not inconsistent with earlier practice which had led the assembly to entrust oversight in the 1560s to superintendents and commissioners, and this arrangement had been explicitly recognised by parliament in 1567 when it approved the rôle of superintendents and 'utheris havand commissioun of the Kirk to that effect' in admitting candidates to benefices.[421]

1584, however, turned out to be a bad year for presbyterians in both Scotland and England. In the southern kingdom, Whitgift began his attack on nonconformity by introducing a subscription which included an acknowledgment of the royal supremacy, the prayer book and the articles of religion; and north of the border the Scottish government followed suit by formulating a subscription in August 1584 which required all beneficed men, ministers, readers, university teachers and schoolmasters, on pain of loss of both benefice and stipend, to subscribe their acceptance of the 'Black Acts' and their obedience to the bishop or royal commissioner. The archbishop arrived home from

[420] Calderwood, *History*, iv, 87.   [421] *APS*, iii, 23.

England at the end of April 1584, but even earlier in March the government issued a proclamation discharging 'all assembleis, as weill civill as ecclesiasticall'; and in May parliament gave its approval to the controversial 'Black Acts', the second of which asserted the supremacy of the crown 'over all statis alsweill spirituall as temporall within this realme'. Nor was there any qualifying clause 'so far as the law of Christ allows'. Such a sweeping declaration of the royal supremacy in matters ecclesiastical was quite without parallel in the history of the reformed church and quite contrary to the first principles of reformation thought in Scotland. But the legislation of 1584 went even further, and after reaffirming the sovereignty of parliament 'of late yeris callit in sum doubt', the 'Black Acts' discharged all jurisdictions and judgments not approved by parliament and all assemblies and conventions held without the king's special licence and command. This effectively subjected the courts of the church and their jurisdiction to the crown-in-parliament.[422]

No longer was the church's jurisdiction to be separate from that of the state, as the first reformers had insisted. Instead, it was made wholly dependent on the power of the crown for all authority under God was held to emanate from the crown alone. No longer was the general assembly to possess an autonomous jurisdiction with power to meet when it chose, as it had done in the past. It could only function when licensed by the crown, and what the crown granted could also be withheld. The church courts, in short, were to operate only at the discretion of the crown; and although kirk sessions continued to meet, presbyteries were proscribed.

Even in its approval of episcopacy, the legislation of 1584 represented a departure from earlier ideas. Whereas the conforming bishops after 1560 had acted as commissioners of the assembly and whereas the Leith episcopate was recognised to be subject in spiritual matters to the assembly, the bishops of 1584 were answerable not to the assembly, which looked like being suppressed, but to the crown alone. The king became, as Adamson explained, 'a bishop of bishops and universall bishop within his realme'; and appeals from bishops were to be directed solely to the king. Despite Adamson's belief in the apostolic authority for bishops, the episcopate in terms of the enactments of 1584 became merely delegates of the crown. As royal commissioners in

[422] *Ibid.*, 292-3, 347; Calderwood, *History*, iv, 20-21, 49, 209.

ecclesiastical causes, the bishops of 1584 were not recognised as commissioned by the apostles to exercise a spiritual jurisdiction, but were stated to be 'appointit be his maiestie to have the exercise of the spirituall jusridictioun'. The source of their jurisdiction sprang purely from the crown, and Adamson accordingly received licence from the king, granting him 'power, authoritie and jurisdictioun to exercise the samine ... by himself, his commissioners and deputs in all maters ecclesiasticall'.[423]

In pressing ahead with this legislation, which threatened to undermine the whole fabric of church order, the government was clearly seen to take the initiative, and by doing so was bypassing the traditional procedure of consulting the church through the assembly or its commissioners; and there is truth in the verdict that 'ever since the reformation nothing concerning the effaires of the kirk was treated or concluded till first the Generall Assemblie was made privie thereto, and their commissioners heard to reasoun and agree to the same'.[424] Both in form and in content, the 'Black Acts' can be seen as a definite departure from reformation practice; and the test of Arran's ecclesiastical measures came with the obligatory subscription. By giving assent to the crown's supremacy in ecclesiastical matters and to a form of episcopacy no longer subordinated to the assembly, ministers were not only departing from earlier practice but, in effect, were condoning a series of innovations which marked a clear breach with the past; and it is not surprising that many ministers, despite the penalties which they might incur, entertained serious misgivings about the terms of the subscription.

Leading ministers who refused to recognise the recent innovations in polity already had fled for safety to England, along with the Ruthven lords. Some ministers declined to subscribe; others agreed to sign only by including a face-saving escape clause which rendered subscription meaningless; and some reluctantly acquiesced in the repressive legislation, only to protest in 1586, after Arran's downfall, against episcopacy and the 'Black Acts', 'no wise allowing of that tyrannicall supremacie of bishops and archbishops over ministers, and their lawes, which directlie repugne to the law of God'.[425] In any event, by 1585, Arran's administration was no longer impregnable, as many began to 'look through

[423] Calderwood, *History*, iv, 144–5, 264; *APS*, iii, 303, 347.
[424] Calderwood, *History*, iv, 62.
[425] J. Kirk, 'The Development of the Melvillian Movement', ii, 465–470.

their fingers' for the banished lords to return and seize power from Arran, which Elizabeth finally allowed to happen, as the exiled nobles recrossed the border in October, 1585. The resulting *coup d'état*, which the nobles effected, ended Arran's rule and resulted in the formation of a coalition government which was likely to be well disposed to the presbyterian ministers who, in exile, had been the political allies of the ultra-protestant lords who now assumed power. Indeed, at their entry into Scotland, the lords had issued a proclamation condemning the misdeeds of the previous regime, and had drawn particular attention to the inhibiting of 'presbytereis and other assembleis, exercises, privileges and immuniteis, ratified by former parliaments, or, at the least, by laudable custome, permitted ever since the first reformatioun within this land'.[426] All in all, the complexion of the new regime seemed sympathetic to the presbyterian cause, and the prospect was that the government would grant the church a wide measure of ecclesiastical independence.

The Bishop in Presbytery

To form a united front with the exiled ministers while in opposition and even to use to their advantage presbyterian support on their return proved easy enough, but once in power the restored lords were either unable or unwilling to concede the full programme of the second Book of Discipline; and having cleared themselves of any possible charge of treason, the lords took care not to antagonise further a king who, in 1586, undertook to prove that there should be bishops in the kirk. In any 'maters of the Kirk that twitched his honour', the king 'wald nocht be controlled thairin, nor grant to na thing bot efter his pleasour; and sa tuk upe a heiche humor against all the guide breithring'. Compromise, therefore, became the order of the day.[427]

Initially, the ministers had hoped 'to recover their synod against the bishops, and so to restore the discipline of the church, if not better, at least as it was before Arran's government'; but the more sanguine expectations of the presbyterians were soon disappointed. After the failure to convene a meeting of the general assembly at Dunfermline in November 1585, which was inhibited by the

---

[426] *CSP Scot.*, viii, nos. 2, 94, 119, 133, 191; Melville of Halhill, *Memoirs*, 302; Melville, *Diary*, 223; *Wodrow Society Miscellany*, i, 437; Calderwood, *History*, iv, 383-9.
[427] Calderwood, *History*, iv, 491; *CSP Scot.*, viii, no. 233; Melville, *Diary*, 225.

provost who claimed to be acting on the king's instructions, the ministers proceeded to Linlithgow where parliament was due to meet. The episcopate, however, was heavily represented on the committee of the articles, and no move was made in parliament to repeal the legislation of 1584. In their hour of triumph, the nobles whom James Melville had once identified as 'our Noblemen' deserted the presbyterians, despite fair promises to the contrary.[428]

A solution to the church's government, acceptable to the king and to the assembly, had still to be worked out, but it was at least plain that Arran's ecclesiastical policies were no longer applicable to the new situation which prevailed. Andrew Melville, credited by the exiles as a man on whom 'all the godly depend',[429] succeeded in interviewing the king in December 1585, and at the king's request the ministers were invited to submit their judgment on the ecclesiastical measures of the preceding regime. This was achieved in a series of 'animadversions', which began by criticising as unnecessarily restrictive the first of the 'Black Acts', which had confirmed only the church's liberty to preach the Word and administer the sacraments, for it failed to recognise the church's exercise of discipline and jurisdiction. The second act, asserting the royal supremacy, was condemned for attributing to the king a sovereignty over church and state alike 'wherein all men of good judgement have justlie found fault with the Pope of Rome, who clameth to himself the power of both the swords, which is als great a fault to a civill magistrat to clame or usurpe'. In commenting on the third act, affirming the authority of parliament, which they found 'obscure', the ministers were willing to concede the expedience of ecclesiastical representation in parliament, in the form of commissioners (not bishops) who might be either ministers or elders; but in opposing the fourth act, discharging all jurisdictions not approved by parliament and all assemblies unauthorised by the king, the ministers insisted that God had entrusted the church with a spiritual jurisdiction, and that it belonged to the church, and not to the king, to 'convocat Assembleis and to hold the same, and to appoint an order, place and time for conveening of the same, to treate upon suche maters as concerne the kirk effaires'. This, it was claimed, applied

---

[428] *CSP Scot.*, viii, nos. 209, 212; Calderwood, *History*, iv, 448–9; Melville, *Diary*, 222, 226, 228.

[429] *Wodrow Society Miscellany*, i, 436–7.

to kirk sessions, presbyteries and synods as well as to general assemblies.

Criticism of the fifth and sixth acts, concerning the deposition of ministers from benefices and the distraction of ministers from their proper duties, centred on points of detail rather than of principle, but exception was taken to those articles which recognised the rule of bishops. Objection was also taken to the twentieth act, empowering bishops and other royal commissioners to act as overseers, first because supervision properly pertained 'to the ecclesiasticall senat and not to anie one man', and secondly because no power was 'committed to a civill magistrat and to whom they please to governe the hous of God, which is his Kirk'. The ministers also protested vigorously at the king's annulment of Montgomery's excommunication, since the power to bind and loose 'can no more perteane to prince or anie civill magistrat, nor to preache the Word of God and ministrat sacraments, for they are both in like maner committed by Christ, our Maister, to the true office-bearers within his kirk'.[430]

All this amounted to a complete repudiation of the legislation of 1584 and to an affirmation of the principles of the second Book of Discipline; and in reply, the king, now somewhat on the defensive, issued a statement giving his own interpretation of the 'Black Acts'. He promised to extend the first act, defining the church's liberty, to include both jurisdiction and polity, and he limited the second act, asserting the royal supremacy, by avowing that all matters of doctrine were 'mere ecclesiasticall and altogether impertinent to my calling; therefore, never sall I, nor never ought they, I meane my posteritie, acclame anie power or jurisdictioun in the forsaids'. On the third act, concerning the authority of paliament, he declared that 'bishops, which are one of the three estats, sall have power, als farre as God's Word and exemple of the primitive kirk will permit', and he rejected the idea that ministers, as commissioners, should represent the spiritual estate in parliament. He remained firm on the fourth act that assemblies should meet only by his special licence; but on the twentieth act, he seemed more flexible and was willing 'after farther conference with some of the ministrie to take a solid order theranent'. On the annulment of Montgomery's excommunication, he replied that he 'must first debate the occasion shortlie';

[430] *APS*, iii, 292–3; Calderwood, *History*, iv, 450–2, 455, 457; Melville, *Diary*, 229–31, 234, 237.

but the statement also gave James an opportunity to define his own attitude to bishops.[431]

What the king proposed, in effect, was a constitutional episcopacy in which the bishop would not 'tyrannize over his brethrein or doe anie thing of himself, but with the advice of his whole diocie, or at least with the wisest number of them, to serve him for a counsell; and to doe nothing him alone, except the teaching of the Word, ministratioun of the sacraments, and voting in parliament and counsell'. Yet such a bishop was not to be mistaken for a mere commissioner of the church, for his office was to be for life and he was also to possess 'some probatioun and dignitie above his brethrein as was in the primative kirk'. There was to be no escaping the true nature of the overseer so defined.

Only in February 1585/6 was a compromise finally effected between the interests of the crown and church, but some of the thinking behind the compromise was already apparent in the king's statement in December 1585. It was now agreed that 'the name of a bishop hath a speciall charge and function annexed to it by the Word'. On presentation by the king and on admission by the assembly to which they remained accountable, bishops were each to serve as a parish minister, act as a constant moderator of the presbytery and conduct visitations within the 'boundis to be appointed to him'. Commissioners, nominated by the king and approved by the assembly, were to assist the bishops in the larger dioceses, and, though they were presumably not to be elected for life, their authority was to be identical to that enjoyed by bishops. In the appointment of bishops to parish charges, congregations were permitted the somewhat negative right of declining to accept the candidate chosen. Presbyteries, instead of being proscribed as under the Arran regime, were once more officially recognised, and the jurisdiction of bishops (and commissioners) in all essential aspects of oversight was carefully restricted and subject to the advice and consent of their presbyteries.[432]

The form of episcopacy advocated was decidedly constitutional not monarchical and appropriately may be described as approximating the concept of the bishop in presbytery. Apart from the use of the title 'bishop', much of what was formulated resembled the visitor's articles of 1576, which the assembly had drawn up

[431] Calderwood, *History*, iv, 459–63; Melville, *Diary*, 239–43.
[432] *CSP Scot.*, viii, no. 276; Calderwood, *History*, iv, 491–4.

after criticism of diocesan episcopacy. There were, of course, no presbyteries in 1576, but the visitor was then expected to work with the exercise, the germ of the later presbytery;[433] but one important distinction between the two sets of proposals was that, unlike the visitor or commissioner, the bishop was not only to be elected for life, and not for a term at the assembly's discretion, but was also to be nominated by the crown and not by the church.

The settlement so effected between the court and some ministers had still to be approved by the assembly, which the king had arranged to meet in May, the first assembly to be so convoked by special licence from the crown. After hesitation, the assembly accepted the compromise with certain misgivings. It claimed that the church possessed the right to convene its own assemblies; it approved the four offices of pastor, doctor, elder and deacon; and, reaffirming earlier practice, it interpreted the name of bishop as 'commoun to all Pastours and Ministers'; but when the king's commissioners made it plain that unless the assembly agreed to at least a reduced form of episcopacy, the king would grant nothing and leave matters as they stood under Arran's rule, the church had no alternative than to accept what concessions it could obtain.

Although it insisted that bishops possessed the same functions as pastors, the assembly recognised that it might lawfully admit a pastor or bishop to a benefice on presentation by the crown. Even so, visitation was still understood to be common to all pastors; and those bishops whom the assembly might appoint as overseers were to act only with assessors and by the counsel and vote of their presbyteries, and by advice of their synods. Nor were they to oversee the whole bounds of the old dioceses, since commissioners, appointed for a term by the assembly, were also to act as visitors with the same powers as bishops; and bishops themselves, though in other respects elected for life, were merely to receive a temporary commission for visitation, renewable only by the assembly.[434]

If bishops were thus equated with pastors, who were also elected for life, and if visitation was common to all pastors commissioned for the purpose by the assembly, then it followed that bishops, as such, had no automatic right to conduct visita-

[433] *BUK*, i, 357–8.
[434] *RPC*, iv, 60–1; Calderwood, *History*, iv, 493, 548, 557–61; NLS, Adv. MS, 6.1.13, fo. 33r.; *BUK*, ii, 645, 652–5; Spottiswood, *History*, ii, 342–3.

tions. The whole trend was to undermine the episcopal office and to substitute the more acceptable office of visitor or commissioner in strict accordance with the assembly's articles of 1576. In the final analysis, oversight was not to be conducted individually but corporately, for in each case the commissioner or bishop was required to act with the advice of the presbytery or synod and with assessors chosen initially by the assembly. Yet if all this was conceded, the church still failed in its attempts to subject the bishop, in life and doctrine, to the presbytery and synod, and the king was adamant that in these matters bishops ought to be subordinated only to the general assembly.[435]

All the elements for compromise and conciliation were no doubt present in the scheme. Even the two offending archbishops were reconciled to the church, though the assembly persisted in defining the functions of church courts in language largely borrowed from the second Book of Discipline; and above all, it still remained to be seen whether or not the church would conscientiously adhere to the letter of the agreement.[436] There is good reason to believe that commissioners worked in close association with presbyteries, in areas where the latter operated, and although presentations to benefices by the crown might continue to be directed to commissioners or bishops, as the recognised agents for collation, a more balanced picture from presbytery records discloses that even with crown presentations, commissioners often acted in conjunction with presbyteries, even to the extent that the commissioner became an instrument of the presbytery, all of which facilitated the tendency, apparent from at least as early as 1583, for presbyteries to appoint their own commissioners to discharge the duties of oversight within their own jurisdictions.[437] Where established, the presbytery's continued ascendancy led to a further diminution in the powers of individual overseers; and in Edinburgh the presbytery, by 1589, declined to admit to the ministry any candidates who had not been recommended by a presbytery.[438] It was thus only in a belated recognition of the growth of presbyterial organisation

[435] *BUK*, ii, 652–4; Calderwood, *History*, iv, 558–60.
[436] Calderwood, *History*, iv, 494; SRO, CH2/121/1. Edinburgh Presbytery Records, 24 May, 7 June, 28 June 1586; 7 Feb., 21 Feb., 21 March 1586/7; 28 March, 1 Aug., 22 Aug., 29 Aug., 5 Sept., 12 Sept., 19 Sept. 1587; *BUK*, ii, 655, 657–8, 662–3, 664–6. See text below, VII. 17–21, 28–31, and notes 116, 125.
[437] J. Kirk, 'Development of the Melvillian Movement', ii, 483–493.
[438] SRO, CH2/121/1. Edinburgh Presbytery Records, 23 Sept. 1589.

that crown presentations began to specify presbyteries as an appropriate agency for collation.

At the same time, the assembly showed a decided disinclination to co-operate in the appointment of further bishops to vacant sees. In June 1587, the assembly condemned and revoked as illegal the consent which Glasgow presbytery had given to the arrangement whereby William Erskine was appointed to the temporality of the archbishopric, ecclesiastical jurisdiction remaining with the church; and it also forbade Robert Pont's election to the bishopric of Caithness, conceding only that he might act as visitor and 'bruik the living only' if he were appointed minister of Dornoch. The same assembly also disregarded the king's insistence in 1586 that bishops should be subject only to the assembly and resolved that 'all Pastours of quhatsoevir sort they be' should be subject to the trial and censure of their brethren in presbyteries and synods as well as in assemblies. All this was in full agreement with the second Book of Discipline's proposals; and, as if to make the ordinance effective, Edinburgh presbytery, in August 1588, received a commission from the assembly to investigate complaints against Patrick Adamson, 'callit bischop of St Androis', who was accused, among other charges of derogating the authority of presbyteries, 'in the quhilk he is fund giltie of error', and so was sentenced 'for ever to be unworthie to brook ony functioun within the kirk of God'.[439] Even the assembly's earlier acceptance, in May 1586, that bishops and commissioners should act as moderators of presbyteries 'quhill farder ordour be tane' does not seem to have been enforced for long, and presbyteries soon reverted to their normal practice of electing their moderators for a half-yearly term, from one synod till the next.[440]

The polity which emerged in the years between 1586 and 1592 was unmistakably presbyterian in character, and the parliamentary ratification which that polity received in 1592 was simply an acknowledgment of the progress which the presbyterians had made in transforming what was at times a somewhat indeterminate polity into one which was thoroughly presbyterian.

[439] *BUK*, ii, 688, 690, 693, 696–9; SRO, CH2/121/1. Edinburgh Presbytery Records, 4 Aug., 15 Oct., 5 Nov., 17 Dec. 1588; 4 March, 11 March 1588/9; 8 April, 15 April, 10 June 1589.

[440] *BUK*, ii, 667; SRO, CH2/121/1. Edinburgh Presbytery Records, 19 April, 11 Oct. 1586; 11 April 1587; CH2/722/2. Stirling Presbytery Records, 16 April 1588.

The Presbyterian kirk by law established

The initiative for the legislation of 1592 came from the assembly in May which drafted a series of articles to be presented to parliament, first and foremost of which was one calling for an annulment of the acts of 1584 and a recognition of the church's constitution in the light of prevailing practice.[441] The legislation which parliament enacted was thus confined to confirming the church's present constitution. It went no further than to establish the existing polity on a sound legal basis. In language borrowed from the assembly's earlier enactment of May 1586, which in turn was largely adopted from the second Book of Discipline, the act of 1592 approved the jurisdiction of synods, and presbyteries, and of kirk sessions of 'particulare kirkis, gif they be lauchfullie rewlit be sufficient ministeris and sessioun'; and it expressly sanctioned the continued existence of the general assembly, which was to convene once a year or oftener *pro re nata*, but the time and place of its meetings were to be determined in first instance by the king or his commissioner if present at the assembly, or, in their default, by the assembly itself. This, of course, was at variance with established practice before 1584, but it would be harder to deny that the proposal was wholly contrary to the conditions which prevailed in the years between 1586 and 1592 when meetings of the assembly were sometimes determined by the king, and sometimes decided by the assembly itself.

There were other areas, too, where the act of 1592 brought statute law into line with prevailing practice. Episcopal jurisdiction was formally transferred to presbyteries, and all presentations in future were to be directed to presbyteries. Earlier relevant legislation was either repealed or amended. The second of the 'Black Acts', confirming the king's power over all estates, was qualified and interpreted not to be prejudicial to 'the privilege that God hes gevin to the spirituall office beraris in the kirk concerning headis of religioun, materis of heresie, excommunicatioun, collatioun or deprivatioun of ministeris or ony sic essentiall censouris speciall groundit and havand warrand of the word of God'; and the twentieth act, granting a 'commissioun to bishoppis and utheris juges constitute in ecclesiasticall caussis' was revoked outright. Episcopacy was certainly eclipsed, and by depriving

[441] *BUK*, ii, 786–7.

bishops of all episcopal jurisdiction granted to them by the crown, parliament came close to abolishing episcopacy. Titular bishops there still might be, in the sense of candidates presented to bishoprics with a legal right, which the assembly contested, to vote in parliament; but as a distinct ecclesiastical function, episcopacy no longer existed, and was recognised neither by the assembly nor by parliament.

Patronage and the system of benefices, on the other hand, remained untouched by the act of 1592. Their abolition had not even been sought in the articles which the assembly had presented to parliament. Here again, parliament can be seen merely to have approved the system then operating; hence the provision that 'presbiteries be bund and astrictit to reseave and admitt quhatsumevir qualifiet minister presentit be his Majestie or uther laic patrounes'. Where a patron failed to present a qualified candidate within six months, the presbytery was recognised to have the right of presentation *iure devoluto*, but where a presbytery refused to admit a qualified candidate, the patron was entitled to retain in his own possession the whole fruits of the benefice. Again, apart from the article amending the second of the 'Black Acts', ecclesiastical independence was neither granted nor denied; it was simply not discussed.[442]

The imperfections and inadequacies of the act, when compared with the far-reaching proposals of the second Book of Discipline, are immediately apparent; but it had not been the assembly's intention in 1592 to press for a comprehensive settlement or for a formal recognition of every aspect of the second Book of Discipline. Even so, major concessions had been granted by the crown to the presbyterians, if only by recognising the *fait accompli* of the years following the repressive legislation of 1584. The act was indisputably a vicory for presbyterian principles, but what it achieved beyond conferring on presbyterianism a legal status and state establishment, it might be hard to say. It neither added to, nor detracted from, existing practice, and so did not materially affect church government. Equally, by upholding a presbyterian system, the king was seen only to be acting in a manner consistent with a 'godly prince'. Yet parliament could later withhold what it once had granted, and much subsequent history in the seventeenth century was concerned with either reasserting or repudiating the principles on which the second Book of

[442] *APS*, iii, 541–2.

Discipline was founded, as each of the two contending parties attempted to adapt for its own benefit the existing system of church government in its hour of triumph.

THE TEXT AND METHOD OF EDITING

The second Book of Discipline first circulated in manuscript form, of which several early copies have survived. Other manuscript copies are to be found not least among the numerous transcripts of the acts of the general assembly compiled in the later sixteenth and early seventeenth centuries; and it was only in 1621[443] that the texts of both the first and second Books of Discipline finally appeared in print. Among the earliest known, individual copies of the second Book of Discipline, still extant (as distinct from copies engrossed among acts of assembly), are the two copies, one of which is defective, of 'Maister James Carmichels Booke' preserved among the state papers in the Public Record Office, London. Both are addressed 'to my lord ambassadour' and are endorsed 'Maister James Carmichels Booke'.[444] One copy is written in a distinctive Scottish hand, resembling Carmichael's, and the other, written in a different hand, is an imperfect copy, defective both in the omission of phrases, for which the scribe has left space for their later insertion, and in the mistranscription of other passages, in sometimes nonsensical fashion.

As minister of Haddington, Carmichael had been appointed to a committee of assembly as early as 1575 to examine the acts of assembly and to make extracts available so that 'all pretext of ignorance may be tane away'. Thereafter, Carmichael was involved in revising the second Book of Discipline, and later resumed work on the acts of assembly; but he was also in touch with Walsingham, Davison and other English puritan diplomats, which explains why Carmichael's copy of the Book of Discipline should come into the possession of the English ambassador, and as a presbyterian exile in England in 1584 he not only related to Walsingham the latest news of Scottish affairs but also set about preparing a statement, on behalf of the exiles, and for this purpose had

---

[443] *STC*, no. 22015; *The First Book of Discipline*, 76.

[444] PRO, SP.52/29 nos. 69–70. The incorrect date '1610', pencilled on both copies, has been deleted in the second (defective) copy, and the date '1580 or 1581' substituted. In *CSP Scot.*, vi, no. 76, the editor has inserted a description of the contents of the second Book of Discipline under the heading 'Parliament in Scotland: (October, 1581)'.

attempted to gather together a series of documents which, significantly, included the second Book of Discipline, the acts of assembly, the acts of parliament for 1584, as well as Knox's History and part of Hume of Godscroft's History.[445] The first of these two versions of the second Book of Discipline which bear Carmichael's name can therefore claim to be among the earliest surviving texts, though the second version is merely a poor copy of limited value.

Another copy, of uncertain provenance, found its way to Trinity College, Dublin, where the English presbyterian leader, Walter Travers, was once second provost of the college, whose library also came to possess a copy of late sixteenth-century statutes for the revised constitution of Glasgow university, among whose principals were to be found at least two presbyterian leaders in Andrew Melville and Thomas Smeaton.[446] A further copy, authenticated by James Ritchie, clerk to the general assembly, which forms the substance of the text offered below, is the copy which Haddington presbytery subscribed in 1591. It also bears the initials and signature of David Laing in the nineteenth century, as well as the stamp of the Library of the Church of Scotland, and is now located in New College Library, Edinburgh. An additional contemporary copy in twelve folios, located in 1937 among papers in the Commissary Office, is preserved in the Scottish Record Office.[447] The text of this copy, in all essential aspects, conforms to that in the Haddington MS.

Besides these, there are also versions in the numerous copies of the acts of assembly, in whose register the second Book of Discipline was engrossed in April 1581.[448] James Carmichael's separate compilation of the acts of assembly from 1560 to 1597 now forms MS. 227 in Aberdeen University Library. Another copy of the acts from 1560 to 1616 came into Robert Wodrow's possession and is preserved as Advocates' MS. 17.1.8. in the National Library of Scotland, which also possesses another

---

[445] *BUK*, i, 325, 398; iii, 815, 856; *Wodrow Society Miscellany*, i, 413–19; Calderwood, *History*, viii, 260–2; *CSP Scot.*, vii, nos. 195, 208, 267.

[446] TCD, MS. 533; Durkan and Kirk, *The University of Glasgow*, 303–4.

[447] The New College MS. has no current classification. It is contained among other ecclesiastical papers which consist of abstracts of acts of assembly, and the 'fforme of sindrie materis to be usit in the elderschip', which David Laing edited for the *Wodrow Society Miscellany*, i, 525ff.; *cf.*, 403. SRO, CH8/35.

[448] *Cf.* D. Shaw, *The General Assemblies of the Church of Scotland, 1560–1600* (Edinburgh, 1964), 1–12.

version in the Wodrow MSS., quarto vol. xxi. The manuscript record of assemblies from 1562 to 1618 compiled by James Melville is contained in Edinburgh University Library, MS. La. III.335; another transcript owned by the Earl of Crawford is to be found in the Scottish Record Office (CH1/1/2); and two further seventeenth-century compilations of the acts of assembly belong to Glasgow University Library (General MSS. 1122, 1132). A Latin version of the book also appears in Archibald Simson's unpublished church history, contained among the Wodrow MSS., quarto vol. xiii, no. 1, fos. 12v.-20r.

In addition, there are the printed texts from 1621 onwards, also incorporated in the histories of Calderwood and Spottiswoode, as well as in James Melville's *Diary*, and in the Bannatyne and Maitland Clubs' joint edition of the *Booke of the Universall Kirk of Scotland*.[449] In compiling another nineteenth-century edition of the acts of assembly, Peterkin resorted to the text of the copy of the second Book of Discipline which Haddington presbytery possessed, but he still succeeded in mistranscribing some of the signatures of the ministers who subscribed the book in 1591.[450]

The text of the copy which belonged to Haddington presbytery has been collated with the versions contained in Aberdeen University Library, MS. 227 (henceforth cited in the notes to the text as AUL); Glasgow University Library, General MSS. 1122, 1132 (GUL); National Library of Scotland, Adv. MS. 17.1.8 (NLS); Public Record Office (PRO), SP. 52/29 (complete version only); Scottish Record Office, CH1/1/2 (SRO); and Trinity College Dublin, MS. 533 (TCD). Grateful acknowledgment is also made to the Librarian of New College for permission to publish the text of the Haddington MS. in his possession.

Variant readings are rendered as notes to the text (prefixed by the abbreviations explained above). Minor discrepancies, grammatical differences and transpositions too numerous to note are not included. The numbering of sub-sections within chapters varies considerably from one text to another, and it has not been thought desirable to indicate these in every instance. For clarity, Roman numerals have been adopted for chapter headings and Arabic numerals for sub-sections, though the Haddington MS.

---

[449] *The First and Second Booke of Discipline, together with some Acts of the Generall Assemblies* (1621); *Heads and Conclusions of the Policie of the Kirk* (1680); Calderwood *History*, iii, 529–555; Spottiswoode, *History*, ii, 233–256; Melville, *Diary*, 87–116; *BUK*, ii, 488–512.

[450] Peterkin, 535–564.

contains Arabic numerals throughout. In transcribing the text, the original orthography has been retained, except for the standardisation of 'u', 'v', and 'w' where relevant. Abbreviated and contracted forms have been extended; punctuation conforms to modern usage; and editorial insertions are contained within square brackets.

As with *The First Book of Discipline*, edited by Professor James K. Cameron, the commentary and notes to the text are intended to draw attention to points of contact with earlier reformed thought and with the ideas of other reformers in Europe, as well as to indicate subsequent attempts to give effect to the programme presented in the second Book of Discipline.

Annotated section of text, VII. 25–27.
By courtesy of the Librarian, New College, Edinburgh

THE SECOND BOOK OF DISCIPLINE
1578

HEADIS AND CONCLUSIONIS OF THE POLICIE OF THE KIRK

The Principall Materis heirin contenit:

I Off the kirk and policie thairof in generall and quhairin it is different frome the civill policie.

II Off the partis of the policie of the kirk and personis or office beirers to quhome the same is committit.

III How the personis that bear ecclesiasticall functioun ar admittit to thair offices.

IV Off the pasturis or ministeris in speciall and thair functioun in the kirk.

V Off the doctouris and scoles.

VI Off the eldaris and thair office.

VII Off elderschippis and assembleis and of discipline.

VIII Off the Deaconis and thair office.

IX Off the patrimony of the kirk and distributioun thairof.

X Off the office of ane Christiane magistrat in the kirk.

XI The present abusis in the kirk quhilk we desyr to be reformit.

XII What kynd of reformatioun we crave.

XIII Off the profitt that sall flow of this reformatioun to all estaitis.

I

OFF THE KIRK AND POLICIE[1] THAIROF IN GENERALL, AND QUHAIRIN IT IS DIFFERENT FROME THE CIVILL POLICIE

1. The kirk of God sumtymis is lairgelie takine for all thame that professis the Evangell of Jesus Chryst, and so it is ane company and fellowschipe, not onlie of the godlie, bot also of hypocrittis, professing alwayis outwartlie ane trew religioun.[2]

2. Other tymis it is takine for the godlie and elect onlie.[3]

3. And symtymis for thame quho exerce the spirituall functioun amang the congregatioun of thame that profes the trewth.[4]

[1] *i.e.* polity or government.

[2] The church defined as a visible institution embracing all those who externally profess faith but who may not possess it is consistent with Bucer's and Calvin's emphasis on the church as an organised and disciplined community. Here a balance is sought between the Roman concept of the visible church hierarchically ordered through the priesthood and the spiritualist and anabaptist belief in the exclusive 'gathered' sect of the elect which repudiated outward forms in church order. No discussion ensues on the marks or notes (usually enumerated in Reformed thought as preaching of the Word, ministration of the two sacraments and the exercise of discipline) by which the true church may be discerned from the false. (*Common Places of Martin Bucer*, ed. D. F. Wright (Appleford, 1972), 202ff.; Bucer, *Martini Buceri Opera Latina*, vol. xv: *De Regno Christi*, ed. F. Wendel (Paris, 1954), 50, 54–6; Calvin, *Institutes*, IV, i, 7; Bullinger, *Decades*, v, 8, 12ff.)

[3] The doctrine of the invisible church as a spiritual assembly of true believers united in faith and known only to God, to which Luther gave primary place, is here subordinated to the idea of the visible church. This tendency in later Reformation thought was already apparent in the modifications to successive editions of Calvin's *Institutes*. Although all may be in the church, all are not of the church, and, purged of the reprobate, the church so conceived in this its inward or invisible aspect is identified with the communion of saints, the elect or redeemed of all ages. Earlier, the Augsburg Confession of 1530 had defined the church both invisible and visible, as did subsequent protestant creeds including the Scots Confession of 1560. (*Luthers's Works*, ed. J. Pelikan and H. T. Lehmann, vol. 41 (Philadelphia, 1966), 144, 150; G. Rupp, *The Righteousness of God* (London, 1953), 312ff.; Calvin, *Institutes*, IV, i, 2; IV, i, 7; Bullinger, *Decades*, v, 7; *Zwingli and Bullinger*, ed. G. W. Bromiley (London, 1953), 265–6; P. Schaff, *The Creeds of the Evangelical Protestant Churches* (London, 1877), 11–12, 219, 271–7, 375–7, 416–22; Knox, *Works*, ii, 108–11; vi, 494.)

[4] This narrower and less characteristically protestant doctrine identifying the church with the ministry and office-bearers appointed to specialised functions within the community of believers may be indicative of the high doctrine of the ministry expressed in Calvin's *Institutes*, where the example set by Oecolampadius and Bucer is developed; but by 1539, even Luther had conceded that 'the church

4. The kirk in this last sence hes ane certane power grantit be God according to the quhilk it usis ane proper jurisdictioun and governament exercit to the comfort of the haill kirk.[5]

5. This power ecclesiasticall is ane auctoritie grantit be God the Fader throcht the Mediator Jesus Chryst unto his kirk gadderit, and having the ground in the word of God, to be put in executioun be thame, unto quhom the spirituall[a] governament of the kirk be lauchfull calling is committit.[6]

6. The policie of the kirk flowing fra this power is[b] ane ordour or forme of spirituall[c] governament quhilk is exercit be the memberis appointit thairto be the word of God, and thairfoir is gevine immediatlie to the office-beirars be quhome it is exercit to the weill of the haill bodie.[7]

[a] *speciall* in both GUL   [b] *hes* in SRO   [c] *speciall* in NLS Adv.

is recognised externally by the fact that it consecrates or calls ministers or has offices that it is to administer ... in behalf of and in the name of the church'. (Calvin, *Institutes*, IV, iii, 1-2; IV, viii, 9; *Luther's Works*, vol. 41, 154.)

[5] The nature of the church's jurisdiction and government, professedly prescribed in scripture, is described below. In 1567 parliament had recognised the ecclesiastical jurisdiction to consist in preaching the Word, administering the sacraments and correcting manners, but it had also appointed a commission to consider what other points pertained to the church's jurisdiction. Erskine of Dun in 1571 claimed for the church its 'owne proper jurisdiction and libertie with the ministratioun of such offices as God hath appointed'; and continued discussion in the general assembly indicates that the matter was by no means resolved. A subsequent commission in March 1574/5 was charged with preparing a form of polity for the church's government, but no enactment followed. (*APS*, iii, 24-5, 89; *BUK*, i, 187, 280, 293, 295-6; Calderwood, *History*, iii, 159.)

[6] The exercise of an independent ecclesiastical jurisdiction through a lawfully-constituted ministry and elected office-bearers, and not by the membership at large, was recognised not only by Calvin and Beza but by other reformers including Bullinger who spoke of 'ecclesiastical jurisdiction which may rightly be called ministerial power, for the church of God uses the authority committed to it for this purpose by its ministers'. The Genevan 'Forme of Prayers' professed that 'the church oght to be gouverned by the pastors and ministers which have charge to preache the Word of God and minister the sacramentes'. (Calvin, *Institutes*, IV, xi, 1-4; IV, xii, 4; Beza, *La Confession de foi*, V, xxxii; Bullinger, *Decades*, v, 42; Bucer, *Opera Latina*, xv: *De Regno Christi*, 54-78, 118-30; Knox, *Works*, vi, 365.)

[7] Calvin had observed that 'this power of jurisdiction is, in one word, nothing but the order provided for the preservation of spiritual polity'. (*Institutes*, IV, xi, 1.) The claim that office-bearers derived their authority immediately of God and not intermediately through the prince, was repeated by the general assembly in 1582. (*BUK*, ii, 582, 600-1.) Such a view contrasts with Archbishop Cranmer's earlier acceptance in England that 'all Christian princes have committed unto them

7. This power is diverslie usit: for sumtymis it is severallie[d] exercit (chieflie be the teacheris),[8] sumtyme conjunctlie be mutuall consent of thame that bear the office and charge eftir the forme of jugement. The former is commonlie[e] callit *potestas ordinis* and the uther *potestas jurisdictionis*.[9]

8. These twa kyndis of power have bayth ane authoritie, ane ground[f] and ane finall caus, bot ar different in the maner and forme of executioun, as is evident of the speiking of our Maister in the 16 and 18[g] of Mathow.[10]

[d] *usit* added in both GUL, and NLS Adv.; substituted for *exercit* in AUL
[e] *onlie* in AUL, both GUL, and SRO   [f] *ane ground* not in NLS Wodrow
[g] *28* in both GUL, NLS Adv., and SRO; *xxviii* in AUL

---

immediately of God the whole cure of all their subjects, as well concerning the administration of God's word for the cure of souls, as concerning the ministration of things political and civil governance'. (Cranmer, *Works*, ii, 116.)

[8] By 'teachers' is meant expositors, instructors or interpreters of the Word, the ministers and doctors of the church. In *Matthew* 16:19, Calvin identified the 'office of teaching' with ministers of the Word. (Calvin, *Comm. Harm.*, ii, 187.)

[9] The distinction between *potestas ordinis*, the authority to preach the Word and administer the sacraments, and *potestas jurisdictionis*, the authority to administer ecclesiastical discipline, was traditional and had been much employed by the conciliarists; it also occurred, for example, in the *Bishop's Book* used in Henrician England. (E. T. Davies, *Episcopacy and the Royal Supremacy in the Church of England* (1950), 7.) The significance here, however, is the claim that whereas *potestas ordinis* is lawfully exercised by individual ministers, *potestas jurisdictionis* pertains not to individuals but should be administered collectively by an ecclesiastical court, defined below as the eldership composed of ministers and elders. The language is reminiscent of Calvin's *Institutes* where it is stated that 'the spitirual power which is proper to the church . . . consists either in doctrine or jurisdiction or in enacting laws'; distinction is drawn between 'the power of the church as existing either in individual bishops or in councils'; and it is shown how in the primitive church this power of jurisdiction was 'not administered at the will of one individual, but by a lawful consistory'. (Calvin, *Institutes*, IV, viii, 1; IV, xi, 1; IV, xi, 5–6.)

[10] These scriptural passages are seen to describe the power of the keys to the kingdom of heaven in different ways. *Matthew* 16:19 is interpreted as bestowing the power of binding and loosing on ministers who through preaching the Word open the door of heaven to faithful hearers. The disciplinary action against offenders discussed in *Matthew* 18:16–18 proceeding from private and public admonitions to excommunication by the church through the assembly of elders is understood to be exercised collectively and not individually. Both Calvin and Beza had commented on the different meaning attached to the 'binding and loosing' of *Matthew* 16 and 18, the former text referring to the authority of teaching and the latter to establishing discipline. (Calvin, *Comm. Harm.*, ii, 187, 189, 228–30; *Institutes*, IV, i, 22; IV, vi, 3; IV, xi, 1–2; Beza, *La Confession de foi*, V, xxxv; V, xliii; Beza, *N. T. Annotations*, 107–8; see also Knox, *Works*, i, 333.) Luther appears to have made no such clear distinction. (*Luther's Works*, vol. 41, 317ff.) See also below, IV. 11, and n. 71.

9. This power and policie ecclesiasticall is different and distinct in the awin nature fra that power and policie quhilk is callit the civille power and appertenit to the civile government of the commoun welth, albeit thay be bayth of God and tend to ane end gif thay be richtlie usit, to wit, to advance the glorie of God and to have godlie and guid subjectis.¹¹

10. For this power ecclesiasticall flowis immediatlie frome God and the Mediatour Chryst Jesus, and is spirituall, not having ane temporall heid in eirth bot onlie Chryst, the onlie spirituall*ʰ* king and governour of his kirk.*ⁱ*¹²

ʰ speciall in TCD   *ⁱ flock and kirk* in both GUL, and NLS Adv.

¹¹ This statement is consistent with the views of Oecolampadius, Bucer, Calvin and Beza in their defence of an independent ecclesiastical jurisdiction. For Oecolampadius, 'there is indeed a great difference between the ecclesiastical power and the secular magistrate even if he be Christian', and Bucer also believed that 'the Church of Christ should have her own discipline and punishment beyond the common discipline and punishment of the secular authority, even though it is entirely Christian and diligent and eager in exercising discipline'. (Cited in A. Demura, 'Church Discipline according to Johannes Oecolampadius in the setting of his Life and Thought' (Princeton Th.D. thesis, 1964), 99, 154.) Calvin found the two jurisdictions to be 'widely different', and Beza concluded that 'il y a une sorte de jurisdiction qui appartient à l'Église. Mais il faut la distinguer totalement de la jurisdiction civile'. (Calvin, *Institutes*, IV, xi, 1; IV, xi, 3–5; IV, xx, 2; *Comm. Harm.*, iii, 26–7; Beza, *La Confession de foi*, V, xxxii.) Such an attitude was evident in Scotland where the general assembly in the 1560s required that 'the jurisdictioune of the kirk may be separate fra that quhilk is civill'; and the idea is again present in Erskine of Dun's comment in 1571 that 'there is a spirituall jurisdictioun and power which God hath givin unto his kirk, and to these who beare office therin; and there is a temporall power givin of God to kings and civill magistrats. Both the powers are of God, and most agreing to the fortifeing one of another, if they be right used'. (*BUK*, i, 140, 146; *RPC*, ii, 7; Calderwood, *History*, iii, 158.)

¹² Such a repudiation of earthly headship, be it of pope or prince, over the church was far from novel in Scotland. While acknowledging that, as regent, Mary of Guise was 'ane minister and servand to God, and hes resavit of him ane office and ministratioun of ane kingdome temporall', the protestant lords of the Congregation in May 1559 had warned Mary to 'tak heid that ye pas nocht the limittis and boundis of your awin office, nother entyr be impir in Christis kingdome usurpeand forther powr unto you nor he hes gevin, ffor thocht all kingdomes bayth temporall and spirituall pertenis to God, yit hes God distributit the ministerie diverslye, that is the temporall kingdomes in the goverment of mortell men, and makis thame princes of the erthe, for the mentenance of commoun welthis and civill polaceis. Bot the goverment of the spirituall and hevinlie kingdome, the kirk of God we mein, he hes onlie committit to his sone Christ, ffor he is the heid thairoff, all uther ar her memberis under him'. (*Spalding Club Miscellany*, iv, 88–9.) The Scots Confession in 1560 had recognised only the 'conservatioun and purgatioun of the religioun' to pertain chiefly to princes and magistrates. (Knox, *Works*, ii, 118.) A denial of earthly headship had been made by Luther,

11. Thairfoir this power and policie of the kirk sould lene upone the word of God immediatlie as the onlie ground thairof, and sould be tane frome the puire fountanis of the Scripturis, heiring the voce of Chryst, the onlie spirituall king, and being *j*rewlit be his lawis.*j*13

12. It is ane title falslie usurpit be antichryst14 to call him self heid of the kirk and aucht not to be attributtit to angell or to mane, of quhat estait soevir he be, saiffing to Chryst, the heid and onlie monarche in this kirk.15

j *allowit be his law* in NLS Wodrow; items 11 and 12 transposed in AUL, both GUL, NLS Adv., and Wodrow, SRO and TCD

who taught in 1520 that 'the first Christendom, which alone is the true church, may not and cannot have an earthly head', and by Calvin, who, no less emphatically observed how 'the apostle teaches that the whole subministration is diffused through the members while the power flows from one celestial Head ... since Scripture testifies that Christ is Head and claims this honour for himself alone'. (*Luther's Works*, vol. 39, p. 71; Calvin, *Institutes*, IV, vi, 9.) See also below I. 12 and n. 15.

13 No distinction is apparently drawn between the Word of God and scripture, the written Word of God. Reformers variously defined the Word of God as the spoken Word of preaching, the visible Word of the sacraments, and the written Word of the Bible. Many protestants, including Calvin who avoided identifying the Holy Spirit with the Word, were highly critical of the spiritualists' subordination of scripture to further divine revelation through the Spirit, independently of the biblical text, as they also were of the Roman emphasis on the tradition and authority of the church's teaching. (Calvin, *Institutes*, I, ix, 1; IV, viii, 2; *Comm. Acts*, ii 103–4; F. Wendel, *Calvin, the Origins and Development of his Religious Thought* (London, 1965), 157.) The claim to found ecclesiastical jurisdiction and polity on scripture had already been made, amongst others, by Calvin who argued that the church's 'only head is Christ under whose government we are all united to each other, according to that order and form of policy which he himself had prescribed'. (Calvin, *Institutes*, IV, vi, 9; *cf.*, IV, iii, 4–5; IV, iv, 1; *CR*, XXXVIII, i, *Calvini Opera*, X, i, 15–17.) Bullinger also affirmed that 'we cannot doubt that the order of the church is perfect and the government absolute if at this day also there remain in the church of God bishops or pastors, doctors also or elders'. (Bullinger, *Decades*, v, 109.)

14 The identification of Antichrist or Satan with the person of the pope and with the papacy as an institution was common practice among protestant reformers (*cf.*, C. Hill, *Antichrist in Seventeenth-Century England* (Oxford, 1971); and Beza cited with approval, as did Bucer, the judgment of St Gregory 'qui dit que le titre d'évêque universel ne convient qu' à l'Antéchrist'. (*La Confession de foi*, V, v; Bucer, *Common Places*, 214.)

15 Leading reformers including Luther, Bucer, Calvin and Beza had rejected the notion of earthly headship over the church (for Luther and Calvin see above n. 12; Bucer, *Common Places*, 203; Beza, *La Confession de foi*, V, v.). In refuting the Catholic claim that 'the church would be without a head if the Pope did not, as head, exercise rule in it', Calvin had shown how Paul 'does not allow this

13. It is proper to kingis, princes and magistrates to be callit
^k lordis and dominatouris over thair subjectis quhom thay
governe civilie, bot it is proper to Chryst onlie to be callit
Lord and Maister in the spirituall government of the kirk,
and all utheris that beris office thairin^l aucht not to usurp
dominion thairin, be callit lordis, bot onlie ministeris, disciplis, and servandis, for it is Chrystis proper office to command, and reull his kirk universall, and everie particular kirk,
throw his Spirit and word, be the ministrie of mene.[16]

^k *heids* added in TCD   ^l *in the kirk* in GUL 1132

---

honour even to angels, and yet he does not maim the church by depriving her of her head; for as Christ claims for himself this title, so he truly exercises the office' (*Comm. Colossians*, 152-3); and elsewhere he attacked the 'blasphemies' which named Henry VIII 'sovereign head of the church'. (Calvin, *Oeuvres*, VII, 13, cited by R. H. Murray, *The Political Consequences of the Reformation* (London, 1926), 96.) In opposing the pretensions of the papacy, Bullinger also maintained, in language which could be equally fatal to the claims of the prince, that Christ alone was 'head of the church', 'the supreme governor of the faithful', a 'privilege, as I think, thou canst give to no creature without blasphemy and sacrilege'. (Bullinger, *Decades*, v, 85-6.) In 1559, John Jewel informed Bullinger that Queen Elizabeth 'is unwilling to be addressed, either by word of mouth, or in writing, as the head of the Church of England. For she seriously maintains that this honour is due to Christ alone, and cannot belong to any human being soever; besides which, these titles have been so foully contaminated by antichrist that they can no longer be adopted by anyone without impiety'. Yet John Parkhurst told Bullinger that the title 'governor' instead of 'head' in practice 'amounts to the same thing'; and Beza's view was that 'the papacy was never abolished in that country but rather transformed to the sovereign'. (*Zürich Letters*, i, 33; 29; ii, 128.) The reluctance of Scots to acknowledge the more modest phraseology of the Eliza- bethan supremacy can be detected in the Scottish oath of 1572 by the deliberate substitution of the phrase recognising King James as 'supreme governour of this realme, als weill in things temporall as in the conservatioun and purgatioun of religioun', so replacing the wording of the English oath affirming Elizabeth 'supreme governor . . . as well in all spiritual and ecclesiastical things or causes as temporal'. (see Introduction above, 40-1.)

[16] This statement recalls the 'two kingdoms' theory enunciated by the lords of the Congregation in May 1559 (*Spalding Club Miscellany*, iv, 88-92). Similarly, in 1548 Henry Balnaves had distinguished the princely office 'having generall administration in the common weale or jurisdiction of others' from 'the office of the administration of the Word of God under whom we comprehend all power ecclesiasticall' (Knox, *Works*, iii, 526). Bucer, too, had shown how 'none of the earthly members of the Church becomes its head; it has its head in Christ in heaven. The princes and magistrates of each locality may of course be called "heads", but only in the body politic and in political government, not in the ecclesiastical sphere'. (Bucer, *Common Places*, 203.) The language here also bears the imprint of Calvin who illustrated how Christ sought 'to distinguish the spiritual government of his church from earthly empires'; how 'even kings do not rightly and truly rule unless they serve; but the apostolic office differs from earthly principalities in that their being servants does not prevent kings and magistrates

14. Notwithstanding, as the ministeris and utheris of the ecclesiasticall estait ar subject to the magistrat civilie, swa aucht the persone of the magistrat be subject to the kirk spirituallie and in ecclesiasticall governament.^m 17

^m *and disciplin* added in PRO

---

from bearing sway and indeed rising above their subjects in magnificent splendour and pomp. . . . But the government of the church permits nothing of this sort. Christ gives to pastors nothing more than that they shall be servants and completely abstain from domination'. (Calvin, *Comm. Harm.*, ii, 274–6.) A similar attitude is apparent in 'A second Admonition to the Parliament' issued by English presbyterians in 1572, and in Thomas Cartwright, who opposed John Whitgift's argument that Christ, as head of the universal church, might delegate authority to princes enabling 'the magistrate to be the head and chief governor of a particular church'. (*Puritan Manifestoes*, ed. W. H. Frere and C. E. Douglas (London, 1907), 106–7; Whitgift, *Works*, i, 391–2; R. Bancroft, *A Survay of the Pretended Holy Discipline* (1593), 205.) The claim that Christ ruled the church through the ministry of the Word had been emphasized by John Knox in 1550, and by James Melville in 1584. (Knox, *Works*, iii, 41; Calderwood, *History*, iv, 151.)

[17] George Buchanan's *De Jure Regni* (1579) asserted that 'just as bishops are subject to kings in their capacity of citizens so kings ought to accept the admonitions of bishops in regard to spiritual matters'. (*De Jure Regni Apud Scotos*, LXVII.) This accorded with earlier Scottish reformation practice and with the first Book of Discipline's insistence on the necessity of ecclesiastical discipline for all offenders a principle enforced by subsequent acts of the general assembly. (*First Book of Discipline*, 164–173; *BUK*, i, 16, 74, 179, 195, 284.) This distinctive approach to discipline, advocated by Oecolampadius, Bucer and Calvin (though not by Zwingli), and adopted by Knox and Scottish reformers, was shared by Cartwright and the English presbyterians (A. Demura, 'Church Discipline according to Johannes Oecolampadius', 154–5; J. Courvoisier, *La Notion d'Église chez Bucer* (Paris, 1933), 24–5, 111ff., and *passim*; R. C. Walton, *Zwingli's Theocracy* (Toronto, 1967), 82, 209, 226; Bucer, *Common Places*, 267; Bucer, *Opera Latina* xv: *De Regno Christi*, 15–17; Calvin, *Institutes*, IV, xi, 4; IV, xii, 7; *CR*, LXXX, *Calvini Opera*, LIII, 223–4; Knox, *Works*, v, 516, 519–20; *RStAKS*, i, 35–6, 41, 60, 270; *CSP Scot.*, ii, no. 45; Travers, *A full and plaine declaration of ecclesiastical discipline* (1574), 185; Whitgift, *Works*, iii, 189, 231–2; *Puritan Manifestoes*, 18). Bullinger had also taught that 'the politic magistrate is commanded to give ear to the ecclesiastical ruler, and the ecclesiastical minister must obey the politic governor in all things which the law commandeth. So then the magistrate is not made subject by God to the priests as to lords, but as to the ministers of the Lord; the subjection and duty which they owe is to the Lord himself and to his law, to which the priests themselves also ought to be obedient, as well as the princes'. (Bullinger, *Decades*, ii, 329.) The Roman claim to clerical immunity from lay jurisdiction was not revived. Although the assembly petitioned the Regent in 1569 for temporary immunity to its members 'that during the time of the Generall Assemblies they be not molested in civil actions', it was still recognised (and stated in 1570) that ministers guilty of 'civil' offences should be punished by the magistrate. (*BUK*, i, 146, 179.) This did not prevent disputes emerging when ministers, accused of exceeding the bounds of their text, declined the privy council's jurisdiction on the grounds that the matter was doctrinal and properly a case for the ecclesiastical courts. (Calderwood, *History*, iv, 5ff.; v, 457ff.)

15. And the exercise of bayth thais jurisdictionis cane not stand in ane persone ordinarlie.[18]

16. The civill power is callit the power of the sword, the uther is callit the power of the keyis.[19]

17. The civile power sould command the spirituall to exercise and do thair office according to the word of God; the spirituall[n] rewlaris sould require the Christiane magistrat

[n] *Christian* in TCD

[18] The Tetrapolitan Confession of 1530, composed by Bucer and Capito, had criticised the promotion of ecclesiastics to offices in the state; Henry Balnaves in 1546 wrote that 'no bishope should mixt him selfe with temporall or seculer busines for that is contrarie his vocation'; Calvin declared likewise; and in 1559 Knox affirmed 'let none that be appointed to labour in Christes vineyearde be entangled with civil affaires'. The first Book of Discipline declared ministers ineligible for membership of the privy council and excluded them from regular attendance at court. In 1573, the general assembly reasserted that 'it is neither aggrieable to the word of God nor to the practise of the primitive kirk that the speciall administratioun of the word and sacraments, and the ministration of the criminal and civil justice be so confoundit that ane person may occupie both the cures'. (A. C. Cochrane, *Reformed Confessions of the Sixteenth Century* (London, 1966), 82; Knox *Works*, iii, 26; Calvin, *Institutes*, IV, xi, 8–9; Knox, *Works*, v, 516, 519–20; *First Book of Discipline*, 178; BUK, i, 267). For Scottish practice, see Introduction above, 37. The same claim was made by English puritans, and denied by Archbishop Whitgift. (*Puritan Manifestoes*, 30, 120; Whitgift, *Works*, i, 153.)

[19] This distinction between the two authorities, the temporal and the spiritual, was traditional. In discussing how 'some magistrates are civil and others ecclesiastical', Melanchthon had indicated that 'the civil magistrate is one who bears the sword and watches over the civil peace. . . . It is the obligation of the sword to enforce the laws against murder, vengeance, etc'. In 1530, Luther expounded his doctrine of *The Keys*, criticising earlier abuses and explaining how the keys 'are an office, a power or command given by God through Christ to all of Christendom for the retaining and remitting of the sins of men'. For Calvin, unlike Luther, it was the ministry which exercised the power of the keys, 'for Christ says that the ministers of the Gospel are like gate-keepers of the kingdom of heaven, because they bear its keys. And secondly He adds that they are endowed with a power of binding and loosing which is effective in heaven'. The Tetrapolitan Confession and Bullinger's sermon 'Of the Holy Catholic Church' recognised the power of the keys to be vested in the ministry. The same point was made by Knox in 1559, and by Erskine of Dun in 1571. The Scots Confession and first Book of Discipline affirmed the magistrate's use of the sword, but to be distinguished from this was the spiritual 'sword granted be God to his church', ecclesiastical censure and excommunication, exercised by the ministry, elders and deacons with consent of the church. (*Loci Communes*, 148; *Luther's Works*, vol. 40, 325–77; cf., 26–7; vol. 39, 86–91; Calvin, *Comm. Harm.*, ii, 187; cf., 189, 228–30; iii, 53; *Comm. Isaiah*, ii, 137; *Institutes*, IV, i, 22; Cochrane, *Reformed Confessions*, 69, Bullinger, *Decades*, v, 42; Knox, *Works*, i, 333; *Spalding Club Miscellany*, iv, 94; Knox, *Works*, ii, 118; vi, 451, 469; *First Book of Discipline*, 166–173.)

to minister justice and punische vyce and to mantene the libertie and quyetnes of the kirk within thair boundis.[20]

18. The magistrat commandeth externall thingis for externall peax and quyetnes amangis the subjectis; the ministerie handlit externall thingis onlie for conscience caus.[o]

19. The magistrat handlit onlie externall thingis and actionis done befoir men; bot the spirituall reularis juge baith inwart affectionis and externall actionis in respect of conscience be the word of God.[21]

20. The civile magistrat cravis and gettis obedience be the sword and uther externall menis, but the ministrie be the spirituall sword and spirituall meanis.[22]

21. The magistrat nather aucht to preache, minister the sacramentis, nor execut the censouris of the kirk, nor yit prescryve ony reull how it sould be done, bot command the ministeris to observe the reull commandit in the word, and punische the transgressouris be civile meanis.[23] The ministeris exerce not

[o] *saik* in both GUL

[20] This point is expanded below, I. 21.

[21] In distinguishing 'the external *forum*' from 'the *forum* of conscience', Calvin observed 'that in man government is twofold: the one spiritual, by which the conscience is trained to piety and divine worship, the other civil, by which the individual is instructed in those duties, which, as men and citizens, we are bound to perform.... The former has its seat within the soul, the latter only regulates the external conduct. We may call the one the spiritual, the other the civil kingdom'. (*Institutes*, III, xix, 15-16; IV, x, 3-5.) Beza also explained that the internal aspects of man's life concerning conscience fell within the ecclesiastical jurisdiction whereas the external aspects fell within the magistrates' jurisdiction. (*De haereticis a civili magistratu puniendis* ..., 26, cited in T. Maruyama, 'The Reform of the True Church' (Princeton dissertation, 1973), 56.)

[22] This amplifies the comment above, I. 16.

[23] The magistrate was not free to prescribe laws to the church but simply obliged to protect it according to the rule of scripture, expounded, of course, by the ministers as official interpreters of the Word. This view, which accords with Calvin's thought, recalls Knox's more forceful pronouncements, and is consistent with Andrew Melville's remark in 1584 that 'it perteaneth not to the prince ather to prescrive religioun to the kirk or discipline to the pastors therof, but by his authoritie to confirme bothe the one and the other, appointed by God, and sincerelie declared out of his Word by the ministrie of his servants'. (Calvin, *Institutes*, IV, xx, 3; Knox, *Works*, v, 519-20; Calderwood, *History*, iv, 165.) Such an emphasis may have owed much to the teaching of Calvin and Beza, but

the civile jursdictioun, bot teaches the magistrat how it sould be exercit according to the word.*p* ²⁴

22. The magistrat aucht to assist, mantene and fortifie the jurisdictioun of the kirk; the ministeris sould assist thair princes in all thingis aggreable to the word, providing thay negleck not thair awin charge be involving thame selfis in civile effairis.²⁵

23. Finallie, as ministeris ar subject to jugement and punis[h]ment of the magistratis*q* in externall thingis, gif thay offend, swa aucht *r*the magistratis to submit thame selfis to the discipline of the kirk gif thay transgres in materis of conscience and religioun.²⁶

p *of God* added in both GUL
q *of the magistratis* not in both GUL, NLS Adv., SRO and TCD
r *they the magistrates* in TCD

Bullinger had also eschewed 'the confounding of the offices and duties of the magistrate and ministers of the church as that we would have the king to preach, to baptize, and to minister the Lord's supper; or the priest, on the other side, to sit in the judgment-seat, and give judgment against a murderer'. He likewise distinguished 'politic laws . . . which the magistrate according to the state of times, places and persons, doth ordain for the preserving of public peace and civility' from ecclesiastical laws 'which, being taken out of the word of God and applied to the state of men, times and places, are received and have authority in the church among the people of God'; and he maintained that 'the proper office of the priests is to determine of religion by proofs out of the word of God, and that the prince's duty is to aid the priests in advancement and defence of true religion'. At the same time, Bullinger recognised, as did the second Book of Discipline (X. 8, below), the magistrate's right to enact certain laws in matters of religion. (Bullinger, *Decades*, ii, 206–7, 329, 331.) For further discussion of the magistrate's office, see below X. 1–9.

²⁴ Calvin, in particular, had shown 'if in this matter we seek the authority of Christ, there can be no doubt that He intended to debar the ministers of His word from civil domination and wordly power'. (*Institutes*, IV, xi, 8.) The minister's right to teach the magistrate his duty had been demonstrated by Knox in 1561 when he preached on 'the duty of all kind of magistrates in a good reformed commonwealth'. (Keith, *History*, ii, 87–88.)

²⁵ The distinctive, though complementary, rôles of minister and magistrate are again emphasized. The phraseology was commonplace among reformers, with the exception of spiritualist and anabaptist writers who repudiated the magistrate's participation. (Calvin, *Institutes*, IV, xx, 2–3; Beza, *La Confession de foi*, V, xliv; Beza, *A Brief and Pithy Sum*, 124v.–125v.; Bullinger, *Decades*, ii, 323–37; Knox, *Works*, ii, 118; Calderwood, *History*, iii, 158; Travers, *A full and plaine declaration*, 187.) See also below, XI. 21 and n. 196.

²⁶ This point is merely a repetition of article I. 14 above.

II

OFF THE PARTIS OF THE POLICIE OF THE KIRK, AND PERSONIS OR OFFICE-BEIRARIS TO QUHOME THE ADMINISTRATIOUN THAIROF IS COMMITTIT

1. As in the civile policie, the haill commoun welth consistith in thame that ar governouris and magistratis and thame that ar governit and subjectis, sa in the policie of the kirk, sum ar appointit to be reularis*s* and the rest of the memberis thairof to be reulit*t* and obey according to the word of God and inspiratioun of his Spirit,[27] alwayis onder ane head and cheif governour, Jesus Chryst.[28]

2. Agane, the haill policie of the kirk consistit in thrie cheif thingis: in doctrene, in discipline and distributioun.[29] With doctrene is joint*u* administratioun of the sacramentis.[30]

s rewlit in NLS Wodrow   *t* rewlaris in NLS Wodrow
u annexit in AUL, both GUL, NLS Wodrow and TCD

[27] The authority of the Word, the written Word of scripture, is authenticated by the witness of the Holy Spirit in the hearts of believers. (*Cf.*, J. K. S. Reid, *The Authority of Scripture* (London, 1957), 46–54.)

[28] The wording here closely follows Erskine of Dun's remark in 1571 that 'in the civile policie we se greit difference betuix men, though all be membris of a commone wealth, be reasone of offices resavit, be the quhilk offices men hes authoritie, power, and honour above utheris; and sa is it in the kirk of God, for it is nocht onlie requerit the evangell of Christ to be haid in estimatioun, bot also the ministeris thairof, sa lang as thai posses the office and travellis faythfullie tharin'. (*Spalding Club Miscellany*, iv, 95–96.) The article also resembles Calvin's comment that 'as no city or village can exist without a magistrate and government, so the church of God . . . needs a kind of spiritual government', which 'is altogether distinct from civil government'. The first Book of Discipline drew a similar distinction; and so did Walter Travers. (Calvin, *Institutes*, IV, xi, 1; *First Book of Discipline*, 165; Travers, *A full and plaine declaration*, 21.) Bullinger also recognised that the function of 'the office of the ministers' was 'to govern the church of God or to feed the flock of Christ'. (Bullinger, *Decades*, v, 145.)

[29] In Beza's Confession of Faith, discussion of the ministries in the church is divided into three sub-sections entitled (a) 'la prédication de la Parole'; (b) 'la dispensation des biens de l'Église'; (c) 'la discipline ecclésiastique'. The first Book of Discipline contained three chapters on doctrine, patrimony and discipline. (Beza, *La Confession de foi*, 116, 123, 127; *First Book of Discipline*, 87–9, 156–173.)

[30] Doctrine was expounded chiefly through preaching the Word which the reformers assigned to a position of co-centrality with the administration of the two sacraments of baptism and the Lord's Supper. The section on doctrine, in the first Book of Discipline, is immediately followed by one on the sacraments. (*First Book of Discipline*, 87–93.)

3. And according to the partis of this divisioun arysit ane thriefald sort of officiaris in the kirk, to wit, of ministeris or preacheris, of eldaris or governouris, of deaconis or distributeris. And all thase may be callit be ane generall word, ministeris of the kirk.³¹

4. For albeit the kirk of God be reulit and governit be Jesus Chryst quha is the onlie king, hie preist and heid thairof, yit he usis the ministrie of men as ane maist necessarie middis*ᵛ* for this purpois.³²

5. For sa he hes fra tyme to tyme befoir the law, under the law, and in tyme of the Evangell for our greit comfort rasit up men indewit with the giftis of theʷ Spirit for the spirituall governament of his kirk exercesing be tham his awine power throw his Spirit and word to the building of the same.³³

ᵛ as most necessar servandis in NLS Wodrow
ʷ his in PRO

³¹ In Scotland, these offices had already been approved. (*First Book of Discipline*, 96ff.; Knox, *Works*, ii, 148; iv, 177; *Spalding Club Miscellany*, iv, 94; *BUK*, i, 305.) Bucer's earlier recognition of the scriptural warranty for the three ministries of preacher, elder and deacon had been adopted and elaborated by Calvin, who observed that as 'three classes of ministers are set before us in scripture, so the early church distributed all its ministers into three orders. For from the order of presbyters, part were selected as pastors and teachers, while to the remainder was committed the censure of manners and discipline. To the deacon belonged the care of the poor and the dispensing of alms'. (Bucer, *Common Places*, 278; F. Wendel, *L'Église de Strasbourg, sa constitution et son organisation, 1532–1535* (Paris, 1942), 45, 50–51, 56, 75, 91; H. Strohl, 'La theorie et la pratique des quatres ministères à Strasbourg avant l'arrivée de Calvin', *Bulletin de la Société de l'Histoire du Protestantisme français*, lxxxiv (Paris, 1935), 123–140; Calvin, *Institutes*, IV, iv, 1.)

³² Christ is understood to govern the church through the preaching of the Word entrusted to the ministry as the chosen instrument for communicating his will. This recalls Erskine of Dun's discussion in 1571: 'In this kirk God regnnes. This kirk he governis, preserves and defendis . . . . To this kirk God hes geffin his eternal word. To this kirk he hes giffin the giftis of his Holie Spreit, and to this kirk hes he giffin the ministratioun of the hevinlie mistereis be the quhilk ministry he quickins the dede, regeneratis his elect, and nurisis his faythfull'. (*Spalding Club Miscellany*, iv, 93; *cf.*, Calvin, *Institutes*, IV, iii, 1–2.)

³³ This accords with those passages in the *Institutes* where Calvin had shown how God had revealed himself first by oracles and visions, and by the ministry of holy men; secondly by the promulgation of the Law (the Ten Commandments and doctrines declared by Moses) and the preaching of the prophets; and thirdly, through Christ who, though known only imperfectly to the Jews under the Law, was manifested under the Gospel. Yet 'as God alone can properly bear witness to his own words, so these words will not obtain full credit in the hearts of men,

6. And to tak away all occasioun of tyranny he will that thay sould reull with mutuall consent of brethrene and equalitie of power, every ane according to thair functionis.³⁴

7. In the New Testament and tyme of the Evangell, he hes usit the ministrie of the apostles, proheitis, evangelistis, pastouris and doctouris in administratioun of the word; the eldarschip for guid ordour and administratioun of discipline; the deaconschip to have the cure of the ecclesiasticall guidis.³⁵

8. Sum of thir ecclesiasticall functionis ar ordinar, and sum extraordinar or temporall.ˣ ³⁶

9. Thair beand thrie extraordinar functionis: the office of the apostle, of the evangelist, and the propheit, quhilk ar not

ˣ *temporarie* in GUL 1132, NLS Adv., and SRO

---

until they are sealed by the inward testimony of the Spirit. The same Spirit, therefore, who spoke by the mouth of the prophets, must penetrate our hearts, in order to convince us that they faithfully delivered the message with which they were divinely entrusted'. (*Institutes*, I, vi, 2; I, vii, 4; II, ix, 1.)

³⁴ The rejection, on scriptural grounds, of a permanent superiority in jurisdiction among ministers and an assertion of their equality had been voiced by Calvin, was repeated in the French and Belgic Confessions of Faith and in the Second Helvetic Confession to which article the Scottish church in 1566 assented, and was reasserted by Beza and English presbyterians. (Calvin, *Institutes*, IV, vi, 10; *Comm. Philip.*, I, 2; Cochrane, *Reformed Confessions*, 155, 212, 274; Knox, *Works*, vi, 544-50; Beza, *La Confession de foi*, V, xxix; *SHS Miscellany*, viii, 102-3; *Puritan Manifestoes*, 106-7, 109, 126; *Zürich Letters*, i, 280-1, 287, 292, 298-9; *The Seconde Parte of a Register*, ed. A. Peel (Cambridge, 1915), i, 207; Whitgift, *Works*, i, 148). In 1548, Bucer had claimed that 'true ministers of Christ . . . have received from the Lord the same spiritual power and authority to exercise the whole ministry of the church, including teaching, the sacraments, penitential discipline and aid to the poor' (Bucer, *Common Places*, 84). Bullinger also recognised that Christ had disallowed that 'any minister should seek any prerogative', that he 'commandeth an equality amongst them all', and that 'of old time an elder or minister and a bishop were of equal honour, power and dignity'. Thus 'men that are pastors of churches are all ministers, and all are equal'. (Bullinger, *Decades*, 87-88.) For earlier Scottish practice, see Introduction, 75ff.

³⁵ This closely follows Calvin's exposition. (*Institutes*, IV, iii, 4-9; *cf.*, Beza, *La Confession de foi*, V, xxiv, xxv, xxx, xxxiv.) Bullinger also distinguished the scriptural offices of apostles, prophets, evangelists, pastors, doctors, bishops or elders and deacons. (Bullinger, *Decades*, v, 105-8.) A similar statement is contained in the Second Helvetic Confession, composed by Bullinger, except for its omission of deacons. (Cochrane, *Reformed Confessions*, 270.)

³⁶ The distinction between temporary (or extraordinary) and permanent (or ordinary) offices had been emphasized by Calvin. (See notes 37 and 39 below.)

perpetuall and have now ceissit in the kirk of God except quhen he pleased*ʸ* extraordinarlie for ane tyme to steir up sum of thame agane.³⁷

10. Thair is four*ᶻ* ³⁸ ordinarie functionis or offices in the kirk of God: the office of the pasture, minister or bischop; the office of the docter; the presbiter or eldar; and the deacone.³⁹

ʸ it pleasit God in AUL, both GUL, NLS Adv., and SRO
ᶻ sum in GUL 1132

³⁷ Luther believed that 'apostles, evangelists and prophets must . . . remain, no matter what their name, to promote God's word and work'. (*Luther's Works*, vol. 41, 155.) Calvin regarded the offices of apostle and evangelist, who preached the gospel among nations, and prophet, who communicated the divine will, as temporary, and so as having ceased, except 'where religion has fallen into decay and evangelists are raised up in an extraordinary manner to restore the pure doctrine which has been lost'. (Calvin, *Comm. Corinth.*, i, 49, 414–5; *Comm. Ephes.*, 280; *Comm. Acts*, i, 69, 468; ii, 27–8, 270; *Institutes*, IV, iii, 4.) Bullinger also taught that 'the order of the apostles, evangelists and prophets was ordained at the beginning by the Lord unto his church for a time, according to the matter, persons and places. For many ages since, and immediately after the foundation of Christ's kingdom in earth, the apostles, evangelists and prophets ceased'. (Bullinger *Decades*, v, 109.) The latter view, also expressed in the Second Helvetic Confession, was affirmed by Beza, by Cartwright and English presbyterians, and by Erskine of Dun. (Cochrane, *Reformed Confessions*, 270; Beza, *La Confession de foi*, V, xxiv; Whitgift, *Works*, i, 471; *Puritan Manifestoes*, 97; *Spalding Club Miscellany*, iv, 94.)

³⁸ The four offices enumerated do not appear to conflict with the 'thriefald sort of officiaris' described in II. 3 above. The four functions are contained within three orders, since pastors and doctors alone exercised ministries of the Word. (See below, V. 1.) This feature is directly borrowed from Calvin. (*Institutes*, IV, iv, 1.)

³⁹ This is a classical exposition of the four permanent offices which Calvin detected in scripture. In function, the two ordinary offices for administering the Word, the pastor of a congregation, and the doctor or teacher, who interpreted scripture, were seen by Calvin as corresponding respectively to the extraordinary offices of apostle or evangelist, and prophet. (*Institutes* IV, iii, 5; IV, iv, 1.) The Reformation rediscovery of the elder as governor and the deacon as financial officer led to their adoption as distinctive offices within Calvinist churches. (See below, VI. 3–4, and VIII. 3.) On the identity of pastor and bishop, see below IV. 1 and n. 60. Bullinger also accepted this definition; he taught that Christ 'laid the foundation of the church, at the beginning, by apostles, evangelists and prophets; he enlarged and maintained the same by pastors and doctors. To these elders and deacons were helpers: the deacons in seeing to the poor; and the elders in doctrine, in discipline and in governing and sustaining other weightier affairs of the church'. (Bullinger, *Decades*, v, 108–9.) Bucer, with greater flexibility, discerned as 'the public ministers of the church, teachers, pastors, rulers, deacons (the stewards of the communal alms), and any others needed for ordering the life of the community of Christ'. (Bucer, *Common Places*, 239.) See also J. Courvoisier, *La Notion d'Église Chez Bucer* (Paris, 1933), 37ff., 141ff.; *CR*, XXXVIII, *Calvini Opera*, X, i, 15–23, 91–103.

11. Thir offices ar ordinarie and aucht to continew*a* perpetuallie in the kirk as necessarie for the government and policie of the same, and na ma offices aucht to be resavit or be sufferit in the trew kirk of God establischit according to his word.⁴⁰

12. Thairfore all the ambitious titles inventid in the kingdome of antichryst and in his usurpit hierarchie, quhilk ar not ane of thais four sortis, togiddir with the offices dependand thairupone, in ane word aucht*b* to be rejectid.⁴¹

a *indure* in NLS Wodrow
b *all utterlie* added in AUL, NLS Wodrow; *utterlie* added in NLS Adv.

⁴⁰ Whereas Lutherans found admissible that which did not contradict scripture, the Calvinist tendency, detectable here, was to admit only that expressly contained in scripture. Despite presbyterian plans to phase out the reader's office, which the reformers introduced on a temporary basis, readers remained, and later further appointments were made (*First Book of Discipline*, 105–7; *BUK*, ii, 455–7, 513).

⁴¹ The utilisation of the ancient benefice structure of the pre-reformation church in the interests of the reformed church meant that ministers on obtaining benefices also acquired the legal (though unscriptural) titles of vicar, parson, provost, dean, archbishop and so forth, which were now condemned. (See below XI. 2–3, 9.) The language used here is similar to that employed in the Negative Confession of Faith, which the king signed in January 1580/1, to condemn 'the usurped authoritie of that Roman Antichrist' and his 'wicked hierarchie'. (Calderwood, *History*, iii, 593–4.)

III

HOW THE PERSONIS THAT BEAR ECCLESIASTICALL FUNCTIONIS AR ADMITTIT TO THAIR OFFICES

1. Vocatioun or calling is commoun to all that sould bear office within the kirk quhilk is ane lawfull way be the quhilk qualifeit personis is promoitit to ane spirituall*c* office within the kirk of God.[42]

2. Without this lauchfull calling it was nevir lesum to ony persone to middle with ony functioun ecclesiasticall.[43]

3. Thair ar two sortis of calling, ane extraordinar be God*d* immediatlie, as wer the propheitis and apostles quhilk in kirkis establishid and weill alreddy reformit hes na place.[44]

4. The uther calling is ordinar quhilk, besyd the calling of God and inward testimony of guid conscience, hes*e* the lauchfull approbatioun and outward jugement of men according to Goddis word and ordour establischid in his kirk.[45]

5. Nane aucht to presume to entir in ony office ecclesiasticall without he have this guid testimony of conscience befoir God wha onlie knawis the hartis of men.[46]

c speciall in TCD
d himselfe added in both GUL and NLS Adv.
e is in both GUL, NLS Adv.; *of conscience is* in SRO

[42] See Calvin, *Institutes*, IV, iii, 10; Bullinger, *Decades*, v, 128; Travers, *A full and plaine declaration*, 17; *First Book of Discipline*, 96; Second Helvetic Confession, art. XVIII, in Cochrane, *Reformed Confessions*, 271.

[43] See Calvin, *Institutes*, IV, iii, 10; 'Ordonnances Ecclésiastiques', *CR*, XXXVIII, i, *Calvini Opera*, X, i, 17, 93; *The Thirty-Nine Articles of the Church of England*, ed. E. C. S. Gibson (London, 1902) art. XXIII; *A Directory of Church-government*, ed. P. Lorimer (London, 1872), Sig. A2–1v.

[44] See Calvin, *Institutes*, IV, iii, 13; *Comm. Acts*, cap. i, 23.

[45] See Calvin, *Institutes*, IV, iii, 11; Erskine of Dun, in *Spalding Club Miscellany*, iv, 98; Travers, *A full and plaine declaration*, 17.

[46] *Cf.*, Travers, *A full and plaine declaration*, 17. At their admission, candidates frequently attested their inward call by God to the ministry. (SRO, CH2/185/1. Haddington Presbytery Records, fos. 9r. 123v.; GCA, Glasgow Presbytery Records, 4 July 1597.)

III: PERSONIS THAT BEAR ECCLESIASTICALL FUNCTIONIS

6. This ordinarie and outward calling hes twa partis: electioun and ordinatioun.⁴⁷

7. Electioun is the chesing out of ane persone or personis maist able to the office that vaikis be the jugement of the eldarschip⁴⁸ and consent of the congregatioun quhom to the persone or personis beis appointit.*ᶠ* ⁴⁹

8. The qualiteis in generall requisit in all thame quha sould beir charge in the kirk consists in soundnes of religioun and godlines of lyf according as thay ar sufficientlie set furth in the word.⁵⁰

9. In the ordour of electioun,*ᵍ* it is to be eschewit that na persone be intrusit in ony of the offices of the kirk contrarie

---

ᶠ presentit and appointit in TCD
ᵍ in this ordinarie election in AUL, both GUL, SRO, TCD

⁴⁷ According to the first Book of Discipline, 'ordinarie vocation consisteth in election, examination and admission'. (*First Book of Discipline*, 96.) Walter Travers' *Ecclesiasticae disciplinae . . . explicatio* (1574) defined the parts of 'lawfull vocation . . . which especially are two' as 'election and ordinacion'. (Travers, *A full and plaine declaration*, 44.) *Cf.*, *Seconde Parte of a Register*, i, 167: 'This calling or vocation hath 2 partes, choosinge and ordeyninge.'

⁴⁸ For the meaning of 'eldership', see below VII. 22 and n. 117. In 1582, the general assembly assigned to 'particular presbyteries' the examination of candidates. (*BUK*, ii, 570.)

⁴⁹ The first Book of Discipline envisaged election by the congregation and examination by 'the ministers and elders of the church', though a later passage indicated admission with 'consent of the people and church' and omitted mention of election by the people. (*First Book of Discipline*, 96–7, 101). Walter Travers believed that 'election is the appointinge by the elders, the rest off the churche allowing it, of a fitt man', adjudged worthy after trial by the elders. (Travers, *A full and plaine declaration*, 44, 56.) On the question of whether 'a minister should be chosen by the whole church or only by colleagues and elders', Calvin favoured congregational consent, with the pastors presiding in examining and judging 'lest any error should be committed'. (*Institutes*, IV, iii, 15; *Comm. Acts*, i, 235). In Geneva, election was by the Company of Pastors, confirmed by the city's Small Council, and approved by the congregation. ('Ordonnances Ecclésiastiques', 1541, in *CR*, XXXVIII, i, *Calvini Opera*, X, i, 17–18, 22–23; R. M. Kingdon, *Geneva and the Consolidation of the French Protestant Movement, 1564–1572* (Geneva, 1967), 38.) For Beza, 'il ne faudra pas élire les pasteurs sans le consentement de toute l'église; mais ce sera aux anciens et au magistrat chrétien – si Dieu l'a donné tel – de conduire le tout par un bon moyen'. (Beza, *La Confession de foi*, V, xxxv.)

⁵⁰ *Cf.*, *First Book of Discipline*, 98; *Spalding Club Miscellany*, iv, 99; Cochrane, *Reformed Confessions*, 106, 271.

the will of the congregatioun to quhome thay ar appointit or without the voce of the elderschip.[51]

10. Nane aucht to be intrusat, or enterit[h] in the places alreddie plantit or in ony rowm that vaikis not for ony warldie respect; and that quhilk is callit the benefice aucht to be nothing els bot the stipend of the minister that is lauchfullie callit and electit.[52]

11. Ordinatioun[53] is the separatioun and sanctifeing of the persone appointit of God and his kirk eftir he be weill tryit and fund qualifeit.

12. The ceremonyis of ordinatioun ar fasting and eirnest prayer, and impositioun of handis of the elderschippe.[54]

[h] *placit* in AUL, both GUL, NLS Adv., SRO; *placeit in the ministrie* in TCD

[51] This accords with both Helvetic Confessions, with the Genevan 'Ordonnances Ecclésiastiques', the French and Belgic Confessions, the French 'Discipline Ecclésiastique' and the first Book of Discipline. (Cochrane, *Reformed Confessions*, 106, 155, 212, 271; *CR*, XXXVIII, i, *Calvini Opera*, X, i, 17; J. Quick, *Synodicon in Gallia Reformata*, (London, 1692), i, 3–4; *First Book of Discipline*, 99. See also *Spalding Club Miscellany*, iv, 95, 98–9; and below, VII. 22, XII. 13. For proceedings against alleged intrusions and irregular admissions, see *BUK*, i, 27, 44; ii, 509; *Synod of Lothian*, 5, 7, 15, 19, 102.)

[52] The criticism here seems to be the promotion of candidates to benefices irrespective of whether they served at the parish church to which the benefice belonged. (*Cf.*, *Spalding Club Miscellany*, iv, 95, 98–99; Calderwood, *History*, iii, 156–162.) Although a minister admitted to a parish might hope to secure the benefice attached, there was no guarantee that he would, for it might be possessed by another. Repeated claims to dissolve the benefice-structure and to reallocate ecclesiastical finances were not realised, and stipends continued to be derived from several sources. (See Introduction, 13ff.)

[53] Owing to its association with pre-reformation practice which the reformers repudiated, the term 'ordination' was replaced by 'inauguration', though by 1577 mention was made of the 'ordinars and inaugurers' of Patrick Adamson as archbishop of St Andrews. (D. Shaw, 'The Inauguration of Ministers in Scotland, 1560–1620', *RSCHS*, xvi, 35–62; *BUK*, i, 386.)

[54] The imposition of hands, replacing the mere 'taking by the hand' of 1561, had been approved by Bucer and Calvin, and was recommended in both Helvetic Confessions, in the French 'Discipline Ecclésiastique' and in Walter Travers' *Ecclesiasticae disciplinae . . . explicatio*. The Second Helvetic Confession envisaged ordination by the elders (*senioribus*), as did some English puritans, but both Calvin and the French 'Discipline' required ordination by ministers; and Erskine of Dun in 1571 understood admission to be by 'pastouris with admonitionis, fasting and prayers passing befoir'. (Knox, *Works*, ii, 149; Bucer, *Opera Latina*, xv: *De Regno Christi*, 69–70; Bucer, *Common Places*, 83, 270; Calvin, *Institutes*, IV, iii, 16; *Comm. Acts*, i, 238, 382, 503; ii, 27–29, 415–16; Travers, *A full and plaine*

III: PERSONIS THAT BEAR ECCLESIASTICALL FUNCTIONIS

13. All thir as thay must be rasit up be God and be him maid able for the wark quhairto thay ar callit, sa aucht they to knaw thair message to be limitat within Godis word without the boundis of the quhilk thay aucht not to pas.⁵⁵

14. All thir sould tak thais titles and namis onlie (least thay be exaltid and puft up in thame selfis) quhilk the Scripturis givis thame as thais quhilk import laubour, travell and work, and ar names of offices and service, and not of idlenes,^i dignitie nor warldlie honour or preheminence,^j quhilk be Chryst our Maister is expreslie reprovit and forbiddine.^k 56

15. All thais office-beraris sould have thair awin particular flokis amangis quhome thay exerce thair charge.⁵⁷

16. All sould mak residence⁵⁸ with thame and tak the inspectioun and ovirsycht of thame, every ane in his vocatioun.^l

17. And generallie thir twa thingis aucht thay all to respect: the

---

^i *idlenes* not in both GUL, and NLS Adv.
^j *dignitie, honour or worldlie preferment* in both GUL, and NLS Adv.
^k item 14 not in PRO   ^l *calling* in NLS Wodrow

---

declaration, 66; P. Schaff, *The Creeds of the Evangelical Protestant Churches*, 221, 280; Quick, *Synodicon*, i, 3; *Seconde Parte of a Register*, i, 87; *Puritan Manifestoes*, 97; *Spalding Club Miscellany*, iv, 100.) 'Eldership' here seems to be equated with 'presbytery'. (See below VII. 22; *cf.*, Whitgift, *Works*, i, 487; Bucer, *Common Places*, 270.) In 1581, there was evidently no 'universall ordour' established for ordinations, though the synod of Lothian included the imposition of hands in its requirements of 1589. (*BUK*, ii, 535–7; *cf.*, iii, 925–6; *Synod of Lothian*, 8–9.)

⁵⁵ The Genevan Confession of 1536 accorded to ministers 'no other power or authority but to conduct, rule and govern the people of God committed to them by the same Word ... without which they neither can nor ought to attempt anything'. (Cochrane, *Reformed Confessions*, 125–6.) Calvin had also shown how scripture 'limits the power which the Pastors of the Church should have and fixes its proper bounds – that they be ministers of the truth'. (Calvin, *Comm. Corinth.*, ii, 339; *Institutes*, IV, viii, 2.)

⁵⁶ See Knox, *Works*, ii, 147, 150; iv, 174; v, 519; Calvin, *Comm. Harm.*, ii, 274–6; Beza to Glamis, *SHS Miscellany*, viii, 102; *Puritan Manifestoes*, 106–7; *cf.*, *Zürich Letters*, i, 51; see also above, I. 13.

⁵⁷ Since the outward call was that of a particular congregation, office-bearers were ordained and admitted only when a specific vacancy occurred. (See below, IV. 2.)

⁵⁸ For action against non-residents, see *BUK*, i, 43, 181, 258, 331, 336, 351; *Synod of Lothian*, 19, 34–5, 37, 39, 41, 45, 49–50, 57, 62, 71–3.

glorie of God and edifeing of his kirk in dischargeing thair dewteis in thair calling.[59]

[59] Cf., *Seconde Parte of a Register*, i, 167: 'In which vocation these two thinges are requyred, to bee called to a certayne place, and to discharge fullye the office wherunto hee is appoynted.'

IV

OFF THE OFFICE-BERARIS IN PARTICULAR, AND FIRST OF THE PASTURIS AND MINISTERIS[m]

1. Pasturis, or bischopis, or ministeris, ar thay quha ar appointit to particular congregationis and kirkis quhilk thay reull be the word of God and ovir the quhilk thay wa[t]che in respect quhairof thay ar callit sumtymis pasturis becaus thay feid thair congregationis, sumtymis *episcopi*, or bischoppis, becaus thay wa[t]che above thair flokis, sumtyme ministeris be reasone of thair service and office, and sumtyme presbyteris and seniouris frome the gravitie in maneris quhilk thay aucht to have in taking cair of the spirituall government quhilk aucht to be moist deir unto thame.[60]

2. Thay that ar callit to the ministrie or that offer thame selfis thairunto aucht not to be electit without ane certane flok be assignit unto thame.[61]

3. Na man aucht to ingeir hime self or usurp this office without laufull calling.[62]

---

[m] *and our ministerie* in AUL

[60] The identity of the New Testament bishop and pastor had been made by many reformers including Calvin who illustrated how 'the name of *bishop* is common to all the ministers of the Word. . . . The titles . . . of *bishop* and *pastor* are synonymous'; 'there is no distinction between a presbyter and a bishop'. (Calvin, *Comm. Philipp.*, 23–4; *Institutes*, IV, iii, 8; *Comm. Tim.*, 75, 85; *Comm. Catholic Epistles*, 145, 293–4.) Calvin had also explained how 'the word Pastor means Elder not by age but by office', how bishops were simply 'persons who watch over the flock', and how 'according to the use of the Scripture bishops differ nothing from elders'. (*Comm. Tim.*, 75; *Comm. Acts*, ii, 255; *cf.*, i, 476.) See also *Luther's Works*, vol. 29, 16, 22–3; 'Ordonnances Ecclésiastiques', 1541, CR, XXXVIII, i, *Calvini Opera*, X, i, 17; Bullinger, *Decades*, v, 85; Beza, *La Confession de foi*, V, xxiv; *N. T. Annotations*, 384, 448; Beza to Glamis, SHS *Miscellany*, viii, 102; Travers, *A full and plaine declaration*, 27; *Puritan Manifestoes*, 126–7. All pastors or bishops, doctors and elders were termed 'presbyters' (see below, V. 1; VI. 2), though 'senior' was usually reserved for the 'lay elder' (see below, VI. 2–3). For Scottish practice, see Introduction, 88ff.; see also below, XI. 18 and n. 191.

[61] This agrees with the requirement of the French 'Discipline Ecclésiastique' of 1559 that 'no ministers shall be ordained without appointing them unto a particular flock'. (Quick, *Synodicon*, i, xix.) *Cf.*, Calvin, *Institutes*, IV, iii, 7; *Seconde Parte of a Register*, i, 167, 258; Whitgift, *Works*, i, 506. See also above, III. 15.

[62] 'Ingeir', *i.e.* 'intrude'. The Genevan 'Ordonnances Ecclésiastiques' of 1541

4. Thay quha ar anis callit be God and dewlie electid be man, eftir that thay have anis acceptid the charge of the ministrie, may not leave thair functionis.⁶³

5. The deserturis sould be admonisched and incaice of obstinacie finalie excommunicat.ⁿ ⁶⁴

6. Na pastour may leave his flok without licence⁰ of the provinciall or nationallᵖ assemblie,⁶⁵ quhilk gif he do eftir admoni[ti]oun not obeyit let the censuris of the kirkᵠ strik upone hime.

7. Unto the pasture appertenis teachingʳ of the word of God in seasone and out of seasone,⁶⁶ publicklie and privatlie, alwayis travelling to edifie and discharge his conscience as Goddis word prescryvis unto hime.ˢ

8. Unto the pasture onlie⁶⁷ appertenis the administratioun of

---

ⁿ item 5 not in both GUL, and NLS Adv. ⁰ *advyse* in NLS Wodrow
ᵖ *or nationall* not in AUL, both GUL, NLS, Adv., SRO, TCD
ᵠ *of the kirk* not in AUL ʳ *preaching* in TCD
ˢ item 7 not in NLS Wodrow and SRO

---

required that 'nul ne se doibt ingerer en cest office sans vocation' (*CR*, XXXVIII, i, *Calvini Opera*, X, i, 17); *cf.*, 'Celuy qui se seroit ingeré, encores qu'il fust approuvé de son peuple, ne pourra estre approuvé des ministres prochains ou autres . . . .' ('La Discipline Ecclésiastique', 1559, in [Beza], *Histoire Ecclésiastique des Églises Réformées au Royaume de France*, ed. G. Baum and E. Cunitz, 3 vols. (Paris, 1883–9), i, 217.) For discussion of this article, see above III. 9 and n. 51.

⁶³ The French 'Discipline', in 1559, stipulated that 'such as are once chosen unto the ministry of the Word must know that their call is during life'. (Quick, *Synodicon*, i, 4.) In 1565, the general assembly decreed that no minister could lawfully 'leave that heavinlie vocation and returne to the profane world for indigence or povertie', and in 1570 ministers at their inauguration were required to 'protest solemnlie that they sall never leave their vocation'. (*BUK*, i, 74, 176; *cf.*, 172–3.)

⁶⁴ See *BUK*, i, 63, 73, 176; ii, 421, 472; *Synod of Lothian*, 3.

⁶⁵ The first Book of Discipline had vested authority to translate a minister in 'the whole church or the most part thereof'; and subsequent acts of the general assembly specified the consent of the superintendent and synod (1562), the 'superintendent or haill kirk' (1564), 'superintendent' (1565), and 'the kirk' (1570). (*First Book of Discipline*, 103–4; *BUK*, i, 29, 50, 61, 173; *cf.*, Calvin, *Institutes*, IV, iii, 7; Quick, *Synodicon*, i, 4.)

⁶⁶ See *II Timothy* 4: 2: 'Preach the word; be instant in season, out of season; reprove, rebuke, exhort with all longsuffering and doctrine.'

⁶⁷ Doctors were prohibited from administering the sacraments (see below,

the sacramentis in lyk maner as the ministratioun of the word, for bacht [*recte*, baith] ar appointit be God as meanis to teache us, the ane be the ear, the uther be the eis and uther sensis, that be baith knawlege may be transferrit to the mynd.[68]

9. It appertenis be the same resone to the pasture to pray for the peple and namelie for the flok committit to his charge and to blis thame in the name of the Lord quha will not suffer the blissingis of his faythfull servand to be frustrat.[69]

10. He aucht also to watche above the maneris of his flok that the better he may apply the doctrene to thame in reprehending the dissolut personis and exhorting the godlie to continew in the fear of the Lord.[70]

11. It appertenis to the minister, efter laufull proceding be the elderschip, to pronunce the sentence of binding and lowsing upone ony persone according to the power of the keyis grantit unto the kirk.[*][71]

[*] items 11 and 12 transposed in SRO

V. 6); so too were readers in the 1560s, though in 1572 they were permitted to baptise, a decision reversed by 1576. (*First Book of Discipline*, 106; *BUK*, i, 82, 124, 211, 276, 372; ii, 438–9; *RStAKS*, i, 177–8.)

[68] The Scottish Book of Common Order explained how at communion services 'some place of the Scriptures is read, which doeth lively set foorth the death of Christ, to the intent that our eyes and senses may not onely be occupied in these outwarde signes of bread and wyne, which are called the visible word; but that our hearts and mindes also may be fully fixed in the contemplation of the Lord's death, which is by this holie Sacrament represented'. (Knox, *Works*, vi, 325.)

[69] *Cf.*, Knox, *Works*, vi, 298ff.

[70] *Cf.*, *First Book of Discipline*, 168ff; Calvin, *Institutes*, IV, iii, 6.

[71] See above I. 8 and n. 10; I. 16 and n. 19. By 'eldership', defined below as an assembly of pastors, doctors and elders (VII. 23), is understood the scriptural 'presbuterion'. The first Book of Discipline had recommended excommunication to proceed 'by the mouth of the minister and consent of the ministry and commandement of the kirk'; and in the 1560s the minister publicly pronounced the sentence of excommunication (or absolution) after judgment by the kirk session (*First Book of Discipline*, 170; *BUK*, i, 75; *RStAKS*, i, 203–5, 266–276; Knox, *Works*, vi, 449ff.). Yet, by the early 1570s the tendency to reserve this power to superintendents, bishops and commissioners caused comment in the assembly; by 1576 the assembly cautioned ministers not to excommunicate 'unadvisedly'. (*BUK*, i, 195, 284, 385.) For further details, see below, VII. 21 and n. 115.

12. It belangis alswa eftir lauchfull proceding in the mater be the elderschip to solempnizat the contract of*u* mariage betwix thame that ar joint thairin and to pronunce the blissing of the Lord on thame that entir in the holie band in the fear of the Lord.⁷²

13. And generallie, all publick denunciationis that ar to be maid in the kirk befoir the congregatioun concerning ecclesiasticall effairis belang to the office of the ministrie,*v* for he is as messinger and herauld betwene God and the people in thais effairis.⁷³

u the contract of not in AUL, both GUL, NLS Adv., SRO and TCD
v minister in the other MSS.

⁷² *Cf.*, Knox, *Works*, iv, 198–202; vi, 326–7. The kirk session, in practice, remained the court with ordinary jurisdiction over parties contracting marriage. (*RStAKS*, Index *sub* 'marriage'.) A disputed section on divorce was omitted from the final version (see Introduction, 48). In 1581, Stirling presbytery forbade all ministers from conducting marriage ceremonies without 'lycence from the elderschip'. (SRO, CH1/722/1. Stirling Presbytery Records, 22 Aug. 1581; *cf.*, 7 Nov. 1581.)

⁷³ *Cf.*, *First Book of Discipline*, 169, 171; 102, where the people are 'exhorted to reverence and honor their ministers, chosen as servants and embassadors of the Lord Jesus, obeying the commandments which they pronounce from God's mouth and book, even as they would obey God himselfe. For whosoever heareth Christis ministers, heareth himself and whosoever rejecteth and despiseth their ministerie and exhortation, rejecteth and despiseth Christ Jesus'.

V

OFF DOCTOURIS AND THAIR OFFICE, AND OF SCOLES

1. Ane of the twa ordinar and perpetuall functionis that travell in the word[74] is the office of the doctour quha may also be callit propheit, bischop, eldar, catechesar, that is, teacher of the cathechisme and rudimentis of religioun.[75]

2. His office is to oppine up the mynd of the Spirit of God within the Scripturis simplie without sic applicationis as the minister usis to the end that the faythfull be instructid, sound doctrene be teachit and the puritie of the Gospell not corruptid throw ignorance and evill opinionis.

3. He is different frome the pasture not onlie in name bot in diversitie of giftis,[76] for to the doctour is gevine the word[w] of knawledg to oppine up be simple teaching the mystereis of

[w] *gift* in NLS Wodrow and TCD

[74] See above, notes 37-39. In 1574, the general assembly recognised that 'in the ecclesiasticall functioun ther is two only distinct offices of teaching, the doctour that interpretes the scriptures, and the minister to preach and apply the same'. (*BUK*, i, 305.) *Cf.*, Calvin, *Institutes*, IV, iii, 4; Bullinger, *Decades*, v, 106; Travers, *A full and plaine declaration*, 158; *Puritan Manifestoes*, 98; *Seconde Parte of a Register*, i, 88.

[75] This follows the teaching of Calvin who had equated the duties of doctor and prophet as interpreters of scripture, had identified 'bishop' with 'all who discharge the ministry of the word', and had discussed Paul's designation of the elders at Ephesus as 'bishops'. (Calvin, *Institutes*, IV, iii, 5; *Comm. Acts*, i, 497-8; *cf.*, *Comm. Corinth.*, i, 415; *Comm. Ephes.*, 279.) Bullinger also commented on how scripture used 'bishop, 'elder' and 'doctor' as interchangeable terms. (Bullinger, *Decades*, v, 108.) The revival of the ancient custom of catechising had been recommended by Calvin amongst others; and the first Book of Discipline emphasized the need in rural parishes lacking schoolmasters for ministers (or for readers) to instruct the youth 'in the first rudiments and especially in the Catechisme, as we have it now translated in the booke of common order called the order of Geneva'. (Calvin, *Institutes*, IV, xix, 13; *First Book of Discipline*, 130-1). In identifying 'doctor' with 'bishop' and 'elder', and in indicating the similarity to 'prophet', Walter Travers described the doctor as 'teacher off the principles off religion', and defined the office as 'expounding the scriptures and cathechizinge off the ignorant'. The equation of 'doctor' and 'elder' was also made in 'A Second Admonition to the Parliament', 1572, where pastors and teachers 'are confounded in the name of elders'. (Travers, *A full and plaine declaration*, 139-141, 147, 155, 158-9; *Puritan Manifestoes*, 98, 125.)

[76] This distinction had been drawn by Calvin, Beza and the English presbyterians. For Beza, 'les docteurs doivent exposer simplement les Écritures pour en avoir

the fayth,⁷⁷ to the pasture the gift of wisdome to apply the same be exhortatioun to the maneris of the flok as occasioun cravit.

4. Under the name and office of ane doctour we comprehend also the ordour of scoles,⁷⁸ in collegis and universiteis quhilk hes bene frome tyme to tyme cairfullie*a* maintenit alsweill

---

a *lawfullie* in GUL 1132

---

le vrai sens . . . . Mais les pasteurs vont plus loin. Car, par des prédications, ils appliquent la doctrine aux nécessités de l'Église pour enseigner, pour reprendre, pour consoler et exhorter en public'. Similarly, Travers in 1574 believed that the doctor ought 'simply to teache oute of God his word', but 'without these vehement speeches wherby the mindes off men are either raised up and comforted or beaten downe and made sadd'; and the general assembly, also in 1574, resolved that 'in the ecclesiasticall functioun ther is two only distinct offices of teaching, the doctour that interpretes the scriptures, and the minister to preach and apply the same'. (Calvin, *Comm. Ephes.*, 279–80; *Institutes*, IV, iii, 4; Beza, *La Confession de foi*, V, xxvi; *Puritan Manifestoes*, 98; *Seconde Parte of a Register*, i, 165; Travers, *A full and plaine declaration*, 158; *BUK*, i, 305.) Bullinger's description of the doctoral office was not markedly dissimilar: 'Doctors or teachers have their names of teaching. Neither do I see what they differ from shepherds, but that they did only teach, and in the meanwhile were not burthened with the care that belongeth to the pastor: of which sort in a manner are the interpreters of scriptures, and governors of christian schools'. (Bullinger, *Decades*, v, 106.)

⁷⁷ The language here, and in V. 2 above, is reminiscent of the wording in the charter of *nova erectio*, embodying Andrew Melville's approach to education, which James VI granted to the university of Glasgow in 1577, where the task of the theology professor (in effect, the doctor) was 'to open up the mysteries of the faith' and so to 'unfold the hidden treasures of the word of God'. (See J. Durkan and J. Kirk, *The University of Glasgow, 1451–1577* (Glasgow, 1977), 285.)

⁷⁸ 'The order of the schools' ('l'Ordre des escoles') was the phrase used in the Genevan 'Ordonnances Ecclésiastiques' of 1541 and 1561 to describe the doctor's office, which included 'the lectureship in theology'; it also occurred in the 'Forme of Prayers'. (*CR*, XXXVIII, i, *Calvini Opera*, X, i, 21, 100; Knox, *Works*, iv, 177.) In Scotland, where school teachers serving under the principal master had long been styled 'doctors' (*cf.*, *Essays on the Scottish Reformation*, ed. D. McRoberts (Glasgow, 1962), 155–6), the general assembly in 1574 decided to appoint commissioners for the north 'to plant ministers, readers, elders and deacons, schoolmasters and others necessar and requisite for erecting of a perfect reformed kirk', and it urged that 'doctouris may be placit in universities'. (*BUK*, i, 305, 311.) Although schoolmasters were regarded as an essential element in a 'perfect reformed kirk', it might seem that here only teachers 'in collegis and universiteis' were to be recognised as doctors in the church. On the other hand, in subsequent sections schoolmasters were said to be 'comprehendit under the clergie' and doctors were 'to have the charge of scoles' in universities, colleges and 'uther places neidfull'. (See below IX. 9, and n. 153; XII. 5 and n. 206.) By 'collegis' is probably to be understood arts colleges or academies on the continental pattern, providing further education beyond the grammar schools, as envisaged in the first Book of Discipline. (*First Book of Discipline*, 131.) In practice, schoolteachers after 1581 sat as members of presbyteries. (See below, n. 153.)

amangis the Jewis[79] and Christianis as amang prophane nationis.

5. The doctour being ane eldar, as said is,[80] sould assist the pasture in the governament of the kirk and concurre with the uther eldaris, his brethrene, in all assembleis be resone of the interpretatioun of the word (quhilk is onlie juge in ecclesiasticall materis) is committit to his charge.[81]

6. Bot to preache unto the peple, to minister the sacraments and to celebrat mariagis pertenis not unto[y] the doctour, onles he be utherwayis ordourlie[z] callit,[a] howbeit the pasture may teache in the scoles, as he quha hes also the gift of knawledge oftintymis meit thairfoir,[82] as the examples of Policarpus[83] and utheris do testifie.

[y] *not onlie unto* in PRO   [z] *ordinarlie* in AUL, GUL 1132, and TCD
[a] *diverslie and utherwayis callit* in NLS Wodrow

---

[79] Calvin had identified the Jewish scribes who were 'teachers or interpreters of the Law in Hebrew usage', with 'public teachers of the Church'. (Calvin, *Comm. Harm.*, iii, 46–7.)

[80] See above, V. 1 and n. 75.

[81] The reason for the doctor's participation in church government is not just that he is an elder, but that he is the expert in interpreting scripture, for it is in the light of scriptural authority that all judgments must be given and all decisions taken, and therefore his presence is regarded as beneficial. Although Calvin had shown how doctors or 'teachers' preside not over discipline', the Genevan 'Ordonnances Ecclésiastiques' had recognised the doctor to be 'most closely associated with the government of the church'; and theology professors seem to have sat as members of the Venerable Company of Pastors in Geneva. (Calvin, *Institutes*, IV, iii, 4; *CR*, XXXVIII, i, *Calvini Opera*. X, i, 21, 100; R. W. Henderson, *The Teaching Office in the Reformed Tradition* (Philadelphia, 1962), 62, 66–68.) The French church in 1563 decided that 'professors of divinity may be admitted as members of consistories and deputed unto synods' (Quick, *Synodicon*, i, 32); English presbyterians assigned the doctor a seat on church courts (*Puritan Manifestoes*, 98; Travers, *A full and plaine declaration*, 159); and in Scotland, university teachers and schoolmasters are known to have sat as elders on kirk sessions from as early as 1561, on presbyteries as doctors from 1581, as well as on synods and general assemblies. (See Introduction, 86ff., and n. 153 below.)

[82] This point had been made by Calvin; and in 1560 the French church resolved that 'the doctor in a church may not baptize, nor administer the Lord's Supper, unless he be ordained a minister as well as a doctor at the same time'. (Calvin, *Comm. Ephes.*, 279–80; *Institutes*, IV, iii, 4; Quick, *Synodicon*, i, 15.) In 1580, and again in 1582, the general assembly found that in certain circumstances 'it is leisum for a minister for a season to superseid the ministrie and use the office of a doctour'. (*BUK*, ii, 469, 597.)

[83] Polycarp, a leading Christian figure in Roman Asia whose only extant

writing is his 'Epistle to the Philippians', was a disciple of the Apostle John and bishop at Smyrna in the earlier half of the second century. The specific reference here is to the Apostolic Fathers, *The Martyrdom of Polycarp*, xvi, 2 where he is described as 'an apostolic prophet, teacher, the Bishop of the Holy Church'. *Cf.*, F. L. Cross and E. A. Livingstone, *The Oxford Dictionary of the Christian Church* (2nd. edn., Oxford, 1974), 1107.

VI

OFF THE ELDARIS AND THAIR OFFICE

1. The word eldar[84] in the scripturis sumtyme is the name of aige, sumtyme of office.

2. Quhen it is the name of ane office, sumtyme it is takine lairgelie, comprehending alsweill the pastouris and doctouris, as thame quha ar commounlie[b] callit seniouris and eldaris.[c] [85]

3. In this our divisioun we call thais eldaris quhome the apostles callis[d] presendentis or governouris.[86]

[b] *commounlie* not in both GUL, SRO and TCD
[c] item 2 not in NLS Wodrow
[d] *titillis* in PRO; *apostlę calles* in SRO

---

[84] Confronted with this philological problem, Luther wrote: 'Earlier I mentioned that "elder" is ambiguous in the Greek. Does it mean one who is older or an official? I take it to mean one who is generally an older person, even though one may take it as a minister.' (*Luther's Works*, vol. 28, 350, cf., 332.) Adopting a different view, Calvin believed that by elders are designated 'pastors and all those who are appointed for the government of the church. But they called them presbyters or elders for honour's sake, not because they were all old in age, but because they were principally chosen from the aged, for old age for the most part has more prudence, gravity and experience'. (Calvin, *Comm. Catholic Epistles*, 143.)

[85] Calvin understood by elders 'generally all those who presided over the church; for pastors were not alone called presbyters or elders, but also those who were chosen from the people to be as it were censors to protect discipline'. (Calvin, *Comm. Catholic Epistles*, 356; *Comm. Tim.*, 138–9; *Comm. Isaiah*, ii, 187; *Comm. Acts*, ii, 27; *Comm. Corinth.*, i, 416–7; *Institutes*, IV, xi, 1.) The equation of 'doctor' and 'elder' had already been made by English presbyterians. (See above, n. 75.) The specific term 'senior', in preference to the generic 'presbyter' (which could denote both 'teaching' and 'ruling' elders), was often used to describe the so-called 'lay' elder, though in Scotland 'elder' remained customary. ('senior': *A Brief Discourse*, 39, 41, 43; *First Book of Discipline*, 174, 176; *RStAKS*, i, 29; *Puritan Manifestoes*, 15, 17; Whitgift, *Works*, iii, 156). In Glasgow from 1583 ministers in the district were elected to sit as 'elders' on the session – a practice unique in the extant records of the period. (SRO, CH2/550/1. Glasgow Kirk Session Records, fos. 2r., 20v., 52r., 80r., 100r., 119r., 137v., 158v., 181r.)

[86] *I Corinthians* 12:28, in its list of functions in the church, speaks of the gift of 'governments', which Calvin interpreted to refer to the 'elders who had the charge of discipline'. (Calvin, *Comm. Corinth.*, i, 416; cf., *Institutes*, IV, iii, 8); Beza also noted that 'Saint Paul les appelle quelquefois *gouverneurs*'; Bullinger understood by 'governors' those 'set in authority concerning discipline and other affairs of the church'; and the 'Second Admonition to the Parliament' regarded 'governors' and 'elders' as synonyms. (Beza, *La Confession de foi*, V, xxxii; Bullinger, *Decades*, v, 107; *Puritan Manifestoes*, 98.)

4. Thair office, as it is ordinary, swa is it perpetuall, and alwayis necessar in the kirk of God.[87]

5. The eldarschip is ane functioun spirituall, as is the ministrie.[88]

6. Eldaris anis lauchfullie callit to the office and having giftis of God meit to exercyse the same may not leave it agane.[89]

7. Albeit sic ane number of eldaris may be chosine in certane congregationis that ane part of thame may releif ane uther for ane resonable space, as was amang the Levittis undir the law in serving of the temple.[90]

[87] This agrees with Calvin who regarded the elder's office to be 'of perpetual duration' and 'necessary for all ages'. The Scottish reformers justified the office as an order which God 'hes now restoired unto us agane efter that the publict face of the kirk hes bene deformed by the tyrany of that Romane Antichrist'. (Calvin, *Institutes*, IV, iii, 8; Knox, *Works*, ii, 153.) See also above II. 10 and n. 39.

[88] The Genevan 'Forme of Prayers' grouped the elders 'with the rest of the ministers'; the English exiles at Frankfort had spoken of the elders' 'ministry or office'; the Scottish reformers recognised how God 'hes always usit the ministry of men, alswell in preiching of thy word, and administratioun of thy sacraments, as in gyding of thy flock, and provyding for the puir within the same'; and in St Andrews the elders and deacons in the 1560s were seen to form part of the 'ministerie'. (Knox, *Works*, iv, 176; *A Brief Discourse*, 186; Knox, *Works*, ii, 153; *RStAKS*, i, 77, 127, 196–7, 199, 205, 266.)

[89] In Geneva, election was annual; in France, as in England, elders were neither to hold 'their office for life' nor 'quit it without leave first obtained from the church'; and in Scotland, where elections to kirk sessions in the 1560s were for a term, usually annually (with substantially the same personnel re-elected), elders appointed to presbyteries in 1581 were elected for life, though elders on kirk sessions continued to be elected for a term. (Kingdon, *Geneva and the Consolidation of the French Protestant Movement*, 39; Quick, *Synodicon*, i, 5; *Directory of Church-government*, Sig. B2–1v.; *First Book of Discipline*, 175; SRO, CH2/722/1, Stirling Presbytery Records, 8 Aug., 22 Aug., 12 Sept. 1581; 16 Jan. 1581/2.)

[90] Though elected for life, elders were not expected to serve continuously. In 1597, the general assembly understood that elders 'are elected *ad vitam* except just causes of deprivatioun interveene. But becaus the kirk-living is so sacrilegeouslie spoyled which sould susteane them, they may not everie yeere leave their occupatiouns, and attend on that office. And, therefore, of a number lawfullie elected successivelie, some releeve other, yitt all abide kirk officers'. (Calderwood, *History*, v, 588.) See also Introduction, 88ff. Although *Deuteronomy* 18: 6ff., treats of occasional duties performed by Levites, here the term is used probably in the sense of 'the priests and Levites', as frequently occurs in the Old Testament and appears to allude to the priests' 'courses' outlined in *I Chronicles*, 24: 1–19, the operation of which is later illustrated in the case of Zechariah in *Luke*, 1: 23 where Zechariah's leaving the temple and returning home seems to imply release from duties until he was due on call again. I am grateful for conversations with Dr R. P. Gordon, Department of Hebrew and Semitic Languages, University of Glasgow.

8. The number of the eldaris in every congregatioun cane not be weill limitat, bot sould be according to the boundis and necessitie of the peple.

9. It is not necessar that all eldaris be also teachearis of the word, albeit thay aucht cheiflie to be sic and swa ar worthie of double honour.⁹¹

10. Quhat maner of personis thay aucht to be we refer to the expres word and, namelie, the canonis wryttine be the apostles.ᵉ ⁹²

11. Thair office is, als weill severallie as conjunctlie, to watche diligentlie upone the flok committit unto thair charge, bayth publicklie and privatlie, that no corruptioun of religioun or maneris enter thairin.⁹³

12. As the pastouris and doctouris sould be diligent in teacheing and sowing the seid of the word, ᶠso the eldaris should be cairfullᶠ in seiking the fruict of the same in the peple.

13. It appertenis to thame to assist the pastour in examinatioun of thame that cumis to the Lordis table⁹⁴ andᵍ in visiting the seik.⁹⁵

ᵉ *the apostle Paul* in AUL, both GUL, NLS Adv., SRO and TCD; *be Paul* in NLS Wodrow
ᶠ *so aucht thay to be faithfull* in NLS Wodrow
ᵍ *item* in AUL, both GUL, and NLS Adv.

⁹¹ This is a commentary on *I Timothy* 5:17, 'Let the elders that rule well be counted worthy of double honour especially they who labour in the word and doctrine'. *Cf.*, Calvin, *Comm. Tim.*, 138–9; *Institutes*, IV, xi, 1. By the 1640s, this scriptural reference caused much debate at the Westminster Assembly, and was discussed in G. Gillespie, *An Assertion of the Government of the Church of Scotland* (1848 edn.), 21–24.

⁹² This is a reference, not to the apostolic canons and constitutions attributed to Clemens Romanus, of which the reformers had not a particularly high estimation, but to the canons or regulations set out in the pastoral epistles. By the 'expres word and, namelie, the canonis' is to be understood the scriptures and, in particular, the canons written in the Pauline and other epistles.

⁹³ *Cf.*, *First Book of Discipline*, 175–6.

⁹⁴ *Cf.*, *First Book of Discipline*, 186; Travers, *A full and plaine declaration*, 156–7.

⁹⁵ See *The Buik of the Kirk of the Canagait*, ed. A. B. Calderwood (1961), 5, 26, 51; *Seconde Parte of a Register*, i, 166. In 1595, St Andrews kirk session ordered that 'the eldaris and deaconis tak triall of sic personis as ar seik'. (*RStAKS*, ii, 806.)

14. Thay sould be cairfull to*ʰ* caus the actis of the assembleis, alsweill particular as provinciall or*ⁱ* generall, to be put in executioun.*ʲ* ⁹⁶

15. Thay sould be diligent in admonisching of all mene ot thair dewteis according to the reull of the Evangell.

16. Thingis that thay cane not correct be privie admonisioun thay sould bring to the assembly of the*ᵏ* elderschip.⁹⁷

17. Thair principall office is to hauld assembleis with the pastouris and doctouris (quha ar also of thair numberis) for establisching of guid ordour and executioun of discipline, unto the quhilk assembleis all personis*ˡ* ar subject that remane within thair boundis.⁹⁸

ʰ be cairfull to not in AUL, both GUL, NLS Adv., SRO and TCD
ⁱ provinciall or not in both GUL, NLS Adv., SRO and TCD
ʲ in executioun carefullie in AUL, SRO and TCD; *and cairfullie* in both GUL, and NLS Adv.
ᵏ assembly of the not in TCD   *ˡ men* in NLS Wodrow

⁹⁶ See below VII. 19.

⁹⁷ The reference here is to the common understanding of *Matthew* 18:15, where private admonition is enjoined as the first step in discipline. This dominical passage was of great importance for all concerned with constitutional authority in the church from the conciliar writers onwards. (See Major in *Advocates of Reform*, ed. M. Spinka (London, 1953), 175–184; Calvin, *Comm. Harm.*, ii, 226ff.) *Cf.*, Stirling kirk session: 'the present assemblie thinks meit that everie eldar and diacun be appointed to oversie ane particular portion of the toun, quha salbe hauldin cheiflie to tak attendence to the maneris of the pepill thairin, that be his privie admonitionis and discipline of the eldarship, thay may be restrainit fra vice and maid obedient to the Word'. (SRO, CH2/1026/1 Stirling Kirk Session Records, 17 Nov. 1597.) See also, Beza, *La Confession de foi*, V, xxxii; Travers, *A full and plaine declaration*, 156. 'Eldership' was often used to denote 'kirk session' and 'presbytery' alike: see Introduction, 102ff.

⁹⁸ Apart from their rôle in kirk sessions, elders in the 1560s were liable to be elected to synods and were said to have been present in general assemblies. (*BUK*, i, 29; *SHS Miscellany*, viii, 105.)

VII

OF ELDARSCHIPIS, AND ASSEMBLEIS AND OF DISCIPLINE

1. Eldarschippis or assembleis*m* ar constitute commounlie of pasturis, doctouris and sic as commounlie we call eldaris that laubour not in the wo[r]d and doctrene, of quhome and quhais severall power hes bene spokine.

2. Assembleis ar of four sortis: for ather ar thay of particular kirkis and congregationis ane or ma, ather of ane province, ather of ane haill natioun, or of all and divers nationis professing ane Jesus Chryst.*n* 99

3. All the ecclesiasticall assembleis have power to convene lauchfullie togidder for treatting of thingis concerning the kirk and pertening to thair chargis.

4. Thay have power to apoint tymis and places to that effect, and ane assemblie to appoint the dyet, tyme and place for ane uther.100

5. In all assembleis, ane moderator sould be chosine be commoun consent of the haill brethrene convenit quha sould propone

m or assembleis not in TCD   *n* professing ane Jesus Chryst not in TCD

99 This graded series of courts or 'elderships' composed of pastors, doctors and elders became a distinctive feature of presbyterianism: the system operated in France, and had been advocated by Beza and by English presbyterians. In Scotland, there already existed kirk sessions, provincial synods and general assemblies, somewhat wider in composition; and the basic unit now postulated was the eldership drawn either from a single congregation or from several, followed by a provincial assembly, a national assembly and an international ecumenical assembly. An exact parallel is to be found in the English puritans' 'Second Admonition' of 1572 and in Walter Travers' *Disciplinae ecclesiasticae . . . explicatio* (1574). In 1576, Beza recommended to lord Glamis the need for three distinct assemblies – national provincial and local, – within a kingdom. (*Puritan Manifestoes*, 107, 109–110; Travers, *A full and plaine declaration*, 178; cf., *Seconde Parte of a Register*, i, 94; Whitgift, *Works*, i, 18; *SHS Miscellany*, viii, 106.) See also below, VII. 13–15, 27, 32, 40–41.

100 Until the 'Black Acts' of 1584, the church courts met and functioned without licence from the crown, a situation which led repeated governments to challenge the general assembly as an illegal convocation of the king's lieges. (Knox, *Works*, ii, 296–7, 395–7, 405–6, 479; *BUK*, i, 38–9, 292; Calderwood, *History*, iii, 306–7; Melville, *Diary*, 45, 61, 68, 209–210, 233.) See further, Introduction, 38–41, 139.

materis, gather the voitis and caus guid ordour be kepit in the assembleis.[101]

6. Diligence sould be tane cheiflie be the moderator that onlie ecclesiasticall thingis be handlit in the assemblie and no melling with ony thingis pertening to the civile jurisdictioun.[102]

7. Everie assemblie hes power to send furth frome thair awine

[101] The need for a moderator to preside at meetings of the exercise (for interpreting scripture) was recognised in 1560 by the Book of Discipline. The appointment of moderators of general assemblies, elected by common consent for the duration of each meeting, is recorded from 1563. Superintendents and commissioners of provinces are understood to have chaired synods from the 1560s; in 1576 the visitors, or commissioners of provinces appointed for a term by the general assembly, were expressly charged to act as moderators of synods; but by the 1580s the procedure in the general assembly was adopted for synods, and moderators were elected for the duration of the synod by plurality of votes; and in 1591 the synod of Lothian decided that the elective office of moderator should change from one presbytery to another. In presbyteries, from 1581 the moderator was elected to hold office on a half-yearly basis from one synod till the next. In kirk sessions, the minister presided; in general sessions with several ministers a moderator was elected for a term, and in Glasgow the presbytery eventually decided that in the session 'heirefter quarterlie everie ane of the said ministeris sall use the office of the moderator *per vices*'; and in sessions where the minister's absence was prolonged, it was not unknown for an elder to act as moderator. (*First Book of Discipline*, 189; cf., Knox, *Works*, iv, 179; *BUK*, i, 38, 52, 157, 243, 357; *Synod of Lothian*, 10, 16, 20, 23, 29; *BUK*, ii, 487, 567; SRO CH2/722/1. Stirling Presbytery Records, 8 Aug., 10 Oct. 1581; 15 May 1582; CH2/424/1. Dalkeith Presbytery Records, fo. 28r, 25 Oct. 1582; CH2/185/1 Haddington Presbytery Records, fo. 4v, 11 Oct. [1587]; CH2/121/1. Edinburgh Presbytery Records, 19 April 1586; cf., St Andrews Presbytery Records, 13 Oct. [1586], 15 April 1590; SRO CH2/550/1. Glasgow Kirk Session Records, 26 Oct. 1598; CH2/448/2. Aberdeen Kirk Session Records, 28 July 1605 (where the synod appointed the moderator of Aberdeen presbytery); *RStAKS*, ii, 823; GCA, Glasgow Presbytery Records, fos, 5r. 63v, 13 March 1592/3, 6 Jan. 1595/6; Ayr Kirk Session Records, fo. 120v, 21 March 1608.) The introduction of moderators agreed with the views of Calvin and Beza, and with the practice of the French church. (Calvin, *Institutes*, IV, iv, 2; Beza, *La Confession de foi*, V, xxix; *SHS Miscellany*, viii, 103, 106; cf., Cartwright in Whitgift, *Works*, ii, 271; *Directory of Church-government*, Sigs. A2-1v., C2r.) See further, Introduction, 115.

[102] The church courts were careful to exclude any cases not regarded as ecclesiastical: in 1560 the general assembly had remitted to parliament a petition on weights and measures; St Andrews kirk session referred civil cases to the magistrates; and in 1583 Stirling presbytery, on finding that Alva kirk session had dealt with criminal matters, admonished the minister 'not to suffer na thingis to be trettit in the said sessioun in tymis cuming bot ecclesiasticall causis'. (*BUK*, i, 5; *RStAKS*, i, 478, 482; SRO, CH2/722/1. Stirling Presbytery Records, 11 June 1583.) See also Beza's advice to lord Glamis (*SHS Miscellany*, viii, 103).

nomber ane or ma visitouris to sie how all thingis be reulit*º* in the boundis of thair jurisdictioun.[103]

8. Visitatioun of ma kirkis is na ordinar office ecclesiasticall in the persone of ane man, nather may the name of ane bischop be attributit to the visitour onlie, nather is it necessar to abyd alwyse in ane manis persone, bot it is the part of the eldarschip to send out qualifeit personis to visit *pro re nata*.[104]

9. The finall end of all assembleis is first to keip the religioun and doctrine in puritie without errour and corruptioun, nixt, to keip cumlines and guid ordour in the kirk.[105]

10. For the ordouris caus, thay may mak certane reulis and

º handlit in PRO

[103] From the 1560s, the power of oversight was recognised to be vested in the general assembly, to which all bishops, superintendents and ministers were subject, and in the subordinate courts, which might delegate authority to individuals, severally or conjointly. The assembly itself from the early 1560s had appointed ministers as commissioners to visit provinces and plant ministers. At no point since the Reformation had visitation been committed solely to either superintendents or bishops, and even with the creation of the Leith episcopacy in 1572, ministers possessing a commission from the assembly continued their work in the majority of dioceses. (See Introduction, 15, 31–2.)

[104] The general assembly's acceptance in 1575 of the identity in function of bishop and minister and its decision that some should 'have power to oversie and visite sick reasonable boundis ... as the General Kirk sall appoint' led to the assembly's appointment of ministers in 1576 to act for a term as visitors of provinces, and it was emphasized how 'the power stands not in the visiter but in the kirk'. At the same time, Beza advised lord Glamis that 'the churches may very well be visited at set times, without any great cost and bishoplike pride, by them whom every eldership hath chosen under the king's majesty's authority'. The assembly proceeded in 1578 to censure bishops 'that they impyre not above the particular elderschips but be subject to the same' and 'that they take no farder bounds of visitation nor the kirk committeth to them'. The visitor of a province, in turn, came under attack in 1580 when the assembly found it obnoxious 'that sick kynd of office sould stand in the person of ane man, quhilk sould flow from presbyteries'; and with the creation of presbyteries in 1581, the assembly resolved in 1582 that presbyteries had power to appoint for visitations 'two or ma, as the presbyterie sall direct, for the necessitie of the matter according to the Booke of Policie'. (*BUK*, i, 342–3, 357; ii, 425, 469, 568; *SHS Miscellany*, viii, 104.)

[105] The Scots Confession of Faith in 1560 had declared that the purpose of summoning a general council or 'generall assemblie' of the church in times past was 'partlie for confutatioun of heresyes, and for geving publict confessioun of thair faith to the posteritie following' and also 'for good policie and ordour to be constitut and observed in the kirk, in whiche ... it becumis all thingis to be done decentlie and into ordour'. (Knox, *Works*, ii, 113.) Similar statements were made by Knox, Bullinger and Beza. (Knox, *Works*, ii, 296; Bullinger, *Decades*, i, 12; *SHS Miscellany*, viii. 105–8.)

constitutionis[106] appertening to the guid behaviour of all the memberis of the kirk in thair vocatioun.

11. Thay have power also to abrogat and aboleisch all statutis and ordinancis concerning ecclesiasticall materis that ar found noysum[107] or unprofitable, or aggrie not with the tyme, or abusit be the peple.[108]

12. Thay have power to execut ecclesiasticall discipline and punischment upone all transgressouris and proud contempnaris of guid ordour and policie of the kirk, and sua the haill discipline is in thair handis.[109]

13. The first kynd and sort of assembleis, althocht thay be within particular congregatiounis, yit thay exerce the power, auctoritie and jurisdictioun of the kirk with mutuall[p] consent, and thairfoir beiris sumtyme the name of the kirk.[110]

[p] *continewall* in NLS Wodrow

[106] From 1560, the general assembly assumed legislative power for the church, and authority was vested in the subordinate courts to make enactments within their respective jurisdictions. In England, convocation had existed as an independent legislature until its virtual abeyance under the Tudors. The church's right to enact its own legislation had also been claimed by Calvin and Beza. (Calvin, *Institutes*, IV, viii, 1; *SHS Miscellany*, viii, 108.) See also below, VII. 20.

[107] *I.e.* harmful.

[108] This resembles the statement in the Confession of Faith disavowing that 'ane policie and ane ordour in *ceremonies* can be appointit for all aigis, tymes and plaicis; for as ceremonies (sick as men hes devised) ar but temporall, so may and aucht they to be changed, when they rather foster superstitioun, then that they edifie the kirk using the same'. (Knox, *Works*, ii, 113; my italics.) Beza had also informed lord Glamis that whereas 'the substance both of doctrine and ecclesiastical discipline abideth whole and unchangeable, yet must the outward circumstances of the order need be changed, for the same reason of the person and places abideth not always'. (*SHS Miscellany*, viii, 108.)

[109] This follows the tradition of Oecolampadius, Calvin and Beza, and was already practised in Scotland where the church courts and their delegates exercised full disciplinary powers in ecclesiastical matters. See above, I. 7-8, 14 and notes 9, 10, 17. Martin Bucer also believed that offenders 'in the church are to be kept in check by excommunication and every form of discipline, to be administered by faithful shepherds and teachers and by elders chosen from ordinary members of the church'. (Bucer, *Common Places*, 206.)

[110] The assembly or eldership 'within particular congregatiounis' envisaged here appears to correspond to the kirk session, with the exclusion of the deacons from that court; but see VII. 14 below, which qualifies this interpretation. As the local manifestation of the universal church, the eldership is understood to embody the authority of the church and to exercise it in name of the universal church.

14. Quhen we speik of eldaris of particular congregationis we mene not that every particular paroche kirk cane or may have thair awin particular eldarschip, especiall to landwart, bot we think thrie or four, ma or fewar, particular kirkis may have ane commoun eldarschip to thame all to judge thair ecclesiasticall causes.[111]

15. Albeit it is meit that sum of the eldaris be chosine out of everie[q] particular congregatioun to concur with the rest of thair brethrene in the commoun assemblie and to tak up the dilationis of offencis within thair awin kirkis and bring thame to the assemblie.[112]

16. This we gadder of the practise of the primitive kirk quhairas eldaris or colleges of seniouris wer constitute in citeis and famous places.[r] [113]

[q] *ilk* in NLS Wodrow   [r] *in famous citeis* in GUL 1132, and NLS Adv.

[111] Unless replaced by another agency, the elimination of individual overseers from ecclesiastical administration meant that kirk sessions would be subject only to the supervision and inspection of biannual synods and general assemblies. A distaste for congregational autonomy, which had its advocates in both France and England, together with an awareness of the need to solve the very practical problem of parishes, still without ministers or sessions, several of which were often grouped together under one minister (though each might possess a reader) led to the solution of 'commoun eldarschips', consisting of ministers, doctors and elders from several parishes. The first Book of Discipline had counselled that elders and deacons from small congregations should be 'joyned to the next adjacent kirks, for the plurality of kirks without ministers and order shall rather hurt then edifie'. In the larger burghs, a general session (composed of the ministers, elders and deacons of the various congregations in the town) already existed; and by the early 1570s the exercise, where ministers and elders gathered for interpreting scripture, began to assume administrative duties, which resulted in the assembly's decision in 1579 that 'the exercise may be judgit a presbyterie'. In practice, presbyteries came to have a dozen or even twenty constituent churches, considerably more than the 'thrie or four, ma or fewer' suggested here. (See Introduction, 102ff.)

[112] All this is consistent with Beza's advice to lord Glamis in 1576 that 'in every parish the pastor may have with him fit men to assist him, who also may, being watchful, salve up the offences not so weighty, leaving the other of greater importance to the whole eldership and that an eldership, made of the pastors of parishes, both of city and country, and a sufficient number of men approved for their godliness and wisdom, lawfully also chosen as is aforesaid, be placed in most fit places'. (*SHS Miscellany*, viii, 102–3.)

[113] Calvin regarded the eldership or presbytery of the early church to be 'ordained by the Spirit of Christ' and described it as the 'consistory of elders which was in the church what a council is in a city'. (*Institutes*, IV, xi, 6; IV, xii, 2; *Comm. Tim.*, 116.) Bullinger also explained how 'governors of cities are both

17. The power of thir particular eldarschippis is to gif diligent laubour in the boundis committid to thair charge that the kirkis be kepit in guid ordour to inquire diligentlie of nauchtie and unrewlie*[s]* personis and travell to bring thame in the way agane, ather be admonitioun or threitining of Goddis judgementis or be correctioun.

18. It pertenis to the eldarschip to tak heid that the word of God be puirlie preachit*[t]* within thair boundis, the sacramentis rychtlie ministrat,*[u]* the discipline*[v]* mentenid and the ecclesiasticall guidis uncorruptlie distribute.

19. It belangis to this kynd of assembleis to caus the ordinancis maid be the assembleis, provinciallis, nationallis*[w]* and generallis*[x]* to be keipit and put in executioun.

20. To mak constitutionis quhilk concerne τὸ πρέπον[114] in the kirk for the decent ordour of thais particular kirkis quher*[y]* thay governe (provyding thay alter na reulis*[z]* maid by the generall and provinciall assembleis and that thay mak the provinciall assembleis foirsene of the reulis that thay sall mak) and to abolesche thame*[a]* tending to the hurt of the same.

21. It hes power to excommunicat[115] the obstinat.[116]

[s] *ungodlie* in PRO   [t] *teichin* in NLS Wodrow   [u] *usit* in NLS Wodrow
[v] *richtlie* added in both GUL, and SRO
[w] *nationallis* not in both GUL, and NLS Adv.
[x] *maid be the generall assemblie provinciall or nationall* in NLS Wodrow
[y] *of the said paroche kirkis quhilk* in NLS Wodrow
[z] *na thing* in both GUL, and NLS Adv.   [a] *constitutionis* in PRO

---

called seniors and senators. And as commonweals have their senators, so hath the church her elders'. (*Decades*, v, 106.)

[114] τὸ πρέπον, i.e. what is seemly, what is fitting.

[115] Calvin and Beza had each emphasized how this power should be exercised neither by a single individual nor by the whole congregation but by the ecclesiastical senate of elders. In England, Travers agreed that excommunication 'is a sentence given by the assembly off the elders'; and likewise Cartwright who argued that this power, which Christ conferred on the church according to the practice of the Jewish synagogue, chiefly belonged to 'the presbytery or eldership'; but Richard Bancroft, though conceding that this power had been exercised only by 'presbiteries in the Apostles tyme', adopted the erastian argument that this jurisdiction had been since transferred to the magistrate. (Calvin, *Comm. Harm.*, ii, 229; *Institutes*, IV, xi, 1; Calvin, *Letters*, ed. J. Bonnet (Edinburgh, 1855-57),

VII: ELDARSCHIPIS, ASSEMBLEIS AND DISCIPLINE

22. The power of electioun of thame quha bearis ecclesiasticall chargis pertenis to this kynd of assemblie within thair awin boundis, being weill erectit and constitut of mony pastouris and eldaris of sufficient[b] habilitie.[117]

[b] *of good* in TCD

---

iii, 67; Beza, *La Confession de foi*, V, xliii; *SHS Miscellany*, viii, 110; Cartwright *A full and plaine declaration*, 116; Whitgift, *Works*, iii, 226, 229; *Tracts ascribed to Richard Bancroft*, ed. A. Peel (Cambridge, 1953), 111.) An erastian solution was rejected in Scotland where the church's right to excommunicate was recognised from 1560 (and explicitly recognised by statute law in 1573). Scottish practice was that a minister should proceed only after advice from the kirk session; in areas lacking ministers, the superintendents, commissioners or bishops assumed responsibility, and by the early 1570s their approval had also to be sought by ministers, which led the Regent Morton in 1576 to enquire whether power lay with ministers and kirk sessions or with bishops, superintendents and commissioners; no answer is recorded; but after 1581 presbyteries soon exercised ordinary, though not exclusive, jurisdiction in such matters: in 1597 the assembly informed the king that 'everie ecclesiasticall judgement, weill constituted, has power to excommunicat within their bounds; howbeit, in respect of the weightinesse of that censure, it is thought good that the sessions proceed not without advice of their presbyterie'. (See above IV, 11, n. 71; *APS*, iii, 71, 73, 82; *BUK*, i, 16, 98–9, 145, 178, 195, 272, 284, 358, 369; *RStAKS*, i, 311–13, 478; ii, 607; SRO, CH2/424/1. Dalkeith Presbytery Records, fo. 23v., 12 Aug. 1582; SRO, CH2/1026/1. Stirling Kirk Session Records, 16 Feb. 1597/8; SRO CH2/521/1. Perth Kirk Session Records, fos. 22r., 110v., 113v.–114r.; 11 May 1579; 11 April, 15 Aug. 1585; *Synod of Lothian*, Index, *sub* 'Excommunication'; *BUK*, ii, 564; Calderwood, *History*, v, 595.)

[116] In 1586 the general assembly adopted the phraseology used in items 17 to 21 above, and applied it to presbyteries. This section was later ratified by parliament in 1592. (*BUK*, ii, 665–6; iii, 808; *APS*, iii, 541.)

[117] The election of office-bearers (ministers, doctors, elders and deacons) for congregations was vested in the eldership or presbytery, but only in such as contained 'mony pastouris and eldaris', which plainly excluded those 'particular elderships' of single congregations recognised in VII. 14 above. Previously, ministers were elected with consent of the congregation and inaugurated after examination by the superintendent, commissioner, bishop or visitor; elders and deacons were (and continued to be) elected from the congregation with the approval of the kirk session and consent of the people; and after 1581 elders were also elected to presbyteries (see above, n. 89), which gradually became the recognised court for supervising the examination and election of ministers. On 4 December 1582, two bailies and kirk session elders of Stirling together with two presbytery elders informed Stirling presbytery that the parishoners had elected a new minister 'according to the powar gevin to thame be ane act of the generall assemblie'; but in 1587 the presbytery attacked the presumption of St Ninians kirk session in proceeding to elect a minister as 'plaine repugnant to God's Word and gude ordur', since 'the admissione of all ministeris is onlie in the handis of the presbyteriis and utheris assembleis of ministeris'. (SRO, CH2/722/1. Stirling Presbytery Records, 31 July 1582, 22 Aug. 1587.)

23. Be eldarschip[118] is meint sic as ar constitut of pastouris, doctouris and sic as now ar callit eldaris.[c]

24. Be the lyk resone, thair depositioun also pertenis to this kynd of assembleis as of thame that teache errone[o]us and corrupt doctrene, that be of sclanderous lyfe and eftir admonitioun desist not, that be gevine to sesme [*recte*, schism] or rebellioun contrare the kirk, manifest blasphemy, simony and all corruptioun of brybis, falset, perjurie, huredome, thift, drunkinnes, fechting, worthie of punischment be the law, usurie, dansing,[d] infamie and[e] all utheris deserves separatioun frome the kirk.[119]

25. These also quha ar fund altogiddir insufficient to exerce[f] thair chargis[g] sould be deposit[120] quhairof uther kirkis wald be advertesit that thay resave not personis deposit.

26. Albeit thay aucht not to be deposit quha throw aige, seiknes or uther accidentis becum unmeit to do thair office, in quhilk cace thair honour sould remane unto thame, thair kirkis sould intertene[h] thame and utheris aucht to be provydit to do thair office.[i] [121]

[c] item 23 not in AUL, both GUL, NLS Adv. and Wodrow, SRO and TCD
[d] *and sic desolutioun, crymes that import civile* deleted in the Haddington MS.
[e] *and sic disholutioun, crymes that importe civill infamie and all utheris that deserva separatioun from the kirk* in PRO
[f] *execut* in NLS Wodrow and SRO
[g] *wha ar unabill altogether to execut thair charge* in TCD
[h] *mentene* in AUL, both GUL, NLS Adv., and Wodrow, SRO and TCD
[i] At item 26, the Haddington MS. contains the following annotation (see plate):
'I Tim. 5: 17 "the eldars that rule wel are worthie of double honour specialie

[118] In 1584, it was affirmed that 'under this name PRESBYTERIE we understand the pastors, doctors, and these who are properlie called elders, ἡγούμενοι, προϊστάμενοι, guiders, leaders, whose office is to rule the Kirk of God'. (Calderwood, *History*, iv, 57.)

[119] *Cf.*, Calderwood, *History*, iv, 56; *BUK*, ii, 666.

[120] See, for example, Stirling presbytery's deposition of James Dalmahoy from the ministry in 1582. (SRO, CH2/722/1. Stirling Presbytery Records, 31 July 1582.)

[121] *Cf., ibid.*, 27 Sept. 1586, where Henry Laing was recommended to Stirling presbytery as coadjutor to Patrick Gillespie, minister at St Ninians, who because of 'grit seiknes and infirmitie' was 'inablle to use and exerceis his offeice'. In 1598, Canongate 'kirk and counsall' petitioned Edinburgh presbytery for the admission of Henry Blyth as 'fellow labourir' with John Brand, 'thair adgit pastor'. (SRO, CH2/121/2. Edinburgh Presbytery Records, 14 Feb. 1597/8.)

27. Provinciall assembleis we call lauchfull conventionis of the pastouris, doctouris and eldaris*j* of the*k* province [122] gadderit for the commoun effairis of the kirkis thairof, quhilk also may be callit the conference[123] of kirkis and brethrene.

28. Thir assembleis ar institut for wechtie materis necessar to be intraitit be mutuall consent and assistance of the brethrene within the provincis as neid requiris.*l*

29. This assemble hais power to handle, ordour and redres all thingis omittit*m* or done amis in the particular assembleis.

---

they who labour in the word and doctrine". "διπλῆς τιμῆς de quibus magis etiam quam de reliquis sumus soliciti. Honoris [enim] appelatione [iam dixi] pium omne officium ac subsidium, Hebraeorum more, significari: et numerus certus pro incerto positus est, ut minime [opus] sit quicquam hic subtilius inquirere". Beza, [*N. T. Annotations*, 459]. Vide Marlor[at], [*Novi Testamenti Catholica Expositio Ecclesiastica*, 914]. "Hoc de victu et reverentia vulgo exponunt. [Probabilius autem videtur hic fieri comparationem inter viduas et presbyteros. Prius jusserat Paulus honorem habere viduis: atqui honore sunt digniores presbyteri quam illae. Quare his duplex honor earum respectu exhibendus.] Æquum enim est ut rebus quae hominum vitae necessariae sunt, abundent, ne harum cura distracti praedicandi munus omittant. Hic quorundam tenacitas et illiberalitas (imo vero malignitas erga Christi servos) carpenda est, qui tenuissimum etiam et utcunque obaesum et gracile stipendium perpetuo invident, cum tamen Paulus duplicem id est, copiosum honorem illis prestandum doceat".' (I am indebted to Dr J. Durkan for help in elucidating this text. Material in square brackets omitted in the annotation is derived from the printed sources.)

j and uthers eldaris in the other MSS.
k ane in the other MSS.
l within that province if neid beis in TCD
m committit in SRO and TCD; *omittit or* not in NLS Wodrow

[122] The envisaged inclusion of elders in synods was no new development. In 1562, it was expected that 'the minister with ane elder or deacon' from each church should attend synods; and this was endorsed by Beza in 1576. (*BUK*, i, 29; *SHS Miscellany*, viii, 106.) Yet, there is little evidence of deacons attending synods, and the intention here is that they should be excluded. For a survey of the evidence, see Introduction, 114ff.

[123] The English classis, which corresponded to the Scottish presbytery, was also known as the 'conference'; and the 'Second Admonition' in 1572 had defined the provincial synod as 'the meeting of certaine of the consistorie of every parishe within a province which is of manye conferences'. (*Puritan Manifestoes*, 109; *Directory of Church-government*, Sig. C2-v.) In Scotland, the meeting of the presbytery was sometimes spoken of as the 'place' or 'house of conference' (NLS, Adv. MS. 6.1.13, fo. 39r.-v.; SRO, CH2/424/1. Dalkeith Presbytery Records, fo. 94v, 13 Feb. 1583/4); and there is mention of the 'brether of the conference' of a synod in 1591 (*Synod of Lothian*, 32).

30. It haith power to depose the office-beraris of that province for guid and just caus deserving deprivatioun.[124]

31. And generallie thir assembleis have the haill power of the particular elderschippis quhairof thay ar collectid.[125]

32. The nationall assemblie (quhilk is generall to us)[126] is ane lauchfull conventioun of the kirkis of the haill realme or nation quhair it is usit and gadderit for the commoun effairis of the kirk and may be callit the generall eldership[127] of the haill kirkis within the realme.

33. Nane ar subject to repair to this assemblie to voit bot ecclesiasticall personis to sic ane number as salbe thocht guid be the same assemblie, not excluding uther personis that will repair to the said assemblie to propone, heir and resone.[128]

34. This assemblie is institute that all thingis aythir omittit[n] or done amis in provinciall assembleis may be redrist and handlit,[129] and thingis generallie serving for the weill of the haill body of the kirk in that realme may be foirsene, intreattid and set furth to Goddis glorie.

[n] *committit* in NLS Adv., SRO and TCD

[124] See *Synod of Lothian*, Index *sub* 'Ministers, deposition of'.

[125] This section (items 28 to 31 above), which answers the Regent Morton's query in 1576 on the synod's jurisdiction, was repeated *verbatim* in the assembly's definition of 1586 (where 'particular eldership' was equated with 'presbytery') and was incorporated in the act of parliament of 1592. (*BUK*, i, 369; ii, 665; iii, 808; *APS*, iii, 542.)

[126] The use of 'national assembly' to denote the general assembly was an attempt to distinguish this court from the international 'generall assemblie or generall counsall of the haill kirk of God' discussed in VII. 40-41 below.

[127] This looks like an attempt to reconcile the existence of the assembly (and other church courts) with the scriptural 'presbyterium', which the Geneva bible translated as 'eldership'.

[128] In 1586, the general assembly 'found that all such as the scripture appointeth governours of the kirk of God, as namelie, pastours, doctours and elders may conveine to generall assemblies and vote in ecclesiasticall matters; and all uthers that hes any sute or uther things to propone to the assemblie may be ther present and give in thair sutes and propone things profitable to the kirk and heir reasoning but sall not vote'. (*BUK*, ii, 650.) For a discussion of the assembly's composition, see Introduction, 116ff.

[129] In 1593, the assembly resolved that 'in tyme cuming to everie generall assemblie the buiks of the synodall assembleis salbe direct be the synodollis to be sychtit and considderit in the generall assemblie'. (*BUK*, iii, 815.)

35. It sould tak cair that kirkis be planted⁰ in places quhair thay ar not planted.¹³⁰

36. It sould prescryve the reull how the uther twa kynd of assembleis sould proceid in all thingis.¹³¹

37. This assemblie sould tak heid that the spirituall jurisdictioun and civile be not confoundit to the hurt of the kirk.¹³²

38. That the patrimony of the kirk be not diminishid*ᵖ* nor abusid.*ᵍ* ¹³³

39. And generallie concerning all*ʳ* wychtie effairis that concerne the weill and guid ordour of the haill kirk*ˢ* of the realme it aucht to interpone auctoritie thairto.¹³⁴

40. Thair is besydis this an uther mair generall*ᵗ* kynd of assemblie quhilk is of all nationis or of all estaitis of personis within the kirk representing the universall kirk of Chryst quhilk may be callit properlie the generall assemblie or generall counsall¹³⁵ of the haill kirk of God.¹³⁶

41. Thais assembleis war appointit and callit*ᵘ* togidder speciallie quhene an greit sisme [*recte*, schism] or controversie in

---

⁰ *placit* in NLS Wodrow   *ᵖ not confoundit* in AUL, both GUL, and TCD
ᵍ not abused nor confounded in SRO   *ʳ uther* added in both GUL
ˢ the kirk universall in PRO; *of the kirk* in SRO
ᵗ uther maner and generall in NLS Wodrow   *ᵘ and gatherit* in NLS Wodrow

¹³⁰ See *BUK*, i, 34, 338; ii, 708, 714; iii, 848–51, 982, 997, 1025–6, 1061.
¹³¹ *Ibid.*, ii, 665.   ¹³² *Ibid.*, i, 140, 146, 267; ii, 540, 600–1, 782; iii, 853.
¹³³ *Ibid.*, i, 7, 107, 164, 253, 360; ii, 417, 455, 457, 513, 601–3, 776.
¹³⁴ *Cf.*, Beza to Glamis, *SHS Miscellany*, viii, 107.
¹³⁵ Both Beza's Confession and the Scots Confession of Faith used 'general assembly' as a synonym for a general or universal council. (Beza, *La Confession de foi*, V, xi; Knox, *Works*, ii, 113.)
¹³⁶ Despite the apparent fragmentation of the universal church as a visible institution, the Scottish church did not lose sight of the church as a catholic institution; and presbyterianism, with its strongly international emphasis, championed the vision of an ecumenical general council. (See above VII. 2, n. 99.) This firm bond with the 'best reformed churches' was implicit in Edinburgh presbytery's support in 1587 for the exiled French church in England as 'memberis of the sam body quhairof we ar'. (SRO, CH2/121/1. Edinburgh Presbytery Records, 26 Sept. 1587).

doctrene did aryse in the kirk and war convocat at command of the godlie emperouris being for the tyme for the avoiding of sismis [*recte*, schisms] within the universall kirk of *God, quhilkis becaus thay pertene not to the particular estait of ane* realme we ceis forder to spek.[137]

* phrase missing in both GUL, and NLS Adv.; *the* added in these MSS.

[137] See Beza, *La Confession de foi*, V, x-xi; *A Brief and Pithy Sum*, 92ff. In 1552, Archbishop Cranmer had proposed convening an international council of reformed churches, since 'nothing tends more injuriously to the separation of the churches than heresies and disputes respecting the doctrines of religion'; and Calvin, in replying, agreed that 'grave and learned men from the principal churches might meet together at a place appointed and, after diligent consideration of each article of the faith, hand down to posterity a definite form of doctrine according to their united opinion'. (Cranmer, *Works*, ii, 431-33.) For many reformers, including presbyterians, the idea for an international meeting sprang from the example of the general councils in the early church which met at Nicaea, Constantinople, Ephesus and Calcedon 'for keeping the soundness of faith, the unity of doctrine and the discipline and peace of the churches'. (Bullinger *Decades*, i, 12ff.; Beza, *La Confession de foi*, V, xi-xv.)

VIII

OFF DEACONIS AND THAIR OFFICE, THE LAST ORDINAR FUNCTIOUN OF THE KIRK

1. The word διάκονος sumtymis is lairglie takine comprehending all thame that beir office in the ministrie and spirituall[w] functioun in the kirk.[138]

2. Bot, now as we speik, it is tane onlie for thame to quhom the collectioun and distributioun of the almous of the faithfull and ecclesiasticall guidis does appertene.[x] [139]

3. The office of the deacone sa takine is ane ordinar and perpetuall ecclesiasticall functioun in the kirk of Chryst.[140]

4. Off quhat properties and dewteis he aucht to be that is callit to this functioun we remit to the manifest Scripturs.

5. The deacone aucht to be callit and electit as the rest of the spirituall officiaris of the quhilk electioun wes spokine befoir.[141]

6. Thair office and power is to ressave and distribut the haill ecclesiasticall guidis unto thame to quhome thay ar appointit.[142]

[w] *speciall* in both GUL
[x] *belong* in both GUL, NLS Adv., and Wodrow, PRO, SRO and TCD

[138] Luther in his lectures on *Timothy* observed that 'deacons were men who also preached occasionally ... although their principal responsibility was to care for the poor and the widows. That custom has long ceased to exist.... There ought to be deacons for the church ...' (*Luther's Works*, vol. 28, 295). Bucer believed that 'the early churches assigned them a rank near to that of the presbyterial dignity and admitted them to a part in the sacred ministry of both teaching and the sacraments'; and Calvin commented how 'the word itself is indeed general, yet it is properly taken for those which are stewards of the poor'. (Bucer, *Opera Latina*, xv: *De Regno Christi*, 145; Calvin, *Comm. Acts*, i, 234; *Institutes*, IV, iii, 8–9; *Comm. Philip.*, 24; see also Beza, *La Confession de foi*, V, xxx.)

[139] This agrees with earlier Scottish reformed practice, and with the teaching of Calvin who affirmed that 'although the term διακονία has a more extensive meaning, scripture specially gives the name of deacons to those whom the church appoints to dispense alms, and take care of the poor, constituting them as it were stewards of the public treasury of the poor'. (*Institutes*, IV, iii, 9.)

[140] This follows Calvin, who taught that the deacon's office was 'of perpetual duration' and 'necessary for all ages'. (*Institutes*, IV, iii, 8).

[141] See above III. 1–17.

[142] Calvinist churches on the continent and puritans in England all recognised the deacon's duties in distributing alms for the poor and caring for the sick

7. This thay aucht to do according to the juigment and appointment of the presbytereis or elderschippis[143] (of the quhilk the deaconis ar not)[144] that the patrimony of the kirk and pure be not convertid in privat mennis use nor wranguslie distributit.[y]

[y] *Deaconis are not of the presbitrie or sessione* added as marginal annotation in NLS Adv.

(CR, XXXVIII, i, *Calvini Opera*, X, i, 23–5, 101–3; *Discipline or Book of Order of the Reformed Churches of France*, ed. M. G. Campbell (London, 1924), 13–15; *Puritan Manifestoes*, 15, 122; Whitgift, *Works*, iii, 61; Knox, *Works*, iv, 176.) From the outset, the Scottish reformers envisaged a very comprehensive rôle for the diaconate in collecting and distributing the whole revenues of the church for support of the ministry, the schools and the poor. (*First Book of Discipline*, 158–9, 163, 178–9.) This approach, reiterated here, had the support of Calvin and Beza (Calvin, *Institutes* IV, iv, 6; Beza, *La Confession de foi*, V, xxx; *cf.*, Travers, *A full and plaine declaration*, 154), but there is little indication of any sustained attempt by deacons to fulfil this wider rôle (yet see *RStAKS*, i, 138): their primary function remained the administration of poor-relief. (*Cf.*, Bucer, *Opera Latina*, xv: *De Regno Christi*, 143ff.) See also *Service in Christ*, ed. J. I. McCord and T. H. L. Parker (London, 1966), 80–135.

[143] According to the first Book of Discipline, the deacons were to discharge their office 'as by the ministers and kirk shall be appointed'; the 'Forme of Prayers' had prescribed 'the consent of the ministers and elders'; the English 'Second Admonition' of 1572 placed the deacons under the supervision of the consistory; and Walter Travers understood that the deacons 'ought to be subiecte' to the pastors, doctors and elders. (*First Book of Discipline*, 178; Knox, *Works*, iv, 176; *Puritan Manifestoes*, 120–22; Travers, *A full and plaine declaration*, 27.) With the creation of presbyteries, kirk sessions continued to supervise the deacons' activities, and presbyteries usually intervened only at visitations.

[144] In the belief that scripture assigned the government of the church to elders, deacons were now to be excluded from 'elderships' in particular and church courts generally. The Genevan consistory consisted only of pastors and elders and this practice was also observed by the English exiles in Geneva; but in France, and in the Dutch church until at least 1574, deacons were permitted a place on church courts, and in 1576 Beza approved the deacons' participation in the courts of the Scottish church, where deacons from 1560 had been allowed to 'assist in judgement with the ministers and elders'. (R. M. Kingdon, *Geneva and the Consolidation of the French Protestant Movement, 1564–1572* (Geneva, 1967), 41; Knox, *Works*, iv, 178; E. G. Léonard, *A History of Protestantism*, ii (1967), 83 and n. 2; Quick, *Synodicon*, i, 2; *SHS Miscellany*, viii, 106; *First Book of Discipline*, 178–79.) Yet practice may not have been uniform: initially, in St Andrews kirk session disciplinary cases were judged by the minister and elders, and only occasionally is the deacons' participation recorded, but by the mid-1560s their inclusion becomes more regular. (*RStAKS*, i, *passim*.) Their attendance at synods and assemblies is hard to document, though, in Elgin as late as 1580, mention was made of the 'ordinances of the synodal assemblies made and statute by the ministers, elders and deacons of this realm in tymes bypast'. (*The Records of Elgin*, i, 155.) No place, however, was accorded to deacons on presbyteries after their creation in 1581. See also Introduction, 97ff.

IX

OFF THE PATRIMONY OF THE KIRK AND DISTRIBUTIOUN THAIROF

1. Be the patrimony of the kirk we mene quhatsumevir thing hath bene at ony tyme befoir, or salbe in tyme cuming, gevin or be consent and universall custome of cuntreis professing Christiane religioun*z* applyit to the publick use and utilitie of the kirk.

2. Swa that onder this patrimony we comprehend first all thingis gevin, or to be gevin, to the kirk and service of God, as landis, bigginis, possessionis, annuall rentis and all sicklyk quhairwith the kirk is doitit ather be donationis, fundationis, mortificationis, or ony uther lauchfull title of kingis, princes or ony personis*a* inferiour to thame, togiddir*b* with the continewall*c* oblationis of the faythfull.

3. We comprehend*d* also all sic thingis as be lawis and custome and use of countreis hes bene applyit to the use and utilitie of the kirk of quhilk sort ar the teindis, mans, glebis and siclyk, quhilk be commoun and be municipall lawis and universall custom ar possessit be the kirk.[145]

4. To tak ony of this patrimony be onlawfull meanis and convert to the particular and prophane use of ony persone we hald it ane detestable sacralege befor God.[146]

z *the true religioun* in both GUL   *a* *ony utheris* in NLS Wodrow and SRO
b *togiddir* not in NLS Adv.   *c* *continuall* not in both GUL, and NLS Adv.
d *apprehend* in both GUL

[145] This comprehensive claim (in items 1–3 above) to the whole goods of the church – consisting of the temporality (*i.e.* lands and their rents), the spirituality (primarily the teinds or tithes, but also including manses and glebes) and, thirdly, the offerings, oblations or obventions of the faithful – surpassed even that of the first Book of Discipline, which had not advanced any claim to the monastic temporalities; and it constituted yet another attempt to check the alienation of church property, which still continued to be secularised after the Reformation despite the protests of the general assembly. (*First Book of Discipline*, 156–64; *BUK*, i, 107–8, 199, 253, 360.)

[146] Bucer had claimed that the goods of the church were 'sacred and not to be converted to other uses, so that whoever deals with them in any other way should be held guilty of sacrilege, under penalty of anathema'. (*Opera Latina*, xv: De

5. The guidis ecclesiasticall aucht to be collectit and distributit be deaconis as the word of God appointis that thay quha beiris office in the kirk be provydit for, without cair and solicitud.[147]

6. In the apostolicall kirk, the deaconis war appointit to collect and distribut quhatsumevir thingis[e] war collectid of the faythfull to be distribut unto the necessitie of the sanctis, sa that na laikit amangis the faythfull.[f] [148]

7. These collectionis war not onlie of that quhilk was collectit in maner of almous (as sum supponis[g]), bot of uther guidis, movable and onmovable, of landis and possessionis, the pryce quhairof was brocht to the feit of the apostles.[149]

8. This office continewit in the deaconis handis quha intromettit with the haill gudis of the kirk ay quhill the estait thairof was corruptit be antichryst, as the ancient canonis beiris witnes.[150]

9. The same canonis mak mentioun of ane fourfald distributioun of the patrimony[151] of the kirk quhairof ane part was

[e] *thingis* not in both GUL, NLS Adv., SRO and TCD
[f] *amangs thame* in PRO and TCD   [g] *propose* in both GUL

Regno Christi, 140.) The general assembly affirmed in 1576 that 'the patrimonie of the kirk quherupon the kirk, the poore, the schooles sould be sustained is *ex jure divino*' and that 'unjust possessours' should be prosecuted'. (*BUK*, i, 360.) This attitude was reiterated by Beza in his letter to lord Glamis. (*SHS Miscellany*, viii, 111.)

[147] See above, VIII. 2, 6 and notes 139, 142.

[148] The deacons in the primitive church, Calvin had observed, served as they had done under the apostles, 'for they received the daily offerings of the faithful and the annual revenues of the church that they might apply them to their true uses; in other words, partly in maintaining ministers, and partly in supporting the poor'. (*Institutes*, IV, iv, 5.)

[149] See above VIII. 6 and n. 142; IX. 6 and n. 148. Bullinger's narrower definition recognised that 'in the primitive church the care of the poor was committed to deacons'. (Bullinger, *Decades*, v, 107.) In 1571, Erskine of Dun had illustrated how 'the faythfull in Jerusalem, convertit be the aspostles doctrin, sauld their landis and possessionis, and laid the price thairof at the apostles feit'. (*Spalding Club Miscellany*, iv, 97.)

[150] See Bucer, *Opera Latina*, xv: *De Regno Christi*, 87–88, 145; and Calvin, *Institutes*, IV, v, 13; IV, xix, 32, where the same point is made.

[151] This had been emphasized by Beza who showed 'par les anciens canons que

IX: THE PATRIMONY OF THE KIRK   211

applyit*ʰ* to the pasturis or bischoppis for thair sustentatioun and hospitalitie, ane uther to the eldars and deaconis and all the clergie,¹⁵² the thrid to the pure, sick personis and strangeris, the ferd to the uphald and uther affairis of the kirk, especiall extraordinar: we add heirto the scoles and schoolmaisteris quhilk aucht and may be weill sustenit of the same gudis and ar comprehendit ondir the clergie,¹⁵³ to quhome we jo[i]ne clerkis of assembleis¹⁵⁴ alsweill particular as generall, syndikis

ʰ appoynted in PRO and SRO

---

les biens ecclésiastiques étaient divisés en quatre parties', and assigned to clerks, the poor, church buildings and other necessities, and, to bishops for hospitality. (*La Confession de foi*, V, xxx; cf., Beza to Glamis, *SHS Miscellany*, viii,111–112.) The subject was also discussed by Calvin and Bucer. (Calvin, *Institutes*, IV, iv, 5; Bucer, *Opera Latina*, xv: *De Regno Christi*, 140.) The first Book of Discipline believed that 'ministers and the poore, together with the schooles... must be susteyned upon the charges of the kirk'. (*First Book of Discipline*, 156.) See also XII. 16 below.

¹⁵² The term 'clergy', the erroneous use of which both Calvin and James Melville had severely criticised (Calvin, *Institutes*, IV, iv, 9; yet see *ibid*., IV, xii, 1; Calderwood, *History*, iv, 517), is employed here in an effort to include certain categories of officers within the terminology used in the early canons.

¹⁵³ The attempt to include schoolmasters, kirk lawyers, clerks and precentors within the category of 'clergy', none of whom apart from teachers who occupied the doctoral office in the church exercised an ecclesiastical ministry is somewhat forced, and (as explained in n. 152 above) was really a means for justifying their financial provision from church patrimony in accordance with the canons of the early church. Nonetheless, the reformed church from the outset had assumed a particular responsibility for supervising schools. (*First Book of Discipline*, 129–136; *BUK*, i, 17, 33–34, 60, 108, 279; *APS*, iii, 24.) Schoolmasters were often elders on kirk sessions, and from 1581 they were assigned, significantly enough, a seat on presbyteries where they were even elected as moderator. (SRO, CH2/550/1. Glasgow Kirk Session Records, fos. 2r., 20v., 52r., 80r., 100r., 119r., 137v., 158v., 181r., (Blackburn); CH2/1026/1. Stirling Kirk Session Records, 17 Nov. 1597 and annually thereafter till 1607 (Yule); St Andrews Presbytery Records, fo. 1r. (Monipenny); GCA, Glasgow Presbytery Records, fo. 148v. (Blackburn as moderator); SRO, CH2/722/1. Stirling Presbytery Records, 31 Oct. 1581 and regularly thereafter (Yule), 21 Oct. 1589 and 9 March 1596/7 (as moderator).)

¹⁵⁴ In St Andrews, the session-clerk was often an elder or deacon whose fees were met from ecclesiastical fines and from a contribution by the town council; a reader served as clerk to Stirling presbytery; in Dalkeith presbytery one of the ministers was elected clerk for a half-yearly term, and it was expected that the modifiers of stipends would provide a salary; and in the general assembly the clerk was also keeper of the Register of Ministers' Stipends with a salary assigned from the thirds of benefices. (*RStAKS*, i, 454; ii, 489, 875–6, 879, 882; SRO, CH2/722/1. Stirling Presbytery Records, 8 Aug. 1581; CH2/424/1. Dalkeith Presbytery Records, fos. 83v., 101r., 111r. and *passim*; D. Shaw, *The General Assemblies of the Church of Scotland* (Edinburgh, 1964), 144–149.)

or procuratouris of the kirkis effairis,[155] takaris up of the psalmis,[156] with siclyk uther ordinar offices[i] of the kirk sa far as thay ar necessar.

[i] *and sicklyk uthers officials* in TCD

[155] The first recorded instance of a solicitor for the kirk is the general assembly's appointment of James Macartney in June 1564. (*BUK*, i, 50; D. Shaw, *General Assemblies*, 150–155.)

[156] In Perth, the master of the song school reported his 'greatt travaillis in teaching of the youthed of this toun in musik, and in takin up of the psalmes, and thatt the consell of the toun had maid him sum titill of rycht to the annuallis of the confraternity alter within this toun'. (SRO, CH2/521/1. Perth Kirk Session Records, 12 Jan. 1578/9; *cf.*, 17 April 1592, 12 Aug. 1594, 21 May 1599, 21 Oct. 1605.) The music teacher also acted as precentor in St Andrews. (*RStAKS*, ii, 833, 908.)

X

OFF THE OFFICE OF ANE CHRISTIANE MAGISTRAT IN THE KIRK

1. Althocht all the memberis of the kirk be hauldine every ane of thair vocatioun and according thairto to advance the kingdome of Jesus Chryst sa far as lyis in thair power,[j] yit cheiflie and namelie[k] Christiane princes, kingis[l] and uther magistratis ar haldine to do the same.[157]

2. For thay ar callit in the Scripturis nurissaris of the kirk, forsamekle as be thame it is, or at least aucht to be, mentenid, fosterit,[m] uphaldine and defendit aganis all that[n] wald procure the hurt thairof.[o] [158]

3. So it pertenit to the office of ane Chrystiane magistrat to assist and fortifie the godlie proceding of the kirk in all behalfis, and, namelie, to sie that the publick estait[p] and ministrie thairof be mantenit and sustenit as it appirtenis according to Goddis word.[159]

[j] *sa far as in them lyis* in both GUL, NLS Adv. and TCD
[k] *and namelie* not in AUL, both GUL, NLS Adv., SRO and TCD
[l] *kingis* not in both GUL, and NLS Adv.
[m] *fosterit* not in TCD   [n] *all these that* in NLS Wodrow; *all thame that* in TCD
[o] *hurt of the same* in PRO   [p] *in namelie the publick estait* in NLS Wodrow

[157] This is consistent with the statement in the Scots Confession of Faith acknowledging that the conservation of religion pertained 'cheiflie and maist principallie' to kings and magistrates; and in Beza's Confession of Faith, the Christian magistrate was also recognised as 'l'un des membres de l'Eglise, et même le principal en son domaine'. (Knox, *Works*, ii, 118; Beza, *La Confession de foi*, V, xliv.) Bullinger also emphasized how 'the care of religion doth especially belong to the magistrate'. (Bullinger, *Decades*, ii, 323ff.)

[158] The text of *Isaiah* 42:23 that 'kings shall be thy nursing fathers and their queens thy nursing mothers' had an appeal for presbyterians and their opponents alike: James VI positively gloried in the notion. (Calvin, *Institutes*, IV, xx, 5; Bullinger, *Decades*, ii, 328; v, 34; Calderwood, *History*, iv, 53, 279; *BUK*, iii, 903; *O.L.*, i, 248; Travers, *A full and plaine declaration*, 189; Whitgift, *Works*, i, 390–1; iii, 189; Jewel, *Works*, iii, 98; Hooker, *Of the Laws of Ecclesiastical Polity*, VII, xxiv, 22; *Basilikon Doron*, i, 80–81.)

[159] This, and the preceding item, recalls the language of Beza's Confession of Faith: 'il s'ensuit, donc, que rien ne doit être en plus grande recommandation aux magistrats chrétiens que d'avoir une Église bien dressée selon la règle de la Parole de Dieu, de maintenir et de défendre son autorité contre tous ceux qui en seraient les contempteurs et les perturbateurs obstinés'. (*La Confession de foi*, V, xliv.) See also above I. 22.

4. To sie that the kirk be not invadit nor hurt be fals teachearis or hyrlingis nor the rowmis thairof occupyit be dum doggis or idill bellies.[160]

5. To assist and mantine the discipline of the kirk and punische thame civilie that will not obey the censur of the same without confounding alwayis of the ane jurisdictioun with the uther.[161]

6. To sie that sufficient provisioun be maid for the ministrie, scoles and the puire,[162] and gif thay have not sufficient to await upone thair chargis to supplie thair indigence evine with thair awine rentis, gif neid requiris, to hauld hand to thame, *alsweill concerning thair awin personis, saiffing thame frome injurie* and oppine violence as concerning*

q alsweill to the saiffing of their persones fra injurie in AUL both GUL, NLS Adv., SRO and TCD
r as to in AUL, both GUL, NLS Adv., SRO, and TCD

[160] Knox affirmed in 1558 that the 'punyshment of false teachers do appertaine to the civile magistrate and nobilitie of any realme'; Erskine of Dun, in 1571, warned against intruding 'in office vitious persones, hyrelingis, or men nocht qualifeit to discharge their conscience'; and in 1585 opponents of Arran's 'antipresbyterian dictatorship' criticised the government for replacing the exiled ministers with 'dumb dogges that cannot barke or hyrelings that . . . in no weill reformed church could be tolerated'. (Knox, *Works*, iv, 485, 491; *Spalding Club Miscellany*, iv, 99; Calderwood, *History*, v, 451.) The language here also recalls the barons' protest in 1571 against bishops intruded by the government whereby the church was 'compelled to admitt dumbe dogges to the office, dignitie, and rents appointed for sustentatioun of preaching pastors, and for other godlie uses.' (Calderwood, *History*, iii, 145.)

[161] See above I. 9, 17, 21–22. Knox, in 1564, spoke of 'the just power whairwith God hes armit his magistratis and lievtenentis to punische syn and mentene vertew'. (Knox, *Works*, ii, 437–8.) Apart from ensuring that obstinate offenders duly submitted to the church, the magistrate was also responsible for inflicting the civil punishment which was liable to accompany ecclesiastical censure and correction. (*BUK*, i, 75–6, 97, 111, 160; *RStAKS*, i, 36, 41, 58, 60, 138, 141, 149, 168, 223, 247, 251, 448, 465, 467.)

[162] The general assembly's repeated petitions for adequate provisions for the ministry, schools and poor (*BUK*, i, 16–17, 30, 34, 59–60, 146, 253, 279) led the government to respond, first, by assigning in 1562 a proportion of the thirds of benefices for the support of the ministry, then, by providing machinery for ministers to succeed to the lesser benefices in 1567 and to the greater benefices in 1572 and, thirdly, by recognising in 1581 that every parish church, including those annexed to prelacies, should have 'thair awin pastoure with a sufficient and ressonable stipend'. (*RPC*, i, 201–3; *BUK*, i, 209ff; *APS*, iii, 211.) The government also made some provision for schools and the poor. (*RPC*, i, 202; *BUK*, i, 214; *APS*, iii, 433 (schools); *APS*, iii, 37–8, 42, 88, 139, 147 (poor).)

thair rentis and possessionis that thay be not defraudit, reavit nor spolzeit thairof.[163]

7. Not to suffir the patrimony of the kirk to be applyit to the prophane and onlauchfull uses or to be devoirit be idle belleis and sic as have na lauchfull functioun in the kirk,[164] to the hurt of the ministrie, the scoles, the puir and utheris godlie uses quhairupone the same aucht to be bestowid.

8. To mak lawis and constitutionis aggreable to Goddis word, for the advancement of the kirk and policie thairof without usurping ony thing that pertenis not to the civill sword[165] bot belangis to the offices that ar mere ecclesiasticall, as is the ministrie of the word and sacramentis, using of ecclesiasticall discipline and the spirituall executioun thairof, or ony part of the power of the* spirituall keys, quhilk our Maister gaif to his apostles and thair trew successouris.[166]

* *power of the* not in both GUL, and NLS Adv.

[163] See *RPC*, ii, 261-4, 313-4, 586; iii, 88, 90-91, 124-5, 273, 276-7, 290; iv, 352, 358, 832.

[164] Despite attempts to curtail the abuse, the alienation of ecclesiastical revenues through the dilapidation of benefices by the granting of feus, tacks and pensions remained an outstanding problem; there was also a legacy of benefices held by unqualified possessors who declined to serve in the ministry and of benefices disponed by simple gift; and added to this was the continued existence of the monastic properties possessed by lay commendators and largely outside the church's control. (See Introduction, 122ff.) Aware of the 'many inconveniences and missordour fallin furth be the ambitioun, covetousnes and indirect dealing of sundrie quho gangs about to entir in the ministrie', the assembly resolved in 1582 'that no man pretend to ecclesiasticall functioun, office, [promotione] or benefice be any absolute gift, collation or admission of the civill magistrate or patrone, be letters of horning and quhatsoevir uther meanes then is established be the Word of God and acts of the generall kirk and hitherto ordinarlie used within the reformed kirk of Scotland'. (*BUK*, ii, 564.)

[165] Though not entitled to 'prescryve ony reull' in matters affecting doctrine or discipline (I. 21 and n. 23 above), the magistrate was nonetheless expected to legislate in the church's interest; and the general assembly, which often met just before parliament, was accustomed to submit recommendations for legislation by both parliament and privy council. This accorded with Melville's belief that 'it perteaneth not to the prince ather to prescrive religioun to the kirk or discipline to the pastors therof but by his authorite to confirme both the one and the other appointed by God and sincerelie declared out of his Word by the ministrie of his servants'. (Calderwood, *History*, iv, 165.) In 1590, the assembly asked the king for a ratification of 'all lawis that hes bein made for the weill of the true kirk togither with ane new act of parliament specially establishing the kirk's jurisdictioun, thair generall and synodall assemblies, presbytries and discipline'. (*BUK*, ii, 772.)

[166] The magistrate's exclusion from exercising ecclesiastical discipline and

9. And althocht kingis and princes that be godlie, sumtymis be thair awin auctoritie (quhene the kirk is corrupt and all thingis^t out of ordour) place ministeris and restoir the trew service of the Lord, eftir the example of sum godlie kingis in Judea^u and divers godlie emperouris and kingis, also in the lycht of the New Testament, yit quhair the ministrie of the kirk is anis lauchfullie institut,^{v} and thay that ar^w placed do thair office faythfullie, all godlie princes and magistratis aucht to heir and obey thair voice, and reverence the majestie of the sone of God^x speiking^y be thame.[167]

^{t} *tymes* in both GUL
^{u} *the quhilk they did be direction of Prophets* added in *BUK* and Melville, *Diary*
^{v} *constitut* in AUL, both GUL, NLS Adv., PRO, SRO, and TCD
^{w} *and aricht are* in NLS Wodrow
^{x} *of the sone* not in both GUL, and TCD ^{y} *spoken* in TCD

notably excommunication (see above I. 8, 16, 20–21 and notes) was at variance with the Zürich or Basel emphasis on magisterial control, but it was consistent with Knox's defence of excommunication in 1559 on the grounds that 'our churche and the trew ministeris of the same have the same power whiche our Maister, Christ Jesus, granted to his Apostles', and with Beza's belief in 'la jurisdiction des clefs données aux apôtres, et en la personne des apôtres, à tous les vrais anciens'. (Bullinger, *Decades*, v, 39ff., 146ff.; Knox, *Works*, i, 333; Beza, *La Confession de foi*, V, xliii.)

[167] This passage is borrowed directly from Bucer, who wrote that 'though pious kings of the world sometimes establish and restore priests of the Lord on their own authority, especially when the priesthood is vitiated and the church depraved (as we read that David, Solomon, Hezekiah, Josiah and many other pious emperors and kings did in the light of the New Testament); nevertheless, when the ministers of the churches have been legitimately established and they rightly fulfill their office, all true kings and princes humbly hear the voice of Christ from the ministers and respect in them the majesty of the Son of God'. (Bucer, *Opera Latina*, xv: *De Regno Christi*, 15–16; *Melanchthon and Bucer*, ed. W. Pauck (London, 1969), 187–8.) See also Bullinger, *Decades*, ii, 329.

XI

OFF THE PRESENT ABUSIS REMANING IN THE KIRK QUHILK WE DESYR TO BE REFORMIT

1. As it is the dewtie of the godlie magistrat to mantene the present libertie quhilk God of his mercie[z] hes grantit to the precheing of his word and the trew ministratioun of the scaramentis within this realme, sa it is to provyde that all abusis as yit remaning in the kirk sould be removit and utterly[a] takine away.[168]

2. Thairfoir, first, the admissioun of men to papisticall titles of benefices sic as servis not nor hes na functioun in the reformit kirk of Chryst, as abbatis, commendatouris, priouris, priouressis and uther titles of abayis, quhais places ar now for the maist pairt be the just jugementis of God demolished and purgit of idolatrie, is plane abusioun and is not to ressave the kingdome of Chryst amangis us, bot rather to refuise it.[169]

[z] *of his mercie* not in AUL, both GUL, SRO and TCD
[a] *outwardlie* in AUL, and both GUL; *utterly* not in NLS Wodrow

[168] The authors of the first Book of Discipline had expected the magistrate to set the 'kirk at freedome and liberty'; and in 1579 the assembly informed James VI that 'God hath chosen you as a singular instrument . . . in offering you so fair occasions to put the kirk of God to full liberty, to purge it from corruption, to establish such decent and comely policie within the same as his word craveth, and to provide for the long during and perpetuity thereof'. (*First Book of Discipline*, 209; *BUK*, ii, 447.)

[169] The monastic houses, which the reformers wished 'to be utterly suppressed' in 1560, were dissolved only in the sense that as religious communities they ceased to function, for they continued to exist as legal and financial entities administered by lay titulars; and the surviving monks continued to receive their 'portions'. The Convention of Leith in 1572 proposed distinguishing the spirituality from the temporality of monastic property, as vacancies occurred, in an effort to secure for ministers who served the cure an adequate stipend from the teinds of appropriated churches, but the temporality and title were still assigned to a lay commendator, who would represent the ecclesiastical estate in parliament, after due examination by the church; he might also act as senator of the college of justice or be engaged in government service. By 1575, the estates decided that the religious houses were unnecessary in a godly commonwealth and that no future appointments should be made until the church's polity was settled. But the process of secularisation was merely confirmed with the crown's annexation of monastic temporalities in 1587 and with their subsequent erection into temporal lordships; and the problem of extricating the teinds still awaited a comprehensive solution. (*BUK*, i, 210; *APS*, iii, 90, 347.)

3. Of the lyk natour ar the deanis, archedeanis,[170] chanteris subchanteris, thesauraris,[b] chancelaris and utheris having the lyk titles flowit frome the paip and canon law onlie quha have na place in the reformit kirk.[c] [171]

4. Siclyk, thay that war callit of auld the chapteris[d] and conventis of abbayis, cathedrall kirkis and lyk places servis for nathing now bot to set fewis and takis (gif ony thing be left) of kirk landis and teindis in hurt and prejudice thairof as daylie experience teached and thairfoir aucht to be alluterlie abrogat and abolischit.[e] [172]

[b] *thesauraris* not in both GUL, and NLS Adv.
[c] item 3 not in NLS Wodrow; items 3 and 4 transposed in AUL, both GUL, PRO, SRO and TCD
[d] *prioris* in PRO   [e] item 4 not in NLS Adv.

[170] *I.e.* archdeacon.

[171] In the pre-reformation church, the dean was administrative head of the body of canons or chapter of a cathedral, or alternatively the head of a college of prebendaries, either canons or chaplains, in certain collegiate kirks. The archdeacon, with his subordinates the deans of Christianity, was responsible to the bishop for supervising the parish clergy within his jurisdiction. In a cathedral, the chanter or precentor, who was next in rank to the dean, instructed the choristers and regulated the music in services; the sub-chanter, or succentor, was the precentor's deputy. The treasurer, fourth in seniority in the chapter, was responsible for the treasure and *ornamenta* of the cathedral; and the chancellor, who was third in dignity in the cathedral chapter, was custodian of the charters, library and common seal of the chapter. (J. Dowden, *The Medieval Church in Scotland* (Glasgow, 1910) 61–2, 74, 106, 213–4, 220–1.) The continued existence after 1560 of the structure of the old church meant that a legal and financial significance was still attached to such titles, though the ecclesiastical offices were no longer regarded as valid by the reformed church. Even with the utilisation of this beneficial structure in the interests of the reformed church, the general assembly in 1572 censured the use of 'certaine names, sick as archbischop, deane, archdeane, chancellour, chapter, quhilks names were found slanderous and offensive to the ears of many of the brethren, appeirand to sound to papistrie: therfor the haill Assemblie in ane voyce, asweill they that were in commission at Leith as uthers, solemnlie protests that they intend not be useing sick names to ratifie, consent and aggrie to any kynd of papistrie or superstition, and wishes rather the saids names to be changeit into uthers that are not slanderous or offensive'. (*BUK*, i, 246.) Similar criticisms were voiced by English presbyterians. (Travers, *A full and plaine declaration*, 26, 43; Whitgift, *Works*, ii, 173–5, 178–80, 543; *Seconde Parte of A Register*, i, 207, 258; ii, 1, 3, 209; *Puritan Manifestoes*, 11, 15–16, 18, 30–31, 102.)

[172] The consent of cathedral, collegiate and conventual chapters was required in the administration or alienation of property pertaining to the bishopric, collegiate kirk and religious house. Though forming no part of the structure of the reformed church, chapters continued to function after 1560, for their consent was still legally required in conveying monastic or episcopal property. But in seeking a solution to the problem of the prelacies, the Leith agreement of 1572 provided that episcopal and monastic chapters should be staffed in future by ministers of the

XI: THE PRESENT ABUSIS REMANING IN THE KIRK

5. The kirkis also quhilk ar unitit and joynit togidder be annexatioun to thair benefices aucht to be seperatid and dividit and gevin to qualifeit ministeris*[f]* as Godis word cravis.[173]

6. Nether aucht sic abuseris of the patrimony of the kirk of Chryst to have voit in parliament nor sit in counsall under the name of the kirk and kirkmen[174] to the hurt and prejudice of

---

[f] *personis, pastouris,* in PRO

---

reformed church. (*BUK*, i, 210, 221–26.) Yet dilapidation was still not averted: the assembly in 1578 required chapters to obtain its consent before acceding to grants of feus and tacks, and Menmuir's 'Constant Platt' of 1596 recognised that 'the dilapidation of the rents of the kirk has proceeded for the most part from the kirkmen themselves, who had over great liberty to sett such long tacks and fewes, and for dueties as they pleased; the solemnity of ordinar chapters serving not to restrain the said dilapidation, for which they were first instituted, but rather to authorize the same; which chapters for the most part be now worn out' and so recommended the presbytery's consent as a pre-requisite to any such disposition (*BUK*, ii, 414, 417, 634; iii, 883).

[173] As well as the legacy of appropriations whereby revenues from most parishes (over 86%) had been annexed before the Reformation to such higher institutions as monasteries, bishoprics and universities (Cowan, *Parishes*, v) there was also the added problem of a shortage of ministers: adjacent churches were often united under the care of a single minister 'according to the corrupted platt of the four kirks', the Regent Morton's device whereby 'the king's revenues by the superplus of the thrids [i.e. thirds of benefices] might be the greater'. (EUL, MS. La.II.14. Visitation of the Diocese of Dunblane, e.g. visitation of Aucherarder, 13 Oct. 1586; Calderwood, *History*, iii, 301.) In 1579, the assembly informed the privy council that the 'ecclesiasticall policie culd not possibillie be well establischit, the kirkis universalie plantit with ministeris, nor they weill and commodiuslie payit and answerit of thair leavingis, quhill the multitude of paroche kirkis annexit in tyme of papistrie and ignorance to bischopreis, abbayis and proyoriis, war separate thairfra, and the saidis gret benefices dissolvit that the ministrie mycht be sustenit upoun the teyndis as maist competent for thame'; and in 1582, the assembly again petitioned the king 'that every kirk have thair awin severall pastour to be sustainit on the teynds of the parochin quher he serves'. (*RPC*, iii, 176–7; *BUK*, ii, 601.)

[174] The problem of abbatial and episcopal representation in parliament became acute after 1560, for the reformed church recognised neither office as such and, indeed, argued for a dissolution of the prelacies. In 1572, however, a compromise was reached when the Convention of Leith confirmed the pre-reformation practice whereby lay commendators as titular heads of religious houses sat and voted in parliament as part of the clerical estate, though not as representatives of the reformed church, and were sometimes appointed privy councillors; and it was understood that the new protestant bishops would also take their seats in parliament and that some might be elected to the privy council, despite the reformers' earlier intentions that the two jurisdictions should remain separate and that ministers should be debarred from secular politics. The subsequent erection of abbatial property into temporal lordships removed commendators from the

the libertie thairof and lawis of the realme maid in favouris of the reformit kirk.[175]

7. Mekleles is it laufull that ane persone amangis thais men sould have fyve, sax, tene, twentie[g] or ma kirkis, all having the charge of the saulis and bruik the patrimony thairof ather be admissioun of the prince or of the kirk in this lycht of the Evangell, for it is bot mockage to crave reformatioun quhair sic hes place.[176]

8. And albeit it wes thocht guid for avo[i]ding gretter inconvenientis that the auld possessouris of sic beneficies quha imbracit the religioun sould enjoy be permissioun the twa

[g] *xv, xvi, xx* in PRO

---

clerical estate in parliament and again raised the question of how and whether the reformed church should be represented. (See further XI. 22 and n. 197.)

[175] See *APS*, ii, 526-35; iii, 23-4, 36-8, 67, 71-2, 76, 79, 90, 137.

[176] The legacy of parish churches appropriated to prelacies meant that the teinds, which should have been assigned to ministers' stipends, were not immediately available, other than as an allocation from the thirds, until provision was made for separating teinds from other revenues pertaining to the holder of the prelacy. As early as 1565, the general assembly had petitioned Mary that none of the greater beneficies 'havand many kirks annexit therto be disponit altogither in any time comeing to any one man, bot at the least the kirks therof be severallie disponit and to severall persons, swa that every man having charge may serve at his awin kirk'. (*BUK*, i, 59-60.) Although parliament later made provision in 1581 for reserving ministers' stipends in future grants of prelacies, the assembly still complained in 1583 that 'abbacies are disponed without any provisioun made for the ministers serving in the kirks annexit therto, directlie against the act of parliament'. (*APS*, iii, 211; *BUK*, ii, 632, 634, 643-4.) In 1586, James VI commented on how 'thair is dyvers parische kirkis annexit to diverse beneficis under prelaceis plattid togidder in the book of modificatione albeit in sindrie partis sum lyis far seperate quhilk can not be otherwayis presentlie convenientlie done in respect it is not yit concludit that sick benefecis sall be dissolvit' and he recommended that the commissioner of Lothian with advice of the synod should 'injoyne and direct the personis provydit in tytle to the haill of the saidis beneficis how and in quhat forme thay sall caus the uther kirkis annexit to thair beneficis and lyand far distant fra thair residence be servit onder thair expensis'. (SRO, CH2/121/1. Edinburgh Presbytery Records, 30 August 1586.) Presbyteries soon undertook negotiations with holders of prelacies for satisfactory stipends (St Andrews Presbytery Records, 2 Dec., 18 Dec. 1591; 6 May 1592; GCA, Glasgow Presbytery Records, fos. 116v., 117v., 148r.; SRO, CH2/121/1. Edinburgh Presbytery Records, 11 Feb., 18 Feb., 25 Feb. 1589/90; 1 June, 15 June, 29 June 1591; *Synod of Lothian*, 19, 64, 71, 80, 97); and the synod of Lothian petitioned the king in 1590 'that the perpetuall and constant plat go forward. That thair be a dissolution of prelaceis and kirk levingis annexit to uther kirkis and that na dispositioun be maid quhill the said dissolutioun be'. (*Synod of Lothian*, 18.)

XI: THE PRESENT ABUSIS REMANING IN THE KIRK

pairt of the rentis quhilk thay possest befoir induring thair lyftymis, yit it is not tollerable to continew in the kirk lyk abuse, and gif thais places and uther benefices of new to als onmeitt[177] men or rather onmetter, quha ar not myndit to serve in the kirk, bot leid and[h] leve ane idle lyf as the utheris did quha bruikit thame in tyme of blindnes.[178]

9. And insafar as in the ordour tane at Leyth in the yeir of our Lord $1^m v^o$ sevintie-ane yeir,[179] it appeiris that sic may be admittit, being fund qualifeit, etc., ather that pretentid ordour[180] is aganis all guid ordour or ellis it must be onderstandit not of thame that be qualifeit to warldlie effairis to serve in the court bot sic as ar qualifeit to teache Goddis word havand thair laufull admissioun of the kirk.[181]

[h] *leid and* not in AUL, both GUL, NLS Adv. and Wodrow, PRO, SRO, and TCD

[177] *I.e.* 'unsuitable' or 'unworthy'.

[178] After the Reformation existing holders were permitted to remain in possession of their benefices for life; and it was only as vacancies occurred through death, resignation or forfeiture that ministers in the reformed church gained access to the lesser benefices from 1567 and to the bishoprics from 1572. At the same time, benefice holders from 1562 had been subject to a levy of a third of their revenues for the support of the crown and kirk, and while parliament in 1573 required the holders of benefices to accept the reformed Confession of Faith and achnowledge the king, there was still no compulsion that they should serve as ministers. Indeed, the continued disposition and possession of benefices by such 'unqualified' persons gave serious grounds for concern. (*APS*, iii, 23–24, 72; *BUK*, i, 209ff.; *RPC*, i, 202; *BUK*, ii, 564, 582, 632, 634, 644, 659; *APS*, iii, 211–12, 309–10, 542–3; Melville, *Diary*, 347–8.) Abbacies and priories were a particular problem: in 1575 the estates declared that titulars and possessors of such benefices had no right to dispone them to their heirs and that gifts of provision, reserving their own liferents, were null and void; and, in language reminiscent of Bucer, the general assembly in 1582 proceeded to argue, though to little effect, 'that of the temporall lands of every abbacie, pryorie, bischoprick, nunrie, etc., so meikle may be applyit to the schooles as may sufficientlie mantaine ane sufficient number of masters and bursers, according as the living may beare, in place of cannons, monks, nunnes or uther idle bellies'. (*APS*, iii, 90; *BUK*, ii, 601–2; Bucer, *Opera Latina*, xv: *De Regno Christi*, 238.)

[179] *I.e.* January 1571/2.

[180] The Concordat of Leith never received parliamentary sanction, despite reports that the Regent was fully prepared 'to have it enacted by parliament as a law' and that there would 'not be great let to have it allowed by parliament'. (*CSP Scot.*, iv, no. 149, p. 134.) In 1576, the settlement was described in the privy council merely as a 'prevate constitutioun as is the said pretendit ordinance maid at Leyth, quhilk is nayther constitute be the Estaittis as a law, nor yit is it ressavit be the ministerie universalie, bot oppugnit and callit in doubt be thame selffis in divers the maist substanciall points of the same'. (*RPC*, ii, 565; *cf.*, *BUK*, i, 371.)

[181] While the Convention of Leith provided machinery for the admission of

10. As to bischoppis, gif the name ἐπίσκοπος be properlie takin, thay ar all ane with ministeris (as was befoir declairit), for it is not the name of superioritie and lordschip, bot of office and watching.[182]

11. Yit, becaus in the corruptioun of the kirk this name as utheris hes bene abusid and yit is lyk to be, we cane not allow the fassioun of thais new chosine bischoppis nather of the chapteris that ar the electeouris of thame to sic office as thay ar chosine.[183]

12. Trew bischopis sould addict thame selfis to ane particular flok (quhilk sindrie of thame refusis)[184] nather sould thay

---

qualified ministers to the bishoprics as they became vacant, and for the admission of 'well learnit and qualifeit' lay commendators to abbacies, priories and nunneries it was nonetheless recognised that the commendators might become senators of the college of justice or 'be employit be the king in the necessar effaires of the common weill'; and on the failure of the chapter to elect a bishop, it was also open to the crown to make a simple gift of the temporalities of the bishopric *iure devoluto*. (*BUK*, ii, 209–10, 690; *RPC*, iii, 474–6.) Exception was now taken to misuse of the church's patrimony, but even this qualified acceptance of the Leith agreement, if operated wholly in the interests of the reformed church, was somewhat at odds with the claim advanced for the subversion of the ancient ecclesiastical structure. (See XII. 14, 16 below.)

[182] See above, IV. 1 and n. 60.

[183] Criticism of the Leith agreement led the assembly in 1575 to debate the question 'whither if the bischops, as they are now in the kirk of Scotland, hes thair function of the word of God or not, or if the chapiter appointit for creating of them aucht to be tollerated in this reformed kirk'; by 1578, after considering the 'great corruption in the estate of bischops', the assembly resolved that 'no bischops salbe electit or made heirafter befor the nixt generall assemblie, dischargeing all ministers and chapiters to proceid any wayes to electioun of bischops in the meanetyme'; and by 1580 the assembly concluded that 'the office of a bischop, as it is now usit and commounly takin within this realme, hes no sure warrand auctoritie nor good ground out of the [Book and] Scriptures of God'. (*BUK*, i, 340; ii, 408, 453.)

[184] An assembly committee reported in 1575 that 'the name of bischop is commoun to all them that hes a particular flock', and in 1576 the bishops of Dunblane, Ross and Moray agreed to accept a parish ministry. (*BUK*, i, 342, 358–9 361.) Archbishop Boyd of Glasgow was less co-operative but did agree 'to haunt to ane particular kirk and to teach therat quhen he dwells in the sheriffdome of Air' and to do likewise 'quhen he is in Glasgow'; in 1577 he finally promised to accept a single congregational charge. (*Ibid.*, 379, 386.) Several years elapsed, however, before the remaining bishops, including Patrick Adamson, submitted to the assembly's injunction requiring them to undertake a parochial ministry. (See Introduction, 130ff.)

XI: THE PRESENT ABUSIS REMANING IN THE KIRK 223

usurp lordship ovir thair brethrene and ovir the inheritance of Chryst as thais men do.[185]

13. Pastouris, in safar as thay ar pasturis, hes not the office of visitatioun of ma kirkis jo[i]nit to the pastureschip without it be gevin to thame.[186]

14. It is ane corruptioun that bischopis sould have fordar boundis to visit nor thay may lauchfullie.[187]

15. Na man aucht to have the office of visitatioun bot he that is lauchfullie chosine be the presbyterie thairto.[188]

16. The elderschippis being weill establishit hes power to send out visitouris ane or ma with commissioun to veseit the boundes within thair elderschippis; and siclyk eftir compt tane of thame ather to continew thame or renew[i] thame frome

[i] *remove* in AUL, NLS Adv. and Wodrow, PRO, SRO and TCD

[185] Although at their admission bishops were required to acknowledge their subordination to the assembly in spiritual matters (*BUK*, i, 209), Archbishop Adamson in 1576 declined to do so. (*BUK*, i, 377, 385–6.) The assembly, in 1578, insisted further that bishops 'impyre not above the particular elderschips, but be subject to the same' and that 'they usurp not the power of the presbyteries' (*ibid.*, ii, 425), while in 1579 the 'usurpit jurisdictioun in the bischopis' was again attacked. (*RPC*, iii, 96.) With parliament's reaffirmation of episcopacy in 1584 James Melville renewed criticism of 'that presumptous and lordlie authoritie over the rest of ther breithring'. (Melville, *Diary*, 212.) Calvin had also condemned the abuse which crept into the early church when, from among the presbyters, bishops 'usurped dominion over the others'. (Calvin, *Comm. Philipp.*, 23–4.)

[186] See above, VII. 8 and n. 104.

[187] The rejection in 1576 of the dioceses as adequate units for visitation, which on the testimony of the bishops themselves were often too large and unwieldy for effective oversight, led to the adoption of smaller areas over which visitors, whose ranks included some bishops, were appointed for a term by the general assembly to have supervision and oversight. (*BUK*, i, 352–59.)

[188] This article seems to envisage the elimination of visitors or commissioners of provinces appointed by the assembly for a term, and the substitution of oversight for smaller areas by visitors appointed by the 'presbytery' or eldership of several contiguous parishes, though, in the same document, it was earlier recognised that 'everie assemblie' had power to elect visitors for 'the boundis of thair jurisdictioun'. (See VII. 7–8 above and notes 103–4.) In 1576, the general assembly insisted that this 'power stands not in the visiter but in the kirk'; and by 1580 it resolved that even the visitor's office was 'ane corruption and [to] sound to tyrranie that sick kynd of office sould stand in the person of ane man quhilk sould flow from presbyteries'. (*BUK*, i, 357; ii, 469.)

tyme to tyme to the quhilkis elderschippis thay salbe also*ʲ* subject.¹⁸⁹

17. The criminall jurisdictioun jo[i]nit in the persone of ane pastoure is ane corruption.¹⁹⁰

18. It aggreit not with the word that bischoppis sould be *ᵏ*pasturis of pasturis,*ᵏ* pasturis of mony flokis,¹⁹¹ *ᵏ*and yit*ᵏ*

ʲ alwayes in AUL, both GUL, NLS Adv. and Wodrow, TCD and PRO; *also* not in SRO

ᵏ not in NLS Wodrow

¹⁸⁹ In 1582, the general assembly reiterated the claim that visitations should be conducted by 'two or ma, as the presbyterie sall direct, for the necessitie of the matter, according to the Booke of Policie'. (*BUK*, ii, 568.) This agreed with Beza's advice to lord Glamis that 'the churches may very well be visited at set times, without any great cost and bishoplike pride, by them whom every eldership hath chosen'. (*SHS Miscellany*, viii, 104.) In areas where presbyteries were not yet established visitors or commissioners continued to operate as before. (*BUK*, ii, 569, 586–7.)

¹⁹⁰ The first Book of Discipline had declared ministers ineligible for membership of the privy council. In the 1560s, the assembly took action against the bishops of Galloway and Orkney for accepting appointment on the privy council and college of justice, thereby confounding the two jurisdictions; and in March 1572/3 the assembly proceeded to the more general affirmation that 'it is neither aggrieable to the word of God nor to the practise of the primitive kirk that the speciall administratioun of the word and sacraments and the ministration of the criminall and civill justice be so confoundit that ane person may occupie both the cures'. Thereafter, the assembly in 1578 expressly charged the bishops 'that they usurp no criminal jurisdiction'. (*First Book of Discipline*, 178; *BUK*, i, 52–3, 112, 114, 131, 162, 267; ii, 425.) Hooper, among others, made a similar point in England. (Hooper, *Later Writings*, 559.)

¹⁹¹ During discussions on the Book of Discipline, it was further explained that 'the name BISHOP is relative to the flocke, and not to the eldership; for he is bishop of his flocke, and not of other pastors or fellow-elders. For the pre-eminencie that one beares over the rest, it is the inventioun of man, and not the institutioun of the holie writt.... A bishop is not the bishop of a bishop, nather yitt the pastor of a pastor; but everie one bishop and pastor of their owne flocke'. (Calderwood, *History*, iv, 57.) This description of the New Testament bishop was widely recognised. Although willing to accept a system of *pastores pastorum* as a human institution, Luther had nonetheless taught in 1527 that 'at the time of the apostles every city had numerous bishops. Then Christianity was in outstanding condition. This meaning of the word "bishop" disappeared, and it was subjected to very long and very distorted abuse. Now it is called the human ordinance by which a man is in charge of five cities.... Every city ought to have many bishops. ... In *Acts* 20: 28 Paul speaks of the bishops of a single church'. (*Luther's Works*, vol. 29, 16–17; H. H. Kramm, 'The "Pastor Pastorum" in Luther and early Lutheranism', in *And Other Pastors of Thy Flock*, ed. F. Hildebrandt (Cambridge, 1942) 124–34.) Zwingli, during the first disputation, understood that bishop 'means nothing else than a guardian or supervisor, who should direct attention and care towards his people, being entrusted to instruct them in the divine faith

without ane certane flok[192] and without ordinar teiching.[193]

19. It aggreit not with the Scripturis that thay sould be exemit fra correctioun of thair brethrene and discipline of the particular elderschip of the kirk quhairas [*recte*, quhairat] thay sould serve, nather that thay sould usurp the office of visitatioun of uther kirkis nor ony uther functioun besyd uther ministeris, *k*bot safar as beis committit to thame be the kirk.*k* [194]

k not in NLS Wodrow

---

and will, that is, in good German, a pastor'. (Walton, *Zwingli's Theocracy*, 25.) Similarly, Cranmer in England agreed that bishop and minister 'were not two things, but both one office in the beginning of Christ's religion'. (Cranmer, *Works*, ii, 117.) In Scotland, the general assembly explained in 1565 that 'every true preacher of Jesus Christ is a Christian bishop'; George Buchanan observed that 'whilst a bishop is said to have only one church, others are commended to his care and all are plundered' (Knox, *Works*, vi, 434; Buchanan, *De Jure Regni Apud Scotos*, XXXI); and, in 1572, Patrick Adamson, then 'a zealus preatchour against bischopes', took as his sermon the three sorts of bishop: the papal prelate or 'my lord bishop', the 'tulchan bishop' who was 'my lord's bishop' and 'the Lord's bishop' who was none other than 'the trew minister of the Gospel'. (Melville, *Diary*, 32; Calderwood, *History*, iii, 206.) See further IV. 1 and n. 60 above.

[192] See above, XI. 12 and n. 184.

[193] The Reformation emphasis on preaching as the bishop's primary rôle was widely recognised (*Luther's Works*, vol. 29, 59; *Zürich Letters*, i, 51; Tyndale, *Doctrinal Treatises*, 229–31; Latimer, *Sermons*, 66; Hooper, *Early Writings*, 19, 480; Knox, *Works*, i, 46, 194, 239; iii, 531–4; v, 518–9; *First Book of Discipline*, 122); but when even 'godly' bishops failed adequately to discharge this duty, some carried criticism further: Knox contrasted 'a lord-like bishop' with the 'painfull preacher' of the Word; in England, Christopher Goodman objected to the 'making of lordly bishops before the realm be provided of necessary ministers', and Thomas Sampson decided: 'let others be bishops; as to myself, I will either undertake the office of a preacher, or none at all'. (Knox, *Works*, vi, 559; *CSP Scot.*, i, no. 554; *Zürich Letters*, i, 63.) In Scotland, the general assembly also censured bishops for their failure to preach (*BUK*, i, 162, 166, 168, 255, 270, 286, 325, 348–9), a practice which encouraged the assembly to explore alternative methods of oversight and to insist that bishops undertake a congregational and preaching ministry.

[194] In language which clearly echoed the newly drafted Book of Discipline, the general assembly, in October 1578, required that bishops 'impyre not above the particular elderschips but be subject to the same', 'that they usurp not the power of the presbytries' and 'that they take no farder bounds of visitation nor the kirk committeth to them'. (*BUK*, ii, 425.) By 'particular eldership' is meant not simply the kirk session but the eldership of several adjacent congregations or presbytery, which the assembly in 1579 identified with the exercise already in existence as an administrative unit. In 1576, visitors (including bishops) whom the assembly subordinated to synods were required to seek the 'advice' of the exercise in urgent cases, and the power of visitation, it was clearly stated, 'stands not in the visiter but in the kirk'. (*BUK*, i, 357.) Some manuscript versions of the

20. Heirfoir we desyr the bischoppis that now ar ather to aggrie with that ordour that Goddis word requiris thame and as the generall kirk will prescryve unto thame not passing that boundis nather in ecclesiasticall nor civile effairis or ellis to be deposit frome all functioun in the kirk.[195]

21. We deny not in the meane tyme bot ministeris may and sould assist thair princes quhen thay ar requirit in all thingis aggreable to the word quhidder it be in counsall or parliament or utherwys, providing alwayis[l] thay nather neglek thair awin chargis, nor throch flatterie of princes hurt the publick[m] estait of the kirk.[196]

[l] *alwayis* not in both GUL, and SRO   [m] *publick* not in both GUL

---

acts of assembly contain a variant reading for the article that bishops 'usurp not the power of the presbyteries' to the effect that they 'usurp not the power of pastors', but 'presbyteries' does appear to be the authentic reading. (See Introduction, 105.)

[195] From 1578, the general assembly required bishops to reform 'the corruption of that estate of bischops in thair persones'; in 1580 it ordered synods to examine 'any usurpit bischops'; and in 1582 subjected them to trial by presbyteries. (*BUK*, ii, 413ff., 453, 593.) See also Introduction, 134ff.

[196] *Cf.*, I. 22, and n. 25 above. Knox's advice to England in 1559 was that 'as touching their [the bishops'] yearly commynge to the parliament, for matters of religion, it shalbe superfluous and vain; if God's true religion be so once established that after it be never called in controversie'; and Beza's advice to Scotland in 1576 was that 'this sitting of the bishops with the authority of the voice in the public estates of the kingdom came in with a manifest abuse, contrary to the Word, and therefore in our mind is to be utterly abolished'. (Knox, *Works*, v, 519; *SHS Miscellany*, viii, 104.) The problem of who should represent the ecclesiastical estate in parliament, conventions and councils was also raised by the Regent Morton in 1576. In discussions on the second Book of Discipline, it was said that 'as to voting in parliament and publict assembleis of the estats of this realme, if the ecclesiasticall effaires were weill ordered and the civill policie rightlie guided, and perfyte in all points . . . pastours sould have no vote therin. But as things are now, and time is, it is needfull to forsee that the kirk be not hurt, and that the lawes which are made be conforme to God's Word'. After exploring the possibility of whether ministers might vote in parliament, the assembly decided in 1578, and again in 1581, that 'none vote in parliament for the kirk, except such as sall have commissioun of the kirk for that effect'. The archbishops of Glasgow and St Andrews continued to defend episcopal representation; and no lasting compromise was effected until the decision, contrived by the king, in 1597 that ministers appointed to the title of a bishopric should have a seat and vote in parliament. (*BUK*, ii, 369, 409, 414, 419, 423, 425, 479, 526–7, 606; Calderwood, *History*, iv, 54, 60, 452; *APS*, iv, 130.) Yet as late as 1604, members of St Andrews presbytery still protested at how one of their number was advanced to the honour of sitting in parliament, council and exchequer. (MS. St Andrews Presbytery Records, 29 March 1604.)

XI: THE PRESENT ABUSIS REMANING IN THE KIRK

22. Bot generallie we say na personis under quhatsumevir title of the kirk and speciallie the abusid titles in papistrie, of prelatis, conventis and chapteris aucht to attempt ony act in the kirkis name ather in counsall, parliament *n*or out of counsall having na commissioun of the reformit kirk within this realme.*n* 197

23. *n*And be act of parliament*n* it is provydit that the papisticall kirk and*o* jurisdictioun sould have na place within the same and na bischop nor uther prelat in tymis cuming sould use ony jurisdictioun flowing frome his auctoritie. 198

24. And agane that na uther ecclesiasticall jurisdictioun sould be acknawlegeit within this realme bot that quhilk is and*p* salbe within the reformit kirk*q* and flowing thairfra. 199

25. So we esteme halding of chapteris in papisticall maner, athir in cathedrall kirkis, abbayis, collegis or uther conventuall places*r* usurping the name and auctoritie of the kirk to hurt the patrimony thairof or use ony uther act to the

---

n not in SRO   *o* *kirk and* not in NLS Wodrow
p *is and* not in NLS Wodrow   *q* *within the realme* added in NLS Wodrow
r *conventuall sates* in SRO

197 By 'prelatis' is understood both the protestant bishops and the lay commendators of the religious houses, whom the assembly in 1578 inhibited from voting in name of the kirk without a commission from the kirk (*BUK*, ii, 419, 425). Yet as late as 1592, the assembly still protested that 'abbots, pryours and uther prelats, pretending the title of the kirk, and votting for the samein, without thair power and commissioun, be not sufferit in tyme comeing to vote for the samein, either in parliament or uther conventioun'; and in 1597 it continued to condemn the presence in parliament of 'sacrilegious persons as abbots, pryours, dumb bischops, voteing in name of the kirk contrair to the lawis of the countrey, quherby the caus of the kirk is damnified'. (*Ibid.*, 787, 875.) In 1578, chapters were discharged by the assembly from proceeding to elect further bishops and from giving their consent to feus or tacks from benefices without the assembly's express approval. (*Ibid.*, 408, 413, 414, 417.) See also above XI. 6, 21 and notes 174, 196.

198 In 1560, the 'reformation parliament' had ordained that 'the bischope of Rome haif na jurisdictioun nor autoritie within this realme in tymes cuming...and that na bischop nor uther prelat of this realme use ony jurisdictioun in tymes to cum be the said bischop of Romeis autoritie'. This statute was confirmed by parliament in 1567. (*APS*, ii, 534–5; iii, 36.)

199 In 1567, parliament recognised the reformed church as the 'trew kirk' and 'no uther jurisdictioun ecclesiasticall acknawlegeit within this realme uther than that quhilk is, and salbe within the same kirk, or that quhilk flowis thairfra'. This act was ratified in 1579. (*APS*, iii, 24–5, 137–8.)

prejudice of the same sene the yeir of our Lord 1560 yeiris to be abusioun and corruptioun*s* contrar to the libertie*t* of the trew kirk and lawis of the realme and thairfoir aucht to be annullat, reducit and in tymis cuming utterlie dischargit.²⁰⁰

26. The dependences also of this papisticall jurisdictioun ar to be abolishid of quhilk sort is the mingled jurisdictioun of the commissaris in safar as thay mell with ecclesiasticall materis and have no commissioun of the kirk thairto, bot war erectit in tyme of our soveranis mother*u* quhen thingis war out of ordour. It is ane absurd thing that sindrie*v* of thame having na functioun in the kirk sould be jugis to ministeris and depose thame fra thair rowmis: thairfoir ather thay wald be dischargit to medle with ecclesiasticall materis or it wald be limitat to thame in quhat materis thay mycht be juges and not hurt the libertie of the kirk.²⁰¹

s *and corruptioun* not in NLS Wodrow
u *soverane lordis mother* in NLS Wodrow
t *weill* in SRO
v *sum* in NLS Wodrow

²⁰⁰ See above XI. 4 n. 172.

²⁰¹ The confusion at the Reformation in determining the authorities competent to exercise the consistorial jurisdiction, particularly in matrimonial matters, was apparent in the rival claims advanced by the existing bishops, the court of session and, not least, by the courts of the reformed church, all of which thought fit to judge matrimonial suits. By March 1561/2, the privy council recognised that a superintendent with the advice of a kirk session 'aucht to discus, discerne and decyde upoun all actionis, of divorce . . . for the cryme of adultrie', and in December, 1561 Mary had directed a matrimonial case for judgment to the superintendent that he 'do justice in the actioun and cause to be intendit before you . . . according to Godis word'. (SRO, GD1/371/1. Warrender Papers, fos. 98r., 95r.) The general assembly's decision in 1562 that the church could 'no longer sustene that burthen' and its recommendation in favour of the appointment of secular judges facilitated the move towards the reorganisation of the commissary courts in 1564 with the establishment on a secularised basis of local commissaries. Besides its particular jurisdiction in all consistorial cases, such as in actions relating to teinds, testaments and defamation, Edinburgh commissary court was endowed with a general jurisdiction for the whole country in specified cases including benefices, matrimony, divorce, bastardy and the confirmation of testaments over a certain value. (*BUK*, i, 23; *RPC*, i, 252; xiv, 304–7.) Although its jurisdiction was thus curtailed, the reformed church by no means relinquished all claims in this area, and indeed in 1571 the assembly argued that judgment in divorce suits ought to fall within the church's competence. (*BUK*, i, 187.) Yet more was at issue than the respective jurisdictions of the ministry and magistracy in matrimonial causes, for commissaries also possessed a competence to try actions relating to ecclesiastical benefices (*cf.*, *RPC*, iii, 394); and added to this was criticism, from the privy council in 1575, of 'sindry abusis and inconvenientis' which had crept into the working of the commissary courts. (*Ibid.*, ii, 455–6.) In 1581, the assembly set up a committee 'anent the jurisdictioun of the com-

27. Thay also that of befoir war of the ecclesiasticall estait in the papis kirk or that ar admittit of new to papisticall titles and now ar tollerat[w] be the lawis of the realme to posses the twa pairt of thair ecclesiasticall rentis aucht not to have ony forder libertie bot to intromet with the portioun assignit and grantit to thame for thair lyftyme and not under the abusit titles quhilkis thay had to dispone the kirk rentis set takis and fewis thairof at thair plesour to the greit hurt of the kirk and pure lauboraris that dwell upone the kirk landis contrarie to all guid conscience and ordour.[202]

[w] *tolerable* in NLS Wodrow

missariat of Edinburgh and quherin they middle with the jurisdictioun of the kirk'; and the bishops in 1581 also advanced a claim to the consistorial jurisdiction which parliament declined to recognise until 1609. (*BUK*, ii, 543; *APS*, iii, 214; iv, 430.) In England, Walter Travers also attacked the practice whereby commissaries 'without any grounde off the worde of God take upon them authoritie to judge off all suche causes as belong to the assemblie off the elders'. (Travers, *A full and plaine declaration*, 26.) As late as 1590, the synod at Glasgow sought advice from the commissaries whether a marriage conducted by a reader, suspended from his charge, was lawful or not (Porteous MS., 34).

[202] See above, XI. 8 and n. 178. The solicitude for the 'poor labourers' on ecclesiastical estates is similar to that displayed by the first Book of Discipline and by earlier acts of assembly. (*First Book of Discipline*, 156; *BUK*, i, 40, 49, 60, 108, 146.) Some agricultural labourers possessed cottars' rights to the portions of land which they occupied but others like ploughmen and shepherds had only their labour for hire; all were liable to exploitation and even oppression. (*APS*, iii, 37, 139, 450; *RPC*, ii, 589; iii, 101.) See also below, XIII. 4.

XII

CERTANE SPECIALL HEIDIS OF REFORMATIOUN QUHILK WE CRAVE

1. Quhatsoevir have bene spokine of the offices of the kirk the severall power, the office-beraris thair conjunct power also, and last of the patrimony of the kirk, we onderstand it to be the rycht reformatioun quhilk God cravis at our handis that the kirk be ordourit according thairto as with that ordour quhilk is maist aggreable to the word of God.[203]

2. But becaus sumthingis wilbe twichit in particular concerning the estait of the cuntrie and that quhilk we principallie seik to be reformit in the same, we have collectit thame in thir heidis following.

3. First, seing the haill cuntrie is devydit in provincis and thir provincis agane ar dividit in parochis alsweill in landwart as in townis, in every paroche of resonable congregationis thay [*recte*, there] wald be placit ane or ma pasturis to feid the flok and na pasture or minister aucht[*x*] to be burdenit with the particular charge of ma flokis or kirkis thene ane allanerlie.[204]

4. And becaus it wilbe thocht hard to find out pasturis or ministeris to all the paroche kirkis of the realme, alsweill in landwart as in borrows to[w]nis,[*y*] we think, be the advys of sik as commissioun may be gevine to, be the kirk and the prince, parochis in landwart or small villagis may be jo[i]nit twa or thrie or ma in sum places togidder and the principall and

---

[*x*] *alwayes* in AUL, both GUL, NLS Wodrow and SRO
[*y*] *in townis* in AUL, both GUL, NLS Adv., and Wodrow, PRO, and SRO; *in burgh* in TCD

[203] The claim to order ecclesiastical polity on the basis of scripture was far from novel. (See Calvin, *Institutes*, IV, vi, 9; *First Book of Discipline*, 86.)

[204] This closely follows the phraseology of Beza's reply to lord Glamis wherein Beza observed that 'first the whole kingdom is to be divided into regions. Again, the regions into parishes, either of cities or country towns: that in places most fit, and of greatest assembly, be placed pastors'. (*SHS Miscellany*, viii, 102.) In 1575, the assembly had petitioned the regent 'that so many ministers as may be had, quhilks as yet are unplaced, may be receivit, asweill in the countrey, to releive the charge of them that hes many kirks, as utherwayes throughout the haill realme'. (*BUK*, i, 338.)

maist commodious kirkis to stand and to be repairit sufficientlie and qualefeit ministeris placet thairat, and the uther *z*kirkis quhilk ar not fund necessar may be sufferit to decay, thair kirk*z* yairdis alwayis being kepit for buriall places, and in sum places quhair neid requiris ane parochine quhair the congregatioun is ovir greit *z*for ane kirk*z* may be devidit in twa or ma.[205]

5. Doctouris wald be appointit in universiteis, collegis and uther places neidfull and sufficientlie provydit for to oppen up the meaning of the Scripturis*a* and to have the charge of scoles and teache the rudimentis of religioun.[206]

6. As to eldaris, thair wald be sum to be censuris of*b* maneris of the peple, ane or ma in everie*c* congregatioun, bot not ane assemblie of eldaris in every particular kirk, bot onlie in the townis and famous places quhair resort of men of jugement and habilitie to that office may be had.[207]

z not in NLS Wodrow
a *for the opening up of the Scripturis* in both GUL, and NLS Adv.
b *to censure the* in both GUL, and NLS Adv.   *c* *ilk* in NLS Wodrow

[205] In 1581, the king reported to the assembly that plans had been prepared by a group of privy councillors and ministers showing 'how elderships may be constitute of a certaine number of parochines [lyand] togither; small parochines to be united, and the great to be divydit, for the better sustentatioun of the ministrie, and the more commodious resort of the commoun peiple to thair kirks'. (*BUK*, ii, 477.)

[206] This recalls the assembly's request in 1574 that the Regent Morton 'take ordour that doctouris may be placit in universities and stipends grantit unto them'. Walter Travers made a similar plea in England: 'let teachers and doctors be provided (suche as we have but a fewe right and lawfull in these our dais) to teache the churches and especially the rude and ignorant. (*BUK*, i, 305; Travers, *A full and plaine declaration*, 139.) See also above, V. 1–6.

[207] Whereas most Reformed churches organised on conciliar or presbyterian lines (such as those of the French, Dutch and English presbyterians) advocated or adopted four courts within a nation, here only three courts are postulated; and the intention seems to have been not to create a new court as such but rather to remodel and extend the jurisdiction of kirk sessions by abandoning an attempt to create elderships for individual congregations and by adopting instead a scheme for establishing communal elderships of neighbouring parishes, a policy consistent with Beza's advice to lord Glamis for elderships 'made of the pastors of parishes both of city and country and a sufficient number of men approved for their godliness and wisdom'. The attempt to link the elderships with 'the towns and famous places where resort men of judgment and ability' recalls earlier efforts in the first Book of Discipline to associate the rural hinterland with 'the best reformed citie and towne', where 'the ministers of the parish kirks in landwart adjacent to every chief town' within a radius of six miles was expected to attend

7. Quhair the eldaris of particular kirkis about may convene togidder and have ane commoun elderschip and assemblie place*ᵈ* amangis thame to treat of all thingis that concerne the congregatioun of quhome thay have the oversycht.*ᵉ* ²⁰⁸

8. And as thair aucht to be men appointit*ᶠ* to unit and devyd the parochis as necessitie and commoditie requiris, sa wald thair be appointit be the generall kirk, with the assent*ᵍ* of the prince, sic*ʰ* ⁱmen as feirith God and knew the estait of the cuntreisⁱ *ʲ*that war able to nominat and designe*ᵏ* places quhair the assembles of*ˡ* particular elderschippis²⁰⁹ sould convene to tak consideratioun of the dioces as thay war dividit of auld and of the estait of the cuntres*ʲ* and provincis of the realme.²¹⁰

ᵈ placeit in TCD; *plantit* in NLS Wodrow   *ᵉ have charge* in NLS Wodrow
ᶠ appointit not in TCD   *ᵍ with advyce* in both GUL, and NLS Adv.
ʰ sic as in NLS Wodrow   ⁱ not in NLS Wodrow
ʲ not in both GUL, and NLS Adv.   *ᵏ denominat and assigne* in PRO
ˡ assembles of not in AUL, NLS Wodrow, and TCD

the 'exercise'. In Geneva, the consistory was composed of the city ministers and twelve elders, but 'the pastors of the surrounding villages were expected to attend whenever there were charges pending against their own parishioners, and could attend at other times'. (*SHS Miscellany*, viii, 103; *First Book of Discipline*, 97, 190; Kingdon, *Geneva and the Consolidation of the French Protestant Movement*, 39.) See also above, VII. 2, 14, 16 and notes 99, 111, 113; and below XII. 8 n. 210.

²⁰⁸ This merely forms a continuation of the preceding sentence in XII. 6 above; 'congregatioun' should presumably be plural.

²⁰⁹ The 'assembles of particular elderschippis' refers to the 'common elderships and assembly places', or presbyteries, mentioned in XII. 7 above.

²¹⁰ In July 1579, the assembly discussed the need for 'a general order to be taken for erecting of presbyteries in places quher publick exercise is used', and by October 1580 an assembly commission was formed for devising a platt for presbyteries in consultation with the privy council. In April 1581, the king's commissioner reported to the assembly that 'ther is, be commandment and advyce of sick of our counsell and the ministers as conferrit in this purpose, some forme drawin how elderships may be constitute of a certaine number of parochines [lyand] togither; small parochines to be united and the great to be divydit'. The king had also directed 'some of the principall noble and gentle men and certaine of the ministers within the bounds of every elderschip to conveine, advyse and report thair advyce to us'. The same assembly proceeded with plans to reduce over 900 parishes to 'sax hundreth kirks to be divydit in fiftie presbyteries, twelve to every presbytrie or therabout', and 'to the effect this ordour of elderships may be establischit in the saids townes with the better expedient and more convenient forme, the kirk hes namit the brethren underwrytin to take care and travells to sie the same constitute betuixt and the last day of May nixt to come'. It also replied to the king 'with thanks to his hienes for the labors which had been taken for constitution of presbyteries, union and divisione of kirks, which the assemblie

XII: CERTANE SPECIALL HEIDIS OF REFORMATIOUN

9. Lykwayis as concerning provinciall and synodall assembleis, consideratioun war easie to be had*[m]* how mony and in quhat places thay war to be haldine and how oftene thay sould convene, aucht to be referrit unto the libertie of the generall kirk and ordour to be appointit thairin.[211]

10. The nationall assembleis of this cuntrie, callit commounlie the generall assembleis, aucht alwayis to be retenit*[n]* in thair awin libertie and to haif thair awin place with power to the kirk to appoint tymis and places convenient thairfoir.[212]

11. And all men, alsweill magistrattis as inferiouris, to be subject to the jugment of the same in ecclesiasticall causis*[o]* without ony reclamatioun or appellatioun to onie*[p]* judge, civile or ecclesiasticall, within this realme.[213]

[m] taken in the other MSS *[n]* receivit in NLS Adv.
[o] effairis in NLS Wodrow *[p]* reclamatioun of onie in NLS Wodrow

---

had so far travelled that certan presbytries ar be them erected'. The next step came in May 1581 when the privy council pressed ahead with a revision of the ancient diocesan and parochial boundaries, in recognition of the difficulties experienced in establishing 'ony formall order thairanent, likly to have continewance to the posteritie, quhill the ancient boundis of the diocyes be desolvit: quhair the parochinnis ar thik togidder and small, to be unitit, and quhair thay ar of ower great and large boundis to be devidit that thairefter presbitereis or elderschippis may be constitute'. (*BUK*, ii, 439, 470, 477, 480–7, 514, 519; *RPC*, iii, 383.) Although thirteen model presbyteries were immediately erected in central and southern Scotland as 'exemplars to the rest'. (Calderwood, *History*, iii, 523; *BUK*, ii, 482), little was achieved by way of reducing over 900 parishes to the envisaged 600; and as a result kirk sessions continued to function alongside presbyteries, both confusingly styled 'elderships'.

[211] In 1581 the assembly resolved that there should be 'thrie of thir presbyteries, or moe or fewer, as the countrey lyis, to make ane diocie, according to ane forme after following, to be considderit of. Of thir number, certaine of presbyteries salbe the synodall assemblie: and ilk synodall assemblie sall appoint the place within that province for thair nixt synodall. Of persons direct from the synodall assemblies sall the general assemblie consist'. (*BUK*, ii, 480ff.)

[212] See above VII. 4, and n. 100.

[213] Despite the Regent Morton's attempts to subordinate the assembly to council and parliament (*RPC*, ii, 346–7, 560, 565; iii, 209–10, 237), the assembly showed no signs of withering away and remained the church's supreme court. In 1567, parliament itself had recognised the assembly (and not, as might have been expected, the privy council or court of session) as the final court of appeal in certain cases involving disputed rights of patronage. (*APS*, iii, 23, c. 7.) As early as 1563, the assembly had recognised an appellate jurisdiction from the subordinate church courts to the assembly, 'fra the whilk it sall not be leisum to the said pairtie to appeale'. The claim was repeated in 1582 (*BUK*, i, 33; ii, 564).

12. The libertie of electioun of personis callit to ecclesiasticall functionis and observit without interruptit continewance salang as the kirk was not corruptit be antichryst we desyr to be restoirat and retenid within this realme.²¹⁴

13. So that nane be intrusit upone ony congregatioun, aither be prince or ony uther inferiour persone, without lauchfull electioun²¹⁵ and the assent*q* of the *r*peple ovir quhom the persone is placet, as the practise of the apostolicall*r* primitive kirk and guid ordour cravis.²¹⁶

14. And becaus this ordour quhilk Goddis word cravis can not stand with patronagis and presentationis to beneficis usit in the papis kirk, we desyr all thame that trewlie feiris God eirnistlie to considder that foralsmekle as the name of patronagis and beneficis togiddir with the effect*s* thairof ar flowand frome the pape and corruptioun of the canone law onlie insafar as thairby ony persone was intrusid and placit ovir kirkis having *curam animarum*, and *t*forsamekle as that maner of proceding hes na ground in*t* the word of God,

q consent in NLS Wodrow   *r* not in GUL 1132   *s office* in NLS Wodrow
t not in NLS Wodrow

²¹⁴ See above III. 7, and notes 48, 49. The protest here is against the exercise of rights of patronage (XII, 14 below), and of crown nomination and capitular election to the greater beneficies. (See above XI. 9, 22, and notes 181, 197.)

²¹⁵ The method of 'lawful election' has to be distinguished from congregational consent. (See above III. 7, 9, and notes 48, 49, 51.)

²¹⁶ When the crown had attempted to appoint bishops in 1571 without consulting the church, Erskine of Dun condemned the action and protested that 'this is the ordour quhilk we requeir to be observit in placeing of men in beneficies quhatsumevir, haifing thairto jonit the office of a pastour. First, we refer, according to the lawis, to the patron the naming or presenting of the persone that sould be placed, quhowbeit we haif it be the Scriptouris and consuetud of the primitive kirk that the congregatione namit the persone. The man being nemit or presented, than it is requirit that sic of the ministerie as hes commissione and cuir to exeme the persone namit, nocht privatlie bot publictlie, be the advyiss and counsall of the haill congregatione, of his conversatione, his fear of God, his lerning and doctrene; and he being fund qualifeit, he to be admitit and resavit be the ministerie foirsaid to the spirituall function, with the consent of the congregatione; for it is requerit that the pastouris of the kirk do all thingis concerning the publict efferis of the kirk with consent of the congregatione, and that the admissioun be publict, be impositione of handis be the pastouris, with admonitionis, fastings and prayers passing befoir. This godlie ordour for preservatione of the kirk in puritie, we wis of God that the prince, the maiestratis, and all people wald admit and authorise, and nocht repyne aganis the samin'. (*Spalding Club Miscellany* iv, 99–100.)

XII: CERTANE SPECIALL HEIDIS OF REFORMATIOUN 235

but is contrar to the same *and to the said* libertie of
electioun thay aucht not now to have place in this lycht of
reformatioun, and thairfoir quhasaevir will trewlie imbrace
Goddis word and desyr the kingdome of his sone Jesus
Chryst to be advancit thay will also imbrace and resave that
policie and ordour quhilk the word of God and upricht
stait of his kirk cravis utherwys it is in vane that thay sould
have professid the samin.[217] Notwithstanding as concerning
uther patronagis of beneficies that have not *curam animarum*
(as thay speik) sic as ar chaplanries, prebendaries fundit upon
temporall landis, and annuallis and siclyk may be reservit*
unto the ancient patronis* to dispone tharupone quhen thay
veak to scolleris and bursaris, as thay ar requirit be the act of
parliament.[218]

15. As to the kirk rentis in generall, we desyr the ordour to be
admittit and mantenit amangis us that may stand with

u not in NLS Wodrow
v not in NLS Wodrow
w reformit in GUL 1122 and NLS Wodrow; *resigned* in SRO
x patronages in TCD

[217] The claim here is for a return to the earlier ideal of subverting the benefice
system, as advocated in the first Book of Discipline, which proposed dissolving
the prelacies, separating spirituality from temporality and reorganising the chaotic
state of ecclesiastical finances. In 1567, the assembly had called for a restoration
of the church's patrimony 'according to the booke of God, and the ordour and
practise of the primitive kirk'; and in 1571 the hope was still expressed that the
prelacies might be dissolved. (*First Book of Discipline*, 158ff; *BUK*, i, 107; Calderwood, *History*, iii, 159.) Such a view, now reiterated, agreed with the statement
in Beza's Confession of Faith that 'tout ce trafic de présentations, de droit de
patronat, de collations, de résignations, et d'autres choses ausi vilaines, procède de
Satan, même si leurs premiers commencements furent, sans aucun doute, meilleurs
et plus louables'. A more flexible note was struck when Beza advised lord Glamis
that the right of patronage might be conceded 'but not without some conditions:
namely, that he which shall be chosen by the free voices of the eldership should
be offered by the patrons to the king's majesty, being also to set upon his charge
after the consenting of his flock'. (Beza, *La Confession de foi*, V, xxxv; *SHS
Miscellany*, viii, 105.)

[218] In 1567, parliament required patrons of provostries, prebendaries, altarages
and chaplainries to present bursars on a vacancy to sustain them in their studies at
university. This measure was ratified in 1581 and again in 1592. (*APS*, iii, 25,
210, 586–7.) For the operation of the act, see Durkan and Kirk, *The University of
Glasgow*, 358ff. In 1581, the assembly complained that some of these livings were
still 'givin to courtiers' and argued that those with the cure of souls attached
should be assigned to ministers and that others should be made available for
school-teachers. (*BUK*, ii, 536.)

sinceritie of Goddis word and practes of the puritie of the kirk of Christ.[219]

16. To wit, as was befoir spokine,[220] in the haill rent and patrimony of the kirk (excepting the small patronagis befoir mentionat) may be devydit in four partis and portionis: ane thairof to be assignit to the pasture for his intertenement and for hospitalitie; ane uther to the eldaris, deaconis[221] and utheris officiaris of the kirk sic as clerkis of assembleis, takaris up of the psalmis,[222] beddallis and keparis of the kirkis[223] safar as thay ar necessar, joyning thairwith also the

---

[219] See above IX. 1–3, and n. 145; XII. 14 n. 217.

[220] See above IX. 9.

[221] In 1560, the first Book of Discipline had decided that a 'publick stipend' for elders and deacons was not necessary 'because their travell continues but for a yeare, and also because that they are not so occupied with the affairs of the kirk but that reasonably they may attend upon their domesticall businesse'. (*First Book of Discipline*, 179.) The second Book of Discipline, which envisaged appointing elders and deacons for life, recommended that they should receive remuneration, in accordance with the canons of the early church. Yet the suggestion here, it would seem, was not that elders and deacons should permanently put aside their occupations but that they should be reimbursed for loss of earnings. In 1597, the church maintained that elders were already elected for life, unless otherwise deprived, and that it was only because no financial assistance was forthcoming that they could not afford to neglect their occupations every year while attending to their ecclesiastical duties. For this reason, some were elected to relieve others, though all remained elders. (Calderwood, *History*, v, 588.)

[222] See above IX. 9, and notes 154–156.

[223] Beadles sometimes acted as executive officers for the kirk session, as was so in St Ninians where two offenders were 'oft tymes callit and lauchfullie summond . . . be the beddall of the eldarship of thair awin kirk of S. Niniane at command thairof'. (SRO, CH2/722/3. Stirling Presbytery Records, 13 June 1599.) Linlithgow town council in 1564 paid the fee 'for rynging of the bellis, keping of the kirk and keping of the basyne and towell for baptysme as salbe appointit be the eldaris' (SRO, B48/7/1. Linlithgow Court Book, 1 March 1563/4); and in Haddington, the council in 1567 acceded to the petition of sir William Wilson who held the parish clerkship and who was prepared to provide 'watter at the ministratioun of the sacrament of baptism, hald the kirk clene, clois and oppin the kirk durris at tymes convenient and to do sic service in the kirk as now appertenis to the clerkschip' if he also undertook 'to sing the psalmis ilk Sonday the tymes usit and be chantur thairto'. (SRO, B30/10/2. Haddington Court Book, 26 March 1567.) In Perth, the kirk session augmented by £8 a year the fee of 'thair officiar and commone servand' who 'sustenis great panes and travellis as also is put to great expensis by daylie tempering of the clock, by awaiting on the sessione and daylie ringing of the bellis both at ordinar and extraordinar tymes'. (SRO, CH2/521/3. Perth Kirk Session Records, 15 March 1602.) In an earlier instance, the session ordered that his fees be paid by the master of the hospital. (*Ibid.*, CH2/521/1. fo. 71v., 10 Jan. 1585/6.) When the kirk of Leith attempted to choose a bellman and church officer in 1591, Edinburgh town

doctouris of scoles to help*ʸ* the ancient fundationis quhair neid requirith; the thrid portioun to be bestowit unto the pure memberis of the faythfull and hospitallis;²²⁴ the fourt for reparatioun of the kirkis and utheris extraordinar chargis as ar profitable for the kirk and also for the commoun welth, gif neid require.²²⁵

17. We desyr thairfoir the ecclesiasticall guidis to be upliftit and distributit faythfullie to quhome thay appertene and that be the ministrie of the deaconis to quhais office properlie the collectioun*ᶻ* and distributioun thairof belangis that the pure

ʸ *hald* in both GUL, and NLS Adv.; *all the doctours and scooles to helpe* in SRO
ᶻ *electione* in both GUL

---

council, 'as superiouris to the town of Leyth', intervened by discharging the candidate and intruding another which led to the presbytery's intervention in the dispute; and similar difficulties were encountered in Glasgow where the presbytery in 1594 declared 'the office of the ringing of the bell to the buriall of the deid to be ecclesiasticall, and that the electioun of the persone to the ringing of the said bell belongis to the kirk according to the auncient canonis and discipline in the reformit kirk'. (SRO, CH1/121/1. Edinburgh Presbytery Records, 16 Nov. 1591; GCA, Glasgow Presbytery Records, fo. 37v., 5 Nov. 1594.)

²²⁴ In Geneva, Calvin distinguished two types of deacon, the *procureur* who collected and administered alms for the poor, and the *hospitallier* who supervised the daily use of revenues gathered for the poor. (*CR*, XXXVIII, i, *Calvini Opera*, X, i, 23–25; Calvin, *Institutes*, IV, iii, 9; R. M. Kingdon, 'The Deacons of the Reformed Church in Calvin's Geneva', *Mélanges d'histoire du XVIᵉ siécle. Offerts à Henri Meylan* (Geneva, 1970), 81–89.) Although no such distinction was observed in Scotland, the church still exercised oversight of the hospitals, and the masters of the hospitals who were usually appointed by the town council, which also contributed to the hospitals' upkeep, were not infrequently members of the kirk session. (*BUK*, i, 44, 46, 60, 291, 339; *RStAKS*, ii, 879–881, 883, 906–7, 922–3, 929; *Edinburgh Burgh Records*, iii, 244–5, 247–8; iv, 54, 63, 80, 147, 403, 508, 554; *Stirling Burgh Records*, 81, 94.) In Perth kirk session, which acquired particular say in the running of the hospital, the names of the masters of the hospital are entered after those of the deacons in the annual election of 'elders and deacons and other officers elected and ordeyned to beare office' in the church. (SRO, CH2/521/2. Perth Kirk Session Records, fos. 2r., 11r., 31v., 41v., 53r., 66v., 85v., 107r., 133v., 160r.; CH2/521/3. fo. 1r.) In Perth and St Andrews, one deacon in particular was appointed 'distributer to the ordinar pure'. (*Ibid.*, 7 Oct. 1594, 12 Oct. 1601, 11 Oct. 1602; *RStAKS*, ii, 887, 906, 923.)

²²⁵ The fourfold division of the church's patrimony, though assigned to the support of the same categories, takes a slightly different form here from that described in IX. 9 above. The suggestion that surplus revenue might be allocated to affairs of the commonwealth recalls Erskine of Dun's compromise of 1571 for assigning 'suche profites as may be spaired above the reasounable sustentatioun of the ministrie of the kirks of suche benefices to the maintenance of the authoritie and commoun effaires for the present'. (Calderwood, *History*, iii, 159.) See also *BUK*, i, 70, 151–2, 154, 232.

may be answerit of thair portioun thairof and thay of the ministrie leve without care and solicitud as also the rest of [the] thesaurarie of the kirk may be ressavit*a* and bestowit to the rycht uses.²²⁶

18. Gif thayis deaconis be electit with sic qualiteis as Goddis word cravis to be in thame, thair is no feir that thay sall abuse thame selfis in thair office as the prophane collectouris did of befoir.*b* ²²⁷

19. Yit becaus this vocatioun appeiris to mony to be dangerous let them be oblist*c* (as thay war of auld) to ane yeirlie compt to the pasturis and elderschip and gif the kirk and prince think expedient lat cautioneris be obleist for thair fidelitie that the kirk rents onnawayis be delapidat.²²⁸

20. And to the effect this ordour may tak place it is to be provydit that all utheris intromettouris with the kirkis rentis, collectouris generall or speciall,²²⁹ quhidder it may be by the appointment of the prince or utherwayis be denudit of

a *resigned* in SRO; *reformit* in NLS Wodrow
b *the prophane did* in TCD   *c* *establisched* in GUL 1132

²²⁶ See above IX. 5, and n. 147.

²²⁷ In 1578, the privy council detected 'certane abusis and corruptionis' among the collectors of thirds of benefices and decided to revoke all pensions granted from the superplus of the thirds. (*RPC*, iii, 29–31.) Deacons, in practice, did not assume any of the collector's duties; and the appointments made at the Convention of Leith show the collectors to have been men of some standing in the community. (*BUK*, i, 234–5.)

²²⁸ Aware of the temptation for 'private men to use in their private business that which appertaines to the publick affaires of the kirk', the first Book of Discipline had required that 'the deacons shall be compelled and bound to make accounts to the minister and elders of that which they received'. (*First Book of Discipline*, 164.) In kirk sessions, it was common practice for auditors to be appointed to scrutinise the accounts rendered by the deacons. (SRO, CH2/450/1. Edinburgh General Session Records, 14 July 1575; CH2/1026/1. Stirling Kirk Session Records, 30 Nov., 7 Dec. 1598.) At a visitation of Kinnellar in 1602, the 'collector' of the penalties and other 'geir' was ordered to give an account of his intromissions to the ministers and elders; and in Edinburgh an elder was appointed treasurer of the general session. (SRO, CH2/1/1. Aberdeen Presbytery Records, 20 Aug. 1602; CH2/450/1. Edinburgh General Session Records, entry preceding that of 1 July 1574, and 3 March 1574/5.)

²²⁹ For collection of the thirds, the country was divided into twelve areas, each with a sub-collector accountable to the collector general who, in turn, accounted to the exchequer. (*Thirds of Benefices*, xv–xvi.) The accounts of the collector general survive from 1561 till 1597. (SRO, E45/1–25.)

forder intromissioun thairof and suffer the kirk rentis in tymis cuming to be haillalie intromettit with þe ministrie of the deaconis and distributit to the usis afoir mentionat.[230]

21. And also to the effect that the ecclesiasticall rentis may suffice to thair usis for the quhilkis thay ar to be appointit, we think it necessar to be desyrid that all alienationis,[a] setting in fewis or takis of the rentis of the kirk, alsweill landis as teindis, in hurt and diminutioun of the auld rentallis be reducit and annullat and the patrimony of the kirk restoirit to the formar and auld libertie.[231]

22. And lykwayis that in tymis cuming the teindis be set to nane bot to the labouraris of the ground or ellis not set at all as it was aggriet upone and subscryvit be the nobilitie befoir.[232]

[a] *abominationes* in both GUL

[230] See above IX. 5 and n. 147. Menmuir's 'Constant Platt' of 1596 recognised the minister's right to the teinds locally assigned, 'with power to the said minister to collect, gather and intromett with, and to make wairnings and inhibitiouns against the possessors of the said tithes, manses, and gleebs, with als great effect as anie parson or vicar, or anie other beneficed person, might have done in anie tyme bypast'; but there was still no practical attempt to assign to the deacons the collection of these revenues. (Calderwood, *History*, v, 425.)

[231] The general assembly continued its campaign against dilapidation of rentals through grants of feus, leases and pensions from benefices (*BUK*, i, 336, 373; ii, 413–4, 455, 601, 603, 632, 634; iii, 848–52, 939); and in an effort to eliminate abuses presbyteries undertook a survey of benefices within their jurisdiction and investigated reports of dilapidation. (SRO, CH2/722/1. Stirling Presbytery Records, 29 Jan. 1582/3, 9 April 1583, 14 Jan., 3 Mar. 1583/4; CH2/722/2. 3 Nov. 1590, 12 Sept. 1592; CH2/722/3. 23 June 1596; CH2/185/1. Haddington Presbytery Records, fos. 113v.–115v.; CH2/424/1. Dalkeith Presbytery Records, 23 Jan. 1583/4, 24 Sept. 1590; GCA, Glasgow Presbytery Records, fo. 61r.; *Synod of Lothian*, 7, 18, 49–50, 77, 83, 88.)

[232] The reform of the teind system in favour of the labourers or farmers, who worked the land, at the expense of the tacksmen or middlemen, who held the teinds, had been proposed by James V and was taken up by the reformers in the first Book of Discipline which laid claim to the teinds in their entirety for financing the work of the reformed church. By removing the middlemen, the farmers were to become directly accountable to the deacons for paying a composition in lieu of their teinds, since 'neither do we judge it to proceed of justice that any man should possesse the teinds of another, but we think it a most reasonable thing that every man have the use of his own teinds, provided that he answer to the deacons'. (G. Donaldson, *The Scottish Reformation* (Cambridge, 1960), 90; *First Book of Discipline*, 158.) Yet no comprehensive attempt was made to carry out these proposals until Charles I embarked on his revocation scheme which provided *inter alia* that 'every man may have his own teinds upon reasonable conditions'. (*RPC*, 2nd ser., i, 228.) The reference here to the nobles who agreed to a reform

of the teinds is an allusion to the convention of nobles and barons which approved the first Book of Discipline in January 1560/1 and to those who subscribed the accompanying act of privy council accepting, with certain reservations, the articles of the Book of Discipline. (*CSP Scot.*, i, nos. 958-9; Knox, *Works*, ii, 128, 297; *First Book of Discipline*, 210-12.)

XIII

THE UTILITIE THAT SALL FLOW OF THIS REFORMATIOUN TO ALL ESTAITIS

[1.] Seing the end of this spiritual government and policie quhairof we spak is that God may be glorefeit, the kingdome of Jesus Chryst*e* advancit and all thay quha ar of his mysticall bodie may leve peciablie in conscience, thairfoir we dar bawldlie affirme that all thay quha have trew respect to thais endis will evin for conscience caus glaidlie aggrie and conforme thame selfis to this ordour*f g*and advance the same safar as lyis in thame that thair conscience*g* being set at rest thay may be replenischid with spirituall gladnes in geving full obedience to that quhilk Goddis word and the testimony of thair conscience dois crave and refusing all corruptioun contrare unto the same.²³³

2. Nixt, we sall becum ane example and patrone*h* of guid and godlie ordour to uther nationis, cuntreis and kirkis professing the same religioun with us that as thay have glorifeit God in our continewing in the sinceritie of the word hitherto without all errouris (prayse be to his name) sa thay may have the lyk occasioun in our conversatioun*i* quhen as we conforme our selfis to that discipline, policie and guid ordour quhilk the same word and puritie of reformatioun craves at our handis,

---

e *mentenit and advancit* in NLS Wodrow   *f* *that* added in NLS Wodrow
g not in NLS Wodrow   *h* *paterne* in both GUL   *i* *life* in NLS Wodrow

²³³ The claim so expressed does not specify the need for parliamentary approval, though the expectation was that all Christians according to their estate should seek to promote and give effect to the book's proposals. Any hopes entertained by the assembly for an early ratification by parliament were diminished with parliament's decision in July 1578 that the book's proposals were of 'great wecht and consequence' necessitating a commission to examine and to compare the proposed polity with the Leith settlement of 1572. The assembly's repeated requests for royal approval also failed to secure a favourable response and led the king to require the assembly to 'let it so rest' until parliament determined the church's polity. Although, in April 1581, the king agreed to further discussion 'of all things requisite that may sett fordwart the Policie quhill the same may be establischit be law', the assembly, in an awareness of the continuing failure to secure the magistrate's approval, decided to register the Book of Discipline among the acts of assembly that 'posteritie sould judge weill of the present age and of the Assemblie of the Kirk'. (*APS*, iii, 105–6, 137–8; *BUK*, ii, 408, 410, 419, 428, 478, 487–8, 514.)

utherwayis this feirfull sentence may be justlie said to us: the servand knawand the will of the maister and not doing it.²³⁴

3. Mairovir, gif we have ony pitie or respect to the puir memberis of Chryst, quha sa greatlie incres and multiplie amangis us, we will not suffer thame to be langer defraudit of that part of the patrimony of the kirk quhilk justlie belangis unto thame, ʲand be this ordour, gif it be dewlie put in executioun,ʲ the burding of thame salbe takine of us to our greit comfort, the streitis salbe clangid of the cryingis and murmuringis of thame, as we salbe na mair sclander to uther nationis, as we have hitherto bene, for not taking ordour with the puir amangis us and causing the word quhilk we profes to be evill spokine of, giving occasioun of sclander to the enemies and offending the consciencis of the simple and godlie.²³⁵

ʲ not in both GUL, and NLS Adv.

²³⁴ In 1572, the Leith settlement was found by some not to conform sufficiently to 'the policies of the best reformed Kirks' (*BUK*, i, 246), and may be said to have deflected the attainment of earlier reformed ideals. In 1566, John Knox had remarked on the 'great puritie God did establisse amangis us his treu Religioun, alsweall in doctrine as in ceremonyes', and had professed a belief that 'as tueching the doctrine taught by our Ministeris, and as tueching the administratioun of Sacramentis used in our Churches, we ar bold to affirme that thair is no realme this day upoun the face of the earth that hath thame in grettar puritie: for all others (how synceare that ever the doctrine be, that by some is taught) reteane in thair churches, and the ministers thairof, some footsteppis of Antichrist, and some dreggis of Papistrie; but we (all praise to God alone) have nothing within oure Churches that ever flowed frome that Man of synne'. The somewhat similar sentiments expressed here were probably made in knowledge of the claims for further reform advanced by English puritans, and particularly by English presbyterians, who were in touch with Scottish opinion and who in their 'Admonition to the Parliament' in 1572 had questioned 'Is a reformation good for France? and can it be evyl for England? Is discipline meete for Scotland? and is it unprofitable for this Realme?' (*Puritan Manifestoes*, 19.)

²³⁵ See above IX. 9 and n. 151; XII. 16 and n. 224. In 1569, the general assembly had urged that 'ordour may be takin for sustentatioun of the poore and that ane portioun of the teinds be appointit for that effect'; and the Leith settlement in 1572 had suggested that a tenth of the teinds of beneficces should be devoted to 'support of the pure in a part'. Parliament took action in March 1574/5 by requiring elders and deacons in towns and 'headsmen' in rural parishes to prepare a yearly roll of the poor and impotent, who were natives or residents for seven years, and to collect a weekly contribution for their support, or, failing this, to license the poor to beg for alms. In August 1575, the assembly petitioned that 'the ordour already tane toward the poore may be put in full executioun: and to that effect, that a portion of the teinds quhilk is thair awin patrimonie asweill of the twa part as of the thrids may be imployit for thair sustentatioun according as necessity craves'. (*BUK*, i, 146, 216, 339; *APS*, iii, 86–9.)

4. Besydis this, it salbe a greit ease and commoditie to the haill commoun peple *k*and releving*k* thame of the beilding and uphalding of thair kirkis, in bigging of briggis and uther lyk publick warkis, to the laubourars of the ground in the payment of thair teindis, and schortlie in all theis thingis, quhairunto thay have bene hitherto rigorouslie handlit be thame that war falslie callit kirkmen, thair takkismen, factouris*l* and extortioneris.[236]

5. Finallie, to the kingis majestie and common welth of the cuntrie, this profit sall redound that the uther effairis of the kirk being sufficientlie provydit according to the distributioun of the quhilk hes bene spoken, the superplus being collectit into the thesaurarie of the kirk may be profitablie employit and liberallie bestowit upone the extraordinar support of the effairis of the prince and commoun welth, and speciallie of that part quhilk is appointit for reparatioun of the kirks.[237]

6. Sa, to conclude, all being willing to apply thameselfis to *m*this ordour,*m* *n*the peple suffering tham selfis to be reulit*n* according thairunto (the princis and magistratis thame selfis not being exemit)[238] and thay that ar placit in ecclesiasticall estait rychtlie reuling and governing, God salbe glorefeit, the kirk edifeit, the boundis thairof enlargit, Chryst Jesus

k in rewling of in NLS Wodrow
l chalmerlandis added in AUL, both GUL, NLS Adv., SRO and TCD
m be orderit in NLS Wodrow   *n* not in NLS Wodrow

[236] See above IX. 9; XII. 16; and XII. 22, n. 232. The claim for a restoration of the church's full patrimony and its redistribution according to the fourfold division of the ancient canons contained an appeal to the commons who would be relieved from undue burdens and exactions. In 1569, the assembly had petitioned that 'the pure labourers of the ground may have intromissioun to lead their awin teinds upon reasonable compositioun', and proceeded in 1572 to criticise the nobility 'that thai be reformit in the wrangous using of the patrimonie of the Kirk, applying the same to their particular use, to the great hurt of the Ministerie, the Scullis and Poore: and that the Commonis may be eased be thame baith in paying of their teinds and utheris dewties in respect of thair great povertie'. (BUK, i, 146, 252–3.)

[237] See above XII. 16 and n. 225. The church had repeatedly recognised that surplus fruits from the church's patrimony, after provision was made for the ministry, poor, schools and churches, might be devoted to the 'publick charges' of the prince and commonwealth; and Beza had advised lord Glamis to similar effect. (BUK, i, 70, 151–2, 154, 232; Calderwood, History, iii, 159–60; SHS Miscellany, viii, 112.)

[238] See above, I. 21–23.

and his kingdome set up, Sathane and his kingdome subvertit,° and God sall dwell in the middis of us to our comfort, throw Jesus Chryst, quha togiddir with the Fader and the Halie Ghaist, abydeth blissit in all eternitie. So be it.[239]

Finis
Deo gratias
Mr J. Riche[240]

[Subscription by Haddington presbytery]

This buik of policie being red apart privatlie be the maist part at sindrie tymis and the penult of September 1591 being [red] publicklie in the elderschip of Hadingtoun was subscryvit be the brethren thairof according to the act of the generall assemblie as followis:

Act 8 *Augusti* 1590
Sessio 10.

Mr Thomas McGhie, minister of Gulane.
Mr James Carmichael, minister at Hadingtoun
James Gibsone, minister at Pencatland.
Mr W. Hay, Bothans
Thomas Greg, minister at North Beruik
James Reid, minister at Garvat kirk
Mr G. Byris, minister of Godis Word at Barow
James Lamb, minister at Boltoun kirk
Mr Johne Ker, minister at Aberladay
Daniel Wallace, minister at Mororme [Morham]

° *abolischit* in NLS Wodrow

[239] The failure to secure for the second Book of Discipline the support of the crown and parliament led the assembly in 1581 to register the Book of Discipline among the acts of assembly. By 1590, the assembly resolved that all ministers 'salbe chargit be every particular Presbytrie quher thair residence is to subscrive the heids of Discipline of the Kirk of this realme at lenth sett downe and allowit be the act of the haill Assemblie in the Book of Policie quhilk is registrat in the Register of the Kirk'. (*BUK*, ii, 487–8; iii, 773.)

[240] The signature of James Ritchie, clerk to the general assembly from 1574 until his death in 1596, authenticates the text of Haddington presbytery's copy of the second Book of Discipline. (See Introduction, 155.)

APPENDIX I

Conference on the second Book of Discipline, 1578.

In December 1578, a conference was held at Stirling castle 'in the utter high chamber, direct above the king's majestie's inner hall' by thirteen commissioners, among whom were included the two archbishops and five ministers to discuss the contents of the second Book of Discipline. Their resolutions were recorded by Calderwood and, with some variations often in less detailed form, by Spottiswoode. Calderwood, however, only related the decisions of the conference to the numbers of the chapter headings and articles of the second Book of Discipline, which do not correspond with the numbering of the articles or sub-sections in the version of the book contained in a later section of Calderwood's *History* among the acts of assembly for April 1581. The correct order of the decisions taken at the conference at Stirling in relation to the enumeration of the articles in the Haddington text of the Book of Discipline, depicted above, has been reconstructed and is presented below.

The thirteen 'commissioners', whom the king invited to take part in the conference, consisted of the earl of Buchan, the archbishops of St Andrews and Glasgow, the commendator of Dunfermline, the lairds of Dun and Seggie, the tutor of Pitcur, George Buchanan and Peter Young, and Robert Pont, James Lawson, John Row and David Linsday. Erskine of Dun was elected moderator for the duration of the conference, which lasted for nine days; and the ministers, who took part, were careful to 'protest' that they convened only at the king's request and not as commissioners authorised by the church to negotiate.[1]

Chapter I:

22 December, 1578

1-3. 'Entering in reasoning and conference, the saids commissioners agreed in one voice unto the first [three] sentences or heeds, as they are writtin, word by word, in the said Booke of Policie presented to the king's Majestie'.

4. 'The [fourth] sentence or article was by one consent remitted to the morne, to receave further reasoning; and

[1] Calderwood, *History*, iii, 433–442; Spottiswoode, *History*, ii, 232–253.

the doctors, with other ancient writters, ordeaned to be brought, who best could informe in that purpose'.

23 December, 1578

'All the said commissioners conveened, and invocatioun of God's name being made, the said sentence was agreed by the whole commissioners, to witt, that the kirk is sometimes taikin for them that exercise the spirituall functioun in particular congregatiouns'.

'To consider how this [fourth] article sould be understood, whether of the particular presbyterie or the generall kirk'.

5. 'The [fifth] article bearing *This power, etc.*, is thought good to be continued to further reasoning and explanatioun. And where it is said *This power floweth from God to his kirk*, whether this sould be understood of the whole kirk or of the office-bearers, or whether it floweth mediatlie or immediatlie'.
6. 'Refered to further reasoning'.
7. 'In the [seventh] article, thir words *The former is called potestas ordinis commounlie, and the other potestas jurisdictionis* are thought not necessar, and therefore to be deleted'.
8. 'Agreed'.
9. 'Agreed'.
10. 'In this article, thir words would be left out *ecclesiasticall floweth immediatlie from God and from the Mediator Jesus Christ*, and say in stead therof, *for this power is spirituall having, etc.*'
11. 'Agreed'.
12. 'Agreed'.
13. 'The [thirteenth] agreed unto, eeking to thir words, *They sall not be called lords over their flocke*'.
14. 'Agreed, onlie changing thir words, *Ecclesiasticall governement*, instead wherof to say *Ecclesiasticall discipline*, according to the Word of God'.
15. 'Refered to further reasoning when the order of bishops sall be discussed'.

24 December, 1578

16. 'Lettin stand over whill they come to the distributioun of the power'.

17. 'Agreed, as it is conceaved in the booke'.
18. 'Differre this to be reasouned with the [16th]'.
19-20. 'Referre thir two'.
21. 'Agreed, that the magistrat nather ought to preache, minister the sacraments, nor execut the censures (which is to be understood, excommunication) of the kirk; and referre the secund part of this answere to further reasoning; and agreed that the minister, as minister, exerce not civill jurisdiction in respect of his ministrie; and referre the last part'.
22-23. 'Refered both'.

Chapter II:
1. 'The name of the kirk in this article is taikin for the kirk in the first significatioun, to witt, for the whole kirk. Agreed with the rest of the article'.
2-3. 'Referred thir two'.
4-5. 'Agreed both'.
6. 'Referred to reasoning at the heed of the Visiters'.
7-12. 'Referred'.

Chapter III:
1-6. 'Agreed unto'.
7. 'Referred'.

25 December, 1578

8. 'Agreed with the generalitie heerof'.
9. 'Agreed, with this additioun at the end of the article, *if the people have a lawfull caus against his life and maners*'.
10. 'Agreed. A supplicatioun be formed, and givin to the king's Majestie and estats in the nixt parliament concerning ministers that travell at kirks where the benefice therof may vaike by deceasse of the old possessors, that in that cace the patrons may preferre the ministers that serve there to all others for that time allenarlie'.
11. 'Agreed, eeking after this word *kirk* thir words *to travell in the spirituall function there*'.
12. 'Agreed, leaving out thir words *of the eldership*'.
13-15. 'Agreed'.

R

16. 'Agreed, and that all ministers of the Word and sacrament sall mak residence'.
17. 'Agreed'.

Chapter IV:
1. 'Agreed, saving this word *bishop* is referred to the place of visitatioun'.
2-5. 'Agreed'.
6. 'Referred to after noone'.
7-8. 'Agreed'.
9. 'Agreed, eeking thir words *to pray for the prince and the people*'.
10. 'Agreed'.
11. 'Agreed that the minister, who is the mouth of God, may pronounce the sentence of excommunication after lawfull proceeding'.
12. 'Agreed with the present order concerning mariage after lawfull proceeding'.
13. 'Agreed'.

Chapter V: 'Refers the whole chapter till further reasoning'.

Chapter VI:
1-2. 'Passed over'.
3-5. 'Agreed upon; the name of elders to be joynned with ministers'.
6-7. 'Referred the perpetuitie of elders to further deliberatioun'.
8. 'Agreed'.
9-10. 'Referred'.
11-17. 'Agreed'.

Chapter VII:
1. 'Agreed that the ministers and elders of everie particular kirk sall have power of everie spirituall thing within their owne jurisdiction consonant to the lawes'.
2. 'Agreed that there sall be particular assembleis of kirks; synodalls in provinces, and nationall, which we call Generall, within this realme, which we crave to be made a law of, and erected in parliament'.

26 December 1578

3-4. 'Agreed that in provinciall or synodall assembleis he that beareth charge of visitation of the kirks of that province, together with the pastors and doctors of the same province, and some of the elders of everie particular congregatioun within the same bounds, being authorized by commission of their congregations, sall resort to the said provinciall assembleis, of which persons it consisteth; and thir assembleis to be twise in the yeere at least, and ofter as occasioun sall crave; and also, thir assembleis to have libertie to appoint times and places of the same, as they sall thinke expedient; and that the Generall Assembleis may be once in the yeer or ofter, as necessitie requireth; and the king's Majesteis authoritie to be craved to be interponed heerunto in parliament. And the visiter of everie province, with the minister and the two elders therof, and a commissioner of everie burgh of the said province, chosin by the synodall assemblie of the same, sall come to the said Generall Assemblie, not secluding therefra other noble and godlie men that please to come thereto, providing that they sall not have libertie to vote above the number of fifteen, with the king's Majesteis commissioners, if it please his Hienesse to send anie thither. And that no sentence of excommunicatioun be pronounced by anie particular kirk or minister, but by consent of him that beareth the charge of visitation within the bounds therof, and by advice of six pastors joynned to the visiter in the provinciall assemblie of the countrie; and the six to be chosin by the provinciall assemblie to be assessors to the said visiter. And this order to be observed also in other maters'.

5. 'Agreed that in all Generall Assembleis a moderator be chosin'.
6. 'Agreed' (in Calderwood); 'referred' (in Spottiswoode).
7. 'Referred'.
8. 'Differred to the heed of Reformation of the Bishops'.
9. 'Agreed'.
10. 'Agreed, joynning in the end of the article thir words *in spirituall things onlie*'.
11. 'Agreed that as they have power to make lawes according

to the Word of God in spirituall things, so as the necessitie of time requireth they may alter and change the same'.

27 December 1578

12–25. 'Referred'.
26. 'An article to be formed for ministers who through age, sickenesse or other accidents are become unable to doe their office; in which cace that suche be provided for during their lyfe-time, notwithstanding the said impediments'.
27–29. 'Referred'.
30. 'Agreed upon that the provinciall assemblie hath this power for suche as sall be agreed upon in the article of depositioun. That with the article of deposition, a supplicatioun be givin in to the king's Majestie and estats, desiring a law to be made that the person so deposed, if it be a beneficed man, the benefice sall vaike and another be placed in his rowme'.
31–32. 'Past over'.
33. 'Answered before'.
34. 'Agreed'.
35. 'Differed to the heed of The Bishops'.
36. 'Differred'.
37. 'Agreed that this Assemblie sould take heed that the spirituall jurisdiction meddle not with civill maters'.
38. 'Referred'.
39. 'Agreed in spirituall maters'.
40–41. 'Referred'.

Chapters VIII and IX: 'Concerning the chapters of the Diaconat, and the patrimonie of the kirk, it is thought good to be superseeded whill the heed of the corruptions be reasouned. That an article be made and givin in to the parliament how the poore may be supported'.

Chapter X: 'The whole chapter is thought good. That an article be formed and givin in to the king's Majestie and estats craving an aid to be made that a speciall punishment be ordeanned for suche as putt violent hands in ministers of the Word of God; and also to crave suche immuniteis and priviledges as sall be thought meet by suche as sall penne the same'.

Chapter XI:
1. 'Agreed'.
2. 'Agreed that a supplication be formed and givin in to the king's Majestie and estats craving dissolution of kirks, benefices, prelaceis and others which are united and givin to one person; and the severall kirks to be givin to qualifeid ministers, at least, after deceasse of the present possessors'.
3–6. 'Past over'.
7. 'Answered by article of Dissolutioun'.
8. 'Agreed, and that an act sall be sought that no united benefice be dispouned to anie person after deceasse of the present possessors; but particular kirks therof to be provided to ministers and pastors, as said is'.
9. 'Differed'.
10. 'Agreed'.
11. 'Differed'.
12. 'Agreed and thought reasonable that everie bishop have his particular flocke'.
13–14. 'Agreed, and an article to be givin in parliament that the dioceis be divided in suche sorte as men may reasonablie visie, and that they have no farther bounds nor they may oversee'.

28 December 1578

15. 'Anent the perpetuitie of the visiters, it is referred to further reasoning and conference that good resolutioun may be takin therin'.
16. 'Past over'.
17. 'Agreed'.
18. 'Agreed, that bishops sall have a certan flocke'.
19–20. 'Past over'.
21. 'Agreed'.
22. 'Referred'.
23. 'Agreed'.
24. 'Agreed'.
25. 'Agreed that an article be made that no possessor of

benefice, als weill prelats as others, or that sall come heerafter, sall hurt or diminishe the patrimonie of the said benefices'.
26. 'Finds good that the kirk advise what maters now handled by the commissioners [*recte*, commissaries] are meete and expedient to be treatted and handled before them'.
27. 'Answered before'.

Chapter XII:
1–4. 'Agreed, and an article to be givin in therupon'.
5. 'Agreed'.

29 December 1578

6–7. 'Differred to the joynning of the kirks'.
8. 'Agreed, as a dependent upon the former'.
9. 'Past before in the mater of the provinciall assembleis
10–11. 'Agreed as before'.
12–13. 'Agreed to this generall'.
14. 'Referred to the article of the Patronage'.
14. [*chaplainries*, etc] 'Agreed, and that an act of parliament concerning the disposition of provestreis, prebendreis and chaplanreis may be reformed, conforme to the article to be givin in therupon'.
15–20. 'Referred to the heed of the Diaconat, and to the provisioun to be made for the poore'.
21. 'Agreed, conforme to the lawes'.
22. 'Referred'.

'To penne an article of non-residence.
That an article be givin in craving a civill punishment may be had against them that admitt an unqualified person to the office of the ministrie of the Word, and of them that make simoniacall pactioun, being convicted by the Generall Assemblie; and that this act strike not onlie upon him that beareth the charge of the diocie, but upon his assessors, so many as consent to the same.
It is thought meet, by supplicatioun to the king's Majestie and estats, it sall be craved that additioun be made to the act of parliament confirming laick patronages, that the said act be extended als weill to the patronage of the king's Majestie as others.

Agreed that an article be formed and givin in parliament, concerning the kirk's libertie to the thrids.

Agreed that the presentations be directed according to to the act of parliament standing therupon.

And that an article be formed and givin in to the king's Majestie and estats in the nixt parliament, and that provisioun be made for visiters till farther order be tane.

Referred the penning of the articles and other things agreed in this conference or that may be found profitable to the kirk, speciallie the caus of Deprivatioun, to the Lord Dunfermline, the Laird of Segie, Mr Robert Pont, Mr James Lowsone, Alexander Hay, Mr David Lindsey to putt them in suche forme as they may be givin in and past in this nixt parliament.'

APPENDIX II

Criticisms of the second Book of Discipline, c. 1585

The following observations on the second Book of Discipline are contained among the Balcarres Papers in the National Library of Scotland (Adv. MS. 29.2.8, fos. 128r.-129v.). They appear to be strictly contemporary, and have been assigned a notional date *circa* 1585. The criticisms, which throw light on the reaction of at least one contemporary observer, are possibly to be identified with the views of John Lindsay of Menmuir, lord Balcarres, who became the king's secretary.

'Chapter 1

In the tent article and elevent it apearis that the policie of the kyrk als weill as the power leinis immediatlie upon the Word of God as the onelie ground theyrof, albeit the contrar apeir to be of trueth and that albeit the power be of God to preache and teache yit the policie and ordour and constitutionis for preservation of the kyrk doeth lene immediatly on men quha do mak this same, utherwayis the book of discipline and maist parte of the actis of the generall assembly war maid in vaine, and for example to institute fasting at certayne tymes, to statute the minister teache indecent [*recte*, in decent] apparell the Worde, to transport ane minister or superintendent frome one place to ane uther, quhair he is meit, perteneth to the policie, and hes not the ground immediatlie of God.

2. Gif the power be immediatlie of God, quhat misteris inauguration, or servis *impositio manum* [sic], quhilk Johne Calvine in his *Institution* dois not denye may be callit ane sacrament albeit not pertening to the holy people.

3. In the xiii article, it appeiris na power is gevin to the prence to command or reull over the kyrk, and als all ministeris of the kyrk, bischoppe and all, are of lyke power and not ane to command ane uther.

4. The haill first chaptour servis rather to appeir to declare the power of the kyrk, and descryving quhat it differis fra the civill power, nor to discreve the policie thairof.

Chapter 2

In the first article, he appeareth to gif sum primacie in reuling the kyrk, albeit the xiii article of his former cheptour he appearis to mak all ministeris alyke in power.

2. In the thrid article, it appeareth that marchandis and craftismen onliteratt in ane seation may be called ministeris seing throch the haill realme sic men are electit elderis and deacones.

3. In the tent article, doctouris in the kyrk are left furth albeit Sainct Paull name theme first, and that mencion also of theyr perpetual function be maid in the fyft chaptour and first article thairof quhilk two places semis to haif repugnance, seing that in the ane he makis two ordinare functiones or offices in the kirk, and in the uther place thrie.

Chapter 3

In the first article vocation or calling and promotion be name of ane minister is requirit, albeit in chapter ii it is said that they haif power immediatly of God, swa appearis *impositio manum* [*sic*] misteris not.

2. Article 10, he makis all benefices to be stipendis quhair I wald speir quha should modifie the stipend sence some benefices are great sum small, for gif he levis not that power to the prince he takis away the kingis patronage.

Chapter 4

In the first article, I find doctouris omittit quha should teache in the sculis.

2. In the fourt article and fyft he concludis sic men as Mr John Scharpe and Mr William Scott of Spensar Feald and Maister Johne Freud, advocates, should be cursed becaus they have left the ministerie.

3. In the sevinth article, I waitt not quhat it menis to preache out of seasoun except he interpreith S. Paules speiking *insta importune* in that maner.

Chapter 5

In the first article, he makis two ordinar functionis and doctouris, albeit chapter 2, article 10, he makis three and doctouris not ane.

Chapter 6

Article quhen he makis the office of ane elder perpetuall, I think it should be so, and yit it is playne contrarie the ordour that hes bene observit quhair eldaris hes bene yeirlie electit through the haill realm.

2. Article 10, I desyre to knawe quaht canonis they are that he callis the canonis of the apostles, for the ministeris will not aggree with mony headis of sic canonis as we half callit the canonis of the apostles.

Chapter 7

In the viii article, the name of ane bischoppe is taken awaye albeit theyr be mony argumentis for defence thairof.

2. In the x article, it is confessit that the kyrk may mak reulis and constitutionis for ordouris caus albeit afoir he ascryvis the haill power to come immediatlie of God and policie also.

3. In the thrid and fourt article abid throch the haill chapter, na power is left to the prince to call the generall assembleis, nor yit knaw I, quhome to the power is left, or quhair we sall haif recours to the kyrk, or yit the prence, quhan he wald haif the assemble callit.

Chapter 9

In the secound article, he makis landis, biggingis, possessionis to be the patrimonie of the kyrk and yit therefter they wald haif all kirk mennis landis annexit to the croun, and sua gif the prence the patrimonie of the kyrk, albeit in the fourt article he haldis it ane detestable sacriledge to tak ony of the said patrimonie.

In the fyft article, quhair he makis deacones collectoris, he appearis to searche in agayne the collectouris quhilk wes of afoir albeit experience teache us how over officiabill they war unto the kyrk.

Chapter [blank]

Article 1, all titillis of beneficit men and chaptouris are takin away.

2. Article 6, the state of the kyrk in parliamentis is taken away and sua two statutis [recte, estates] of parliament are left, les the ministeris theyr selfis wald enter in the thrid.

3. Article 9, quhair he accuis the ordour tane at Leyth, he dois accuis the kyrk becaus the kyrkis commissioneris aggreit theyrto and the commissionar is yit in place.

4. Article [1]2, he astrictis ilk bischoppe to ane particular kirk, and leiffis pastouris and visitouris to haif power over ma kyrkis

and ever wald haif the bischoppis subiectit to the particulare assemblie albeit the ministeris theyr selffis affirmes they should assist the prince in parliament and not the bischoppis and that jurisdiction should proceid frome theme.
5. It is concludit that all few[s] sett thir xvii yeiris bygane shalbe annullit reduced and alluterly dischargit.
6. The commissioneris [*recte*, commissaries] are also designit to be dischargit and theyr power to cum frome them and to be limitat. Chapter 12 [*blank*]'.

APPENDIX III

The Election of Commissioners to the General Assembly

A study of the appointment of commissioners to the general assembly based on an examination of record evidence from synod, presbytery and kirk session registers has never been undertaken. The following appendix containing material extracted in the main from presbytery records available only in manuscript is offered as a contribution towards a more exact understanding of the assembly's composition and of the procedures adopted in electing commissioners by the courts of the church during a period of presbyterian ascendancy and in the light of the second Book of Discipline's proposals. Apart from these ecclesiastical sources, burgh records, with printed extracts from relevant entries, provide further information on commissioners from towns;[1] and the procedure for appointing university commissioners is forthcoming from the rector's book for St Andrews university.[2]

Any exclusive reliance on the acts of assembly is clearly bound to give an imperfect picture, for they are not necessarily an accurate guide to practice. In 1568, the assembly had acknowledged the synod as the appropriate body for appointing commissioners to the assembly, and it was not till March 1597/8 that the assembly regulated presbyterial appointments by requiring each presbytery to elect three ministers and a baron as commissioners to the assembly;[3] but from a study of presbytery records it emerges that certain presbyteries were accustomed to elect their own commissioners from as early as 1582. Entries tend to be somewhat haphazard and irregular; the only surviving synod records for the late sixteenth century – those of Lothian and Tweeddale – contain a solitary entry (4 April 1593) on the appointment of commissioners, though presbytery records usually reveal whether elections were conducted by synods or by presbyteries; and Edinburgh presbytery from 1588 remarked that its commissioners were chosen 'according to the laudable use and custome observit within everie presbiterie of this realme'. Presbyteries, of course, were still not in universal operation, and in certain areas the synod remained the appropriate body for conducting elections.

[1] *Edinburgh Burgh Records*, iii, 138, 161, 175, 211, 226; iv, 167-8 (see also below, 281ff.); *Glasgow Burgh Records*, i, 286, 451; *Stirling Charters*, 211, 220.

[2] St Andrews University Archives, MS. Acta Rectorum, ii, 74, 75, 92, 98.

[3] *BUK*, i, 124; iii, 947-8.

The number of commissioners elected varied considerably from one presbytery to another and fluctuated even within any one presbytery. Whereas Glasgow presbytery chose only one commissioner in 1595, Edinburgh by contrast chose six; and on one occasion St Andrews decided that 'the hail presbetrie' should attend the assembly. The variations are partly to be explained by the geographical distribution of presbyteries. The majority of assemblies met in or near Edinburgh, which permitted commissioners from the Lothians and Fife to attend in considerably larger numbers than their counterparts from the west and the north. Since ministers from Glasgow had to pay their own expenses travelling to the assembly, it is not altogether surprising that that particular presbytery sent no more than two ministers at most, and more usually only one, to assemblies held in the east. Even Peebles presbytery seems to have been unable or unwilling to send any more than two ministers as commissioners to the assembly. Edinburgh presbytery, on the other hand, succeeded in electing four ministers and three lairds to the assembly appointed to be held at Aberdeen in July 1591 but when the place of the assembly was changed instead to Edinburgh, the presbytery increased its representation to six ministers and eight lairds. At the same time, it should be noted that Edinburgh and St Andrews presbyteries were larger than most, each with six times as many ministers as Glasgow.

Before the assembly's act of 1598, there was apparently no limitation on the number of commissioners who might attend. In one instance, eight ministers and doctors with twenty-seven lairds and burgesses were elected from the bounds of St Andrews presbytery alone, and on another occasion more than twenty-eight commissioners, including nine ministers and doctors, were chosen 'out of the boundis of the presbiterie of Sanctandros'. It is all too evident that in some presbyteries the gentry often outnumbered the ministers elected. This tendency, apparent in St Andrews, is also revealed in Dalkeith where it was not unknown for twice as many lairds as ministers to be chosen; and there were instances in Stirling presbytery, too, where the gentry numerically outweighed the ministers nominated to the assembly. Nor was the lay element restricted to the ranks of the gentry and burgesses. On two occasions, the earl of Morton figured among commissioners from Dalkeith presbytery, and in 1596 Stirling presbytery chose as two of its representatives the earls of Argyll and Mar. In

Edinburgh presbytery, however, there is no record of earls as commissioners, and it was exceedingly rare in that presbytery for the gentry to surpass the number of ministers commissioned to attend the assembly.

Although the form of commission which ministers and other delegates received seems to have given them freedom to vote in assemblies according to their conscience and the Word of God, there is nonetheless some indication that commissioners were accountable to their presbyteries for the way in which they voted in assemblies. In 1597, when the king appointed an assembly to be held at Perth, Edinburgh presbytery after choosing three ministers as commissioners proceeded to give them a detailed list of instructions; Stirling presbytery charged its commissioner 'gif any thing beis concludit in this nixt assemblie against the actis of the generall assemblie to protest against it', and then found fault with him on his return for failing to protest 'against thais thingis thair concludit'; and Peebles presbytery also sought to discover whether its commissioner had 'past the boundis of his commissioun or not'.

St Andrews kirk session records are really the only surviving kirk session records for the period to give a clear indication of the procedure which a kirk session adopted in the choice of burgh commissioners; and it is significant that in St Andrews the kirk session, and not the town council, determined the choice of commissioners who also turned out to be members of the session. In Edinburgh, however (where the session records are extant only for 1574-5), the town council retained its say in the choice of commissioners from the burgh, though in at least three recorded instances the kirk session's advice was sought in the selection of commissioners.[4]

In the following presbytery records, the gentry who were appointed as commissioners are never styled elders; but it can be shown that many lairds were elders of either kirk sessions or presbyteries, and one contemporary account indicates how it was customary for 'gentlemen elders' to be elected to the assembly from presbyteries.[5] In Dalkeith presbytery, the lairds who were elders were termed 'gentlemen', or 'gentlemen elders' or 'gentlemen and elders'; and in 1587 Edinburgh presbytery 'thocht good

---

[4] *RStAKS*, i, 367-8, 406, 459, 478-9; ii, 526, 748-9, 798, 921; see below, 281ff.
[5] J. Kirk, 'The Development of the Melvillian Movement', i, 310-17; NLS, Adv. MS, 6.1.13, fo. 40r.-v.

that the baronis and gentilmen quha wer chosin to be eldaris at the first erecting of the presbyterie salbe desyrit be the brethren of the ministrie to be present' at a presbytery meeting.[6] It is observable, too, that the same small tightly-knit groups of gentlemen were repeatedly returned as commissioners to be assembly.

All in all, it was neither Melville nor the proposals of the second Book of Discipline which sought to overturn the assembly's composition, but the action of the king threatened to do so when, in November 1596, he discharged all barons and other lieges from attending presbyteries and 'other ecclesiastical judgements' without express approval.[7] Despite the act of assembly in 1598 permitting three ministers and a baron to be elected to the assembly from each presbytery, none of the entries in presbytery records beyond 1596 indicates the appointment of lairds as commissioners. It is evident, however, that the gentry continued to attend assemblies in one capacity or another but they were certainly not commissioned by presbyteries; and it was not until 1600 when 'the baronis convenit haive chosen be them selfis the yong laird of Dersy their commissioner to the generall assemblie' that St Andrews presbytery decided to ask them to be present in future 'at synodall assembleis to the intent the ancient forme of election of commissioneris may be kepit'.

Synod of Lothian[8]

4 April 1593: 'The assemble, understanding the generall assemble of the kirk is to be convenit at Dundie in this instant moneth of Apryle, appointis thair brether, of the presbyterie of Dunbar Mr Robert Hepburne, Mr Alexander Hum; of the presbyterie of Hadintoun Mr James Carmichel, James Gibsoun, Mr Walter Hay; off the presbyterie of Dalkeyth, Mr Georg Ramsay, Mr Johnn Nimbill, Mr Archibald Sympsoun; off the presbyterie of Edinburgh Mr Robert Bruce, Mr David Lyndsay, Mr Robert Pont, Mr James Balfour, Mr Michael Cranstoun; off the presbyterie of Peblis Mr David Narne; off the presbyterie of Linlythgow Mr John Spottiswood, Mr James Law and Mr Patrik Scharpe, thir foirsaid brether thair commissioneris to compeir before the assemble generall for thame and in thair names to vote, ressone and conclude all thingis that concernis the glorie of God and weill of his kirk ffirme and stable, etc.'

[6] See above, 112.
[7] Calderwood, *History*, v, 465.
[8] *Synod of Lothian*, 59.

Dalkeith Presbytery[9]

19 April [1582]: 'The quhilk day thair wes sum commissioneris chosin according to the decre of the synodall assembele to pas to Sanctandrois to the generall assemble quhilk is to be haldin thair the xxiiij of Apryle 1582 to the intent thai may reasone of thair awin particular effaris and also to sute and request sum reformatioun of thingis out of use and also for the furthering of sum publict effaris with the advertesment of the generall [assemblie] of sum enormiteis to be reddressit within our presbiterie ... [and to reason upon all things] bayth particular and generall as occasioun sall serve ... ffor Dalkeyth thair is appoyntitit [sic] to pas [blank] of ministeris within the said eldership thair is ordanit Mr George Ramsay, moderator, Mr Adam Johnestone, Mr Johnne Bennat, Johnne Herres, James Gibsone'.

18 April 1583: 'The moderator proponit quha suld be elected to go to the generall assemble to assist the sam in all godlie effaris concerning the glorie of God and weill of his kirk, and eftir reasoning haid heirupone be the brethren they all togyther with conformitie of votis nominates, electis and chese the lardis of Ormestoun and Cokpen, Thomas Megget of Newbottill, Robert Wilsone, M[aiste]ris George Ramsay, Jhone Bennet, Adam Jhonestoun, Gilbert Tailyour and Jhone Hereis with James Gibsone ordaining thame to be present in Edinburgh the xxiiij at the said assemblie to await upon for the causis foirsaid giffin thame full power in all thair names to reassone, vote and conclude in all matteris treated in the sam concerning the glorie of God and weill of his kirk according to Godis law and guid conscience'.

26 February 1589/90: 'Item that day commissioneris to the generall chosin, naimle, ministeris M[aiste]ris Adam Johnestone, Georg Ramsay, Johne Bennet, Georg Lundye; utheris, the erll of Morton, the lord of Newbottill, the lairdis of Dalhowssye, Ormistoun, Newbyris, Lugtoun, Hatharindaill younger'.

29 July 1590: 'The quhilk day also becaus the generall assemblie approcheit the brether thocht gud according to the ordour to chuse commissionaris authorisit with thair powar thairto bayth

[9] SRO, CH2/424/1.

gentillmen and ministeris and to that effect nominat my lord of Newbottill, the laird of Ormestoun, the laird of Newbyris, David Crychtoun of Lugtoun, the lard of Bruntstoun, Mr Adam Johnestoun, George Ramsay and Jhone Bennet with Jhone Hereis ordaining the brether to foirwarn the gentillmen of the day of the assemblie and to travell ernistlie with thame to be present thairat bayth for the glorie of God, quyetnes of the kirk and commounwealth of the countrie'.

1 July 1591: 'Becaus the generall assemblie wes to be this nixt Tysday the brethren choosis Mr Adam Jhonston, Mr Jhone Bennet and Mr Jhone Nymble to be ther commissioneris to the said assemble to vote and conclud in ther names in actiones spirituall aggreing with the word of God'.

18 May 1592: 'The brether having put in leittis a sevi[n]th or aucht of thair awin nominationes to mak chose of them to be commissioneris to the generall assemble, thair vottis inclynit to M[aiste]rs Adam Jhonsoun, Georg Ramsay, Jhone Nimble, the moderatour being glaid, with full power to vot and ressoun at the said future generall assemble'.

2 May 1594: 'The quhilk day war nominat commissionares to the general assemble: of the ministrie, Mr Adam Jonstoun, Mr George Ramsay and Mr Andro Blackhal; and of nobil men, baronnes and gentl men, my lord of Mortoun, Sir George Douglas, the laird of Dalhoussy, Cokpen and Smeytoun with the gudman of Carbury and Mentoun.'

Edinburgh Presbytery[10]

28 May 1587: 'Anent the commission gevin the secund of this instant to Mr David Lyndsay, Mr Robert Pont and Johnn Duncansoun to speik the kingis majestie for licenciating a generall assemble be convocat of the ministrie of this realme and a speciall day to be appointit for that effect, quha declaring his majestie good will yit as of before and that his majestie had appointit for that effect the xix of Junii nixt, quhairof the presbytere being certefeit appointis Mr Robert Pont, ane of the ministeris of Edinburgh, Mr Patrik Symsoun, Johnn Brand and ane of the kingis ministeris for the kingis houss commissioneris for the nixt

[10] SRO, CH2/121/1-3.

generall assemble to be convenit the said day with power to thame in thair names to voit and ressoun in all matteris ecclesiasticall concerning the glory of God and weill of his kirk that sall come before thame and generally to use and exerce all thingis that sall come before thame *promittere de rato* etc.'

19 December 1587: 'The brethren of the presbiterie being surelie informit of the bissines of the Jesuittis laitlie cum furth of the realme of France travelling to pervert religioun, to corrupt the hartis of the noble men and utheris of the countre, and to draw thame away from obedience of the gospell to idolatry and superstitioun ffor remeid quhairof and for resisting of papistrie and of uther unhappie coursis tending to the dishonour of God and wrak and destructioun of thame quha professis the gospell, it is concludit and ordanit that Mr Robert Bruce, Mr Robert Pont, Mr David Lyndsay, Mr Gualter Belcanquel, Mr Johnn Craig, Mr Robert Rollock and Johnn Brand pas to the kingis maiestie his chanceller and justice clark craving of his maiestie a licence that bayth ministeris, barronis and burrowis may convene for ressoning and concluding upon the best way and mein to resist sick dangerous procedingis. And for this purpos efter finall conclusioun takin that thay may be send as commissioneris to his maiestie craving thair advyse to be exequute. Item, to crave that his maiestie wald grant libertie bayth to ministeris and gentilmen to pas throw the countrey to exhort men to continew in the professioun of the religioun and to resist thame that opponis thame selfis aganis the sam alsweill be preiching as persuasioun. Item, that his maiestie wald grant libertie to exequut discipline and censures ecclesiasticall against papistis, Jesuittis and utheris notwithstanding of ony charge purchest fra his maiestie on the contrare'.

4 August 1588: 'According to the laudable use and custome observit within everie presbiterie of this realme to nominat and appoint thair commissioneris to compeir for thame and in thair names before [the] generall assemble, the brether of the presbiterie convenit hes thocht meit and be thair ordinance statute that Mr Robert Bruce, Mr Gualter Belcanquel, Johnn Brand, Mr Patrik Sympsoun, Mr Johnn Hall, Mr Robert Rollock, Mr Johnn Craig, Mr Andro Blakhall, the lardis of Merchinstone, Pilrik, Braid, Colingtoun, the guidman of Carbarry, Smetoun and Mr

James McKgill, compeir befoir the nixt generall assemble to be haldin at Edinburgh the vj of this instant for thame as commissioneris'.

10 June 1589: 'According to the laudable use observit and keipit in all the presbytereis of the kirk of this realme to appoint commissioneris to everie generall assemble of the kirk, the presbiterie understanding the generall assemble of the kirk for to be convenit in Edinburgh the xvij of this instant hes nominat and appointit commissioneris for thame and in thair names the lardis of Merchinstoun, Pilrik, Colintoun, Braid, Carberry, Smeton, M[aiste]rs Johnn Davidsoun, Robert Rollock, Patrik Sympsoun, Robert Pont, the kingis majesteis ministeris, John Hall, Mr Gualter Belcanquel, Johnn Brand, ordaning to compeir before the said assemble etc.'

25 February 1589/90: 'According to the laudable use observit and keipit in all the presbiteries of the kirk of this realme to appoint commissioneris to everie generall assemble of the kirk, the presbytere be ressoun the generall assemble of the kirk is to meit the v of Merche nixtocum in Edinburgh hes nominat and appointit commissioneris for thame and in thair names Mr Robert Pont, Mr Robert Bruce, Mr James Balfour, Mr Robert Rollock, Mr John Davidsoun, Mr Patrik Sympsone, the lairdis of Merchinstoun, Pilrik, Braid, Corstorphin, Colintoun, James Richesone of Smetoun, the gudman of Carbarry ordaining thame to compeir before the said assemble, etc., *promittere de rato*, etc.'

1 June 1591: 'According to the laudable use observit and keipit in all the kirkis of this realme to appoint commissioneris to every generall assemble of the kirk, the presbytere be ressoun the generall assemble of the kirk is to meit at Abirden in the moneth of July nixt hes nominat and appointis commissioneris for thame and in thair names viz., Mr David Lyndsay, Mr Robert Bruce, Mr Robert Pont, Mr James Balfour, the laird of Braid, the laird of Pilrik, James Richesoun of Smetoun, ordaining thame to compeir before the said assemble and for this end hes appointit a commissioun to be gevin to thame'.

29 June 1591: 'The presbytere notwithstanding the first of this instant appointit thair commissioneris to the nixt generall

assemble quhilk at that tyme was supposit to be haldin at Abirden in the moneth of July nixt, and now seing the place of the assemble is alterit hes nominat of new thair commissioneris to the said assemble Mr Robert Bruce, Mr David Lyndsay, Mr Robert Pont, Mr James Balfour, Mr John Craig, Mr John Hall, the lardis of Braid, Colintoun, Pilrik, Merchinstoun, Dammahoy, the gudeman of Carberry, James Richesoun of Smetoun, Gilbert Hay of Mont Hall'.

16 May 1592: 'According to the laudable use observit and keipit in all the presbytereis of this realme to appoint commissioners to everie generall assemblie of the kirk, the presbytere in respect the generall assemblie of the kirk is to meitt heir in Edinburgh the xxii of this instant nominattis and appointis commissioners for thame and in thair names viz., Mr Robert Bruce, Mr Robert Pont, Mr David Lyndsay, Mr Walter Belcanquell, Mr James Balfour and the kingis ministers ordaning thame to compeir before the said assemblie and for this end hes appointit a commissioun to be gevin thame'.

30 April 1594: 'The generall assemble of the kirk being to convene the vii of May nixt heir in Edinburgh, the presbytere appointis thair brether Mr Robert Pont, Mr Robert Bruce, Mr David Lyndsay, Mr Robert Rollock, Mr Walter Belcanquell, Mr James Balfor, the lardis of Merchistoun, Pilrik, Colintoun, Dammahoy, Braid and Andro Logan of Cotfeild thair commissioners to compeir before the said assemblie in thair names to vote, ressoun and conclude in all thingis that concernis the glorie of God and weill of his kirk, ffirme and stable, etc.'

10 June 1595: 'Forsamekle as the generall assemblie of the kirk is to convene the xxiiij of this instant at Montros, the presbyterie hes appointit and directit in commissione thair brether the lard of Colintoun, the lard of Dammahoy, Mr Robert Bruce, Mr David Lyndesay, Mr Robert Pont and Mr James Balfour and for this purpos ordanis a commissioun to be written to the effect foresaid.'

16 March 1595/6: 'Forsamekle as thair is a generall assemblie of the kirk to be haldin heir at Edinburgh the xxiii of this instant the presbyterie appointis as commissionaris for thame to be present at the said assemblie Mr Robert Bruce, Mr Robert Pont, Mr David

Lyndsay, Mr John Hall, Mr James Bennet, the kingis majesteis ministeris, the lardis of Braid, Merchinstoun, Colintoun, Dammahoy, Pilrik and Brunstoun'.

8 February 1596/7: 'Anent the lettre directit from the kingis majestie in effect declaring that his majestie had appointit ane assemblie generall of the kirk to convene at Perth the last of this instant and thairfore willit the presbytere to direct thair commissioneris to be present at the said assemblie, the presbytere continewis quhill the xxii of this instant to be advysit quhat brether sall ga'.

22 February 1596/7: 'Anent the conclusioun takin the viij of this instant in the quhilk it was concludit that this day commissionaris suld be nominat to convene at the nixt generall assemblie to be convenit at Perth the last of this day, the presbyterie for obedience of his maiestie lettre hes direct in commissioun to the said assemblie thair brether Mr David Lyndsay, Mr Patrik Galloway and John Duncansoun, and to deall according to the injunctiounis that salbe gevin thame in wrait'.

26 February 1600: 'The presbyterie understanding that the generall assemblie of the kirk is to convene at Montros the xviii of Merche nixt hes nominat and appointit and be thir presentis nominatis and appointis thair brether Mr Robert Bruce, Mr Henrie Blyth and Mr Michael Cranstoun to compeir for thame and in thair names as thair commissionaris to vot reassoun and conclude in all thingis that concernis the glorie of God and weill of the kirk promesing to hald ferme and stable quhatsoever thair commissionaris foresaid sall do in the premissis'.

4 March 1600: 'Instructionis for the commissionaris of the generall assemble. Ordanis the commissionaris direct in commissioun to ga to the nixt generall assemblie to observe in discharging thair commissioun the instructiounis efter following. 1. Concerning the questioun to be nominat in the nixt generall assemblie that thair said commissionaris keip thame selfis within the boundis of the actis of the provinciall assemblie haldin at Innerask the moneth of July 1598. 2. Gif ony thing sall happin to be concludit in the said mater (as God forbid) aganes the word of God, actis of parliament, grantit in favouris of the kirk, book of

disciplin be act of generall assemblie ratefeit and subscryvit be all the presbytereis of Scotland, or the said actis of the said provinciall assemblie or remanent actis of the said assembleis, provinciall and generall concludit in the said mater, that in that cais they in the name of the presbyterie protest in the contrar. 3. Incais the congregatioun of Leyth mak requeist to the generall assemblie for ane uther minister that they protest that the assemblie reserve to the presbyterie thair awin liberty to plant the said kirk unto the tyme they have occasion to find falt with the said presbytery quhilk they hope they sall not have. 4. Because the brether appointit upon the wark of the constant plat haifing convenit thair brother Mr Robert Bruce before thame quha willingly (albeit he neidit not) consentit for planting the kirkis of Arbroth to quyt a greit part of his pensioun, quhairupon the brether appointit for the said wark of the plat agreis as haifing commissioun of the haill kirk of Scotland and in takin of thair agrement subscryvit with thair handis, quhais deid the last generall assemblie haldin at Montros ratefeit that the said Mr Robert suld enjoy the rest of his pensioun during his lyftyme that tharefore the assemblie wald requeist his majestie that the same may be keipit to the said Mr Robert, and also command the brether of the ministry not to hurt the said Mr Robert'.

29 April 1601: 'The presbytere understanding the nixt generall assemblie is to convene at Bruntisland the xii of May nixt gives full power and commissioun to thair brether Mr Peter Hewat, Mr William Arthour and Mr James Mureheid to compeir for thame and in thair names before the said assembly as thair commissioneris and in all thingis to vot, ressone and conclude that concernis the glory of God and weill of his kirk'.

27 October 1602: 'The presbytery nominatis and appointis thair brether Mr James Balfour, Mr Walter Belcanquell and William Ard commissionaris for thame and in thair names to compeir before the nixt generall assemblie of the kirk to be convenit in Edinburgh the ix of November nixt'.

Glasgow Presbytery[11]

5 March 1594/5: 'Quhilk daye the moderator and brethrene of the presbiterie of Gl[asgw] maid and constitut as be thir presentis

[11] GCA, Glasgow Presbytery Records, vol. i.

makis and constitutis thair weilbelovit Mr Patrik Scharp, principall of the college of Glasgow, minister at Go[van], thair very lauchfull, undoutit, irrevocabill commissioner geving and committand to him thair full power to compeir for thame and [in thair name] in the assemblie of the kirk tobe haldin at Edinburcht the ... with continuatioun of dayes, and thair to reasoun voite [and conclud in all materis] agg[reab]ill to Goddis word. To the sayming and ... moderator and brethrene gevis to the said Mr Patrik thair commission ... said thair full power'.

17 June 1595: 'The quhilk day the presbiterie of Glasgw inrespect of the age, sicknes and present inhabilitie of Mr David Wemes appointit in the last synodall commissioner to the nixt generall assemblie hes appointit be thir presentis appointis Mr Alexander Rowat commissioner in his steade to the generall assemblie and thain to do in all thingis according to the commissioun of the said last synodall'.

17 February 1595/6: 'The presbiterie makis and constitutis Mr Patrik Scharp, principal of the colledge of Glasgw, and Mr John Couper, ane of the ministeris, thair commissioneris to the nixt generall assemblie to convein in Edinburcht upone the xxiii daye of Marche instant, thair to aggrie and condiscend to all thingis that salbe voitit and concludit thair that salbe found consonant and aggreabill to the Word of God for Godis glorie and weale of his kirk within this realme'. [*In margin*: 'Certane gentilmen to be desyrit to be commissioneris to the nixt general assemblie'.]

'Quhilk daye the presbiterie ordenis Sir Matthew Stewart of Mynto, knycht, William Levingstoun younger of Kilseythe, the lardis of Craigbernat and Banclocht tobe desyrit to ryid to Edinburcht agane the xxiiij daye of Merche instant unto the nixt generall assemblie and the said lardis of Campsie to be warnit be the minister of Campsie to the effect foirsaid'.

'The said presbiterie ordenis the letter send fra the kirk of Edinburcht anent the desyre of certane tobe present with the ministeris in the nixt general assemblie to be producit befoir the sessioun of Glasgw the nixt Thurisday'.

16 March 1595/6: 'The presbiterie ordenis the commissioner for

thame quha salbe voitit heireftir pas and ryid on his awin expensis without ony contributioun fra his brethrene'.

11 March 1600: 'Put on lytes to be commissioner to the nixt generall assemblie:

Mr John Bell, minister at Cader
Mr Patrik Scharp.

The presbiterie electit Mr Patrik Scharp, principall of the college of Glasgw to be commissioner to the nixt generall assemblie to be haldin at Montros.

Mr Alexander Rowat [1 vote]
Mr Archibald Glen [6 votes]
Mr Andro Boyde [no votes]

The presbiterie hes chosen Mr Archibald Glen to be commissioner with Mr Patrik Scharp, principall of the college of Glasgw, to the nixt generall assemblie to be haldin as said is.'

'Quhilk daye the moderator and brethrene of the presbiterie of Glasgw hes maid and constitut, as be thir presentis makis and constitutis, thair weilbelovit brethrene Mr Patrik Scharp, principal of the college of Glasgw, minister at Govane, and Mr Archibald Glen, minister at Ruglen, conjunctlie and severalie thair verie lauchfull undowttit commissioneris gevand, grantand and committand to thame conjunctlie and severalie, as said is, thair full power to compeir for thame and in thair name in Muntros upone the auchtein daye of Merche instant with contineuatioun of dayes in the generall assemblie of the kirk thair to be haldin God willing and thair to propone, heir, ressoun, voitt, conclud and aggrie to all and sindrie materis and actionis that salhappin to fall furthe in the said assemblie quhilk salbe consonant and aggreabill to Godis word and for the weale of his kirk within this realme and quhatsumever thing the saidis Mr Patrik and Mr Archibald commissioneris foirsaid conjunctlie and severalie sall do or leid to be done in the premissis the said moderator and brethren foirsaid sall abyd thairat fulfill and underly the same but contradictioun.'

16 September 1600: [An extract of minutes from the synod held at Glasgow on 16 September 1600, contained in the presbytery

records.] 'Put on lytes to be commissioneris in the next generall assemblie:

Maister William Birnie	[1 vote]
Thomas Lindsaye	[no votes]
Mr Johnne Hewesoun	[18 votes]
Mr Robert Darroche	[8 votes]
Mr Johnne Couper	[10 votes]
Mr Johnne Bell, minister at Cader	[no votes]
Mr Johnne Haye	[13 votes]
Mr Walter Stewart	[4 votes]

The synodal assemblie be voittis prevaleand hes nominat Mr John Heweson, minister at Cambuslayng, and Mr Johne Haye, minister at Renfrew, commissioneris for thame the nixt generall assemblie and ordenis thair commissioun to be imbuikit.'

'Quhilk daye the brethrene of the ministerie within the presbiteries of Lanerk, Hammiltoun, Glasgw, Paslaye and Dumbartone hes maid and now be thir presentis makis and constitutis thair weilbelovit brethrene Mr Johnne Hewesoune, minister at Cambuslayng, and Mr Johnne Haye, minister at Renfrew, thair verie lauchfull, undowtit, irrevocabill commissioneris gevand, grantand and commitand to thame conjunctlie and severalie thair full power, expres bidding, command and charge to compeir for thame and in thair name in the nixt generall assemblie of the ministerie to be haldin God willing in the toun of Edinburcht upone the fourtein daye of October nixtocum, and thair to voit, conclude, ressoun and aggrie to all and sindrie materis that salhappin to be intreatit in the said assemblie quhilk salbe fund consonant and aggreabill to Godis word and tending to his glorie and weale of his kirk within this realme, and specialie to deploir the advocatioun be our souverane lordis lettres usit be incestuous persones, adulteraris and excommunicat persones fra the discipline of the kirk to the lordis of secreit counsale and sessioun seing fornicatouris ar chasticed and the haynous sclanderaris escapis, and to deploir that mariages unlauchfullie ar maid be persones haveing na calling in the kirk, quhilk marriages unlauchfull in the self ar ratefeit be the commissaris of Edinburcht to the hurt of the discipline of the kirk, and to lament that the donatioun of benefices quhilk of befoir be actis of parliament pertenit to his M[ajestie] ar now devolvit in particular menis handis to the hurt of the ministerie, and to lament anent the new erectionis of benefices (*decimis inclusis*) in temporal lordshipes specialie of the abbacie of Paslaye quhair vicares pensionares within the said abbacie everie ane of theme of auld had yeirlie to everie kirk fyve or sex chalder of victuall now the minister at everie kirk is reducit to thre or four chalder of victuall yeirlie to the greit prejudice of the kirk, and to meane {deploir, *deleted*] the restitutioun of the bishop of Glasgw aganis the actis of parliamentis to the greit prejudice of the ministerie and schullis within the boundis of the bischoprik of Glasgw, and to meane [deploir, *deleted*] that excommunicat persones ar recept in nobill menis housis to the greit contempt of the discipline of the kirk, and crave uniforme ordor of buriallis to be establischit in the nixt parliament, and ane securitie for thair stipends that ar perrillit be the restitutioun of the bischop of Glasgw, and to crave that ane act of parliament be maid in the nixt parliament that all the takis of teindis be reduced allanerlie to ane nynetein yeir tak or lyfrent tak eftir the making of the said act for the weale of the ministerie and poore within this realme, and for the planting of the kirkis within the same, and quhatsumever thing the said commissioneris conjunctlie and severalie sall do or leid to be done in the premisses the brethrene of the ministerie within the said presbiteries convenit in thair synodall assemblie faythfullie promises to underly, fulfill and obey but contradictioun under the pain of defamatioun'.

'Quhilk daye the presbiterie of Glasgw willis the commissioneris appointit in the last synodall assemblie haldin in Glasgw quha ar to pas, God willing, to the nixt generall assemblie to be haldin in Edinburcht the xiiij daye of October instant to propone incase thair be restitutioun of the bischop of Glasgw that the pensionis gevin to the ministerie and schullis within the bischoprik of Glasgw quhairin thai stand in possessioun be ratefeit be act of parliament, to wit, twa chalder victuall to Mr Johnne Couper out of the thriddis of the said bischoprik, uther twa chalder to Mr Johnne Bell out of the said thriddis, twentie pundis yeirlie to Mr Johnne Allansone, readare in Glasgw, furth of the said thriddis, fyve chalder victuall to Mr Alexander Rowat, minister in the parochin of Glasgw, furth of the twa part of the said bishoprik, seven chalder victuall to Mr Archibald Spittell, minister at Driman, furth of the said bischoprik, [*blank*] to Mr Thomas Muirhead, minister at Cannathane [*i.e.* Cambusnethan], furth of the said bischoprik, ane chalder of victuall to the college of Glasgw for the sustentatioun of ane bursar furth of the mylne of

ELECTION OF COMMISSIONERS TO GENERAL ASSEMBLY 273

Partik and the toone of Glasgw to the said college, and to meane the greit abuse the pepill ar brocht into be the setting out and prenting of the buikis of prognosticatioun quhairby thai ar driven to beleve the secund cause'.

Haddington Presbytery[12]

4 June [1589]: 'The quhilk day the brethrene nominat commissioneris for the generall assembly, to wit, my lord Yester, Alexander Howme of Northberwik, the lairdis of Trabroun, Elphinstoun, Saltcottis, Blanshe and Cashkelpie. Ministeris, Mr James Carmichaell, Mr Thomas Macgy and Thomas Greg. Ordanis the brethrene speik the baronns and gentilmen to compeir at the generall assemblie to be haldin at Edinburgh the xvij of Juni nixtocum.'

25 February [1589/90]: 'Commissioneris to the generall assembly my lord Yester, the lairdis of Clarkintoun, Hirmanstoun, Elphinstoun, Fadounsyd, George Hammiltoun, Mr James Carmichaell, Mr Thomas Macghie, James Gibsone, Alexander Forrester'.

[July, 1590]: '[Commissioneris to the generall] assemblie, the lairdis of Clerkingtoun, Elphinstoun, Cas[?hkelpie] ... [Mr James Carmichaell, Mr] Thomas Macghie, Thomas Greg'.

24 April [1594]: 'The presbyterie understanding that the generall assemblie appoyntit to be haldin in Edinburgh wes to begin upone [the nixt Tyisday the last of April, *deleted*] the vij of May appoyntis Mr Walter Hay, Mr Thomas Makghie and James Gibsone commissioneris unto the same for thame'.

11 June 1595: 'Forsamekle as the generall assembly to be haldin at Montros is to begin the xxiiij Junii instant, the presbyterie gives commissioun to thair brother Mr Walter Hay to go to the said assembly to resson, vote and conclude as if thai wer all present thameselvis'.

25 February 1595/6: 'Anent the letter directit from the commissioneris of the generall assembly desyring us that, seing for sundrie caussis thair is ane generall assembly to be haldin and to

[12] SRO, CH2/185/1-2.

begin the xxiii of Merche nixt following not only of ministeris bot of the best affectit noblemen and gentlemen of this realme to appoynt some commissioneris bayth of the ministrie and of the best affectit gentlemen within our boundis, the presbyterie appoyntis commissioneris for thame of the ministrie thair brethren Mr James Carmichael, Mr Walter Hay, James Gibson and Mr Jhone Davidsoun and Mr Thomas Makghe to awayt upon the said assembly and everie minister to wairne the gentlemen within thair parochin to be present heir this day aucht dayes for accomplishing of the uther part of the letter touching commissioneris to be chosin of the gentlemen'.

3 March 1595/6: 'Anent the ordinance maid the last day touching the warning of the gentlemen to compeir this day to the effect as is contenit in the said ordinance in respect of the few number that is convenit the presbyterie continewis farder dealing in the said matter quhill this day aucht dayes desyring the gentlemen present to resort againe and ordaines the rest to be warnit and requeistit ernistlie to be present the said day'.

10 March 1595/6: 'Anent the ordinance maid the last day . . . of the gentlemen of this presbyterie to be present this day for ch[oosing] commissioneris of thame to the generall assembly, ane grat number [of] thame being present, with uniforme consent it was aggreit that thai . . . sould give thair presence to the said assembly upon the xxiii of this insta[nt] and that thay sould meit the said day at thrie efter noone among thamselvis to chuse out some commissioneris in thair names to awayt quhill the said assembly sould be endit'.

27 April 1597: 'Forsamekle as the generall assemblie to be haldin at Dundie [is to] begin upon Tyisday the tenth of May nixtocum, the presby[terie] gives commissioun to thair brethren Mr Thomas Makghe, Mr J[ames] Carmichael and Mr Walter Hay to pas to the said assemblie and in thair name to ressoun, vote and conclude in all thingis not prejudiciall to the libertie we have bene thir monie yeiris and ar presentlie in possessioun of, and na furder'.

29 April 1601: 'The quhilk day Mr James Carmichell and James Gibsone war chosin commissionars to the generall assemblie'.

ELECTION OF COMMISSIONERS TO GENERAL ASSEMBLY 275

6 July 1608: 'The quhilk day the B. considering the generall assemblie of the kirk of Scotland to [be] holden at Linlithgow upon Tuisday the 26 of July instant did by electione appoynt Mr Archibald Orswald, Mr John Adamsone, Mr John Ker their commissioneris to compeir in thair name at the said assemblye day and place foirsaidis. ...'

Paisley Presbytery[13]

14 October 1602: 'The brethren of the presbytre of Paslay assembling in thair sessioun hous within the kirk of the saming efter invocatioun of God his name consyddering the generall assemble of the kirk of Scotland is appoyntit to convein at Edinburgh the nixt day of this instant quhair the commissionares of the said presbytre are requssit to be present, they have ordanit lykas be thir presents they ordane thair weilbelovit brethren M[aiste]ris Johne Hay, Andro Knox, William Brisbane to repair to the said assemble geving full commissioun, power and credeit to thame to concurr with the brethren of the said assemblle and in the nam of the said presbytrie to ressoun, vott and conclud in all matters quhilk salbe proponit thair tending to the glorie of God and weill of his kirk'.

Peebles Presbytery[14]

17 February 1596/7: 'Forsamekill as his majesties lettre being presentit to us in our conference efter exerceis at Peblis the xvii day of Februar instant craving our commissionaris to be derect to the conventioun to be haldin at Perthe the last of this moneth, ffor obeying his majesties requeist the brethrene althocht ffew in number hes appointit and ordanit Mr Archibald Douglas, minister at Peblis, to pas to the said conventioun or assemble gif ony be to concure withe the commissionaris of the rest of the presbitreis to heir and sie his majesties will and weill affectit mynd conserning the polacie of the kirk alreadie establischit and reformit be sindre actis of parliament and to report the samyn bak agane to us that we may be readie to consentt withe his majestie ffor establisching and concluding of thais thingis that sall tend to the glorie of God, weill of his kirk, and standing of his majesties persoun and estait at sic tyme as salbe thocht maist expedient and to this effect giffis and grantis to the foirsaid Mr Archibald power and commission be thir presenttis sub-

[13] SRO, CH2/294/1. [14] SRO, CH2/295/1.

scryvit be our moderatour and clerk as followis the day foirsaid, 1596.

> Adam Hepburne, moderator of the presbyterie of Peblis.
> Hector Cranstoun, clerk of the presbyterie of Peblis'.

14 April 1597: 'The quhilk day the presbyterie ordanis according to the act of the provinciall assemble to try Mr Archibald Douglas, minister at Peblis, commissionar to the generall assemble haldin at Perthe to sie gif he past the boundis of his commissioun or not'.

'The presbyterie ordanis the nixt day ane commissionar to be apointit to the generall assemble'.

12 January 1597/8: 'The quhilk day the presbyterie resavit ane lettre direct frome his majestie concernyng commissionaris to be direct to the generall assemble continewis the electioun of thame to the nixt day'.

26 January 1597/8: 'The quhilk day the presbyterie appoynttis Adam Hepburne and Maister Robert Levingstoun, commissionaris to the generall assemble'.

6 March 1600: 'The presbyterie appoynttis Mr Johnne Wemis commissionar to the generall assemble'.

St Andrews Presbytery[15]

31 July 1590: 'Commissioneris appoyntit to the generall assemblie: M[aiste]ris Androw Moncre[iff], Johne Robertsoun and David Monipenny'.

19 April 1593: 'The Roll of the names of the commissionares nominat out of the boundis of the presbitrie of Sanctandros to pas to the generall assemble to be halden at Dundie, commissionares for the townn and landwart of the paroche of Sanctandros, Mr David and William Russelss, Mr William Cock, Duncane Balfour, Charles Watsoune, David Dalgleishe, Mr Robert Zuil, Andro Wood of Stravithie, Mr Johne Aittoun of Kinnadie; for Crail Wilmestoun, Cambo; for Kilrennie, William Barclay, Robert Strang; for Kilconchar, Rires; for Ceres, Largo younger,

---

[15] Holy Trinity Parish Church, St Andrews, St Andrews Presbytery Records, vol. i.

Lundie; for Leuchars, Colluthie, Durie, Ear[l]shall. Commissionares to the general assemble of the presbitrie: Mr David Black, Mr Robert Wilkie, Mr James Melvill, Mr Nicol Dalgleish, Mr Robert Durie, Mr Andro Melvill, Mr Johne Johnsoun, Mr Patrik Melvill, Mr Andro Moncref'.

2 May 1594: 'Commissionares to the generall assemble, gentlemen, borrowis and ministrie: provest of Sanctandros, Andro Wood of Stravithie, Craighall, George Ramsay, Carnbie younger, James Traill, Wilmistoun, Pitmillie younger, Cambo younger, Ardrie, William Barclay, Robert Strang, Mr William Scott, Bufrey, Balcormo, Balrimonth, Kilconchar, Rires, Kincraig, Sandfurd, Mr Andro Sandilandis, Largo, Lundie, Kirktoun, Durie, Kembok, Blebo, Mr[is.] Nicol Dalgleish, Robert Wilkie, Robert Durie, David Mernis, Homar Blair, David Black, James Melvill, the Rector'.

11 March 1595/6: 'M[aiste]ris Andro Melvill, Nicoll Dalgleische, James Melvill, Robert Wallace, Robert Durie being put on leittis and being votit quhilk thre of them suld pase commissioner to the generall assemble it wes concludit that be pluraletie of vottis that M[aiste]ris Andro and James Melvill, with Nicol Dalgleishe suld be commissionaris to the assemble'.

26 January 1597/8: 'Commissionaris to the general assemble, the hail presbetrie'.

6 March 1600: 'The same day the baronis convenit have chosen be them selfis the yong laird of Dersy the commissioner to the generall assemblie quhairwith the presbyterie aggreit for that tyme, and ordanis this to be remembred that the baronis be adverteist in all tymis heirefter to be present at synodall assembleis to the intent the ancient forme of electioun of commissioneris may be kepit'.

26 July 1604: 'The presbitrie chuissis and appoyntis M[aiste]ris James Melvill, William Erskyne and William Murra thair commissioneris to the generall assemblie appoyntit to be holden in Aberdene this moneth geving them ther full commissioun and expres charge to pas to Aberdene and thair for the said presbytare and in thair name to reason, vote and conclude in sic thingis as salbe handlit in the said assemblie, and to do quhatsumevir uther

thingis belongis to the weill of the kirk promeising to ratifie and approve quhatsumevir the saidis commissioners sall do thairintill according to the Word of God'.

Stirling Presbytery[16]

10 October 1581: 'The moderator schew to the lairdis of Garden and Keir and Mr James Pont that thai war appointit be the provinciall assemblie to be commissionaris to the generall assemblie to be haldin in Edinbrugh the xvii day of this instant and desyrit thame to keip the samin'.

10 April 1582: 'The brethrein of the presbyterii of Striviling electit and nominat Patrik Gillaspie, Mr Andro Yung and Mr William Stirling, ministers, Alexander Bruce of Airthe or his sone Mr Robert Bruce, James Kinross of Kippenross, Umphra Cunynghame, commissar of Striviling, and Mr James Pont, commissar of Dunblane, barronis and gentill men commissionaris to the nixt generall assemblie to be haldin in Sanctandrus the xxiiij day of Aprill instant for the said presbyterii to concur with the said assemblie for treatting of thais thingis concerning the weill and gude ordur to be observit within the kirkis of the said presbyterii and also quhatsumevir thingis salbe trettit in the said assemblie that may tend to the glorie of God and weill of his haill kirk plantit of his mercie within this realme'.

9 April 1583: 'The quhilk day the brethrein of the presbyterii of Striviling electit and nominat James Andirsone, Patrik Gillaspie and Johnne Duncanson, ministeris, Sir James Stirling off Keir, knycht, provest of Striviling and Alexander Forester of Garden, barronis, commissionaris for thame to pas to the nixt generall assemblie of the kirk to be haldin in Edinburgh the xxiiij day of Aprill instant with full powar to concur with the said assemblie for treatting of thais thingis concerning the weill and gude ordur to be observit within the kirkis of the said presbyterii and also quhatsumevir thingis that salbe trettit in the said assemblie that may tend to the glorie of God and weill of his haill kirk plantit of his mercie within this realme'.

13 June 1587: 'The samin day the brethrein hes electit and nominat Mr Arthur Fethie and Andro Forester ministeris to pas with

[16] SRO, CH2/722/1-3.

James Andirsone, minister, commissionar within the boundis of this province, as commissionaris for this presbyterii to the nixt generall assemblie of the kirk to be hawldin in Edinbrught the xx day of this instant moneth of Junii to concur with the said assemblie for traittein of thais thingis concerning the weill and gude ordur to be observit within the kirkis of the said presbyterii and haill kirk within this realme that may tend to the glorie of God and promotione of his Word within the samin'.

16 May 1592: 'The quhilk day the brethrein nominatis commissionaris to the nixt generall assemblie for this presbyterii, of gentilmen: Alexander Bruce of Airth and William Mentayth of Cars to concur with the brethrein of the ministrie nominat commissionaris for this presbyterii to the said assemblie be the last synodall'.

17 April 1593: 'The commissionaris nominat to the nixt generall assemblie for this presbyterii ar admonesit to be thairat in Dundy the nixt Tuysday the xxiiij day of Aprill instant and ar desyrit to be cairfull to thais thingis concerning the weill of the kirk namelie within thir boundis and according to the commissione of the last synod nominatis Alexander Bruce of Airth, Williame Mentayth of Cars and Johnne Murray of Touchadame, zealus barronis, commissionaris for this presbyterii to convein with the said assemblie, reassone and voit in sic materis as salhappin to be treated thairin and ordanis the clark to mak everie ane of thame adverteisit heirof and request thame in the brethreinis name to keip the said assemblie'.

3 March 1595/6: 'The quhilk day thair being producit ane misseive letter direct to this presbyterie from the commissionaris of the generall assemblie appointed to the plat and otheris brethrein conveinit with thame in Edinburgh makand adverteisment that the Spanish armie ar of deliberat purpois with all possiblle diligence to arryve in this cuntrie and extinguish all trew religione in this Ill, to conques the samin, and thairin to erect up idolatrie and thairfor hes thocht meit that thair be ane generall assemblie conveinit at Edinburgh the xxiii day of Merche instant of the maist grave, wyse and godlie professoris of the treuth within this cuntrie alsweill of the nobilitie, barronis, commissionaris of brughis as of the ministrie as lykwys hes thocht meit that thair

be observit oulklie everie Sabboth a publict humiliatioun with ane fast at all the kirkis within this realm ay and quhill we receave sum confortablle effect of our humiliatioun and that the said exerceis of humiliatioun and fasting be observit everie day thrughout that haill oulk quhilk is appointed for the generall assemblie. According to the quhilk advys, the brethrein of this presbyterie hes electit and nominat commissionaris for thame to the said assemblie: Archibauld, Erlle of Argyll, Lord Campbell and Lorne; Johnne Erlle of Mar, Lord Erskein and Gariocht; Adame, commendator of Cambuskynneth; Sir Archibauld Stirling of Keir, knycht; Johnne Murray of Touchadame; James Saittone of Tullibody; Sir William Mentayth of Kers, knycht; and James Shaw of Sauchie; off ministeris Mr Patrik Simsone, Mr William Stirling and Mr Henrie Levingstone to concur with the said assemblie as commissionaris foirsaidis to consult, reasone and conclude how the just wrath of God sa neir approching may be turned away from us by ane universall and trew convertione of all estaitis from thair sinis to repentence, and to condiscend upon sum gude and ordinar meinis for the mantenance of the libertie of the trew religione and cuntrie against thair violence and for resisting of thair invasionis as also to give thair advys and opinione in sic uther materis as salbe treated in the said assemblie tending to Godis glorie and promotione of his Evangell within this cuntrie, and siclyke ordanis that ane humiliatioun and fast be observit at everie kirk within ther boundis ilk Sabboth during the said spaic and in the brugh of Stirling and cietie off Dunblane ilk day of that oulk appointed for the generall assemblie according to the judgment of the saidis commissionaris and uther brethrein conveinit with thame'.

16 February 1596/7: 'The brethrein nominatis and constitutis Mr William Stirling thair commissionar to convein with the remanent commissionaris of the kirk at Perth to desyr of his Majesteis letter, thair to heir quhat beis proponit, and report againe that this presbyterie may caus answer be maid thairto at the next generall assemblie of the kirk to be conveinit in Sanctandrus and gif any thing beis concludit in this nixt assemblie against the actis of the generall assemblie to protest against it'.

9 March 1596/7: 'The quhilk day Mr William Stirling commissionar directit to Perth for this presbyterie is askit gif he hes

done any thing thair besyd and attour the commissione gevin to him, he ansores that his voit was nevir soght and that he ansored not and gave na voit to any thing, and being askit gif he protested against thais thingis thair concludit he ansored negative for the quhilk he is now fund fault with'.

20 April 1597: 'The samin day the brethrein nominatis and constitutis thair brother Mr Andro Yung, minister of Dunblane, thair commissionar to convein in thair name with the nixt generall assemblie of the kirk in S. Andros the last Tuysday of Aprill instant thair to propone sic thingis as he is appointed, reassone, voit and conclude upone all materis treatit in that assemblie according to Godis Word and to that effect the said presbyterie commitis the said Mr Andro thair full powar, *promittere de rato*, etc.'

4 May 1597: 'The quhilk day the brethrein nominatis and constitutis thair brethrein Mr Patrik Simsone, Mr Adame Bellenden, Mr Richard Wrycht, Mr Henrie Layng, Mr James Duncansone, Mr Malcolme Henresone thair commissionaris to convein in thair name with the nixt generall assemblie of the kirk in Dundy the secund Tuysday of Maij instant thair to propone sic thingis as is appointed unto thame, reassone, voit and conclude upone all materis treatit in that assemblie according to Godis Word and to that effect the brethrein of this assemblie commitis thair full powar to thair saidis commissionaris, *promittere de rato*, etc.'

Edinburgh Town Council[17]

24 June 1562: 'The provest, baillies and counsale constitutis and nominatis James Barroun, Edwerd Houpe and James Young, cutler, commissioneris for this burgh to compeir and to be present at all tymes neidfull with the kirk, presentlie convenit within this said burgh, and for this hale toun to ressoun and aggrie with thame in all godlie caussis concernyng religioun'.

18 June 1563: 'The baillies and counsale ordanis Andro Murray of Blakbaronye and Jhonn Adamsoun to pas with the minister, Jhonne Knox, to the assemblay of the kirk to be haldin in Sanct Jonistoun the xxv of this instant moneth of Junii, and gyffis thame

[17] Edinburgh City Archives, MS. Edinburgh Town Council Records, vols. 4–11.

full commissioun and power to treit and conclude upoun the caussis of the said kirk'.

24 December 1563: 'The provost baillies and counsale befoir writtin, understanding that the generale counsale of the kirk is to be haldin at this present within the tolbuith of this burgh and the nobilitie for that purpois convenit, and becaus thai have sum materis to prone tuiching the glorie of God and thair commoun weill in the said conventioun, thai constitute and ordanit James Barroun, Maister Clement Littill and Maister Johne Merioribankis to compeir for thame to ressone and propone in thair caussis and sik utheris as sall occur, and geifis thame full commissioun sa to do, and siclike ordanis Richart Trolhope and the gild officeris to wait on the keiping of the tolbuith dure induring the tyme of the said assemblie and conventioun, and that the dene of gild se thame furneist in candill, fire and uther necessaris upoun the tounnis expenssis'.

30 May 1565: 'The quhilk day the baillies and counsale ordanis Maister Jhonn Spens and James Barroun to pas to the conventioun laitlie to be haldin in Pairthe and thair to trait in the causis of the kirk and commounweall of this burght, and ordanis ane commissioun to be maid to thame....'

24 December 1565: 'The provest, baillies and counsale ordanis Maister Thomas Makcalyeane and Maister Jhonn Prestoun to convene the morne with the generale kirk, in the counsalhous, and with thame to treit, ressoun and conclude upoun the caussis of the said kirk'.

21 June 1566: 'The quhilk day the provest, baillies and consall names and constitutis James Broun and Mr Alexander Sym and failzeing of James Broun, Adam Foullertoun, thair commissioneris to compear for thame with the assemble of the kirk now convenit within this burght, and thair to reasone, decyde and end for thair partis upoun sic effaris as pertenis to the kirk and all utheris thingis to do that thai mycht do thameself gif thai wer present in propir persone thameselfis....'

20 December 1566: '[The town council appoints] James Barroun, merchand, and Maister Richert Strang, lawer, thair commissaris

and procuratouris, to compeir in the townis name in the generall assemble of the kirk presentlie convenit within this burgh'.

20 June 1567: 'The quhilk day the provest, baillies and counsall names and constitutis Maister Clement Lytill, Maister Richart Strang, Alexander Clerk and Maister Jhone Prestoun, or onye tua of thame, to compeir in thair name with the generall assemble of the kirk as thair commissionaris, and ordanis ane commissioun to be maid thame'.

2 July 1568: 'The quhilk day the provest, baillies and counsale nominatis, constitutis and ordanis Mr Clement Litle and James Barroun thair commeissaris for thame in the assemblie of the kirk to compeir and upoun the caus thairof to ressone and conclude, and ordanis this thair commissioun to be extendit in uberiore forma, promeisand to hald ferme and staible, etc.'

24 December 1568: 'The baillies and counsale nominatis Alexander Clerk, baillie, and Maister Clement Litill thair commissioneris for thame to compeir in the generale assemble of the kyrk and thair to ressoun and conclude as thay mycht do thame selfis, promissand ferme and stable to hald'.

1 July 1569: 'The quhilk day the baillies and counsale makis Maister Thomas Makcalzeane and Edward Houpe commissioneris for thame to compeir in the generale conventioun of the kirk within this burght upoun [*blank*] nixt, and thair with the said kirk to ressoun, agrie and conclude in all causis concernyng the glorie of God and the commoun weill, promissand to hald ferme and stabill'.

1 February 1569/70: 'The baillies and counsall namis, constitutis and ordanis Alexander Clerk and Adame Foulertoun thair commissaris, grantand and giffand to thame thair commissioun and power for thame and in thair names with the lordis of nobilite to convene, and with thame to conclud the caussis concernyng the glorie of God, the Kingis weill, and commoun of the realme'.

30 June 1570: 'The quhilk day the baillies and counsale nominattis, constitutis and ordanis Adam Foullertoun and Maister Thomas

Makcalzean thair procuratouris and commissioneris, gevand thame full power to convene in this next assemblie of the kirk within this burght and thair for thame to ressoun and in the causis of the kirk to conclude, promissand to hald ferme and stable etc.'

28 February 1570/1: 'The quhilk day the baillies and counsale nominatis Adam Foullertoun, deane of gild, and Maister Jhonne Prestoun with avise of the kirk thair commissioneris to convene in the counsalhous of this burght with the remanent commissioneris of burrois in the generale assemblie thair and with thame in the causis of the kirk to ressoun and conclude etc., promissand ferme and stable, etc.'

28 March 1571: 'The baillies and counsall ordanis Mr Jhone Prestoun to ryd with Nycholl Uddart commissionaris of the kirk to Streveling to my lord regentis grace, and thair with thame to ressoun and conclude etc., and my lord thesaurarer to answer him of his expensis'.

4 August 1574: 'The samyn day the baillies and counsale makis Maister Clement Lytill and Maister Mychaell Chisholme thair procuratouris to compeir for thame in the generale assemblie of the kirk haldin in this burght vj$^{to.}$ instantis, gevand thame power to ressoun and conclude in all causis concernyng the glorie of God and weill of the kirk, promissand ferme and stable etc.'

4 March 1574/5: '[The town council] nominattis and makis Jhonne Adamsoun and Adam Fullertoun thair procuratouris and commissioneris, gevand thame power to convene in thair names in this present conventioun of the kirk to ressoun, conclude etc., promissand ferme and stable etc.'

19 October 1576: '[The town council] makis Maister Jhonn Merjoribankis, Adam Foullertoun, thair commissioneris, gevand thame power to convene upoun Wednisday next in the generale assemble of the kirk in this burght and thair in the causis of the kirk to ressoun and conclude, promissand ferme and stable etc.'

24 April 1578: 'The samine day the lettres and counsale nominattis Maister Jhonne Prestoun and Jhonne Jhonnstoun of Elphins-

ELECTION OF COMMISSIONERS TO GENERAL ASSEMBLY 285

toun thair commissioneris to convene in the conventioun of the kirk and promiss ferme and stable haldand and for to hald'.

17 October 1578: 'The quhilk day the provest, bailleis and counsell at the desir and request of the kirk and ministeris nominattis Mr Clement Litle and Johne Johneston, merchand, thair commissioneris conjunctlie and severalie for thame to convene in the assemble appointit in [Stirling, *deleted*] Edinburgh the xxiiij day of October instant, promissend to hald ferme and stable etc.'

3 July 1579: 'The quhilk day the baillies and counsale nominatis and ordanis Mr James Lawson, minister, Alexander Clark and Johne Adamson thair commissioneris, geving them power for thame to convene in the generall assemblie appointit to be had in this burght upoun Tyisday nixt and ordanis to gif to them sufficient commissioun, promesand to hald ferme and stabill'.

1 July 1580: '[The town council] namet and constitute, with avyse of the minister, eldares and deikynes of the kirk of this burgh, Maister James Lowsoun, minister, and Jhone Jhonestoun of Elphinstoun thair procuratouris and commissioneris in the Generall Assembly of the Kirkis of this realme to be haldin and begun in Dundie the xij of this instant, with power to voit, conclude and determinat with the rest of the commissioneris and ministeris of this realme in all thingis concerning the glory of God and welfair of the kirk'.

14 October 1580: 'The same day etc., names and constitutes Mr David McGill, advocat, and Mr Jhone Prestoun, merchant, thair commissioners to the generall assembly. . . .'

14 April 1581: 'The same day etc., electis and nominatis Mr James Lowsoun, minister, Jhone Jhonestoun, collectour, thair commissioners to the generall assembly to begynn and halden at Glasgw the xxiiij of this instant to intreat, ressoun and conclude annent all things belanging to the promotioun of religioun and weill of the realme, and ordanis ane lettre to be maid heirupoun under thair seill of caus'.

13 October 1581: 'The quhilk same day etc., electis and constitutis Mr Thomas Craig and Jhone Jhonestoun, collectour, to be

commissionaris for the guid towne in the assembly of the kirk to begin in this burght the xvii of October instant, and ordanis ane commissioun to be direct heirupoun under their seill of caus'.

18 April 1582: 'The same day etc., makis and constitutes Mr James Lowson, minister, and Jhone Jhonestoun, collectour, commissioners for thame to the nixt generall assembly of the kirk to be haldin at St Androes and in the xxiiij of this instant, gevand thame power to resson, intreat and conclude in all things concerning the glory of God and welfare of the realme....'

15 October 1582: 'The sam day etc., names and constitutes Mr Jhone Skene, advocat, and Henry Chairters thair commissioners to this present generall assemblie of the kirk haldin within this burght, and ordains ane lettir to be maid thairupon under their seill of caus'.

24 April 1583: '[The town council] makis and constitutes Jhonn Adamesoun and Jhonn Jhonestoun thair commissioneris in the generall assembly of the kirk of this realme to beginn and haldin within this burght this present day with power etc., promittere de rato, and gif neid beis ordanis ane lettre or commissioun to be maid heirupoun under thair seill of caus'.

4 October 1583: 'The sam day the foresaidis provest, bailyeis and counsall electit and nominat Jhonn Adamsoun, merchant, and Jhone Jhonestoun, collectour, thair commissioneris to the generall assemblie of the kirk to begyn within this toun the x of October instant....'

6 May 1586: 'The quhilk day thair being the names of personis presentit unto thame on the behalff of the sessioun of the kirk to be and out thairof twa be chosin to be commissioneris to the generall assembly to be halden in this burght the [blank] day thereof, this instant electis furth of the said names Jhonn Jhonestoun, brothir of the laird of Elphinstoun, and attour the said names electis Edward Hairt, goldsmyth, quha wes not contenit thairin to be commissioners as said is'.

14 June 1587: 'The quhilk day the foresaid provest, bailyeis and counsall names and constitutes Henry Charteris and Edward

Galbrayth commissioneris for the guid toun to the generall assembly to be haldin within this burght the [blank] day of [blank] promittere de rato'.

2 February 1587/8: 'The quhilk day Jhonn Arnott, provest, the baillies, dene of gild, thesaurer and maist part of the counsall being convenit maid and constitute Mr Jhonn Lindsay, persoun of Memmure [recte, Menmuir], ane of the Senatouris of the College of Justice, and Jhonn Jhonestoun, collectour, commissioneris for the guid toun in the generall assembly of the kirk to be haldin within this burgh'.

2 August 1588: 'The sam day furth of the lytes presentet to thame on behalf of the sessioun of the kirk of this burgh electet and chusit Jhonn Jhonesoun, collectour, and Edward Galbrayth commissioneris for the toun in the generall assembly haldin within this burgh'.

13 June 1589: 'The sam day electis and constitutes Henry Charteris, Gilbert Primrose, Jhonn Jhonestoun and Patrick Sandelands commissioners for the guid toun to the generall assembly to be haldin within this burgh'.

27 February 1589/90: 'The quhilk day Jhonn Arnott, provest, the baillies, dene of gild, counsall and deykins of crafts for the maist part beand convenit maid, creat and constitute Jhonn Adamesoun, merchant, and Alexander Ousteane, tailyeour, commissioners for the guid toun in the generall assemblie to begun and haldin within this burgh the secund of Marche nixtocum promittentes de rato'.

31 July 1590: 'The sam day makis and constitutes William Littill, Alexander Oustanne, Edward Galbreyth commissioners for the guid toun in the generall assembly of the kirk of this realme to be begun and haldin within this burgh on Tysday nixtocum'.

30 June 1591: 'The quhilk day Jhonn Arnott, provest, the baillies, dene of gild, thesaurer and counsall for the maist part beand convenit makis and constitutes Jhonn Jhonestoun and Patrick Sandelands commissioneris for the guid toun to the generall assembly to be haldin within this burgh promittere de rato'.

APPENDIX III

18 April 1593: 'The sam day makis and constitutes Clement Cor, merchand, and Jhonn Bannatyne, skynner, commissioners for the guid toun in the generall assembly of the kirk to be haldin at Dunde'.

3 May 1594: 'The sam day makis and constitutes Jhonn Adamsoun and Alexander Lyndsay commissioners for the guid toun in the generall assembly of the kirk presently within this burgh with power etc., promittere de rato'.

18 June 1595: 'The samyn day makis, creats and constitutes Jhonn Jhonestoun and James Barclay, commissioners for the guid toun to the generall assembly of the kirk to be haldin at Montrose the 24 of this instant'.

24 March 1595/6: 'The quhilk day the baillies, dene of gild and ane part of the counsall being convenit makis and constitutis Alexander Home of North Berwik, provest, and Alexander Oustean, tailyeour, and in absence of my lord provest Clement Cor, baillie, with the said Alexander Ousteane thair commissioners to the generall assembly of the kirk haldin within this burgh promittere de rato'.

23 February 1596/7: 'The sam day makis and creatis and constitutes Henry Nesbet and Jhonn Watt thair commissioners to compeir at Perth [at the general convention of estates] . . . to intreatt and resolve anent all questiouns standing in difference betuix the civile and ecclesiasticall jugements or ony wayis concerning the civile policie and ecclesiasticall governing of the kirk . . . and siclyke to compeir in the conventioun and generall assembly of the ministry to begin and haldin at the said burgh the said day and to vote and conclude in all maters to be proponit thairin promittere de rato, and ordanis thair commissions to be maid thairupoun in dew and competent form'.

2 March 1597/8: 'The quhilk day Henry Nesbet, provest, the baillies, deyne of gild, thesaurer, the maist part of the counsall being convenit, they electet, creat and constitute my lord provest, Rychert Doby and Alexander Myller thair commissioners to the generall assembly of the ministry of this realme to be begun and haldin at Dundie the [blank] day of Merche instant'.

6 May 1601: 'The quhilk day the baillies, deyne of gild, thesaurer and maist part of the counsall being convenet, electes and constitutes Jhonn Jhonestoun of Elphinstoun and George Hereott, elder, goldsmyth, thair commissioners to the generall assembly of the kirk to be begun and haldin at Sanctandrois the xij of May instant promittere de rato'.

St Andrews University[18]

'Vigesimo tertio Februarii 1568[/9]: Quo die academia Andreapolitana per rectorem convocata ad eligendum commissarium, qui universitatis nomine ad comitia publica generalis ecclesie huius regni vigesimo quinto Februarii Edinburgi indicta proficisceretur unanimi omnium consensu designatus est Magister Joannes Douglas, rector, ut universitatis nomine consultet ac cum reliquis commissariis urbium ac provinciarum deliberet aliaque singula agat que ad dei gloriam ecclesie utilitatem et academiae libertatem pertinent excepta questione controversa inter Magistrum Jacobum Carmechaell et eius collegas adversus dominum rectorem et ceteros quos in criminationem vocant de qua si quid agat tanquam a privato agi statuit datum anno et die supra dictis ex collegio [novo, *deleted*] Mariano'.

Vigesimo septimo Februarii anno 1569 [1570]: In scholis Marianis conclusum fuit a domino rectore et suis assessoribus ordine collegiorum commissarium eligi debere qui generalibus ecclesie commitiis adsit et universitatis nomine consultet et cum reliquis commissariis urbium ac provinciarum deliberet aliaque singula agat que ad dei gloriam et ecclesie utilitatem pertinent quo die vir prudentissimus Mr Joannes Retorfortis, Salvatoriani collegii prepositus, electus fuit ut comitiis die primo Martii Edinburgi futuris adesset et pro sumptibus suis quadraginta solidos a dicto collegio acciperet, deinde ut e collegio Leonardino commissarius eligeretur et ut eidem quadraginta solidos pro suis expensis persolveret decretum fuit tertio vero ordine eligendus erit commissarius ex collegio novo Mariano qui ex euisdem collegii erario quadraginta solidos pro suo commeatu similiter recipiat, et ut hic ordo perpetuis futuris temporibus per curriculum recurrat statutum fuit'.

'Quarto Julii 1577 [*recte*, 1578]: Quo die comitiis academie

[18] St Andrews University Archives, MS. Acta Rectorum, ii, 74, 75, 92, 98.

habitis in cubiculo superintendentis M. Jacobus Wylkie, rector universitatis, designatus est qui mandato academie Strevelingum servet ad comitia ecclesiastica, et dominos parliamenti ubi eidem impense ex erario publico decretae sunt omnium dierum quos ultra 14 mensis predicti in eodem negotio conficeret et nominati que de postulatis academie ad parliamentum deferendis consilium caperent cum rectore, dominus superintendens, M. Robertus Hamiltoun, M. Jacobus Martyne, M. Guilielmus Skein, M. Thomas Brown, M. Joannes Robertsone, M. Guilielmus Walwod, M. Robertus Wilkie, M. Joannes Kar die 8 euisdem mensis et loco eodem'.

'Quarto Julii [1579]: Quo die conclusum est matura deliberatione prehabita a domino rectore et eius assessoribus commissarium eligendum esse suffragiis domini rectoris pro tempore et suorum assessorum qui ad comitia ecclesie generalia mittatur liberaque potestas rectori et assessoribus conceditur ut virum quem maxime iudicaverint idoneum designent pro eorum arbitrio idgue per vices collegiorum'.

BIBLIOGRAPHY

I Manuscript Sources

Aberdeen
    Aberdeen University Library
        MS. 227 Acts of the General Assembly

Dublin
    Trinity College
        MS. 533 The Second Book of Discipline

Edinburgh
    Edinburgh City Archives
        MS. Edinburgh Town Council Records, vols. 4–11
    Edinburgh University Library
        MS. Dc.3.54 Acts of the General Assembly
        MS. Dc.6.45 Melvini Epistolae
        MS. La.II.14 Visitation of the Diocese of Dunblane
        MS. La.III.335 James Melville, Manuscripts of the Kirk of Scotland, 1560–1605

    National Library of Scotland
        Advocates MS. 6.1.13
        Advocates MS. 17.1.8.
        Advocates MS. 29.2.8 (Balcarres Papers)
        Wodrow MS. folio vol. xlii
        Wodrow MSS. octavo vols. ix, xxxiv
        Wodrow MSS. quarto vols. ix, xiii, xxi, lxxvii, lxxxiv

    New Register House
        Old Parochial Records:
        Aberdeen, OPR. 168^{A}/12
        Anstruther Wester, OPR. 403/1
        Errol, OPR. 351/1
        Fossoway, OPR. 461/1

Monifieth, OPR. 310/1
Tealing, OPR. 322/1
Scottish Record Office
Aberdeen Kirk Session Records, CH2/448/1-3
Aberdeen Presbytery Records, CH2/1/1
Accounts of the Collector-General of Thirds of Benefices, E45/1-25
Acts of the General Assembly, CH1/1/2
Ayr Kirk Session Records, CH2/1026/1
Burntisland Kirk Session Records, CH2/523/1
Dalkeith Presbytery Records, CH2/424/1
Dundonald Kirk Session Records, CH2/104/1
Edinburgh General Session Records, CH2/450/1
Edinburgh Presbytery Records, CH2/121/1-3
Elgin Kirk Session Records, CH2/141/1
Ellon Presbytery Records, CH2/146/1
Haddington Burgh Court Book, B30/10/2
Haddington Presbytery Records, CH2/185/1-2
Linlithgow Burgh Court Book, B48/7/1
Paisley Presbytery Records, CH2/294/1
Peebles Presbytery Records, CH2/295/1
Perth Kirk Session Records, CH2/521/1-4
Register of Acts and Decreets, vol. xlv
Register of Presentations to Benefices, CH4/1/2
Register of the Privy Seal, PS1/59, etc.
Second Book of Discipline, CH8/35
Stirling Kirk Session Records, CH2/1026/1
Stirling Presbytery Records, CH2/722/1-3
Warrender Papers, GD1/371/1

Geneva

Bibliothèque Publique et Universitaire Genève MS. Fr. 410

Glasgow

Glasgow Presbytery Office
Porteous Manuscript
Strathclyde Regional Archives incorporating Glasgow City Archives
Glasgow Presbytery Records
Glasgow University Archives
Blackhouse MS. 422

Glasgow University Library
  General MSS. 1122, 1132
  Wodrow's MS. Biographies

London
  British Library
    Additional MSS. 32092
    Harleian MSS. 7004
  Public Record Office
    State Papers, SP/59. Two copies of the Second Book of Discipline

Rome
  Vatican Archives
    Registra Supplicationum, 2962, 2963, 2972

St Andrews
  Holy Trinity Parish Church
    St Andrews Presbytery Records
  St Andrews University Archives
    Acta Rectorum, vol. ii

Zürich
  Staatsarchiv des Kantons Zürich
    MS. E.II. 382

II Primary Printed Sources

Aberdeen Council Letters, ed. L. B. Taylor, vol. i. (Oxford, 1942)
Accounts of the Collectors of Thirds of Benefices, 1561–1572, ed. G. Donaldson (SHS, Edinburgh, 1949)
Acta Facultatis Artium Universitatis Sancti Andree, 1413–1588, ed. A. I. Dunlop, 2 vols. (SHS, Edinburth, 1964)
Acts of the Parliaments of Scotland, eds. T. Thomson and C. Innes, 12 vols. (Edinburgh, 1814–75)
Advocates of Reform, ed. M. Spinka (London, 1953)
The Apostolic Fathers, ed. K. Lake, 2 vols. (London, 1912–13)
AYMON, J. *Tous les synodes nationaux des Églises reformées de France*, 2 vols. (The Hague, 1710)
BANCROFT, R. *A Survay of the Pretended Holy Discipline* (1593)
BANNATYNE, R. *Memoriales of Transactions in Scotland*, ed. R. Pitcairn (Bannatyne Club, Edinburgh, 1836)

The Basilikon Doron of King James VI, ed. J. Craigie, 2 vols. (STS, Edinburgh, 1944, 1950)

BEZA, T. *A briefe and piththie* [sic] *summe of the Christian faith made in forme of a Confession*, tr. R[obert] F[yll] (London, 1565)

—— *Epistolae Theologicae* (1574)

—— *Confession de foi du chrétien*, in *Revue réformée* (1955)

—— *Theodori Bezae Annotationes Maiores in Novum Dn. Nostri Iesu Christri Testamentum* (1594)

—— *Tractatus Pius et Moderatus de vera Excommunicatione et Christiano Presbyterio* (1590)

—— *Historie Ecclésiastique des Églises Réformées au Royaume de France*, eds. G. Baum and E. Cunitz. 3 vols. (Paris, 1883–9)

BILSON, T. *The Perpetual Government of Christ's Church* (1593), reprinted Oxford, 1842

—— *The True Difference between Christian Subjection and Unchristian Rebellion* (1585)

The Booke of the Universall Kirk. Acts and Proceedings of the General Assemblies of the Kirk of Scotland, 1560–1618, ed. T. Thomson, 3 vols. and appendix vol. (Bannatyne and Maitland Clubs, Edinburgh, 1839–45)

The Booke of the Universall Kirk of Scotland, ed. A. Peterkin. 1 vol. edn. (Edinburgh, 1839)

A Brief Discourse of the Troubles at Frankfort, 1554–1558 A.D., ed. E. Arber (London, 1908)

BUCER, M. *Opera Latina*, ed. F. Wendel, vol. xv. (Paris, 1954)

—— *Scripta Anglicana* (1577)

BUCHANAN, G. *De Jure Regni*, translated by D. H. MacNeill in *The Art and Science of Government Among the Scots* (1964)

—— *Opera Omnia*, ed. T. Ruddiman (Edinburgh, 1715)

The Buik of the Kirk of the Canagait, 1564–1567, ed. A. B. Calderwood (SRS, Edinburgh, 1961)

BULLINGER, H. *The Decades of Henry Bullinger*, ed. T. Harding (Parker Society, Cambridge, 1849–1852)

COCHRANE, A. C. *Reformed Confessions of the 16th Century* (London, 1966)

CALDERWOOD, D. *An Answer to M. I. Forbes of Corse, His Peaceable Warning* (1638)

—— *The History of the Kirk of Scotland*, ed. T. Thomson (Wodrow Society, Edinburgh, 1842–49)

Calendar of State Papers relating to Scotland and Mary, Queen of

Scots, 1547–1603, ed. W. K. Boyd, *et al.* 13 vols. (Edinburgh, 1899–1970)

CALVIN, J. *Commentary upon the Acts of the Apostles*, 2 vols. ed. H. Beveridge (CTS, Edinburgh, 1844)

—— *Commentaries on the Book of Joshua*, ed. H. Beveridge (CTS, Edinburgh, 1854)

—— *Commentary on the Book of the Prophet Isaiah*, ed. W. Pringle (CTS, Edinburgh, 1856)

—— *Commentaries on the Catholic Epistles*, ed. J. Owen (CTS, Edinburgh, 1855)

—— *Commentary on the Epistles of Paul the Apostle to the Corinthians*, ed. J. Pringle, 2 vols. (CTS, Edinburgh, 1848–9)

—— *Commentaries on the Epistles of Paul the Apostle to the Galatians and Ephesians*, ed. W. Pringle (CTS, Edinburgh, 1854)

—— *Commentaries on the Epistle of Paul the Apostle to the Hebrews*, ed. J. Owen (CTS, Edinburgh, 1833)

—— *Commentaries on the Epistles of Paul the Apostle to the Philippians, Colossians and Thessalonians.* ed. J. Pringle (CTS, Edinburgh, 1851)

—— *Commentaries on the Epistle of Paul the Apostle to the Romans*, ed. J. Owen (CTS, Edinburgh, 1849)

—— *Commentaries on the Epistles to Timothy, Titus and Philemon* (CTS, Edinburgh, 1856)

—— *A Harmony of the Gospels*, eds. D. W. Torrance and T. F. Torrance 3 vols. (Edinburgh, 1972)

—— *Institutes of the Christian Religion*, ed. H. Beveridge, 3 vols. (CTS, Edinburgh, 1846); another edition, eds. J. T. McNeill and F. L. Battles (London, 1961)

—— *Letters*, ed. J. Bonnet, 3 vols. (Edinburgh, 1855–57)

—— *Ioannis Calvini Opera... omnia*, in *Corpus Reformatorum*, eds. G. Baum. E. Cunitz and E. Reuss (Brunswick, 1869–96)

—— *Tracts*, ed. H. Beveridge. 3 vols. (Edinburgh, 1844–5)

Canones Concilii Provincialis Coloniensis (Paris, 1547)

Catholic Tractates of the Sixteenth Century, ed. T. G. Law (STS, Edinburgh, 1901)

Charters and uther Documents relating to the Royal Burgh of Stirling, ed. R. Renwick (Glasgow, 1884)

Common Places of Martin Bucer, ed. D. F. Wright (Appleford, 1972)

Correspondence of Matthew Parker, ed. J. Bruce (Parker Society, Cambridge, 1853)

COWAN, I. B. *The Parishes of Medieval Scotland* (SRS, Edinburgh, 1967)
COWAN, I. B. and EASSON, D. E. *Medieval Religious Houses Scotland* (London, 1976)
CRANMER, T. *Works*, ed. J. E. Cox, 2 vols. (Parker Society, Cambridge, 1844-6)
Dictionary of the Bible, ed. J. Hastings (Edinburgh, 1909)
A Directory of Church-government drawn up and used by the Elizabethan Presbyterians, ed. P. Lorimer (London, 1872)
Discipline or Book of Order of the Reformed Church of France, ed. M. G. Campbell (London, 1924)
A Diurnal of Remarkable Occurrents that have passed within the Country of Scotland since the Death of King James the Fourth till the year MDLXXV, ed. T. Thomson (Bannatyne and Maitland Clubs, Edinburgh, 1833)
DURKAN, J. and Ross, A. *Early Scottish Libraries* (Glasgow, 1961)
Evidence, oral and documentary, taken by the Commissioners appointed by King George IV for visiting the Universities of Scotland, 4 vols. (London, 1837)
Extracts from the Council Register of the Burgh of Aberdeen, 1570-1625, ed. J. Stuart, vol ii. (Spalding Club, Aberdeen, 1848)
Extracts from the Records of the Burgh of Edinburgh, vols. iii-v, ed. J. D. Marwick, vol. vi, ed. M. Wood (Edinburgh, 1875-1927)
Extracts from the Records of the Burgh of Glasgow, eds. J. D. Marwick and R. Renwick, vol. i. (Glasgow, 1876)
Extracts from the Records of the Royal Burgh of Stirling, ed. R. Renwick. 2 vols. (Glasgow, 1887-9)
Fasti Aberdonenses, Selections from the Records of the University and King's College of Aberdeen, ed. C. Innes (Spalding Club, Aberdeen, 1854)
Fasti Academiae Mariscallanae Aberdonensis, vol. i. (New Spalding Club, Aberdeen, 1889)
Fasti Ecclesiae Scoticanae, ed. H. Scott, 8 vols. (Edinburgh, 1915-50)
Fasti Ecclesiae Scoticanae Medii Aevi ad annum 1638, ed. D. E. R. Watt (SRS, Edinburgh, 1969)
FERGUSON, D. *Tracts by David Fergusson, Minister of Dunfermline* (Bannatyne Club, Edinburgh, 1860)
The First Book of Discipline, ed. J. K. Cameron (Edinburgh, 1972)
The First and Second Booke of Discipline, together with some Acts of the Generall Assemblies (1621)

GARDY, F. and DUFOUR, A. *Bibliographie des oeuvres théologiques, littéraires historiques et juridiques de Théodore de Bèze* (Geneva, 1960)
GILLESPIE, G. *An Assertion of the Government of the Church of Scotland* (1641)
Heads and conclusions of the policie of the Kirk (1680)
The Historie and Life of King James the Sext, ed. T. Thomson (Bannatyne Club, Edinburgh, 1825)
HOOKER, R. *Works*, ed. I. Walton, 2 vols. (Oxford, 1865)
HOOPER, J. *Early Writings*, ed. S. Carr (Parker Society, 1843)
—— *Later Writings*, ed. C. Nevison (Parker Society, 1852)
HUME OF GODSCROFT, D. *History of the Houses of Douglas and Angus* (Edinburgh, 1644)
JEWEL, J. *Works*, ed. J. Ayre 4 vols. (Parker Society, Cambridge, 1845–50)
KENNEDY, W. P. M. *Elizabethan Episcopal Administration* 3 vols. (London, 1924)
KNOX, J. *John Knox's History of the Reformation in Scotland*, 2 vols., ed. W. C. Dickinson (Edinburgh, 1949)
—— *Works*, ed. D. Laing, 6 vols. (Wodrow Society, Edinburgh, 1846–64)
LASCO, J. à. *Opera*, ed. A. Kuyper, 2 vols. (Amsterdam, 1866)
LATIMER, H. *Sermons*, ed. G. E. Corrie (Parker Society, Cambridge, 1844–45)
LESLIE, J. *The Historie of Scotland*, vol. 2 (STS, Edinburgh, 1895)
LINDESAY OF PITSCOTTIE, R. *The Historie and Cronicles of Scotland*, vol 2, ed. E. J. G. Mackay (STS, Edinburgh, 1899)
The Two Liturgies ... with other Documents ... in the Reign of Edward VI, ed. J. Ketley (Parker Society, Cambridge, 1844)
Luther's Works, eds. J. Pelikan and H. T. Lehmann, 55 vols. (Philadelphia, 1955–69)
Melanchthon and Bucer, ed. W. Pauck (London, 1969)
MELVILLE, A. *Scholastica diatriba de rebus divinis* (Edinburgh, 1599)
MELVILLE, J. *The Autiobiography and Diary of Mr James Melvill*, ed. R. Pitcairn (Wodrow Society, Edinburgh, 1842)
MELVILLE OF HALHILL, *Memoirs*, ed. A. F. Steuart (London, 1929)
Miscellany of the Scottish History Society, viii. (Edinburgh, 1951)
Miscellany of the Spalding Club, vol. iv. (Aberdeen, 1849)
Miscellany of the Wodrow Society, vol. i. ed. D. Laing (Edinburgh, 1844)

Original Letters relating to the Ecclesiastical Affairs of Scotland, 2 vols. ed. D. Laing (Bannatyne Club, Edinburgh, 1851)
Original Letters relative to the English Reformation, 1531–58, ed. H. Robinson, 2 vols. (Parker Society, Cambridge, 1846–7)
The Oxford Dictionary of the Christian Church, eds. F. L. Cross and E. A. Livingstone (2nd. edn., Oxford, 1974)
The Presbyterian Movement in the Reign of Queen Elizabeth as Illustrated by the Minute Book of the Dedham Classis, 1582–1589, ed. R. G. Usher (London, 1905)
Puritan Manifestoes: A Study of the Origin of the Puritan Revolt, eds. W. H. Frere and C. E. Douglas (London, 1907)
QUICK, J. *Synodicon in Gallia Reformata*, 2 vols. (London, 1692)
Records of the Burgh of Kirkcaldy, ed. L. MacBean (Kirkcaldy, 1908)
The Records of Elgin, 1234–1800, eds. W. Crammond and S. Ree, 2 vols (New Spalding Club, Aberdeen, 1904–8)
The Records of the Synod of Lothian and Tweeddale, 1589–1596, 1640–1649, ed. J. Kirk (Stair Society, Edinburgh, 1977)
Register of the Great Seal of Scotland: Registrum Magni Sigilli Regum Scotorum, ed. J. M. Thomson, vol. iv. (Edinburgh, 1886)
Register of the Minister, Elders and Deacons of the Christian Congregation of St Andrews, ed. D. H. Fleming, 2 vols. (SHS, Edinburgh, 1889–90)
Register of the Privy Council of Scotland, eds. J. H. Burton and D. Masson, 1st ser., 14 vols. (Edinburgh, 1877–1898); 2nd ser., vols. i-ii. (Edinburgh, 1899–1900)
Register of the Privy Seal of Scotland: Registrum Secreti Sigilli Regum Scotorum, ed. G. Donaldson, vols. v-vii. (Edinburgh, 1957–1966)
Registres de la Compagnie des Pasteurs de Genève au temps de Calvin, ed. J. -F. Bergier, *et al.*, 5 vols. (Geneva, 1962–1976)
Row, J. *The History of the Kirk of Scotland* (Wodrow Society, Edinburgh, 1842)
RUTHERFORD, S. *The Due Right of Presbyteries* (London, 1644)
The Seconde Parte of a Register, ed. A. Peel, 2 vols. (Cambridge, 1915)
Select Biographies ed. W. K. Tweedie, 2 vols. (Wodrow Society, Edinburgh, 1845, 1847)
Selections from the Records of the Kirk Session, Presbytery and Synod of Aberdeen, ed. J. Stuart (Spalding Club, Aberdeen, 1846)
A Short-Title Catalogue of Books Printed in England, Scotland and

Ireland, and of English Books Printed Abroad, 1475–1640, eds. A. W. Pollard and G. R. Redgrave (London, 1956)
Spiritual and Anabaptist Writers, ed. G. H. Williams (London, 1957)
SPOTTISWOODE, J. *The History of the Church of Scotland*, ed. M. Russell, 3 vols. (Spottiswoode Society, Edinburgh, 1851–65)
Statutes of the Realm, ed. A. Luders et al., 11 vols. (London, 1810–28)
STRYPE, J. *Annals of the Reformation*, 4 vols. (Oxford, 1824)
The Thirty-Nine Articles of the Church of England, ed. E. C. S. Gibson (London, 1902)
Tracts ascribed to Richard Bancroft, ed. A. Peel (Cambridge, 1953)
TRAVERS, W. *Ecclesiasticae Disciplinae ... Explicatio* (1574)
—— *A full and plaine declaration of Ecclesiastical Discipline* (1574)
TYNDALE, W. *Doctrinal Treatises* (Parker Society, Cambridge, 1848)
UDALL, J. *A Demonstration of the Truth of that Discipline*, etc., ed. E. Arber (London, 1895)
WHITGIFT, J. *Works*, ed. J. Ayre, 3 vols. (Parker Society, Cambridge, 1851–3)
WIED, HERMANN VON, *A simple and religious consultation of us Herman by the grace of God, Archbishop of Collone and prince Electoure*, etc. (London, 1548)
WINZET, N. *Certane tractatis for reformatioun of doctryne and manneris in Scotland*, ed. D. Laing (Maitland Club, Edinburgh, 1835)
WODROW, R. *Collections upon the Lives of the Reformers and most eminent Ministers of the Church of Scotland*, 2 vols. (Maitland Club, Glasgow, 1834–1848)
The Zürich Letters, ed. H. Robinson, 2 vols. (Parker Society, Cambridge, 1842–5)
Zwingli and Bullinger, Selected Translations, ed. G. W. Bromiley (London, 1953)

III Secondary Sources

AINSLIE, J. L. *The Doctrines of Ministerial Order in the Reformed Churches in the Sixteenth and Seventeenth Centuries* (Edinburgh, 1940)
ALLEN, J. W. *A History of Political Thought in the Sixteenth Century* (Edinburgh, 1957)
BORGEAUD, C. *Histoire de l'Université de Genève: L'Acadèmie de Calvin, 1559–1798* (Geneva, 1900)

BOUVIER, A. *Henri Bullinger* (Neuchâtel, 1904)
BUCHANAN, W. *Treatise on the Law of Scotland on the subject of Teinds or Tithes* (Edinburgh, 1862)
BRUNTON, G. and HAIG, D. *An Historical Account of the Senators of the College of Justice from its Institution in MDXXXII* (Edinburgh, 1832)
BURLEIGH, J. H. S. 'The Presbyter in Presbyterianism', *Scottish Journal of Theology*, ii. (1949), 293-309.
BURNS, T. *Church Property: The Benefice Lectures* (Edinburgh, 1905)
CANT, R. G. *The University of St Andrews* (Edinburgh, 1946 second edn. 1970)
CHOISY, E. *L'état chrétien calviniste à Genève au temps de Théodore de Bèze* (Geneva, 1902)
—— *La théocratie à Genève au temps de Calvin* (Geneva, 1897)
CHRISTENSEN, T. L. 'Scots in Denmark in the sixteenth century', *SHR*, xlix. (1970), 138-40.
CHRISMAN, M. U. *Strasbourg and the Reform* (New Haven, 1967)
COLLINSON, P. *The Elizabethan Puritan Movement* (London, 1967)
CONRADT, N. M. 'John Calvin, Theodore Beza and the Reformation in Poland'. Unpublished Ph.D. thesis (Madison, Wisconsin, 1974)
COURVOISIER, J. *La Notion d'Église chez Bucer* (Paris, 1933)
CUMING, G. J. *A History of Anglican Liturgy* (London, 1969)
DAVIES, E. T. *Episcopacy and the Royal Supremacy in the Church of England in the XVI Century* (Oxford, 1950)
DAVIES, R. E. *The Problem of Authority in the Continental Reformers* (London, 1946)
DEMURA, A. 'Church Discipline according to Johannes Oecolampadius in the Setting of his Life and Thought'. Unpublished Th.D. thesis (Princeton Theological Seminary, 1964)
DONALDSON, G. 'The Attitude of Whitgift and Bancroft to the Scottish Church', *Transactions of the Royal Historical Society*, 4th ser., xxiv. (1942), 95-115
—— 'Bishop Adam Bothwell and the Reformation in Orkney', *RSCHS*, xiii. (1959), 85-100
—— '"The Example of Denmark" in the Scottish Reformation', *SHR*, xxvii. (1948), 57-64
—— *Scotland: James V to James VII* (Edinburgh, 1965)
—— 'Scottish Presbyterian Exiles in England, 1584-1588', *RSCHS*, xiv. (1963), 67-80

DONALDSON, G. *The Scottish Reformation* (Cambridge, 1960)
DOWDEN, J. *The Medieval Church in Scotland* (Glasgow, 1910)
DUNKLEY, E. H. *The Reformation in Denmark* (London, 1948)
DURKAN, J. and KIRK, J. *The University of Glasgow, 1451-1577* (Glasgow, 1977)
EELLS, H. *Martin Bucer* (New Haven, 1931)
Essays on the Scottish Reformation, ed. D. McRoberts (Glasgow, 1962)
FALLOW, T. M. *The Order of Baptism ... illustrated from the Use of Salisbury, the Religious Consultation of Herman* (London, 1838)
FISHER, J. D. C. *Christian Initiation: The Reformation Period* (London, 1970)
FITTIS, R. S. *Ecclesiastical Annals of Perth to the period of the Reformation* (Perth, 1885)
GEISENDORF, P.-F. *Théodore de Bèze* (Geneva, 1949)
GRAVES, F. P. *Peter Ramus and the Educational Reformation of the Sixteenth Century* (New York, 1912)
HENDERSON, G. D. *The Burning Bush: Studies in Scottish Church History* (Edinburgh, 1957)
—— *The Founding of Marischal College, Aberdeen* (Aberdeen 1946)
—— *Presbyterianism* (Aberdeen, 1954)
—— *The Scottish Ruling Elder* (London, 1935)
—— 'The Witness of the Laity', *Scottish Journal of Theology*, ii. (1949), 174–186
HENDERSON, R. W. *The Teaching Office in the Reformed Tradition* (Philadelphia, 1962)
HILDEBRANDT, F. (ed.) *And Other Pastors of Thy Flock* (Cambridge, 1942)
HILL, C. *Antichrist in Seventeenth-Century England* (Oxford, 1971)
HOPF, C. *Martin Bucer and the English Reformation* (Oxford, 1964)
An Introduction to Scottish Legal History, various contributors (Stair Society, Edinburgh, 1958)
KEITH, R. *An Historical Catalogue of the Scottish Bishops*, ed. M. Russel (Edinburgh, 1824)
—— *History of the Affairs of the Church and State in Scotland*, ed. J. P. Lawson, 3 vols. (Spottiswoode Society, Edinburgh, 1844–50)
KINGDON, R. M. 'The deacons of the Reformed church in Calvin's Geneva', *Mélanges d'histoire du XVIe siecle. Offerts à Henri Meylan* (Geneva, 1970)

KINGDON, R. M. *Geneva and the coming of the Wars of Religion in France, 1555–1563* (Geneva, 1956)
—— *Geneva and the Consolidation of the French Protestant Movement, 1564–1572* (Geneva, 1967)
KIRK, J. 'The Influence of Calvinism on the Scottish Reformation', *RSCHS*, xviii. (1974), 157–179
—— 'The Development of the Melvillian Movement in late sixteenth-century Scotland' (Unpublished Edinburgh Ph.D. thesis, 1972)
KNOX, S. J. *Walter Travers: Paragon of Elizabethan Puritanism* (London, 1962)
LAU F. and BIZER, E. *A History of the Reformation in Germany to 1555* (London, 1969)
LEONARD, E. G. *A History of Protestantism*, ed. H. H. Rowley, vols. i–ii (London, 1965–67)
McCRIE, T. *The Life of Andrew Melville* (Edinburgh, 1899)
MACGREGOR, G. *Corpus Christi* (London, 1959)
MACGREGOR, J. G. *The Scottish Presbyterian Polity* (Edinburgh, 1926)
McNEILL, J. T. *The History and Character of Calvinism* (New York, 1962)
McROBERTS, D. (ed.) *Essays on the Scottish Reformation* (Glasgow, 1962)
MARUYAMA, T. 'The Reform of the True Church, The Ecclesiology of Theodore Beza'. Unpublished Th.D. thesis (Princeton, New Jersey, 1973)
MAXWELL, A. *The History of Old Dundee* (Dundee, 1884)
MEEK, D. E. AND KIRK, J. 'John Carswell, Superintendent of Argyll: a reassessment', *RSCHS*, xix. (1975), 1–22
MITCHELL, A. F. *The Scottish Reformation*, ed. D. H. Fleming (Edinburgh, 1900)
MONTER, E. W. *Calvin's Geneva* (New York, 1967)
MUIRHEAD, I. A. 'M. Robert Lokhart', *Innes Review*, xxii, 85–110.
MURRAY, R. H. *The Political Consequences of the Reformation* (London, 1926)
PANNIER, J. 'Calvin et l'épiscopat', *Revue d'Histoire et de philosophie religieuses*, vi. (Paris, 1926)
PAUCK, W. 'Calvin and Butzer', *Journal of Religion*, ix (1929)
PEARSON, A. F. S. *Church and State: Political Aspects of Sixteenth-Century Puritanism* (Cambridge, 1928)

PEARSON, A. F. S. *Thomas Cartwright and Elizabethan Puritanism, 1535–1603*, (Cambridge, 1925)
REID, J. K. S. *The Authority of Scripture* (London, 1957)
RIDDELL, J. *Scottish Peerages and Consistorial Law*, vol. i. (Edinburgh, 1842)
ROSS, J. M. 'The Elizabethan Elder', *Journal of the Presbyterian Historical Society of England*, x, 59–70, 126–138
RUPP, G. *The Righteousness of God* (London, 1953)
SCHAFF, P. *The Creeds of the Evangelical Protestant Churches*, vol. iii. (London, 1877)
SCHWARZ, W. *Principles and Problems of Biblical Translation* (Cambridge, 1955)
Service in Christ, eds. J. I. McCord and T. H. L. Parker (London, 1966)
SHAW, D. *The General Assemblies of the Church of Scotland, 1560–1600* (Edinburgh, 1964)
—— 'The Inauguration of Ministers in Scotland: 1560–1620', *Records of the Scottish Church History Society*, xvi. (1966), 35–62
STEPHENS, W. P. *The Holy Spirit in the Theology of Martin Bucer* (Cambridge, 1970)
STEVENSON, J. H. and WOOD, M. *Scottish Heraldic Seals* (Glasgow, 1940)
STROHL, H. 'Bucer et Calvin', *Bulletin de la Société de l'histoire du protestantisme français*, lxxxvii. (Paris, 1938)
—— 'La théorie et la pratique des quatres ministères à Strasbourg avant l'arrivée de Calvin', *Bulletin de la Société de l'histoire du protestantisme français*, lxxxiv. (Paris, 1935)
SYKES, N. *Old Priest and New Presbyter* (Cambridge, 1957)
TELFER, W. *The Office of a Bishop* (London, 1962)
THOMPSON, J. V. P. *Supreme Governor* (London, 1940)
TORRANCE, T. F. *Kingdom and Church, A Study in the Theology of the Reformation* (Edinburgh, 1956)
WALLACE, R. S. *Calvin's Doctrine of the Word and Sacrament* (Edinburgh, 1953)
WALTON, R. C. *Zwingli's Theocracy* (Toronto, 1967)
WENDEL, F. *Calvin, the Origins and Development of his Religious Thought* (London, 1965)
—— *L'Église de Strasbourg, sa constitution et son organisation, 1532–1539* (Paris, 1942)
WHALE, J. S. *The Protestant Tradition* (Cambridge, 1955)
WILLIAM, G. H. *The Radical Reformation* (London, 1962)

INDEX

Abbacies, 220–22; appointments to, 22; dilapidation of, 33. *See also* Prelacies
Abbeys, 19, 33, 135, 218, 219, 227, 272. *See also* Monasteries, Priory
Abbot, 38, 122, 128, 217; term to be changed (1572), 28. *See also* Commendators
Aberdeen, 46, 86, 98, 259, 265, 266, 277; bishop of, *see* Cunningham, David; King's college, 43, 86, 125; Marischal college, 86; moderator of presbytery of, 196; St Machar's, 86
Aberlady, 96, 244
Adamson, John, 275
 John, merchant in Edinburgh, 281, 284–88
 Patrick, archbishop of St Andrews, 51, 68, 71, 93, 112, 115, 121, 134, 137, 143, 144, 150, 180, 226, 245; his initial criticism of episcopacy, 30, 55, 82, 225; grants of episcopal property by, 34; his ecclesiology, 137ff.; his comments on the second Book of Discipline, 93; assents to same, 125; declines to submit to general assembly, 130, 223; submits to same, 130, 222; accusations against, 151; deposed, 151
Aird, William, minister of St Cuthbert's, Edinburgh, 268
Airth, 108; laird of, *see* Bruce, Alexander
Allanson, John, reader in Glasgow, 272
Alms, 6, 97, 98, 174, 176, 207, 237. *See also* Poor
Alva, 107; kirk session of, 196
Anabaptism, 5, 8; anabaptists, 163, 172
Anderson, James, minister at Stirling, 278, 279
Angus, 46; earl of, *see* Douglas, Archibald 6th earl; superintendent of, *see* Erskine of Dun, John; synod of, 115

Anstruther, kirk session of, 91
Arbroath, 268; postulate of abbey, *see* Douglas, George
Arbuthnot, Alexander, principal of King's college, Aberdeen, 46, 50, 51, 86, 125, 127
Archbishop, 21, 55; office criticised, 25, 27–28, 177. *See also* Bishops, Episcopacy
Archdeacon, 25, 27–28, 218
Ard, William *see* Aird, William
Ardrie, laird of, 277
Ardrossan, 19
Argyll, bishop of, *see* Campbell, Neil; earls of, *see* Campbell; superintendent of, *see* Carswell, John
Arnott, John, provost of Edinburgh, 287
Arran, earls of, *see* Hamilton, James 3rd earl *and* Stewart, James
Arthur, William, minister at Corstorphine, 268
Assembly, general, *see* General Assembly; international, 101, 195, 200, 205, 206
Athelstaneford, 71
Ayr, 4, 100, 222; presbytery of, 134
Aytoun of Kinnaldy, John, 276

Balcanquhal, Walter, minister in Edinburgh, 264–66, 268
Balcarres, lord, *see* Lindsay of Menmuir, John
Balcormo, laird of, 277
Balfour, Duncan, burgess of St Andrews, 276
 James, minister in Edinburgh, 261, 265, 266, 268
Balnaves, Henry, 37, 60, 65, 76, 168, 170
Balrimonth, laird of, 277
Bancleroche (Banclocht), laird of, 269
Bancroft, Richard, 139, 200
Bannatyne, John, skinner in Edinburgh, 288

Barclay, James, in Edinburgh, 288
  William, in Kilrenny, 276, 277
Baro, 69, 244
Barron, James, merchant in Edinburgh, 281–83
Basel, 216
Bassandyne, Thomas, printer in Edinburgh, 61
Beaton, James, archbishop of Glasgow, 14, 18, 19, 272
Bell, John, minister at Cadder, 109, 270–2
Bellenden, Adam, minister at Falkirk, 281
Benefices, 6, 13, 15, 17, 18, 22, 27, 28, 38, 43, 44, 48, 122, 123, 133, 140, 142, 147, 149, 153, 177, 180, 214, 217, 219, 220, 221, 228, 229, 235, 237, 239, 242, 247, 250, 255, 256, 271, 272; admission to, 22, 23, 32, 106, 132, 217, 221, 251; dilapidation of, 215, 219, 220, 239; dissolution of, 14, 17, 251; presentations to, 149, 150, 152, 234, 235, 253; thirds of, 16, 17, 18, 211, 214, 219, 220, 221, 253; collectors of thirds of, 21, 238
Bennet, John, minister at Heriot, 262, 263
  James, minister at Liberton, 267
Beza, Theodore, 9, 44, 45, 52, 53, 64, 97–99, 113, 114, 118, 124, 127, 164–8, 171, 175, 176, 179, 187, 191, 195–200, 203, 208, 210, 216, 224, 226, 230, 231, 243;
  Annotationes, 114; Confession of Faith, 64, 173, 205, 213, 235
Bible, Genevan and Authorised versions of, 110
Birnie, William, minister at Lanark, 271
Bishops, 9, 21, 22, 24, 27–31, 35–37, 43–45, 63, 68, 74ff., 78, 80–81, 84, 97, 103, 105, 124–8, 131, 133–4, 138, 141–53, 169, 185, 187, 197, 201, 211, 214, 218–9, 222–9, 234, 246, 248–51, 254, 256, 257; Catholic, 14–16; conforming, 14, 15, 38, 77, 78, 131, 143; and superintendents, 27, 36–37, 78; criticism of, 22, 29–31, 35, 53, 131; subject to general assembly, 23, 27, 36, 131, 143, 148, 150; decline to submit, 56; 'true' and 'false', 55, 75, 76, 80, 123, 222, 225; identity with parish minister, 51, 53–55, 74–77, 80, 82, 123, 130, 149, 167, 175, 176, 183, 197, 222, 224, 225, 251, 256; of human ordinance, 77, 80, 81, 224; of apostolic ordinance, 79, 138; tulchan, 55. *See also* Episcopacy
Bishoprics, 14, 18–23, 27, 35, 131–2, 218, 219, 221, 222; dilapidation of, 31, 33–34, 135. *See also* Prelacies
'Black Acts' (1584), 101, 111, 142–4, 146, 147, 152, 153, 195
Black, David, minister at St Andrews, 95, 277
Blackbarony, laird of, *see* Murray, Andrew
Blackburn, Peter, regent at Glasgow; minister at Aberdeen, 85
Blackhall, Andrew, minister at Musselburgh, 263, 264
Blair, Homer, regent in St Salvator's college, St Andrews, 88, 277
Blairlogie, laird of, 93
Blanshe, laird of, 273
Blebo, laird of, 277
Blyth, Henry, minister of Canongate, 202, 267
Bologna, 4
Bolton, 244
Bonar, John, 71
Bonn, 6, 8
Book of Common Order, 8, 88, 185
Book of Common Prayer, 142
Books of Discipline, first and second, *see* Discipline, Books of
Borthwick, Alexander, 73
Bothans, 70, 244
Bothkennar, 108
Bothwell, Adam, bishop of Orkney, 33, 37, 76, 78, 131, 224
Boyd, Andrew, minister at Eaglesham, 70, 270
  James, archbishop of Glasgow, 30, 32, 34, 46, 47, 55, 79, 119, 130, 132, 222, 226, 245
  Robert, lord, 30
Braid, laird of, 264–7
Brand, John, minister of Canongate, 50, 202, 263–5
Brechin, 115; bishop of, *see* Campbell, Alexander; bishopric of, 14; presbytery of, 134

Brisbane, William, minister at Erskine, 275
Brown, James, in Edinburgh, 282
  Thomas, regent in St Andrews, 290
Bruce of Airth, Alexander, 278, 279
  Robert, minister in Edinburgh, 71–72, 261, 264, 266–8, 278
Brunstane, laird of, 263, 267
Bucer, Martin, 5–8, 10, 42, 64, 65, 72, 74, 114, 163, 166–70, 174, 175, 180, 198, 207, 209, 211, 216, 221; *De Regno Christi*, 8, 64
Buchan, earl of, *see* Douglas, Robert
Buchanan, George, 61, 76, 77, 225, 245; *De Jure Regni*, 169
Bufrey, laird of, 277
Bullinger, Heinrich, 9, 58, 74, 164, 167–70, 172, 173, 175, 176, 187, 188, 191, 197, 199, 210, 213
Burghs, commissioners from to general assembly, 117–20, 249, 260, 281–9
Burghley, lord, *see* Cecil, Sir William
Burntisland, 99, 268; elders in, 92; kirk session of, 91
Bursars, 235, 272
Byres, George, minister at Baro, 69, 244

Cadder, 47, 270, 271
Caithness, 46; bishop of, *see* Stewart, Robert *and* Pont, Robert
Calderwood, David, 48, 49, 156, 245
Calling, *see* Vocation
Calvin, John, 4, 5, 8, 9, 42, 53, 55, 58, 62, 63, 67, 72, 74, 80–82, 88, 93, 97, 114, 163, 164, 166–76, 179, 180, 181, 183, 187, 189, 191, 192, 196, 198–200, 206–208, 210, 211, 223, 237; *Institutes*, 4, 55, 163, 165, 254; *Psychopannychia*, 4
Calvinism, 3–5, 7, 9, 10, 57, 102, 176, 177
Cambo, laird of, 276, 277
Cambridge, 4
Cambuskenneth, commendator of abbey of, 280; *see also* Erskine, Adam
Cambuslang, 271
Cambusnethan, 272
Campbell, Alexander, bishop of Brechin, 18, 32, 34, 130, 134
  Archibald, 5th earl of Argyll, 21, 30, 33, 34, 136

  Archibald, 7th earl of Argyll, 259', 280
  John, bishop of the Isles, 130, 134–6
  Neil, bishop of Argyll, 130
Campsie, laird of, 269
Canongate, kirk session of, 202
Canterbury, archbishops of, *see* Cranmer, Thomas; Parker, Matthew; Whitgift, John; Bancroft, Richard
Capito, Wolfgang, 170
Carberry, goodman of, 263–6
Carmichael, James, minister at Haddington, 50, 95, 105, 129, 154–5, 244, 261, 273, 274, 289
Carnbee, laird of, 277
Carswell, John, superintendent of Argyll; bishop of the Isles, 18, 78, 136
Cashkelpie, laird of, 273
Cathedral, 122, 218, 227; *see also* Chapters
Catholicism, *see* Roman Catholicism
Cartwright, Thomas, 169, 176, 200
Cecil, Sir William, lord Burghley, 75
Chalmer, John, regent at Aberdeen, 86
Chancellor, 25, 218
Chanter, 218
Chapters, 24, 25, 27–31, 122, 131, 132, 218, 219, 222, 227, 256
Charles I, King of Scots, 239
Charteris, Henry, merchant in Edinburgh, 286, 287
Chisholm, Michael, merchant in Edinburgh, 284
Christ, Jesus, headship of, 58, 59; the Mediator, 58, 62, 164, 166, 246
Christison, William, minister at Dundee, 4, 46
Church, abuses in, 217–29; courts of, 58, 101ff., 195–206; definitions of, 57, 101, 163, 246; office-bearers in, 74ff.; political doctrines of, 61, 65. *See also* England, Church of; Scotland, Church of; *and* Ecclesiastical Jurisdiction; Keys, power of the; Polity, ecclesiastical; Royal Supremacy
Churches, collegiate, 24, 218, 227; parish, 24, 76, 104, 106, 108, 134, 181, 219, 220, 230–3, 252
Civil Magistrate, 10–13, 29, 38, 40, 41, 43, 49, 59, 61–65, 95, 102, 127, 138, 146, 147, 164–6, 168–72, 200,

213-17, 228, 233, 243, 247, 254. See also Royal Supremacy
Clark, Alexander, merchant in Edinburgh, 283, 285
Classis, 113-15, 203
Clerkington, laird of, 273
Cock, William, in St Andrews, 276
Cockburn, Patrick, minister at Haddington, 4
Cockpen, laird of, 93, 262, 263
Colinton, laird of, 264-7
College of Justice, 24, 36, 37, 217, 222, 287. See also Court of Session
Colluthie, laird of, 277
Colmonell, 47
Cologne, 5-8; archbishop and elector of, see Wied, Hermann von
Colt, Oliver, regent at Edinburgh; minister of Canongate, 85
Commendators, 24, 38, 122, 125; 215, 217, 219, 222, 227. See also Abbot, Prior
Commissary Courts (and commissaries), 48, 123, 228, 229, 252, 257, 271, 278
Commissioners for visitation, 15, 31, 32, 37, 38, 54, 56, 77, 79, 82, 84, 106, 115, 119, 136, 138, 142, 143, 148-50, 185, 188, 196, 201, 220, 223, 279. See also Superintendent and Visitor
Conference, 113, 114, 203. See also classis
Confessions of Faith, Augsburg (1530), 163; Belgic (1561), 175, 180; Beza's (1559), 64, 173, 205, 213, 235; French (1559), 175, 180; Genevan (1536), 181; first Helvetic (1536), 180; second Helvetic (1566), 68, 175, 176, 180; Negative (1581), 133, 177; Scots (1560), 5, 11, 64, 163, 166, 170, 197, 198, 205, 213, 221; Tetrapolitan (1530), 170
Consistory, congregational, 7, 58, 66, 80, 99, 109, 110, 113, 114, 165, 189, 199, 203, 208, 232
Cor, Clement, merchant in Edinburgh, 288
Corstorphine, laird of, 265
Cotfield, laird of, see Logan, Andrew
Couper, John, minister in Glasgow, 267, 271, 272
Court of Session, 228, 233, 271. See also College of Justice

Coverdale, Miles, 4
Craig, John, minister of Canongate; at Aberdeen, 4, 46, 48-51, 53, 264, 266
Thomas, advocate in Edinburgh, 285
Craigbarnet, laird of, 269
Craighall, laird of, 277
Crail, 276
Cranmer, Thomas, archbishop of Canterbury, 3, 42, 77, 164, 206, 225
Cranston, Hector, reader at Peebles, 276
Michael, minister at Cramond, 261, 267
kirk session of, 100
Crichton of Lugtoun, David, 262, 263
Crown, see individual monarchs; Civil Magistrate and Royal Supremacy
Cunningham, Alexander, 5th earl of Glencairn, 19, 20, 30
Alexander, son of 5th earl, 19
Cuthbert, 19
David, minister at Cadder; bishop of Aberdeen, 47, 55, 134
Humphrey, commissary at Stirling, 278
James, son of 5th earl, 19, 20
of Drumquhassill, John, 19
William, 6th earl of Glencairn, 136

Dacre, lord, 4
Dairsie, laird of, see Lermonth, James
Dalgleish, David, in St Andrews, 276
Nicol, minister at Pittenweem, 277
Dalhousie, laird of, 262, 263
Dalkeith, 95, 100, 119; presbytery of, 69, 71, 93, 110-12, 114, 128, 130, 136, 211, 260-3
Dalmahoy, laird of, 266, 267
James, minister at Clackmannan, 202
Darroch, Robert, minister at Kilmarnock, 109, 271
Davidson, John, minister at Prestonpans, 70, 85, 265, 274
Davison, William, English diplomat, 155
Deacons, 6, 7, 9-11, 13, 16, 48-50, 73-75, 90, 91, 97-100, 103, 108, 115, 122, 124, 127, 149, 170, 174-6, 188, 194, 199, 201, 203, 207, 208, 210, 211, 236-9, 242, 250, 252, 256; ministerial, 9, 36

INDEX

Dean, 6, 25, 27, 28, 177, 218; of Christianity, 218
Deaneries, 24, 114
Denmark, 9
Dioceses, 23, 28, 32, 132, 223, 233, 251
Discipline, ecclesiastical, 4, 7, 10, 15, 28, 37, 40, 43, 58, 59, 61, 62, 64, 74, 77, 80, 82, 90, 98, 101-3, 106, 108, 110, 113, 125, 141, 142, 145, 146, 163-6, 169, 170, 172, 173, 175, 189, 191, 194ff., 198, 200, 214, 215, 243, 246, 247, 271, 272
Discipline, first Book of (1560), 3, 5-11, 13-18, 22-25, 29, 36, 37, 45, 58, 62, 66, 67, 74, 78, 90, 97-100, 124, 169, 170, 173, 179, 180, 184, 185, 187, 188, 199, 208, 209, 211, 217, 229, 231, 235, 236, 238-40
second Book of (1578), 4, 8; origins and drafting of, 42ff.; authorship of, 45ff.; contents of, 57ff.; fourfold ministry of, 74ff.; final version of, 48; approved by general assembly, 51, 128, 129, 241, 244; subscription to, 72, 124ff., 128-30, 244, 267-8; discussions on, 124-5; king's conference on, 120, 126-7, 245-53; submitted to parliament but not ratified, 124-6, 130, 241, 244; Adamson's commentary on, 93; criticism of (1585), 254; copies to be made, 128; copies extant, 154-6; Carmichael's copy, 129, 154; first printed (1621), 129; effecting proposals of, 130ff.
second new Book of (1557), at Frankfort, 92
Distribution, 74. See also Deacons and Patrimony
Divorce, 43, 48, 49, 186, 228
Dobie, Richard, merchant in Edinburgh, 288
Doctor, office of, 49, 66, 74, 84-88, 94, 97, 101, 103, 104, 110, 111, 114, 115, 120, 121, 126, 140, 149, 165, 167, 175, 176, 183, 184, 187-9, 191, 193-5, 199, 201-4, 208, 211, 231, 237, 246, 249, 255, 259
Dornoch, 151
Douglas, Archibald, 6th earl of Angus, 30
Archibald, minister at Peebles, 275, 276

George, postulate of Arbroath; bishop of Moray, 29, 30, 32, 52, 53, 130, 134, 222
Sir George, 263
James, 4th earl of Morton, 29-31, 34, 38-41, 43, 44, 48, 50, 51, 56, 124-6, 142, 201, 204, 219, 221, 226, 230, 231, 233
John, principal of St Mary's college; archbishop of St Andrews, 3, 20, 21, 29, 30-1, 85, 289
Robert, earl of Buchan, 245
William, 7th earl of Morton, 259, 262, 263
Dublin, Trinity college, 155
Dumbarton, 19; presbytery of, 114, 271; provostry of, 19
Dunbar, presbytery of, 114, 130, 261
Dunblane, 47, 107, 130, 278, 280, 281; bishop of, see Graham, Andrew; bishopric of, 30; exercise at, 106
Duncanson, James, minister at Alloa, 281
John, minister at Stirling, 46, 50, 51, 263, 267, 278
Dundee, 4, 46, 261, 274, 276, 279, 281, 285, 288; presbytery of, 134
Dunfermline, 16, 145, 245; commendator of abbey, 245, 253; presbytery of, 134
Dunkeld, 47; bishop of, see Paton, James; bishopric of, 21, 30; presbytery of, 134
Durie, laird of, 277
John, minister in Edinburgh, 47, 53, 54, 136
Robert, minister at Anstruther Wester, 277
Dutch reformed church, 208, 231
Drymen, 272

Eaglesham, 70
Earlshall, 277
Ecclesiastical Jurisdiction, 10, 12, 13, 36, 37, 39-43, 47-49, 57-61, 63, 83, 126, 128, 137, 138, 143, 146, 147, 153, 164-72, 196, 205, 215, 219, 224, 227, 228, 233, 246-8, 250, 254, 288. See also Civil Magistrate and Keys
Eddleston, 46, 84
Edinburgh, 5, 31, 46, 92, 95, 124, 125, 127, 136, 137, 228, 229, 236, 259, 262, 263, 265, 266, 268, 269, 271-3,

275, 278, 279, 285, 289; college of, 85; kirk session of, 100, 110, 238, 260; parishes of, 71; presbytery of, 70, 73, 87, 110, 112, 114, 129, 130, 134, 136, 150, 151, 202, 205, 237, 258–61, 263–8; 'privy kirk' of, 90; town council of, elections to general assembly, 281–9; Trinity college in, 47

Elders, 6, 7, 9–11, 16, 48, 49, 56, 58, 61, 66, 73–5, 84, 86–97, 100, 101, 103, 104, 107–116, 118–121, 126, 139, 140, 146, 149, 165, 167, 170, 174–6, 179–80, 183, 187–9, 191–6, 198–204, 208, 211, 224, 229, 231, 232, 236, 238, 242, 248, 249, 255, 256, 260, 261. *See also* Seniors

Elderships, 45, 49, 55, 58, 62, 66, 67, 80, 82, 83, 94, 97, 99, 100, 101–110, 113–16, 123, 139, 140, 165, 175, 178, 180, 181, 184–6, 191, 194–201, 204, 208, 223–6, 231–3, 235, 238, 247, 248. *See also* Presbytery

Elgin, 208; kirk session of, 98, 109

Elizabeth I, Queen of England, 75, 77, 145, 168

Elphinstone, laird of, 273

England, 3, 4, 8, 9, 19, 26, 38, 42, 58, 59, 77, 115, 129, 139, 141–4, 165, 192, 199, 202, 203, 205, 207, 208, 224, 226, 229, 231, 242; exiles from, 67, 92; Church of, 4, 8, 9, 35, 36, 71, 168; Convocation of, 41, 139, 198; Ordinal of, 9, 72; conformity with, 35–6, 39, 41, 141, 142; presbyterians in, 82, 113, 114, 169, 175, 176, 187, 189, 191, 195, 203, 208, 218, 231, 242; puritans in, 170, 180, 195, 207, 242

Episcopacy, 6, 30, 35, 45, 47, 53–55, 74–77, 79–82, 123, 127, 128, 130, 131, 134, 137, 140, 143, 148, 223, 225. *See also* Bishops

Erastus, Thomas, 62

Erastianism, 3, 4, 42, 102, 137, 164–5, 200, 201

Erskine, Adam, commendator of Cambuskenneth abbey, 93, 280
John, 6th lord, 1st earl of Mar, 19, 20, 22, 36, 75
John, 2nd earl of Mar, 259, 280
of Dun, John, superintendent of Angus, 4, 21, 22, 26, 32, 41, 46, 48–51, 57, 60, 62, 68, 75, 78, 79, 99, 115, 164, 166, 170, 173, 174, 176, 180, 210, 214, 234, 237, 245
William, titular archbishop of Glasgow, 151, 277
William, minister at Dunino, 277

Excommunication, 6–8, 42, 43, 45, 48, 62, 63, 83, 110, 133, 147, 152, 165, 170, 184, 198, 200, 201, 216, 247–9, 271

Exercise, for interpreting scripture, 8, 56, 69, 72, 73, 86, 105, 106, 114, 115, 145, 149, 196, 199, 225, 232, 276

Exhorter, office of, 10, 36, 83, 84

Faldounside, laird of, 273
Falkirk, 107, 108
Feast days, *see* Holy days
Ferguson, David, minister at Dunfermline, 33, 48–50, 75, 76
Ferme, Charles, minister at Fraserburgh, 86
Fethie, Arthur, minister at Airth, 278
Fife, 46, 70; superintendent of, *see* Winram, John; synod of, 72, 87, 115, 116, 277
'Forme of Prayers', *see* Geneva
Forrester, Alexander, minister at Tranent, 273
of Garden, Alexander, 93, 278
Andrew, minister at Falkirk, 278
Henry, minister at Larbert, 69
Fossoway, 107
France, 3, 4, 12, 14, 20, 52, 59, 66, 67, 81, 88, 118, 195, 199, 208, 242, 264; reformed church in, 3, 66, 67, 99, 101, 113, 189, 192, 196, 231; exiled church in London, 137, 205; 'Discipline Ecclésiastique', 180, 183, 184
Francis II, King of France, 12
Frankfort, 92
Fraserburgh, college at, 86
Freud (*or* Frude), John, advocate, 255
Fullerton, Adam, merchant in Edinburgh, 282–4

Galbraith, Edward, skinner in Edinburgh, 286–7
Galloway, bishop of, *see* Gordon, Alexander
Patrick, minister at Perth; at Edinburgh, 72, 267

INDEX

Garden, laird of, *see* Forrester, Alexander

Garvat, 244

General Assembly, 10–13, 15, 18–21, 23–26, 28–32, 34–37, 43, 45, 50, 55, 56, 61, 66, 68, 70, 72, 75, 78, 82, 94, 96, 101–3, 105–7, 109, 111, 115–21, 124–31, 133–6, 138–40, 144–53, 164, 166, 169–70, 184, 187–9, 192, 194–201, 204, 205, 208–10, 214, 215, 217–25, 228–33, 235, 239, 240, 242–6, 248, 252; origins of, 10–11, 13, 116; composition of, 13, 38–40, 48, 116–21, 126–7, 139, 204; commissioners to, 87, 88, 116, 117, 119, 136, 249, 258–90; king's commissioner at, 249; legality questioned, 38, 39, 41, 45, 139, 143, 195; existence justified, 39–40, 45, 51, 116; moderator of, 26, 51, 81, 115, 117, 139, 196, 249; those subject to, 37, 40, 54, 78; summoning of, 45, 48, 139, 143, 147, 149, 152, 233, 249, 256; clerk of, 128, 129, 155, 211, 236, 244. *See also* Commissioners for visitation

Geneva, 3, 8, 9, 44, 45, 52, 59, 67, 80, 81, 83, 88, 92, 113, 137, 179, 192, 204, 208, 232, 237; 'Forme of Prayers' at, 67, 88, 92, 164, 188, 192, 208; 'Ordonnances Ecclésiastiques', 67, 180, 183, 188, 189; venerable company of pastors in, 113, 179, 189

Germany, 4

Gibson, James, minister at Pencaitland, 244, 261, 262, 273, 274

John, minister at Athelstaneford, 71

Gillespie, George, 72

Patrick, minister at St Ninians, 202, 278

Glamis, lord, *see* Lyon, John

Glasgow, 20, 46, 47, 55, 137, 222, 272, 285; archbishops of, *see* Beaton, James; Porterfield, John; Boyd, James; Montgomery, Robert; Erskine, William; archbishopric of, 18–20, 31, 114, 132, 272; kirk session of, 86, 88, 108, 109, 121, 191, 269; presbytery of, 70, 73, 87, 100, 108, 109, 114, 135, 151, 237, 259, 268–73; superintendent of, *see* Willock, John; synod of, 70, 114, 229, 270–2; university of, 47, 52, 70, 84–88, 109, 132, 155, 188, 269, 270, 272–3

Glebe, *see* Manse and Glebe

Glen, Archibald, minister at Rutherglen, 270

Glendevon, 107

'Golden Act' (1592), 105, 128

Goodman, Christopher, 3, 4, 225

Gordon, Alexander, bishop of Galloway, 29, 37, 78, 224

Govan, 70, 85, 269; minister at, *see* Melville, Andrew; Smeaton, Thomas; Sharp, Patrick

Gowrie, earl of, *see* Ruthven, William

Graham, Andrew, bishop of Dunblane, 30, 32, 34, 52, 53, 130, 134–5, 222

John, 3rd earl of Montrose, 30

Greig, James, minister at Colmonell, 47

Thomas, minister at North Berwick, 244, 273

Gullane, 96, 244

Haddington, 4, 129, 134, 236, 244, 245; kirk session of, 95; presbytery of, 69, 71, 109, 114, 129, 130, 134, 155, 156, 244, 261, 273–5

Hall, John, minister at Colinton, 264–7

Hamilton, presbytery of, 114, 271

Gavin, commendator of Kilwinning abbey, 19

George, 273

James, 3rd earl of Arran, 16

John, archbishop of St Andrews, 3, 9, 20

Robert, principal of St Mary's college; minister in St Andrews, 46, 85, 290

Hart, Edward, goldsmith in Edinburgh, 286

Hawthorndale, laird of, 262

Hay, Alexander, 253

Andrew, minister at Renfrew, 47–51, 55, 109

George, minister at Eddleston; at Rathven, 46, 47, 49–51, 53

of Mont Hall, Gilbert, 266

John, minister at Renfrew, 271, 275

John, Jesuit, 79

Theodore, regent at Glasgow; minister at Peebles, 85

Walter, minister at Bothans, 70, 244, 261, 273, 274
Heidelberg, 62
Henry VIII, King of England, 58, 59, 139, 167; *The Bishop's Book*, 165
Henryson, Malcolm, minister at Kilmadock, 281
Hepburn, Adam, minister at Stobo, 69, 276
  Alexander, bishop of Ross, 30, 130, 222
  John, minister at Brechin, 115
  Robert, minister at Prestonkirk, 261
Herdmandston, laird of, 273
Heriot, George, goldsmith in Edinburgh, 289
Herries, John, minister at Newbattle, 262, 263
Hesse, 8
Hewat, Peter, minister in Edinburgh, 268
Holy days, 6, 7, 68
Holyrood, abbey of, 33
Holy Spirit, 58, 67, 72, 73, 80, 84, 167, 173–5, 199
Home of North Berwick, Alexander, 273, 288
  Alexander, minister at Dunbar, 261
Hooker, Richard, 80
Hooper, John, 77, 224
Hope, Edward, merchant in Edinburgh, 281, 283
Hospitals, 122, 123, 237; master of, 236, 237
Howie, Robert, principal of Marischal college, Aberdeen, 86
Howieson, John, minister at Cambuslang, 271
Hume of Godscroft, David, 155

Imposition of hands, 28, 66–72, 92, 180, 234, 254, 255. *See also* Ordination
Innocent VIII, Pope, 142
Inveresk, 267
Iona, abbey of, 135
Irvine, 134
Isles, bishops of, *see* Carswell, John; Campbell, John

Jack, Thomas, minister at Eastwood, 109
James III, King of Scots, 142
James V, King of Scots, 239
James VI, King of Scots, 17, 41, 71–2, 86, 87, 91, 94, 106, 113, 120, 126–8, 141, 145–50, 152, 153, 168, 188, 201, 213, 216, 217, 219, 220, 231, 232, 241, 245, 247, 249–52, 260, 261, 263, 264, 267, 268, 271, 276, 280
Jedburgh, 4
Jewel, John, 77, 168
Johnston, Adam, minister at Crichton, 262, 263
  of Elphinstone, John, 284, 286, 289
  John, merchant in Edinburgh, 285
  John, collector in Edinburgh, 285, 286
  John, 286–8
  John, regent at St Andrews, 87

Keir, lairds of, *see* Stirling
Kelso, abbey of, 19
Kemback, laird of, 277
Kennedy, Quintin, 57
Ker, John, regent at St Andrews; minister at Aberlady, 244, 299
  John, minister at Prestonpans, 275
Keys, power of the, 62, 165, 170, 184, 215, 216. *See also* Ecclesiastical Jurisdiction
Kilconquhar, 276; laird of, 277
Kilmarnock, 19, 109
Kilrenny, 276
Kilsyth, 100; laird of, *see* Livingston, William
Kilwinning, abbey of, 19
Kincraig, laird of, 277
Kingask, 5
Kingdoms, two, theory of, 51, 58–60, 166, 168
Kinglassie, 5
Kinnaldy, laird of, *see* Aytoun, John
Kinnellar, 238
Kinnoull, 46
Kinross of Kippenross, James, 278
Kippen, 107
Kirk Session, 10, 29, 35, 56, 69, 86, 88, 94, 97, 100–5, 107–10, 113, 115, 116, 119, 120, 136, 140, 147, 152, 185, 186, 189, 192, 195, 198, 199, 201, 208, 211, 225, 228, 231, 233, 237, 238, 255, 258; moderator of, 196. *See also individual towns*
Kirktoun, laird of, 277
Knox, Andrew, minister at Paisley, 275
  John, 3, 5, 9, 17, 20, 24–27, 37, 38,

43, 47, 51, 53, 62, 64, 75–77, 88, 92, 109, 116, 118, 138, 169, 170–2, 197, 214, 216, 226, 242, 281; attitude to episcopacy, 22, 27, 30, 55, 225; *History*, 155

Lamb, James, minister at Bolton, 244
Laing, Henry, minister at St Ninians, 202, 281
Lanark, presbytery of, 114, 271
Larbert, 69
Largo, laird of, 276, 277
Lasco, John à, 92
Law, Andrew, minister at Neilston, 70
   James, minister at Kirkliston, 261
Lawrie, Blaise, regent at Glasgow, 86
Lawson, James, sub-principal at Aberdeen; minister at Edinburgh, 46–48, 50, 51, 53, 85, 138, 245, 253, 285, 286
Leith, 47, 236, 237, 268; settlement of (1572), 22–28, 31, 33, 36, 38, 43, 47, 53, 54, 56, 63, 68, 75, 77, 82, 83, 118, 123, 126, 130, 133, 143, 197, 217–19, 221, 238, 241, 242, 256
Lennox, earls of, *see* Stewart
Lermonth of Dairsie, James, 261
Lesmahagow, priory of, 19
Leuchars, 277
Levites, 89, 93, 191, 192
Lindsay, Alexander, in Edinburgh, 288
   David, minister at South Leith, 47–51, 53, 79, 245, 253, 261, 263–7, 271
   of Menmuir, John, lord Balcarres, 94, 254, 287; his 'Constant Platt', 219, 239, 268
   Patrick, 6th lord, 136
   Thomas, 271
Linlithgow, 134, 146, 236, 275; presbytery of, 114, 129, 130, 261
Little, Clement, advocate in Edinburgh, 47, 48, 282–4
   William, merchant in Edinburgh, 287
Livingston, Alexander, minister at Kilsyth, 100
   Henry, minister at St Ninians, 97, 280
   Robert, minister at Drumelzier, 69, 276
   of Kilsyth, William, 269
   William, 73
Logan of Cotfield, Andrew, 266
Logie, 107; kirk session of, 109

London, 92, 114, 137, 141
Lothian, 46, 106; superintendent of, *see* Spottiswoode, John; and Tweeddale, synod of, 56, 68–9, 83, 105, 113, 114, 116, 129, 134, 181, 196, 220, 258, 261
Lugtoun, laird of, *see* Crichton, David
Lundie, laird of, 47, 277
   George, minister at Pentland, 262
Luther, Martin, 8, 163, 166, 170, 176, 191, 207, 224
Lutheranism, 4, 8, 10, 177
Lyon, John, 8th lord Glamis, 43–45, 47, 99, 113, 118, 195, 197–9, 210, 224, 230, 231, 235, 243

Macartney, James, solicitor for the kirk, 212
McCalzean, Thomas, advocate, 282–4
McGhie, Thomas, minister at Gullane, 244, 273, 274
McGill, David, advocate, 285
   James, advocate, 265
Magistracy, *see* Civil Magistrate
Maitland of Lethington, William, 15, 39
   of Thirlestane, John, 128
Manses and glebes, 134, 209, 239
Mar, earls of, *see* Erskine
Marjoribanks, John, merchant in Edinburgh, 282, 284
Marlorat, Augustin, 203
Marriage, 6, 10, 24, 43, 83, 123, 186, 189, 228, 229, 248, 271
Martin, James, regent at St Andrews, 290
Martyr (Vermigli), Peter, 9, 77
Mary of Guise, 59, 166
Mary, Queen of Scots, 12, 15, 17, 20, 39, 41, 117, 220, 228
Megget of Newbattle, Thomas, 262
Melanchthon, Philip, 5, 170
Melville, Andrew, 47–52, 60, 68, 84–88, 93, 113, 121, 124, 127, 129, 133, 138, 140, 146, 155, 171, 188, 215, 261, 277; attitude to episcopacy, 52–55; principal at Glasgow, 85; minister at Govan, 85; excluded from presbytery, 86; at synod, 87; on kirk session, 91
   James, 53, 55, 85, 87, 93, 105, 115, 141, 146, 156, 169, 211, 223, 277
   Patrick, regent at Glasgow; at St Andrews, 86, 87

Menmuir, lord, *see* Lindsay, John
Menteith, Port of, 108
  of Carse, William, 279, 280
Mentoun, laird of, 263
Merchinston, laird of, 264-7
Merlin, Jean-Raymond, 59
Mernis, David, minister at Carnbee, 277
Methven, Paul, minister at Jedburgh, 4
  Thomas, prebendary, 4-5
Milan, 4
Miller, Alexander, in Edinburgh, 288
Ministers, 5-11, 38, 56-58, 63, 74ff., 83, 94, 106, 119, 165, 171, 176-7, 183-6, 220, 248, 252; parity of, 44, 51, 53, 56, 81, 82, 175, 255; ministers of king's household, 263, 265-7
Ministry, 9, 10, 12, 55, 56, 58, 62, 64-73, 83, 96, 106, 123, 147, 152, 174, 178, 180, 181, 184, 202, 204, 222-4, 233, 253, 255; admission to, 7, 43, 65-73, 110, 122, 150, 178ff., 201, 233, 252; provision for, 13, 15-17, 45, 106, 214, 217, 243, 272
Minto, laird of, *see* Stewart, Sir Matthew
Moderator, 71, 81, 82, 99, 195, 196. *See also* General Assembly, Synod, Presbytery *and* Kirk Session
Monasteries, 217, 219. *See also* Abbeys, Priory
Moncreiff, Andrew, minister at Kilconquhar, 276, 277
Monipenny, David, minister at Kemback, 276
Monks, 217, 221
Montgomery, Robert, archbishop of Glasgow, 132-5, 142, 147, 150
Montrose, 46, 115, 266-8, 270, 273, 276, 288; earl of, *see* Graham, John; presbytery of, 134
Moray, bishop of, *see* Douglas, George; bishopric of, 29; earl of, *see* Stewart, James
Morély, Jean, 99
Morham, 244
Morton, earls of, *see* Douglas
Muckhart, 107
Muirhead, Thomas, minister at Cambusnethan, 272
Murehead, James, minister at North Leith, 268

Murray of Blackbarony, Andrew, 281
  of Touchadam, John, 97, 279, 280
  William, minister at Crail, 277

Nairn, David, minister at West Linton, 69, 261
Neilston, 70
Nesbit, Henry, provost of Edinburgh, 288
Newbattle, lord, 262, 263
Newbyres, laird of, 262, 263
Newcastle, 5
Nigg, 96
Nimble, John, minister at Cranstoun, 261, 263
Nîmes, synod at, 99, 101
North Berwick, 244, 273
Nunneries, 221, 222
Nuremberg, 8

Oecolampadius (Hausgen), Johannes, 10, 42, 114, 163, 166, 169, 198
Ordination, 7, 55, 65-70, 72, 73, 91, 92, 99, 110, 126, 138, 178, 180, 181, 189. *See also* Imposition of hands
Orkney, bishop of, *see* Bothwell, Adam
Orléans, 4
Ormiston, laird of, 262, 263
Oswald, Archibald, minister at Pencaitland, 275
Oustean, Alexander, tailor in Edinburgh, 287, 288

Paisley, 73; abbacy of, 272; presbytery of, 114, 271, 275
Paris, 4, 46
Parish churches, *see* Churches
Parker, Matthew, archbishop of Canterbury, 75
Parliament, 18, 21-23, 26, 46, 124-7, 130-3, 137-9, 142, 143, 146, 147, 152, 153, 164, 196, 201, 204, 215, 219-21, 229, 233, 235, 241, 242, 247-53, 267, 271, 272, 275; ecclesiastical estate in, 24, 36-38, 45, 48, 122, 138, 146-8, 217, 219, 220, 226, 227, 229, 256, 257. *See also* 'Black Acts' *and* 'Golden Act'
Pastor, *see* Minister
Paton, James, bishop of Dunkeld, 21, 30, 32-34, 134
Patrimony, ecclesiastical, 7, 10, 13, 15-18, 20, 21, 23, 24, 33, 45, 48, 49, 64, 77, 91, 101, 122ff., 127,

128, 140, 173, 200, 205, 207–12, 218–20, 222, 227, 235–7, 239, 242, 243, 250, 251, 256, 257, 272
Patronage, ecclesiastical, 13, 22, 24, 48, 49, 122, 123, 127, 132, 140, 153, 233–6, 247, 252, 255
Paul IV, Pope, 4
Peebles, 275; presbytery of, 69, 114, 130, 259–61, 275, 276
Pencaitland, 244
Perth, 24, 46, 72, 118, 260, 267, 275, 276, 280–2, 288; master of song school of, 212; kirk session of, 236, 237; presbytery of, 134
Pilrig, laird of, 264–7
Pitcur, tutor of, 245
Pitmilly, laird of, 277
Pittenweem, commendator of priory of, *see* Stewart, James
Poland, 80
Policarp, 189
Polity, ecclesiastical, 11, 18, 22, 35, 36, 41ff., 47, 52, 53, 57, 74ff., 77, 125, 130, 137, 138, 141, 142, 147, 151, 164, 166, 167, 173, 217, 219, 230, 240, 254, 275, 288
Polwart, Andrew, minister at Cadder, 109
Pont, James, commissary of Dunblane, 278
— Robert, minister of St Cuthbert's, Edinburgh, 47–51, 151, 245, 253, 261, 263–6
Poor, suffort for, 7, 10, 13, 16, 24, 45, 97, 100, 122, 123, 174–6, 207, 208, 210, 211, 214, 215, 237, 242, 252, 272. See also Alms *and* Deacons
Porterfield of that Ilk, John, 19
— John, minister at Kilmaronock; archbishop elect of Glasgow, 19, 20, 30
Portmoak, prior of, *see* Winram, John
Prebendaries, 218, 235, 252
Precentor, 211, 212, 218, 236
Prelacies, 18, 22, 24, 27, 45, 122, 127, 214, 219, 220, 235, 251. *See also* Abbacies *and* Bishoprics
Presbyter, 55, 74, 80, 81, 110, 114, 174, 176, 183, 191, 223
Presbyterianism, 79, 85, 102, 108, 152, 195, 205
Presbytery, 55, 66, 69, 70, 72, 84, 87, 102, 104, 105, 109–15, 120, 128–30, 133, 140–2, 145, 147, 148, 152, 179, 181, 188, 189, 192, 194, 196, 197, 199–204, 208, 211, 215, 220, 223, 224, 239, 244, 246; origins of, 86, 104, 106, 107, 132–4, 232, 233; clerk of, 276; commissioners to general assembly, 258, 262–89; composition of, 111, 112; deacons excluded from, 98; doctors in, 86–87; elders in, 92; lairds at, 139, 261; and bishops, 145ff., 148, 152, 223–6; moderator of, 96, 112, 129, 142, 151, 196, 211, 262, 263, 270, 276, 278; prohibited, 112, 137, 143; presentations to, 150–3; visitations by, 95, 96. *See also* Eldership *and individual towns*
Preston, John, merchant in Edinburgh, 282–5
Prestonpans, 70
Primrose, Gilbert, physician in Edinburgh, 287
Prior, 28, 122, 128, 217, 219
Priory, 221, 222
Privy Council, 12, 15–17, 21, 23, 29, 36, 37, 39, 48, 63, 95, 106, 118, 122, 124, 125, 127, 131–4, 169, 170, 215, 219, 221, 224, 227, 228, 232, 233, 238, 271
Procurators for the church, 212
Provincial assembly, *see* Synod
Provost, ecclesiastical office of, 6, 9, 177
Provostries, 24, 235, 252

Rait, David, principal of King's college, Aberdeen, 86
Ramsay, George, minister at Lasswade, 261–3, 277
Ramus, Peter, 99
Rathven, 46
Reader, office of, 6, 7, 10, 24, 36, 83, 84, 100, 103, 122, 136, 142, 177, 185, 187, 188, 199, 211, 229, 272
Reformation, the, 3, 9, 13, 14, 44, 52, 60, 74, 82, 118, 131, 142, 144, 145, 197, 209, 219, 221, 228
Reid, James, minister at Garvat, 244
Renfrew, 109, 271
Reres, laird of, 276, 277
Rhind, William, minister at Kinnoull, 46
Richardson of Smetoun, James, 263–6
Ritchie, James, clerk of general assembly, 129, 155, 244

Robertson, George, regent and minister in Edinburgh, 85
  John, regent in St Andrews, 87, 276, 290
Rochelle, La, synod at, 99, 101
Rollock, Robert, principal and minister in Edinburgh, 85, 86, 95, 264–6
Roman Catholicism, 4, 5, 9–11, 14, 25, 27–29, 44, 45, 55, 57, 58, 76, 79, 133, 139, 140, 146, 163, 167–9, 177, 192, 218, 219, 227–9, 234, 242, 264
Ross, bishop of, *see* Hepburn, Alexander
Row, John, minister at Perth, 3, 46–51, 127, 245
Rowat, Alexander, minister in Glasgow, 269, 270, 272
Royal Supremacy, 36, 40–42, 58, 60, 128, 137, 138, 140, 142–4, 146, 147; not conceded, 40–41, 51, 58, 59, 61, 166–9. *See also* Civil Magistrate
Russell, David, in St Andrews, 276
  William, advocate in St Andrews, 276
Rutherford, John, principal of St Salvator's college, St Andrews, 46, 289
  Samuel, 72
Rutherglen, 270
Ruthven, lord, 118; William 4th lord, 1st earl of Gowrie, 136
'raiders', 128, 136, 137, 144

St Andrews, 3, 4, 16, 26, 46, 47, 85, 95, 98, 262, 278, 280, 281, 286, 289; archbishop of, *see* Hamilton, John; Douglas, John; Adamson, Patrick; Spottiswoode, John; archbishopric of, 20, 21, 29–31, 85, 114; kirk session of, 86, 90–92, 98, 108, 116, 119, 192, 193, 196, 208, 237, 260; session clerk, 211; precentor in, 212; presbytery of, 86, 87, 96, 108, 111, 113, 116, 120, 129, 134, 226, 259, 261, 276–8; priors of, *see* Stewart; sub-prior of, *see* Winram, John; provost of, 277; university of, 84, 258, 277, 289–90; colleges: St Leonard's, 4, 47, 85, 120, 289; St Mary's, 3, 46, 85, 87, 120, 289; St Salvator's, 46, 88, 289
St Ninians, 97, 107, 202; kirk session of, 109, 201, 236
Saltcoats, laird of, 96, 273
Sampson, Thomas, 77, 225
Sandford, laird of, 277
Sandilands, Andrew, 277
  Patrick, in Edinburgh, 287
Schools, 10, 13, 45, 56, 122, 126, 188, 189, 210, 211, 214, 215, 221, 231, 235, 237, 243, 255, 272
Schoolmaster, 63, 84, 86, 87, 122, 134, 142, 187, 188, 211, 235
Scotland, Church of, 8, 9, 75. *See also* Church; Ecclesiastical Jurisdiction; Polity
Scott of Spencerfield, William, advocate, 255, 277
Segy, laird of, 245, 253
Seniors, 110, 139, 183, 191, 199, 200. *See also* Elders
Seton, Alexander, friar, 76
  of Tullibody, James, 280
Sharp, John, advocate, 255
  Patrick, principal at Glasgow; minister at Govan, 70, 85, 86, 88, 269, 270
  Patrick, minister at Strathbrock, 261
Shaw of Sauchie, James, 280
Simony, 33, 133, 252
Simson, Andrew, minister at Dalkeith, 119
  Archibald, minister at Dalkeith, 95, 110, 119, 156, 261
  Patrick, minister at Cramond; at Stirling, 263–5, 280, 281
Skene, 96
  John, advocate, 286
  William, commissary in St Andrews, 290
Skirling, 69
Sloan, George, 73
Smeaton, Thomas, principal at Glasgow, 86, 133, 155
Smetoun, laird of, *see* Richardson, James
Spens, John, advocate in Edinburgh, 282
Spittall, Archibald, minister at Drymen, 272
Spottiswoode, John, superintendent of Lothian, 3, 51, 79
  John, minister at Mid Calder; archbishop of St Andrews, 51–53, 156, 245, 261
Stevenston, 19

Stewart, Esmé, earl and duke of Lennox, 128, 132, 133, 136, 137
James, illegitimate son of James V, earl of Moray, 3, 4, 13, 18, 19, 169
James, earl of Arran, 112, 121, 128, 137, 144–6, 148, 149, 214
Matthew, 4th earl of Lennox, 19, 20
of Minto, Matthew, 269
Robert, bishop of Caithness, 34, 131
Walter, minister at Kilpatrick, 271
Stipends, 12, 14–16, 24, 108, 122, 142, 180, 214, 217, 220, 236, 255, 272
Stirling, 20, 22, 46, 97, 107, 108, 124, 126, 127, 245, 278, 280, 284, 285, 290; kirk session of, 108, 109, 194, 201; presbytery of, 69, 93, 96, 106, 107, 109, 111, 129, 134—6, 186, 201, 202, 259, 260, 278–81; clerk of presbytery, 211
of Keir, Archibald, 280
James, 278
William, minister at Kippen, 278, 280
Strang, Richard, advocate in Edinburgh, 282, 283
Robert, 276, 277
Strasbourg, 8, 74
Stravithie, laird of, *see* Wood, Andrew
Sub-chanter (succentor), 218
Superintendent, office of, 6, 7, 10–12, 14, 16, 18, 21–24, 27, 29, 31, 32, 35–38, 43, 56, 77–80, 82, 96, 115, 117, 119, 131, 138, 142, 184, 185, 196, 197, 201, 228, 254, 290; court of, 10, 35, 56; *see also* Angus, Argyll, Fife, Glasgow, Lothian
Switzerland, 3, 4, 52. *See also* Basel, Geneva, Zürich
Syme, Alexander, advocate in Edinburgh, 47, 282
Synod, provincial, 6, 11, 35, 56, 66, 87, 96, 99, 101, 102, 105, 110, 112–16, 119, 120, 126, 136, 147, 150, 151, 152, 184, 189, 194–6, 199, 200, 203, 204, 208, 215, 225, 233, 248–50, 252, 258, 261, 262, 267, 268, 276, 278, 279; moderator of, 87, 115; national in France, 59, 66, 118; in England, 113. *See also* Fife, Glasgow, Lothian, synods of

Taylor, Gilbert, minister at Penicuik, 262
Teacher, *See* Doctor, Schoolmaster

Teinds, 13, 15–17, 22–24, 33, 45, 123, 209, 217–20, 228, 239, 242, 243, 272
Touchadam, laird of, *see* Murray, John
Trabroun, laird of, 273
Traill, James, 277
Tranent, 96
Travers, Walter, 113, 155, 173, 187, 188, 200, 208, 229, 231; *Disciplinae ecclesiasticae . . . explicatio*, 97, 98, 179, 180, 195
Treasurer, office of, 218
Trolhope, Richard, in Edinburgh, 282
Tullibody, kirk session of, 109
Tyndale, William, 77

Uddart, Nicol, merchant in Edinburgh, 284
Ulm, 8
Universities, 10, 24, 45, 56, 117, 119, 120, 122, 126, 142, 188, 189, 219, 231, 235. *See also* Aberdeen, Glasgow, St Andrews

Viret, Pierre, 9
Visitor, office of, 6, 32, 35, 37, 54, 79, 82, 106, 127, 136, 142, 148–50, 196, 197, 201, 223, 225, 247, 249, 251. *See also* Commissioner
Vocation, 62, 65ff., 72–73, 83, 90, 92, 94, 100, 126, 178, 181–4, 213, 238, 255

Wallace, Daniel, minister at Morham, 244
Robert, minister in St Andrews, 277
Walsingham, Sir Francis, 154
Watson, Charles, in St Andrews, 276
William, minister in Edinburgh, 70–71
Watt, John, in Edinburgh, 288
Welwood, William, regent at St Andrews, 290
Wemyss, David, minister in Glasgow, 269
John, minister at Kilbucho, 276
Westminster, Assembly of Divines, 84–85, 193
Whiteford, Walter, 73
Whitgift, John, archbishop of Canterbury, 71, 139, 141, 142, 169, 170
Wied, Hermann von, archbishop of Cologne, 5

Wilkie, James, principal of St Leonard's college, St Andrews, 47, 290
　Robert, minister and principal of St Leonard's college, St Andrews, 85, 277, 290
Willock, John, superintendent of Glasgow, 3, 14
Wilmistoun, laird of, 276, 277
Wilson, Robert, minister at Newbattle, 262
　William, in Haddington, 236
Winram, John, superintendent of Fife, 3, 13, 21, 46, 78
Withers, George, 62

Wood of Stravithie, Andrew, 276, 277
Wright, Richard, minister at Clackmannan, 281

Yester, lord, 273
York, archbishop of, 141
Young, Andrew, minister at Dunblane, 278, 281
　James, cutler in Edinburgh, 281
　Peter, 245
Yule, Robert, reader in St Andrews, 276

Zürich, 3, 8, 9, 77, 137, 216
Zwingli, Ulrich, 8, 169, 224

www.ingramcontent.com/pod-product-compliance
Lightning Source LLC
Chambersburg PA
CBHW032017230426
43671CB00005B/120